Implementing
and
Managing
eGovernment

Implementing and Managing eGovernment

AN INTERNATIONAL TEXT

Richard Heeks

SAGE Publications
Los Angeles • London • New Delhi • Singapore

First published 2006
Reprinted 2006, 2007

 SAGE Publications Ltd
1 Oliver's Yard
55 City Road
London EC1Y 1SP

SAGE Publications Inc.
2455 Teller Road
Thousand Oaks, California 91320

SAGE Publications India Pvt Ltd
B1/I 1 Mohan Cooperative Industrial Area
Mathura Road, New Delhi 110 044
India

SAGE Publications Asia-Pacific Pte Ltd
33 Pekin Street #02-01
Far East Square
Singapore 048763

British Library Cataloguing in Publication data

A catalogue record for this book is available from
the British Library

ISBN: 978-0-7619-6791-0 (hbk)
ISBN: 978-0-7619-6792-7 (pbk)

Library of Congress Control Number: 2005926977

Typeset by C&M Digitals (P) Ltd., Chennai, India
Printed and bound in Great Britain by Athenaeum Press Ltd., Gateshead Tyne & Wear
Printed on paper from sustainable resources

Contents

List of Figures

List of Tables

Introduction

eGovernment is a rapidly-growing pheno-menon. It has an increasing impact on the work of the public sector. It absorbs an increasing proportion of public sector bud-gets. It promises (perhaps overpromises) a solution to many public sector problems.

This book studies the implementation and management of e-government. It defines e-government in a broad sense: all use of information technology in the public sector. It covers a broad range of managerial issues: from high-level strategy to detailed tactics; from the technicalities of data flows and process mapping to the politics of e-government.

The text is divided into two main parts:

- Part 1 looks overall at Managing eGovern-ment: the range of issues that public sector managers, private sector providers, consul-tants and others face in planning and operating e-government. These issues include management of strategy and pro-jects; data security, privacy and quality; managing the people, money and policies that are integral to e-government; and dealing with political challenges.
- Part 2 focuses on Implementing eGovern-ment: the more specific actions required to introduce a new e-government system. This explores a set of activities such as feasibility study; system analysis; system design; construction; introduc-tion; and post-implementation tasks such as marketing.

These parts are 'topped and tailed' by Chapter 1, which introduces a set of fun-damental models and ideas that enable e-government to be understood; and Chapter 12, which expands one of the core themes of the book: the notion of 'hybrids'.

Wherever possible, this book weaves a number of these core themes – some more explicit, some more implicit – into its dis-cussion. Five of these will be flagged here:

- *eGovernment hype is not e-government real-ity*: Behind the rose-tinted façade of press releases lies the truth that e-government is difficult to implement, hard to man-age, and often fails. This book sees the positive potential of new technology, but also exposes the real obstacles.
- *eGovernment systems are information systems*: They handle data and hope to deliver information to support decisions and transactions. This book's under-standing of e-government and its manage-ment is thus based on an understanding of information and information systems.
- *eGovernment systems sit within a broader context*: Of people, management, public agencies, IT vendors, politics, culture, and so on. Not only does e-government affect these factors; it is also affected by these factors. Ignore them, and they will swing in to derail your plans. This book's discussion of managing e-government therefore takes account of the broader context.
- *eGovernment is not e-business*: You cannot simply transplant private sector ideas into the public sector. This book recognizes the difference between these sectors, and tries to draw out the particular challenges that face public sector projects.
- *eGovernment may best be implemented and managed by hybrid methods*. Chapters 1 and 12 particularly explain more about the notion of the hybrid approach: not a panacea, but a way through some of the tensions that beset e-government.

To help reinforce these themes and the other ideas presented in the book, there is significant use of figures and boxed cases and examples. A series of activities is also provided at the end of each chapter. These can be used by any readers, but they are particularly aimed at those readers using the book as a textbook; that is, as a facilitator to learning. The activities are divided into categories, described below. In all cases, the activities are labeled to indicate which section or sections they relate to.

The first set of activities is particularly aimed at readers using the book in class teaching: for example, as part of a module on an undergraduate or postgraduate program, or within a shorter training program.

- *In-class activities*: These are quick action- or reaction-based exercises, designed to stimulate ideas or discussion, or to give a brief opportunity to try out a skill. Length of activity will vary but might typically be around 20 minutes. Many of the activities can be undertaken through individual reflection, paired or group discussion/action, plenary debate, or some combination.
- *Assignment questions*: These can be set as written and graded assignments, and are intended to test out understanding of key issues, including some of the core themes of the book.

Each chapter also provides a set of 'Practitioner Exercises'. These are provided for those working in or with the public sector, and using the book – possibly as a self-study guide – to deepen their own e-government knowledge and skills. These exercises prompt the practitioner to relate key chapter ideas to the specific public agency with/in which they work.

Chapters in Part 2 also have a further set of 'eGovernment Project Development Exercises'. These are intended for use by individuals or groups who are working on the live implementation of a new e-government system. They provide a structured set of actions that put chapter ideas into practice.

Finally, all of the chapters have an 'Online Appendix'. This provides a set of web-based materials that expand upon, illustrate, or provide more detail about e-government issues in the text. Each chapter's Online Appendix begins with a set of 'Longer Group Activities'. These relate to sections in the main text and might typically require one or two hours of work, or time away from class. They are intended to develop a deeper understanding of a particular topic. Those marked [I] are seen as most suitable for in-class group work. Those marked [A] are more likely to need some period of assigned activity outside of class. Each of the subsequent Online Appendix sections also has related activities and exercises.

TERMINOLOGY

As noted above, the term 'e-government' as used in this book has a broad definition. It is *not* merely confined to use of the web and/or Internet-based applications in government. Instead, it encompasses all use of digital information technology (primarily computers and networks) in the public sector. (In terms of spelling, the convention adopted here is 'eGovernment' at the start of a sentence; 'e-government' elsewhere.)

A corollary is that no issue is made here of the difference between 'government' and 'public sector'. The latter term is used more generally, but they are used interchangeably. The same is also true of 'public agency' and 'public sector organization': in some contexts these two terms mean specific and different things. Here, though, they do not: an agency is shorthand for any public sector organization.

1

Understanding eGovernment

Key Points

- Most e-government initiatives fail due to poor implementation and management.
- eGovernment is the use of information technology (IT) by public sector organizations
- eGovernment systems are information systems that are socio-technical: combining the technical and the human.
- eGovernment systems can be summarized through the ITPOSMO structure checklist and the CIPSODA process checklist.
- eGovernment systems can be managed by hard, soft or hybrid approaches.
- Gaps between design and reality help to explain why e-government systems succeed or fail.
- eGovernment is not the same as e-business.

Most e-government projects fail.

They are either *total failures*, in which the system is never implemented or is implemented but immediately abandoned; or they are *partial failures*, in which major goals for the system are not attained and/or there are significant undesirable outcomes. Only a minority of e-government projects can be properly called successes (Heeks and Bhatnagar, 2001; Fulton, 2003; UNDESA, 2003a). Estimates of the proportion falling into the failure categories range from 60 percent (Gartner, 2002) through 60–80 percent (UNDESA, 2003b) up to 85 percent (Symonds, 2000).

Thus, there is a huge gulf between the rose-tinted hype about information technology's (IT) role in the public sector, and the actual reality. The overall result is a massive wastage of financial, human and political resources, and an inability to deliver the potential gains from e-government to its beneficiaries. This, despite an estimated global spend on IT by government (excluding public sector health, education and utilities) of some US$3 trillion during the decade of the 2000s (Gubbins, 2004).

These problems are the result of poor management. If the processes and projects and systems of e-government were managed better, failure and waste would be much rarer (Brown, 2000; Gupta et al., 2004).

This book therefore looks at ways in which to improve the management of e-government. Part 1 looks at a range of general issues in the tactical and strategic management of e-government. Part 2 looks specifically at managing the process of developing new e-government applications. We must start, though, by building a better understanding of what e-government is.

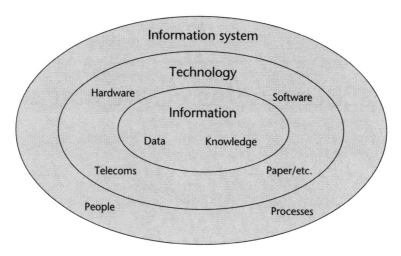

Figure 1.1   eGovernment systems as information systems: Structural view

1.1 UNDERSTANDING ɛGOVERNMENT AS INFORMATION SYSTEMS

eGovernment is the use of IT by public sector organizations. eGovernment is therefore not just about the Internet. And e-government has been with us for many decades: long before the terminology of 'e-government' was invented. eGovernment means office automation and internal management information systems and expert systems, as well as client-facing web sites.

To understand e-government, we must therefore understand IT. What does IT do: it handles data to produce information. The next step to understanding e-government, then, is to understand that *e-government systems are information systems*. At their heart lie data and information (the latter being defined as data that has been processed to make it useful to a recipient). These are handled by digital (and sometimes non-digital) information technologies.

But this does not make a 'system'. A system is a collection of elements that works and has a purpose. To understand e-government as an information system, we must add in some notion of activity and purpose. That can only come if we bring people into the equation. For e-government to be a working information system, it must be seen as much more than just the technical elements of IT. Instead, it must be seen to consist of technology *plus* information *plus* people who give the system purpose and meaning *plus* work processes that are undertaken. We can therefore produce an initial model of an e-government system, as illustrated in Figure 1.1.

Figure 1.1 shows e-government systems can be described as 'socio-technical systems' because they combine both the social – that is, people – and the technical (Avison and Fitzgerald, 2003). This is a first indication that, when managing e-government, both social and technical (otherwise known as *soft* and *hard*) issues will have to be dealt with. As will be seen later in this book, shortcomings in managing the soft aspects are more often a cause of failure than problems with the technology.

The model in Figure 1.1 is a good start, but it is incomplete. eGovernment systems don't just float around like satellites in

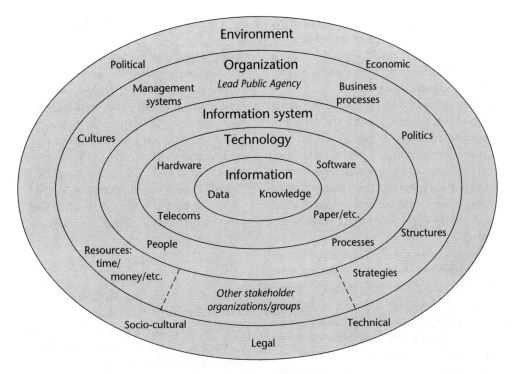

Figure 1.2   Full model of e-government systems

space. Most are embedded within public sector organizations that provide, for example, the management systems and the organizational resources that support e-government. These organizations also provide things like the political and cultural milieu within which e-government operates. Many e-government systems also reach out to other groups (citizens, businesses); a few involve other public agencies. In turn, all these groups and organizations are themselves embedded in institutional environments: a broader context of laws and values, economic systems and technological innovations that affects both the agencies/groups and the systems – including e-government systems – that serve them.

Our full model of e-government must embrace these factors, as shown in Figure 1.2 (adapted from Heeks and Bhatnagar, 2001).

The ITPOSMO Checklist

In fully describing and understanding an e-government system, we could refer to every one of the 20 separate factors identified in Figure 1.2 (and probably to other factors that even this model has not included). But that would be complex. In this book, therefore, we will make more use of a slightly simpler checklist of key items drawn out from this 'onion-ring' model:

• Information: The formal information held by the digital system and the informal information used by the people involved with the system.
• Technology: Mainly focuses on digital IT but can also cover other information-handling technologies such as paper or analogue telephones.

- Processes: The activities undertaken by the relevant stakeholders for whom the e-government system operates, both information-related processes and broader business processes.
- Objectives and values: Often the most important dimension since the *objectives* component covers issues of self-interest and organizational politics, and can even be seen to incorporate formal organizational strategies; the *values* component covers culture: what stakeholders feel are the right and wrong ways to do things.
- Staffing and skills: Covers the number of staff involved with the e-government system, and the competencies of those staff and other users.
- Management systems and structures: The overall management systems required to organize operation and use of the e-government system, plus the way in which stakeholder agencies/groups are structured, both formally and informally.
- Other resources: Principally, the time and money required to implement and operate the e-government system.

This ITPOSMO checklist can be used for describing and understanding any e-government system and stakeholder organizational context. It will be used continuously in this book to help understand e-government systems.[1]

In some cases, it may be important to also describe the wider context, by expanding the checklist to ITPOSMOO, adding an eighth dimension:

- Outside world: The political, economic, socio-cultural, technological and legal factors that impinge on the relevant e-government stakeholders.

The CIPSODA Checklist

Given that e-government systems are information systems, we can draw on one further model/checklist to help us understand e-government. This understands an e-government application in terms of its information-related tasks: a process view to go alongside the structural view offered above. These tasks are summarized by the CIPSODA checklist, illustrated in Figure 1.3.

The checklist of tasks can be explained in some further detail, using the example of part of an e-tax system:

- Capture: Gathering the raw data necessary for the e-government system. The taxpayer obtains the basic data on their various sources of income.
- Input: Entering the data onto the system. The taxpayer types the data into an e-form on the revenue agency's web site.
- Process: Altering the data via calculation, classification, selection, and so on. The e-tax system uses the different tax rates for different income types to calculate the total tax owed.
- Store: Holding raw and processed data on the system. The e-tax system stores all details entered and calculated about this taxpayer.
- Output: Issuing the processed data. The total tax calculated is displayed to the taxpayer.
- Decision: If the processed data is useful enough to be seen as information, it is used for decision making. The taxpayer determines whether to challenge or accept the calculated tax sum.
- Action: Implementation of the decision. If all is well, the taxpayer authorizes payment of the tax owed.

Note there is also an eighth task implicit within the model: the communication of data between each of the other tasks.

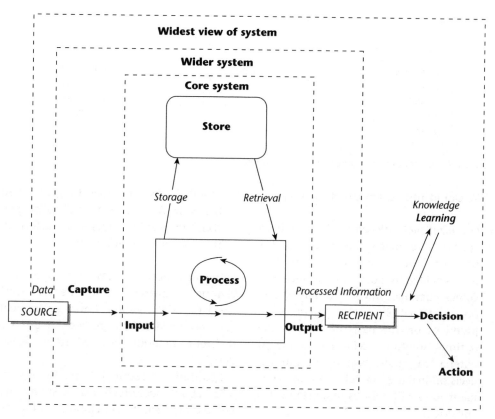

Figure 1.3   eGovernment systems as information systems: Process view

While Figure 1.2 uses an information systems perspective to explain what an e-government system *is*, Figure 1.3 explains more what an e-government system *does*. The main system activities are described by the CIPSO elements, but the actual public value only comes when we add in the D & A elements. This understanding of e-government systems will be drawn on at various stages within this book.

1.2 UNDERSTANDING ɛGOVERNMENT MANAGEMENT

Figure 1.2 shows up two important lessons for the management of e-government. Each will be discussed in turn.

Approaches to Management

Figure 1.2 has shown that e-government systems are socio-technical systems: combinations of hard and soft components. Unfortunately, not all approaches to management are socio-technical. Instead, different approaches can be placed at different locations on the continuum shown in Figure 1.4.

Hard approaches tend to be management science – or even engineering-inspired. They will tend to emphasize the formal, the quantitative and the technical aspects of organizations. Soft approaches tend to be social science-inspired. They will tend to emphasize the informal, the qualitative and the human aspects of organizations.

Soft	Socio-Technical	Hard
Social Science Subjective Qualitative Human Systemic/Holistic	Hybrid	Engineering 'Objective' Quantitative Technical Reductionist

Figure 1.4   Continuum of approaches to management

We can identify examples of each type:

- *Organizational rationality*: This is a hard approach to management. It assumes that behavior (including decision making) is guided by a desire to produce outcomes that best meet formally stated organizational objectives. Outcomes are produced on the basis of what is the optimal solution according to logical criteria. An understanding of rational decision-making models and management roles will help us understand this approach.
- *Personal politics*: This is a soft approach to management. It assumes that behavior (including decision making) is guided by a desire to produce outcomes that best meet personal (often covert and informal) objectives. Outcomes are produced on the basis of compromise between conflicting personal objectives. That compromise will be based upon a mix of the objectives of major stakeholders, their bargaining skills, and the political resources (such as power and attention) that they can bring to bear. An understanding of self-interest and informal groupings will help us understand this approach. Although not used in its title, this approach does have an innate sense of rationality. That is to say, as with organizational rationality, it explains a set of underlying objectives which organizational actors could

rationally use in order to guide their behavior. But this is an individual, personal rationality rather than a formalized, impersonal rationality.

Differences between these two approaches can be summarized using the ITPOSMO checklist. Table 1.1 shows how e-government systems would differ if initiated by the two different methods (adapted from Heeks, 2001).

Returning to Figure 1.2 and the discussion about socio-technical systems, we could draw a simple conclusion: both organizational rationality and personal politics are wrong for e-government. eGovernment is a mix of hard and soft, so it needs a mixed management approach that encompasses both hard and soft.

In this book, a management approach that mixes and/or compromises between two extremes will be called a *hybrid* approach. The socio-technical approach to management of e-government would be one example of a hybrid style. In later chapters, other examples will be encountered, such as a hybrid style that mixes centralized and decentralized approaches to the management of e-government.

Is that it then? Solely hard or solely soft management approaches cause e-government failure. Socio-technical and other hybrid styles of management are the answer to e-government success. The end.

Table 1.1   *Differences between two hard and soft management approaches*

Dimension	Organizational rationality approach	Personal politics approach
Information	Emphasis on standardized, formal, quantitative information	Emphasis on contingent, informal, qualitative information
Technology	A simple enabling mechanism	A complex, value-laden entity: status symbol for some, tool of oppression for others
Processes	Stable, straightforward and formal; decision outcomes as optimal solutions based on logical criteria	Flexible, complex, constrained and often informal; decision outcomes as compromises based on 'power games'
Objectives and values	Formal organizational objectives	Multiple, informal, personal objectives
Staffing and skills	Staff and other users viewed as rational beings	Staff and other users viewed as political beings
Management systems and structures	Emphasis on formal, objective systems and structures	Emphasis on informal, personalized systems and structures
Other resources: time and money	Used to achieve organizational objectives	Used to achieve personal objectives

Unfortunately, life is not quite so simple and we move on to the second lesson from Figure 1.2.

Design and Reality

Figure 1.2 shows that the context for all public sector systems – not just e-government systems but also management systems – is important. In that case, we must be cautious about generalizing from one situation to another. A system might work well in a context, say, of political harmony, of a culture of informality, and of clear organizational strategy. However, that system may not work at all in a context of political conflict and a culture of formality where there is no clear strategy.

We can analyze this a bit more systematically by understanding the difference between two things. On the one hand, reality: how things really are in any given public agency. On the other hand, design: the requirements or assumptions built into a particular system, be it a management approach or an e-government application. Case analysis shows that the greater the gap between system design and agency reality, the greater the likelihood of a system failure. Conversely, the smaller the design–reality gap, the greater the chance of success.

Hard approaches – such as organizational rationality – are popular among public managers dealing with e-government systems (Grönlund, 2002). They (wrongly) associate e-government with technology, and technology with objectivity, formality, and rationality. Thus they follow a hard approach. But there will often be a gap between the requirements and assumptions of organizational rationality (a hard approach to design) and the reality of public agencies. For, in practice, the reality of many public agencies is a reality closer to the 'personal politics' perspective, as has long been recognized:

> [A] government agency is a political system of partly conflicting interests in which decisions are made through bargaining, power, and coalition formation. In general, there appear to be a few elementary rules for operating in a political system. Power comes from a favorable position for trading favors. Thus it comes from the possession of resources ... If you have valued resources, display them. If you don't have them, get them – even if you don't value them yourself. (March, 1986: 314)

Organizational rationality and related hard approaches will therefore run into difficulties when their requirements and assumptions mismatch public sector realities.

This is not to say that such approaches to the management of e-government will always be wrong. Some public agencies – or some parts of some public agencies – may well operate both in theory *and* practice according to organizationally-rational guidelines (Lenk et al., 2002). In these contexts, a hard approach will fit well.

And what of hybrid approaches? A hybrid approach that mixes hard and soft, will work at least to some extent in a broader set of public sector situations than a wholly soft or wholly hard approach will. There are also (as described in Box 1.1) probably a growing number of situations where a hybrid hard–soft mix will fit very well, since this matches the realities of organizational culture and procedures.

Box 1.1   Between Organizational Rationality and Personal Politics: 'Rational Politics'

Some public agencies seem to work in a way that is half-way between organizational rationality and personal politics (Andersen, 2001). Take the example of an agency trying to win a competition or a bid for central funds. There is a certain amount of rationality involved as laid down by the competition/bid parameters. However, there is also a certain amount of politicking involved: schmoozing with key decision makers, finding out who else is competing, using political resources and bargaining. This politicking can be seen as not in the interests of any individual but in the interests of the whole organization (though one might argue about the extent to which those can be disentangled). This, then, is the half-way house of 'rational politics'.

Rational politics has a number of fractions. Towards the rational end of the spectrum is a characteristic of reformed public agencies, which have a focus on 'whatever it takes to get the job done'. There may be a focus on problem solving and innovation, and a focus on team-working and flexibility (Hafeez and Savani, 2003). The agencies may be characterized by what is known as a 'task culture'.

Towards the politics end of the spectrum is that classic inter-agency battle: the turf war. In this, different public agencies seek to defend their power and resources against the encroachment of other agencies, often to the detriment of 'customer-centric' service delivery (Bannister, 2003).

While recommending hybrid approaches, though, this book falls short of seeing them as a guaranteed prescription for success. Instead, its underlying philosophy is a contingent one. This argues first for an analysis of current public sector realities; and second for an assessment of which management and e-government system designs will best fit this reality.

Before finishing, one further upshot of this contingent philosophy will be noted. It recognizes that – despite the best efforts of various neo-liberal reformers – the public sector remains fundamentally different from the private sector:

> Government is not a business. Forcing government managers into private sector thinking usually causes more problems than it solves. (Goddard and Riback, 1998)

The sectors differ in many ways, including their espoused objectives (broader in the public sector); their view of 'customers' (more holistic in the public sector); their relation to 'customers' (mixed with roles as citizens and compliers in the public sector); their accountabilities and perceived stakeholders (broader in the public sector); their human and technological infrastructure (weaker in the public sector); the politicization of their processes (greater in the public sector); and the scale and nature of competition (smaller and political in the public sector) (Heeks and Bhatnagar, 2001).

Because these two sectors are different, the contingent model tells us that what works in one sector will not necessarily work well in the other. In other words, just as government is not business, so e-government is not e-business. Ideas, lessons and applications can be passed between the two sectors, but you cannot just pick up an e-business package and successfully shoehorn it into the public sector. Contingency means significant changes in the design of business systems are needed before they will operate within the context of public sector realities.

Returning to our starting point, then – the failure of so many e-government systems – we can see that one root cause will be management approaches and designs that mismatch the realities of specific public agencies and that mismatch the socio-technical realities of e-government. Adopting more realistic and more hybridized management approaches and designs will improve e-government success rates. The remainder of the book investigates what this means in practice.

ACTIVITIES

Shorter In-Class Activities[2]

Chapter Introduction

a. Discuss why the widespread failure of e-government projects is not well reflected in most books and articles on the topic. Who stands to gain (and who – if anyone – stands to lose) from portraying e-government as a success story?

b. Discuss whether e-government failure has any benefits. If it does, discuss whether we should still worry about trying to avoid failure.

Section 1.1

a. Select two or three IT applications that can be used to support e-government (email, intranets, decision support systems, transactional web pages, SMS, geographic information systems, ERP and many others are examples). For each application, give an example of what an information system (that is, IT plus information plus people plus work processes) would be.

b. Select one type of e-government application. Explain how that application works in CIPSODA terms.

Section 1.2

a. Discuss whether there are other approaches to management than the organizational rationality, personal politics, and hybrid/socio-technical approaches identified in this section.

b. Identify one or two public sector organizations – or parts of public sector organizations – where each of the approaches described below would be likely to be found: organizational rationality, personal politics, rational politics.

c. Hard approaches like organizational rationality are popular among managers dealing with e-government systems because hard approaches are associated with technology. Can you think of any other reasons why some public managers like hard approaches to systems management?

d. Think of a well-known failure: it doesn't have to be related to either IT or government, and doesn't have to be recent. Analyze how differences between design and on-the-ground realities contributed to the failure.

Assignment Questions

Section 1.1

a. Identify two fairly-detailed e-government case studies, and analyze the components

and context of each into the eight ITPOSMOO dimensions. Then, analyze your use of the checklist: for example, has ITPOSMOO left out critical factors? Did it force you to shoehorn items into dimensional headings that were not really appropriate? Did it provide any insights or added value compared to the original case study?

b. Locate a case study of e-government failure. Analyze how differences between assumptions/requirements within e-government design and actual public sector realities contributed to the failure. Use the ITPOSMO(O) checklist to help you.

Section 1.2

a. eGovernment is just e-business by another name. Discuss.

Practitioner Exercises

Chapter Introduction

a. Use discussions with colleagues and other informal data-gathering techniques to estimate the percentage of e-government projects with which your organization is involved that end in total or partial failure. Does your estimate suggest that anything should be done about these failures?

Section 1.1

a. Identify two or three of the key e-government systems operating within your organization. Analyze these as information systems into their main component parts: IT, information, people and work processes.

b. Select one of the key e-government systems that you are working on. Analyze it according to the ITPOSMOO checklist. Reflect on whether or not this analysis has provided any additional insights or value.

Section 1.2

a. Note down which of the following perspectives explains or fits more of your organization and its activities than the others:

- *Organizational rationality*: For example, where decisions are made on the basis of formal steps and logical criteria.
- *Personal politics*: For example, where decisions are made on the basis of self-interest.
- *Rational politics*: For example, where decisions use political thinking to achieve organizational goals.
- *Other*: Some other perspective.

What implications do your findings have for management and e-government in your organization?

b. Analyze the different aspects of management for e-government in your organization. Identify various different dimensions along which management could be said to be 'hybrid' (even if it currently is not hybrid within your organization).

c. Think back to a failure of e-government in your organization. Analyze how differences between system design and on-the-ground realities contributed to the failure.

d. In what ways is your organization different from a private sector company? What implications does this have for the management of e-government?

NOTES

1. Examples of this checklist being applied to real-world e-government cases are provided in the Online Appendix for Chapter 10.

2. Details of longer group activities are provided in the Online Appendix to this chapter.

Part One
Managing eGovernment

2

Approaches to Management
of eGovernment Systems

Key Points

- The management of e-government systems involves managing data, technology, people and processes.
- There are three possible approaches to e-government management: centralized, decentralized, and hybrid.
- Centralized, top-down approaches may be efficient but can be unworkable or ineffective.
- Decentralized approaches may match organizational realities but be high cost and/or low scope.
- Hybrid approaches may be effective by compromising between central and local or by dividing responsibilities between central and local.
- Ultimately, resources, values and politics determine how e-government is managed in particular organizations.

Chapter 1 talked generally about the management of e-government systems. We can break this down into a more detailed set of e-government management responsibilities, drawing partly on the notion that e-government systems are information systems that contain data, technology, people and processes:

- *eGovernment systems planning*: The priorities set for new e-government systems, for the applications of new IT, and for other systems-related changes.
- *Organizational structures and staffing*: The organizational structures used to support the e-government function, and the staffing of that function.
- *Data management*: The way in which data is structured and controlled in the organization.

- *Computing and data management architecture*: The way in which IT is spread and connected throughout the organization, and the way in which data structures and processing are divided across the IT.
- *Systems development*: The who and how by which new e-government systems are analyzed, designed, constructed and implemented.
- *Procurement*: What IT is procured and how it is procured.
- *Training*: What skills are required in training, how that training is to be delivered, and to whom.
- *Technical support*: The way in which IT for e-government is installed, maintained, repaired and otherwise supported in its operation.

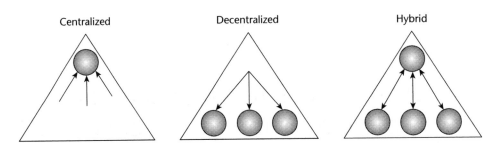

Figure 2.1   Different approaches to e-government systems responsibilities

As outlined in Chapter 1, there are different ways in which management for e-government can be understood. In this chapter, we focus on organizational level, and identify three possible approaches to e-government responsibilities (see Figure 2.1):

- *Centralized*: Decisions are taken at the most senior or central level.
- *Decentralized*: Decisions are taken at some level lower than the most senior; typically by individual work units within the organization or even by individual staff. The latter may also be referred to as *end-user computing*, where the individuals within the public sector who make use of outputs from e-government systems (the internal end users) are also those who operate and/or develop and/or manage those systems.
- *Hybrid*: Decisions are taken at *both* senior and lower levels, either separately or in an integrated manner. This approach is called *federal* or *federated* in some governments.

2.1 THE CENTRALIZED APPROACH TO ᴇGOVERNMENT SYSTEMS RESPONSIBILITIES

Examples of a Centralized Approach

Some examples can be given of what a centralized approach to e-government would mean. In terms of computing and data management architecture, a centralized computing architecture would be one which involves a large central computer with *dumb terminals* or *network computers* attached. That represents an internal view of architecture. An external view sees centralized data architecture in terms of portals: single central web locations through which all data is routed to users. Such a view is reflected in the Box 2.1 case.

Under a centralized approach, e-government systems are typically developed by a team from the central IT unit, or by external contractors under central IT unit control. The content and timing of individual projects can be drawn from any e-government strategy that has been developed (see Chapter 3). That strategy could also be used to guide procurement, where organization-wide standards would be set for hardware, software and telecommunications equipment. Typically a central group is responsible for setting standards, arranging contracts with suppliers, policing standards, and giving final approval on all IT purchase requests. Purchases of IT and IT budgets are routed through a central control point.

In a centralized approach, training is planned and prioritized organization-wide to fit in with e-government plans. Like technical support, it may be delivered by external providers or by specialist staff from the central IT unit. Centralized approaches to some of the other responsibility areas are discussed elsewhere: systems strategic planning in Chapter 3 and organizational structures and staffing in Chapter 5.[1]

Potential Benefits of a Centralized Approach

Many public sector organizations began their 'computing careers' by adopting a centralized approach, and there are continuing drives to maintain centralization. The growth of IT in the public sector means increasing expenditure within a political environment that often prioritizes cost-cutting. Centralized approaches are then attractive because they promise opportunities for reducing costs (Bocij et al., 2003; Wittkemper and Kleindiek, 2003):

- *Achievement of scale economies*: Centralized approaches allow most activities to be undertaken more cheaply per unit. Items purchased externally – computers, software packages, consumables, staff training, systems development, consulting, and so on – can be decided upon once and then bought in greater bulk. Activities undertaken internally – from system development to implementation and maintenance, and management of all these processes – cover a greater number of staff.
- *Avoidance of duplication*: One main intention of centralized approaches is to have a single version of any particular e-government system for the whole organization, and to store any item of data once and only once. As a result, there is no wasted effort, no wasted storage capacity, and no inconsistency of data. For example, only one accounting application needs to be developed for the whole agency. Similarly, if dealing with a set of external clients (such as businesses in the Box 2.1 case), each client's name and details are captured once for use on a single, shared database. If these details change or if the required data structure changes, only one set of amendments needs to be made. The database represents the single authoritative source of digital information in the organization. This saves money, and can also improve data quality; an issue taken up again in Chapter 4.
- *Sharing resources*. A well-planned centralized system holds data used across the organization in one place, allowing all staff to access it. This makes it cheaper, faster and easier to undertake organization-wide activities. Central planning and operation also allows compatible technology and skills to be introduced. Exchange of hardware, software and staff between organizational systems and units therefore becomes much easier and less costly.

The growth of IT also means increasingly pervasive impacts associated with e-government,

---

Box 2.1 Centralized Approach to Business Registration via eGovernment in Nova Scotia, Canada

The Nova Scotia Business Registry (NSBR) is a centralized system that draws together previously separate business registration activities spread across three different federal and provincial agencies (Holmes, 2001). External users benefit because businesses now have to register only once via a central portal. There are internal benefits also. The portal and related back-office software for registration had to be designed only once. The federal agency centrally dispenses a single identification number (previously a business could be issued with six different numbers), which ensures that data is held only once and can be shared easily across the various agencies.

and – as systems increasingly link agencies with citizens and businesses – increasing political fallout from failure. Centralized approaches are then attractive because they promise greater senior manager control over system outcomes including issues such as security or data privacy. Such approaches provide an organizational focus for learning and for control. This may well produce more successful (and cheaper) e-government systems by avoiding the decentralization problems of non-functioning or malfunctioning systems; by avoiding the decentralization problems of inadequate security, maintenance and documentation; and by allowing technology purchases and system developments that are not organizational priorities to be blocked.

It may also produce e-government systems that meet the needs of groups rather than individuals and of the central/senior management rather than peripheral interests. In this sense, there is a greater fit between e-government systems and 'organizational needs'.

Constraints to Centralized Approaches

Centralized approaches to e-government management are beset by constraints (Fountain, 2001; Holmes, 2001; Huang and Smithson, 2003; Mahler and Regan, 2003). Many are the challenges of creating centralized network-based systems, of sharing, and of collaborating. We can categorize some of those constraints in terms of the ITPOSMO dimensions of e-government systems introduced in Chapter 1.

Information, Technology and Process Constraints

Where decentralized information systems, manual or computerized, are already in place, barriers to centralization may be severe. In order to centralize, changes may need to be made to the organization's whole information systems architecture: new data fields and formats, new hardware and software, new processes by which to handle data, and new processes by which to make decisions and take actions.

The perception of information itself is also a constraint to centralized approaches. Information is intangible, and public managers rely heavily on informal information in their decision making (Cohen and Eimicke, 2002). Information is therefore perceived in a way that makes it hard for senior public managers to appreciate some of the key tenets of a centralized approach: that information is an organization-wide resource; that it has a cost; that it can provide value for the public sector; that it needs to be managed; and so on.

Objectives and Values Constraints

Centralization means changes in flows of resources: of people, of money, of technology, of information. Those public managers who perceive themselves as potential resource losers will resist centralization. With data, for example, staff find it hard to think of 'my data' or 'our data' becoming 'the organization's data'. This is a particular problem for the public sector given the political antagonisms caused by the need to fight over limited resources.

Differences between the objectives and values (that is, the cultures) of particular groups in the public sector also cause a problem. One can perceive a four-way gap, as summarized in Figure 2.2 (adapted from Knight and Silk, 1990)

Each of these groups can be analyzed in more detail, to see how all their differing views constrain the development of centralized approaches. We can present some generalizations that – while stereotyped – are still widespread in the public sector (Heeks, 2000b):

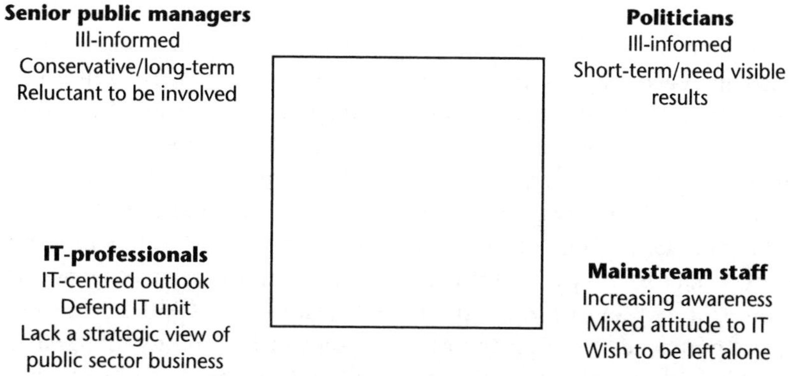

Senior public managers
Ill-informed
Conservative/long-term
Reluctant to be involved

Politicians
Ill-informed
Short-term/need visible
results

IT-professionals
IT-centred outlook
Defend IT unit
Lack a strategic view of
public sector business

Mainstream staff
Increasing awareness
Mixed attitude to IT
Wish to be left alone

Figure 2.2   The 'IT square' of gaps between different public sector staff cultures

- *Politicians*: Have a limited understanding of IT, but want quick and visible results. They may resist large-scale centralized approaches and prefer smaller, citizen-oriented initiatives that have a lower risk and shorter time-scale.
- *Senior public managers*: Have limited understanding of IT or its possible uses in their agency. They may resist any centralized approaches they fear they cannot understand or control.
- *IT professionals*: Do not understand the public organization's business and are only really interested in the technology. This prevents centralized approaches being business-led, and leaves them being technology-led. Such approaches to e-government, if developed at all, therefore address only IT, not data or information systems or business objectives.
- *Mainstream staff* can be divided into:

  o *computer illiterates*: a declining number who feel threatened by IT, the jargon of e-government and its association with change and the unknown; they will resist centralized approaches because of their fears, and
  o *computer literates*: a growing number who want to pursue their own agenda without seeing the need for

co-ordination of IT activities or for 'interference' from IT staff; they will undermine centralized approaches by trying to develop their own e-government systems.

- In addition, there may be members of the most difficult staff group – *semi-literates* – who think they know all about IT and e-government, are vocal in expressing their opinions, but who in practice understand little about the technology and nothing about information systems. Their ignorance may undermine centralized approaches.

In addition to the specific constraints that each group brings, the gaps between groups are a serious constraint since centralized approaches encompass all groups and must either compromise or override group differences. Yet these differences of objectives and values run deep, and are reflected in inter-group gaps of knowledge, of culture, of language and of trust. It is these that partly create the design–reality gaps identified in Chapter 1, and discussed in more detail in Part 2.

*Staffing and Skills, and
Other Resources Constraints*

Centralized approaches require the commitment of four key resources – money, time, people, and skills – all in short supply in the public sector. For many public organizations, a centralized approach may not be possible because of financial constraints; because staff are too busy on other things; or because no-one has the confidence or capabilities to undertake the necessary planning and coordination tasks. Sometimes, skills and awareness may be present within the organization, but not in the right place. Centralized approaches require involvement of senior staff, yet it is they who are often the last in the public sector to pick up IT or systems skills.

Partly related to this is the perception of costs and benefits. The costs of decentralized approaches – of wasted efforts, of organizational inflexibility, of staff time diverted from other activities – are frequently hidden. The benefits, such as managers being able to do what they like, are fairly obvious. For centralized approaches, by contrast, the equation is often the other way round. The resources needed for the implementation of centralized approaches require an overt, up-front commitment. The benefits, though, may be rather intangible, and it can be difficult to shift the perceived cost/benefit balance in favor of centralization. This is particularly an issue because so many public sector budgets follow stovepipes and it can be very hard to get new money for centralized, 'cross-stovepipe' initiatives.

*Management Systems and
Structures Constraints*

Existing division of responsibilities between different functional units within a public sector organization, or different agencies within government, can constrain centralized approaches. In the US, for example, responsibility for IT-based systems was traditionally divided between four agencies (Wolfe, 2001): the General Accounting Office (now Government Accountability Office), covering audit; the Office of Management and Budget, covering policy; the General Services Administration, covering procurement; and the National Institute of Standards & Technology, covering technical standards. This restricted both the potential for, and the effectiveness of, centralized approaches to e-government in the US. Even where one agency appeared to take a lead, as OMB did in the early 2000s (some details of recent OMB activity are given below in Box 2.6), others will be constantly jockeying to get back in the race.

Structural divisions can be exacerbated during reform processes of decentralization, privatization and outsourcing that lead to fragmentation of public sector organizations. We are then faced with the paradox that public sector reform may simultaneously increase the requirement for, but decrease the possibility of, centralized approaches to the management of e-government.

These structural barriers spill over into other areas. Like the four groups of the IT square, decentralized units develop different ways of working, different mindsets that create quite different views of the world between groups; different jargon used in communication; and different issues and people that are valued. Structural differences therefore create information, process and objectives/values differences. This makes it hard to centralize. In the US, for example, OMB's efforts to maintain ownership for centralized initiatives have the feel of trying to put Humpty-Dumpty back together again. Even relatively small centralized e-government initiatives have required (OMB, 2002):

- a Managing Partner from the President's Management Council;
- a Program Office established by the partner;
- a Portfolio Management Office within OMB, itself reporting to an Associate

Director and thence to the OMB Director who gives final approval;

- a Portfolio Steering Committee formed by the CIO Council and related councils; and
- an Integrated Project Team reporting to a Portfolio Manager.

Summary of Constraints

Some of these barriers also exist to decentralized approaches, and we should recognize them as *barriers to change in general* rather than to one or other management approach. However, the barriers to centralized e-government approaches appear greater and, the more strategic and centralized the approach, the greater these barriers are likely to be. In part, this difference arises from the extent to which centralized approaches are associated with organizational rationality, and decentralized approaches with personal politics.

Despite the public sector's ongoing love affair with grand designs, then, centralized approaches to e-government may be particularly hard to implement. The broader and larger the scope of centralization, the harder it is to implement in practice.

Potential Disadvantages of Centralized Approaches

Even if the listed constraints were to be overcome, centralized approaches can produce some disadvantageous outcomes. One obvious disadvantage of a centralized approach – as already noted above – is the high level of overt resource costs. Other disadvantages are described in Box 2.2 and also below.

Heavy Time Consumption

Centralized decisions and actions can be more time-consuming than for a decentralized approach because of: the additional time it takes for information to flow up the organization as an input to centralized decisions; the additional time it takes to collate information from a variety of different decentralized locations as an input to centralized decisions; and the additional time it takes for implementation information to flow down the organization. The result can be inordinate delays in the process of systems development, as seen in practice with, say, large-scale centralized aviation systems in the US public

---

Box 2.2 Problems with a Centralized Approach to Public Healthcare Information Systems

The Ecuadorian government has been committed to decentralization of its public healthcare system, with greater emphasis on primary care institutions such as health centers and county hospitals (Salazar, 2001). Part of this commitment included an e-government project that would use IT to support the work of primary care managers. Unfortunately, due to a long tradition of centralized decision making in Ecuador's public sector, this project was undertaken via a top-down, centralized approach.

As a result, the new e-government system – which took more than 15 months to introduce – was based around the needs and agendas of senior staff in the Ministry of Public Health. It focused on resource costing and budgeting issues that were Ministry priorities, and could not be adjusted to support the day-to-day work of health center and county hospital managers. The project did succeed in putting IT infrastructure in place at some sites, but actual use of the system 'was, at best, partial and, at worst, nonexistent.' The project was then abandoned, to be reinitiated two years later following a more decentralized approach.

sector and social security systems in the UK public sector (Margetts, 1999; HCTI, 2003).

Limited Ability to Meet User Needs

Centralized approaches necessarily mean that priority goes to those e-government systems which are seen as important by some select and centralized staff group. The priorities of the periphery – both individuals and individual work units inside government, as well as clients outside government – may not be addressed. Thus, in the Box 2.2 case, the needs of local managers, let alone their patients, were not met.

Consequences of this failure to meet internal and external user requirements may include a backlog of user applications awaiting development; limited use or even total failure of centrally planned e-government systems because their design does not match user realities; and poor quality of data within these systems, since users will not be motivated to maintain data quality (see Chapter 4).

The frequent outcome is that end users subvert central controls and impose a de facto decentralization. This was certainly the outcome in Ecuador. Individual managers continued to use their own manual or locally computerized information systems, and made little or no use of the central system. Any data they did feed up to the ministry for its purposes was of limited value.

Inflexibility

The greater the amount of central planning that has gone into an e-government system decision, and the longer that decision is therefore intended to provide guidance for the organization, the less flexibility it offers the organization to cope with differences between local units, or with internal or external changes. Yet the pace of environmental change is continuously increasing for public sector organizations as technology, society, the legal framework, and so on, change.

Increased Dependence and Vulnerability

In general, centralized approaches to e-government systems make public sector organizations more dependent and more vulnerable since they create greater numbers of staff and clients relying on single management units, and greater reliance on a few key staff who plan, develop and run e-government.

2.2 THE DECENTRALIZED APPROACH TO ᴇGOVERNMENT SYSTEMS RESPONSIBILITIES

Examples of a Decentralized Approach

Examples of a decentralized approach to managing e-government systems responsibilities can be provided. In terms of computing and data management architecture, a truly decentralized computing architecture would be one that involves standalone computers or, possibly, a peer-to-peer network. Decentralized approaches are commonly associated with the spread of personal computers throughout an organization. An external view would see multiple web sites and other routes through which data could be accessed.

Under a fully decentralized approach, e-government systems would be developed within organizational work groups, focused on their requirements, or even by individual end users. Decentralized procurement means that individuals or groups select and procure whichever technology best suits their particular needs. Similarly, a decentralized approach to training means that individuals or small groups plan their own training needs. It is likely that training takes place on the job or through informal coaching of one staff member by another.

The same approach could be taken to technical support, though such tasks are often too specialized to be provided by individual staff, so provision may be left to

IT vendors or to specialized staff within individual work units. In a similar way, the planning and prioritization of e-government systems could be left to individuals or work units but it would more typically be centralized, at least to the level of the individual public sector organization, as discussed in Chapter 3. Data management is discussed in Chapter 4. Organizational structures and staffing are discussed in Chapter 5.

Potential Benefits of a Decentralized Approach

It would seem from Section 2.1 that centralized management approaches to e-government are highly problematic. What, then, of decentralized approaches such as those just described? As the technology behind e-government has become smaller, cheaper, easier-to-use, more reliable, and more powerful, so decentralized approaches seem to be an increasing possibility.

Decentralization may itself be driven by public sector politics, such as a desire by managers of individual units and departments to wrest control of e-government away from the central IT unit. Those central units often have an image problem with other public servants: being seen as out-of-touch, slow, and costly (Malstrom, 1999; Turban et al., 2001). Decentralization switches this round, with a number of perceived benefits, which include those listed below (Heeks, 2000b; Jessup and Valacich, 2006).

Greater Fit between Systems and Local Needs

The closer the proximity of user and developer, the less the communication gap and the more likely it is that the developed system meets the users' real needs. External client users have yet to be employed as systems developers, but internal users of both internal and external e-government systems

are being allowed to develop such systems (e.g. Jorgensen and Cable, 2002). Where this happens, the approach is far more likely to meet their requirements than when their systems are developed by someone else.

In many ways, then, the more decentralized the approach, the smaller the gap is likely to be between system design and user reality. As Chapter 1 outlined, this will have predictable results on the success rate of e-government systems, explaining why decentralized approaches (such as end-user computing) have been associated with such dramatic growth in IT use.

Users will also be better motivated by such approaches. As seen in Chapter 4, together with designs that better match user realities, this will positively impact data quality which, in turn, should improve learning and decision making.

Faster System Development

The less the organizational distance between system user and system developer, the faster development of that system is likely to be. Again, taking an extreme of end-user development, there will be no delay for the development of mutual understanding and no clash with higher priority e-government systems developments. This can help to overcome the staffing constraints and systems development backlog that often afflict centralized IT units. Other aspects of system use such as implementation, operation, troubleshooting and maintenance are also likely to occur more quickly under a decentralized regime.

Perceived Lower Costs

The past decade has been characterized by a growing realization that the costs of decentralized approaches are greater than anticipated because of many initially unrecognized indirect costs (Eggers, 2003). Nevertheless, it could still be argued that decentralized approaches present lower costs than centralized approaches in certain areas. This is thanks to faster development, less miscommunication, greater fit to local needs through smaller design–reality gaps, the greater emphasis on smaller computers, the greater emphasis on buying software packages rather than developing software in-house, and so on.

Constraints to a Decentralized Approach

As already noted, many of the ITPOSMO constraints to centralized approaches described above are, in fact, constraints to change in general. They are therefore also constraints to a decentralized approach and will not be reiterated in detail. Examples include:

- *information, technology and process constraints*, such as heavy existing investments in a centralized system;
- *objectives/values constraints*, such as the unwillingness of those at the center to change information flows, resource flows and associated organizational power;
- *staffing and skills constraints*, such as a lack of skills to support decentralized decision making and action on e-government systems.

However, it is rare for these constraints to be completely insurmountable, partly because of the great motivation of staff and individual work units to take some control over IT. At least some elements of decentralization of the e-government function are therefore found in almost all public sector organizations.

Potential Disadvantages of a Decentralized Approach

Even if constraints can be overcome, decentralized approaches can produce some

disadvantageous outcomes, as exemplified by the case study in Box 2.3.

Potential disadvantages include:

Barriers to Sharing Data

Decentralized approaches can create e-government systems in different work units that are mutually incompatible. The resulting 'electronic concrete', like its centralized counterpart, constrains the scope of activities that public agencies can undertake, or imposes substantial additional time and financial costs on those activities. In particular, strategic, organization-wide activities are constrained. This can lead to anything from a difficulty in aggregating basic financial information across the organization, to an inability to implement any strategic plans, including the delivery of one-stop services for external clients. In the case of the US agencies discussed in Box 2.3, it constrained the type of data-matching exercise necessary to identify likely terrorist suspects.

Barriers to Sharing Other Resources, Including Human Resources

There may also be an inability to share other resources if work units are allowed to set up their own separate e-government systems. It may be hard to exchange hardware and software. Perhaps more importantly, each individual system requires a unique set of skills for system development, implementation and operation. This makes it more difficult for staff to move between different e-government systems.

Duplication of Effort

Apart from constraining what public organizations can do, decentralized approaches also tend to be very costly because units will often duplicate what others are doing, as those in the FBI, INS and other agencies did

> ## Box 2.3   Decentralized Approaches Cause Problems
> ## for US Homeland Security
>
> The US Department of Homeland Security (DHS) was created in the wake of the 2001 attacks on the World Trade Center and Pentagon. It is understandable that data-sharing problems would exist, as the DHS brought together 22 separate agencies. More troubling, though, was the discovery that decentralized approaches within individual agencies meant those agencies could not access their own data properly:
>
> > Historically, software systems have been developed independently, servicing only each specific unit's needs. ... The same data in different systems ... usually have different names, codes, and formats. ... the FBI has had no enterprise-wide architecture but rather had separate databases for more than 50 applications, which are written in various languages and running on disparate systems. (Laudon and Laudon, 2005: 261)
>
> Similar problems beset the Immigration and Naturalization Service (INS). It was unable to locate many of the foreigners wanted for questioning by the FBI, and had lost track of thousands from countries where al-Qaeda operates. The main problem was a decentralized approach that had allowed 'more than 16 separate database systems to capture data on aliens, including a Non-Immigrant Information System, an Asylum Prescreening System, a Student Exchange Visitor Information System, an Arrival Departure Information System, a Student and Schools System, a Deportable Alien Control System, and a Refugees, Asylum and Parole System.' (Laudon and Laudon, 2005: 262) These systems overlapped to some degree both in their functions, and in the foreigners on whom data was being kept.

in the Box 2.3 case. Duplication covered analysis, design and implementation of e-government systems; gathering and administration of data; and system operation, support and maintenance. In addition, computer input, processing, storage and output capacity all had to be duplicated.

The unnecessary duplication of data (known as *data redundancy*) tends to be particularly problematic. Yet it is quite common in the public sector. As seen in the Box 2.3 case, immigration agencies often store details of the same foreigner several times. Likewise, local government often stores basic details of the citizens in its area many times over. It stores data on paper and on computer, and it stores data for education, for health, for social welfare, for housing, etc. It is estimated that the average local government offers 300 different services and

holds 35 separate address databases covering addresses in its jurisdiction (Leslie, 1999; Leenes, 2002).

This imposes extra costs in gathering, maintaining and updating data. In addition, because data about similar entities is held simultaneously in two or more different locations, it tends to become inconsistent. This has been a particular problem in the fight against terrorism. No-one then knows which, if any, version of the data is the most accurate or up-to-date. Trying to put together a reliable record becomes immensely time-consuming if not practically impossible.

All of this internal duplication also has a knock-on for citizens and other clients of the public sector: they have to duplicate their efforts in interacting with the public sector through different system interfaces.

Lack of Learning and Control

In addition to the extra direct costs that duplication imposes, there is an indirect cost of lost learning opportunities and limited cross-fertilization of ideas. Decentralized management approaches also necessarily mean limited central ability to plan and control, leading to a tendency for some decentralized e-government systems to be developed and used without due care. The result may be a system that never works or does not work properly, with compromised data quality or system security.

There may also be a tendency to develop applications that are personal or group priorities but not organizational priorities: e-government systems may be developed with the intention of furthering a political powerbase or a personal career rather than of producing benefits for the organization and its clients.

Failure to Achieve Scale Economies

As already noted, there are scale economies in e-government systems management covering data, people, hardware and other resources. Decentralized approaches make many e-government-related activities more costly, from buying computers, to gathering data, to training staff, to system operation and maintenance.

Summary of Problems

All of these problems can be largely summarized as: higher-than-desirable costs and/or a lower-than-desirable scope of public sector activities. The intangibility of many of the problems means that costs are not always recognized. For example, only in recent years have the true costs of end-user microcomputer ownership begun to emerge, with estimates up to US$8000 or more per computer per year (Bocij et al., 2003). Much of this is the cost of staff time taken up when ordinary staff provide support to other users, and when PCs are used for non-job-related or other unproductive activities. Training, maintenance and administration costs also contribute. Large, centralized computing systems are estimated to cost something like one-third to one-half of this amount per user per year (CBR, 2001).

More critical still, though, is the reduced scope of the public sector, preventing it from undertaking a proper role in a modern society.

2.3 RESOLVING THE CONTRADICTIONS VIA A HYBRID APPROACH TO eGOVERNMENT

The foregoing review of public sector experience presents some challenging contradictions. Both the centralized and the decentralized approach to managing e-government can provide benefits for public organizations. Yet, at the same time, such approaches can be hard or impossible to implement, and can produce serious disadvantages for the organization.

What is the way out of this quandary? One way forward is the adoption of a hybrid approach that attempts to reconcile the push of the centralized approach with the pull of the decentralized approach. It does this in two ways. First, through *integration*: drawing the centralized and decentralized approaches together into some kind of unified or compromise approach (see Box 2.4). Second, and more commonly, through *division*. This accepts that both centralized and decentralized approaches will be found, and then attempts to set some demarcation lines that will keep the two separate, thereby allowing them both to be accommodated.

As noted in Box 2.4, the hybrid approach is not a panacea. It can suffer from some of the constraints and disadvantages outlined above. If handled poorly, in seeking some compromise between, or combination of, centralization and decentralization, it may

---

**Box 2.4   Australia's Business Entry Point:
Hybrid Cross-Tier eGovernment**

Most activity and most discussion of central, local or hybrid approaches to e-government tends to focus *within* specific layers of government. However, there is growing emergence of hybrid, cross-tier initiatives that link together two or more of: international, national, regional, state and local governments.

One example is Australia's Business Entry Point – a single web point of access that draws together online data and services from three tiers of the Australian government: Commonwealth (national), State, and local (Santos and Heeks, 2003; Turner, 2003). Unlike the example in Box 2.1, it has not imposed a central model in the back office, thus creating a combination of centralized portal with decentralized service systems. This has been a good example of a hybrid approach helping to meet user needs. However, it has been hampered by 'old school' thinking that finds it hard to envisage the new models of governance that cross-tier approaches can enable.

---

end up providing the worst of both worlds rather than best. For example, an unsuccessful hybrid policy for procurement will leave standards sufficiently loose to generate problems of incompatibility and high training and maintenance costs. Yet, at the same time, it will constrain staff from buying the technology that meets their particular needs.

However, if handled well, a hybrid approach to e-government can be feasible and provide distinct benefits. A decentralized approach may be *most economic* for public organizations, because it saves on overt input costs. A centralized approach may be *most efficient*, because it avoids waste and duplication. But a successful hybrid approach may be *most effective* because it can simultaneously provide:

- the control necessary to share key resources (including data), to avoid duplication, and to achieve economies of scale; and
- the freedom necessary to meet user needs, and to overcome blocks to IT usage and system development.

Hybrid Approach Content

What does all this mean in practical terms? It can mean separating whole functions. In the

US State Department, for example, successful progress on e-government has come from retaining computing and data management architecture under control of a central IT office, while decentralizing systems development responsibilities (Fulton, 2003). In other cases, it can mean hybridizing individual functions. Examples of this will now be described. As noted before, details of this type of hybrid approach are also discussed elsewhere: in Chapter 3 relating to e-government systems planning, in Chapter 4 relating to data management, and in Chapter 5 relating to organizational structures and staffing.

*Computing and Data
Management Architecture*

The most common hybrid computing architecture is the client/server model, in which computing power is divided between the central servers and the local client workstations. This architecture has now been adopted by vast numbers of public sector organizations worldwide (Turban et al., 2001).

The underlying networks are also part of the IT architecture. Persuading individual departments to join centralized networks has not been easy. The Canadian government – in response to such difficulties – has developed the hybrid concept of a 'federated architecture' (d'Auray, 2003). This allows departments to build their own networks but then provides a simple common infrastructure that can link those networks together. That infrastructure incorporates a computing architecture to allow the technology to plug together, and an information architecture allowing data to be exchanged. It has also moved further to try to promote a business architecture that would allow reuse of processes for service delivery.

A similar hybrid approach to portals creates a single main portal which merely links through to an existing set of sub-portals. Users are still free to go direct to the sub-portal if they wish, and main data management responsibilities are retained at the sub-portal level. This approach has been used for federal government portals in a number of countries such as the US and Germany: they just provide links to the sub-portals that are still run by individual ministries and departments (Wittkemper and Kleindiek, 2003).

Systems Development

A hybrid approach to systems development can involve a division of responsibilities; for example, defining certain types of e-government system as suitable for central development, and others as suitable for decentralized/end-user development. Decisions about how to classify project proposals for particular systems can be made by a joint team of managers with technical staff input. This team will allocate central resources only to projects meeting agreed criteria.

Candidates for central development (which could be outsourced under central control) might be those systems where one or more of the following applies:

- the system is critical to the functioning of the organization;
- the system is to be used by or from more than one department, such as a one-stop portal;
- data is drawn from several different sources; and/or
- there are particular technical issues, such as a very large database or a need for a fast response time.

Such e-government systems are seen as too important, too cross-cutting, and/or too skill-intensive to be appropriate for decentralized development.

Candidates for decentralized development might be those systems where one or more of the following applies:

- the system is relevant only to the individual user or department;
- data is drawn only from an existing centrally-managed database or from a proposed locally-managed database; and/or
- processing or reporting requirements are subject to frequent change.

Such e-government systems are seen as too small and/or too specific to be appropriate for central development.

A slightly different perspective would aim to create a division of responsibilities within the development of each individual e-government system. Ordinary staff in decentralized units might be responsible for systems analysis, training, documentation, and ongoing support. Centralized IT staff or staff from an external contractor might be responsible for design, construction, implementation, operation and maintenance of the system.

Alternatively, the central role may just be one of quality assurance: decentralized staff or work sections are responsible for developing an application, but quality is assured in some way by the central IT unit. This may involve central guidelines on anything from development methods to data structures, or central testing of programs or documentation. This approach was used when the city government in Boulder, Colorado created a new e-government system to support building and construction licensing and inspection (Harris, 2003). 'Power users' in the departments for Public Works, and Planning/ Development Services undertook design and programming work; while colleagues in the city's IT department had an overall responsibility for managing the project, including its quality and technical components.

Finally, a hybrid approach may also attempt to bridge internal divisions and have shared responsibilities for systems development. It might do this by creating structures that bring different groups together or through processes that allow these groups to communicate with each other. Such structures may involve participatory or prototyping techniques of systems development, as discussed further in Chapter 10.

Procurement

Standards for procurement bring many immediate and obvious benefits to public agencies. Unfortunately, they may be resented by local staff and can be circumvented relatively easily by those who have any local control over finances. This is a sensitive area because those who control the IT tend to control the information held by that technology. This, in turn, is a component of organizational power.

A hybrid approach to acquiring IT therefore typically involves a mixture of 'carrot and stick': encouraging local staff to follow standards, and providing some limited sanctions for those who do not. It also typically involves a flexible approach to

standards that allows users some local leeway within a set of boundaries. The US General Services Administration and the UK's Office of Government Commerce both make use of this approach, essentially providing public agencies with a shopping list of discounted items via central framework agreements. This is an 'opt in' model by which agencies can use these channels if they wish, but are not bound to do so.

Other elements of this approach may include:

- Reserving purchase of certain types of hardware (that is, servers or all network hardware) for central decisions, or reserving purchases above some financial threshold for central approval, but allowing other purchases to be made by individual units. One intention here is to retain central control over the hardware that will form an organization-wide technology backbone for e-government, such as telecommunications, but to relax other controls.
- Limiting the size of decentralized IT budgets. This avoids the extreme of a wholly centralized budget, which antagonizes users and leads them to spend other budgets on IT. It also avoids the extreme of a wholly decentralized IT budget, which can lead to an unwillingness to fund any central services.
- Disseminating a set of minimum functional requirements (memory, disk size, chip, operating system capability, network functionality, etc.) that all computers should meet, but allowing freedom of choice of model and supplier. Sometimes this is restricted further by use of an approved supplier list.
- Providing central advice, bulk purchase, installation assistance, training, and maintenance and repair services only for standardized hardware and software,

but allowing individual units to diverge from this if they are willing to support themselves.

- Setting organizational standards for IT on a committee with strong representation from individual work units.

Other Components

A common hybrid approach is to centralize the planning of training for core e-government systems. Other training needs may be met, as requested, by end-user support centers or by informal training methods. There may also be central provision of access to open and flexible learning systems such as CD-ROM- or Internet- or intranet-based training packages.

Technical support requires special consideration in relation to hybridization. Given the very specialist nature of many repair and maintenance tasks, there are very high costs in leaving them to individual staff. Many organizations, therefore, have at least one IT support employee per department who takes on this role. Centralizing this role even further – for example via outsourcing – can lead to response times and prioritization that may seem poor from a user perspective. However, the more specialized the role, the more the arguments for centralization.

In the case of both training and technical support (and other activities), consideration will have to be given to charges levied on work units or staff for centrally provided services. The benefit of charging (even a nominal sum) is that it induces users to take the services seriously. It will also transfer resources to the central IT unit. The problem of charging is that users may decide not to use the service, possibly creating additional costs for the organization if equipment is then not used properly or wrongly repaired or left in an unusable condition.

2.4 APPROACH TRENDS AND DETERMINANTS

As illustrated in Box 2.5, contradictory trends are at play in the public sector.

Thus we see an undeniable growth of dispersed responsibilities, yet at the same time we see continuing progress towards centralization. Perhaps even more confusingly, the overall chronological pattern of management approaches to IT in the public sector for some organizations is that shown in Figure 2.3. (e.g. Barrett and Greene, 2001; DOI, 2003)

How can we explain this, given the simultaneous trends favoring both centralization *and* decentralization? The first key is to understand the hybrid approach as consisting of the two separate strands described above: integration and division.

Integration

Integration is not really compatible with simultaneous trends of centralization and

---

Box 2.5   Contradictory Trends in Government

E-government structures also reflect overall government structures ... in many OECD countries, administrations have decentralized. (OECD, 2003a)

We are running back very fast to centralisation ... in the USA we have three distinct levels of government, there are trends towards centralisation in each one. (Caffrey, 2003: 4–8)

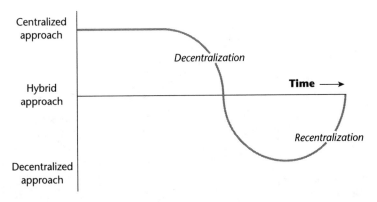

Figure 2.3   Chronology of overall approach to IT in the public sector

decentralization. Rather, it requires a single trend towards integration that, in some ways, represents an attempt to bridge the gap between top-down and bottom-up. This is not always easy to achieve and it is relatively limited in the public sector, but it can be seen in the idea of joint staff teams involving frontline staff, senior managers and IT staff.

Division

Division is compatible with – indeed, is defined as – simultaneous centralization and decentralization. It can be seen in the possible division of responsibilities described for systems development. It can also be seen in the division of responsibilities between client and server computers. In some ways, this is an attempt to let two different paradigms co-exist within different parts of the same organization. It is far more common in the public sector.

We can therefore redraw the post-centralization part of Figure 2.3 to show the two trends of integration and division, as in Figure 2.4. After being initially strong, centralization declines and decentralization takes off. At some point, though, while decentralization remains strong, centralization begins to increase, leading ultimately to a situation of combined centralization and

decentralization that characterizes much of the hybrid approach. (There are weaker strands of compromise and integration between the two.) In these situations, then, there is a trend towards the hybrid approach made up largely from a division of responsibilities between the simultaneous trends of centralization and decentralization.

The second key to understanding is to appreciate that the initial and the later centralized approaches may be dissimilar, as Figure 2.4 indicates. The initial one, which we can call a *technical* or *IT centralization*, was based around (Margetts, 1999):

- mainframe technologies that were so costly that the organization could only afford one, housed in a purpose-built central facility;
- limited telecommunications links that prevented a dissemination of computing power;
- skills that were so specialized that they had to be focused on a small core of IT staff; and
- almost universal ignorance of the role and language of computers among mainstream staff.

Later centralization, which we can call a *managerial* or *information systems centralization*, reflects Nolan's (1979) well-known 'stages of

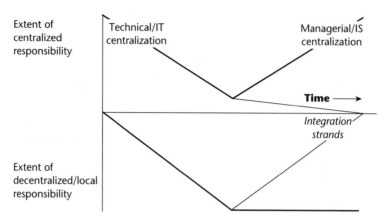

Figure 2.4   Integration and division within the hybrid approach

growth' model, summarized in Figure 2.5. It shows the gradual increase in managerial attempts to control the information systems (which would include e-government systems) within an organization. Nolan's model has been criticized for a lack of predictive power and a generality that fails to match individual organizational experience. However, its core sense of increasing managerial engagement with IT does appear sound.

Thus, while one type of centralized approach may be in decline, another may be in the ascendancy. This is a reminder – reflected in Figure 2.6 – that the notion of a hybrid approach to e-government management is multi-dimensional. One dimension – the main focus of this chapter – relates to central and local; another – discussed elsewhere in this book – relates to technical versus managerial, with the latter arguably needing to be divided further into bureaucratic and political as per the ideas of the IT square in Figure 2.2 (Drake et al., 2003)

Going back to the overall pattern shown in Figure 2.3, we should not claim that it will fit all public agencies. Some agencies maintained an existing level of centralization even as decentralized approaches emerged. This, for example, has been a characteristic of public agencies in Sweden, such as tax, land survey

and vehicle licensing (Hesselmark, 2002). In a number of cases, this centralism has remained technology-led and has not shifted the locus of IT responsibility across the organization. Other public sector organizations, which only computerized in earnest with the advent of microcomputers, began with decentralism. All this reinforces Chapter 1's message about the need for a contingent approach to management ideas; a point now examined further.

Selecting an Approach to eGovernment Management

Which of the three approaches described is best? As you may guess, there is no straightforward answer. Instead, a contingent answer is required: what suits one particular public organization at one particular time will not suit a different organization at the same time or the same organization at a different time. Perhaps more importantly, what may be best for one group in the organization may be worst for another. Having said that, we can still make three generalizations.

Problems of Mismatch

Minor customizing of different management tasks may be beneficial (Broadbent, 2002);

Stage 1: INITIATION
(First basic, routine applications are introduced)

Stage 2: CONTAGION
(Increasing numbers of applications are introduced without
control or planning)

Stage 3: CONTROL
(Increasing demand for information from managers leads to some planning,
some documentation and initial ideas about analyzing problems and designing
systems, though controls can stifle new system developments)

Stage 4: INTEGRATION
(Initial attempts are made to build cross-organizational applications, though
these are often frustrated by lack of standards and lack of overall view)

Stage 5: DATA ADMINISTRATION
(Use of information is planned strategically, recognizing it as an
organizational resource)

Stage 6: MATURITY
(Organization-wide strategic planning and analysis takes place and changes the
structure of the organization)

Figure 2.5   Stages of information systems growth

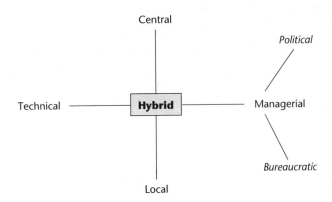

Figure 2.6   Two dimensions of hybrid e-government management

for example, to have architecture decisions more centralized while systems development is more hybrid. However, there will be problems if there is a serious mismatch between locations of responsibility for some of the different elements described above. If, say, all systems development is completely centralized while all procurement is completely decentralized, the outcome will be chaos.

Matching the Approach to the Organization

Certain approaches do seem to fit particular organizational circumstances. For public agencies that are embarking on initial forays into e-government, decentralized approaches have something to recommend them.

There is an implicit assumption in much advocacy of centralized approaches that decentralized approaches are the result of sloppy, willful or politicized management (Curthoys and Crabtree, 2003). This is not necessarily so, where decentralized e-government systems are initial computerizations of previously manual systems, or initial 'webizations' of previously non-networked systems. Those earlier systems were not organization-wide, and so the possibility and benefits of an organization-wide approach to e-government systems were not readily perceived.

More crucially, just adding IT or the web to those earlier systems, rather than completely redesigning them according to centralized specifications of need, is often the only way to ensure that e-government succeeds. In these circumstances, decentralized approaches are more likely to match reality rather than imposing unrealistic organizational rationality. They therefore avoid the many risks of, and constraints to, significant change that would ensue from centralized approaches.

Apparently piecemeal e-government may therefore be logically a better choice than centralized planning for many public sector organizations in the early stages of automation or 'webization'. It is likely to create a mess but it will work, which other approaches may not at this early stage in the organization's computing or web 'career'.

A decentralized approach will also help to spread IT awareness and skills, and even some understanding of the informational aspect of e-government, in a way that other approaches might not. For some public agencies, it is the lack of just such awareness, skills and understanding that represents a key barrier to effective use of IT in government.

As these organizations continue to develop e-government systems, a solely decentralized approach is unlikely to last. The pressure of problems will mount until a head of steam builds to support some form of centralization, within the bounds of previously-described constraints. This typically leads to a hybrid approach.

Conversely, for a public agency with a history of centralized approaches, those are unlikely to last as pressures mount against them. The centralized approach can either be modified by planned decentralization that leads to a hybrid approach, or by the de facto decentralization of work sections that ignore and circumvent it, leading to a more chaotic outcome.

The Flaws of Total Centralization

It is hard to imagine circumstances in which a wholly centralized approach to e-government would be workable. In the microcomputing-based, web-enabled era, the logical flaws and practical constraints to centralism mean that some variant of the hybrid approach seems more viable.

Determining Which Approach is Used

The approach to e-government that best fits an organization's circumstances is, however, not the same as the approach actually selected within that organization.

One particular approach may seem, to an outsider, logical and reasonable for an organization to adopt. However, we have already seen in this book that there are tensions between the somewhat theoretical notions of organizational rationality, and the more real forces of politics in government. Hence, rational logic may play only a minor role in determining which approach is used.

What factors will, then, determine the approach to e-government that is adopted by a public sector organization? Given what we know about constraints and trends, and about the gaps between organizational rationality and reality, we can expect that the approach selected will be partly determined by the realities of factors drawn from the ITPOSMOO list (Barrett and Greene, 2001).

For example, the approach adopted will be shaped by the organization's technology (e.g. whether the computing architecture is already centralized or decentralized); staffing and skills (e.g. what skills are available); management systems and structures (e.g. whether the main organization has a centralized or decentralized structure) and other resources (e.g. the availability of finance).

Stakeholder values will also play a role, such as their perceptions, their awareness of the costs and benefits of particular approaches, and their historical experiences. For instance, the recent experiences of staff with e-government systems create either a satisfaction that is inertial, or a dissatisfaction that demands change.

However, above all – as with so much about e-government – it is organizational politics and its roots in the self-interest of particular stakeholders that will help determine what management approach to e-government is selected (Atkinson and Leigh, 2003; Lazer and Binz-Scharf, 2004). To take just one example, centralization of

the IT unit's location may be an outcome of political conflict in various circumstances:

- Senior public managers or politicians want greater control over e-government resources, and so mainstream the IT unit away from the IT manager towards themselves.
- The IT manager wants more power and greater visibility within the organization, and so uses the political clout of senior management allies to elevate the IT unit's position.
- As the result of a dispute, one group of senior staff wishes to punish the manager within whose department the IT unit currently sits (e.g. the finance director), and so they take the unit under central control.

Four familiar political constituencies (see Figure 2.2) can be identified, whose conflict or compromise within organizations helps to determine which approach is chosen: senior managers, politicians, IT staff, and mainstream staff.

In many cases, IT staff and mainstream staff find themselves supporting centralized and decentralized approaches respectively. The attitude of senior officials – both managers and politicians – is then crucial, not least because they normally hold greater organizational power than the other two groups.

According to a model of personal politics, what senior officials consider their self-interest concerning e-government is therefore critical in determining the preferred approach. In part, this self-interest may be shaped by the other factors described here, such as their resources, their historical experience, and environmental factors.

In some cases, senior officials' self-interest leads them to a hands-off position, for example, when lack of skills or confidence makes them avoid computerized systems. The two other groups are left to slug it out. When the outcome of this political process is one of compromise, it may lead to some kind of hybrid approach. When the outcome is one of conflict and victory by one of the two groups, a more clearly centralized or decentralized approach may result.

In other cases, when senior officials do choose to become involved, it is quite possible that experiences and pressures push them to support some kind of centralized approach (Coursey and Killingsworth, 2000). As we have seen, though, this will not necessarily be successful in delivering the hoped-for results.

Broader, often political, pressures from the outside world – ranging from national political initiatives to dominant ideologies/philosophies – also play their part. Staff in public sector organizations are subject to continuous external pressures, that include (Barrett and Greene, 2001; Abramson and Morin, 2003):

- Pressure to conform to the requirements of external bodies, such as central government bodies and funding agencies. An e-government unit run by central government may, for example, be pushing a department to adopt certain centralized 'best practices': see, for example, Box 2.6.
- Pressure through (mis)perception of what other organizations are doing, which may be transmitted through informal contacts, management texts and training programs, or dealings with consultancy organizations.
- Pressure from private sector IT vendors to purchase particular technologies and systems.

For many public agencies, it is these pressures that have strongly shaped growing centralization of e-government responsibilities. The agencies are subject to increasing scrutiny of

---

Box 2.6   Maneuvering for eGovernment Centralization in the US Federal Government

Central bodies seeking responsibility for IT across government face two challenges: first, competition from other central agencies; second, tensions between themselves and the main departments and ministries of government.

The ultimate location and degree of centralization of e-government responsibilities will, in large part, be the outcome of a political process. In the early part of the 21st-century in the US, the Office of Management and Budget (OMB) worked hard for increased centralization of IT-related responsibilities in federal government, and for itself to be the main recipient of those responsibilities. This hard work included a lot of networking and consensus- building with e-government stakeholders.

Its political efforts were rewarded with a series of measures, chief of which was the 2002 eGovernment Act, which has provided a set of political and other resources to OMB (2003):

- legitimization, codification and expansion of its leadership role in e-government;
- authorization for oversight of e-government initiatives in other departments; and
- approval control over projects to be funded from a central e-government fund.

It does, of course, have to use these resources with care since they have both a rational and a political value. Clumsy interference in the affairs of dozens of agencies risks a political backlash, renewed decentralization, and a loss of powers from OMB. (Development from OMB, 2003)

their e-government activity by apex public bodies. This, in turn, drives agency managers to try to control that activity by centralizing it.

Finally, remember that none of these factors is static. Resource endowments, technology and organizational structures all change with time. So, too, do experiences, external pressures, perceptions of self-interest and the political balance of power.

All those involved will constantly be on the look-out for levers – decrees, regulations, Acts, funds, bad publicity, and so on – to advance their favored position (see Box 2.6). We can therefore expect continuous change in the intended location of e-government managerial responsibility, with a dynamic ebb and flow of centralization and decentralization.

ACTIVITIES

Shorter In-Class Activities²

Chapter Introduction

a. A hybrid approach means either division or integration between center and periphery. But what is center and what is periphery? To investigate this, identify a typical public sector organization and briefly discuss different definitions of center and of periphery. In plenary, discuss the implications of these different definitions for the feasibility and outcomes of a hybrid approach to e-government management.

Section 2.1

a. In relation to the Box 2.1 case, discuss which are more important in justifying a centralized approach: the external or the internal benefits?

b. Review the IT square: does it really identify the key stakeholders with an influence on e-government systems?

c. Draw two lessons for e-government management from the Box 2.2 case.

d. You have to make the case for a centralized approach to e-government to a group of senior officials. In pairs or small groups, develop a two-minute 'pitch' in support of a centralized approach.

Section 2.2

a. Draw two lessons for e-government management from the Box 2.3 case.

b. You have to make the case for a decentralized approach to e-government to a group of senior officials. In pairs or small groups, develop a two-minute 'pitch' in support of a decentralized approach.

Section 2.3

a. 'The hybrid approach to e-government management looks good in theory. But it can never work in practice.' Discuss in small groups, or use as a quick debate topic.

b. You have to make the case for a hybrid approach to e-government to a group of senior officials. In pairs or small groups, develop a two-minute 'pitch' in support of a hybrid approach.

Sections 2.1 to 2.3

a. Divide the class into two sets of small groups. One set is allocated centralized, the other set is allocated decentralized. Choose one of the eight e-government responsibilities (e.g. procurement). Each centralized group must identify two benefits of a centralized approach, and two constraints and two disadvantages of a decentralized approach *specific to the chosen responsibility*. Each decentralized group does the mirror image, identifying two benefits of a decentralized approach, and two constraints and two disadvantages of a centralized approach specific to the chosen responsibility. Report back one item at a time from each group and list them under headings. Discussion of the pros and cons of a hybrid approach to that responsibility can follow.

b. Provide theoretical or real-world examples for each cell in the matrix shown below.

Section 2.4

a. Look at the models shown in Figures 2.3 to 2.5. Discuss whether they are more valuable as description (showing how things are) or prescription (showing how things should be).

b. Read Box 2.6. What advice would you offer the head of OMB about the best way forward for management of e-government?

Assignment Questions

Sections 2.1 to 2.3

a. Identify a public sector organization. Which of the three approaches – centralized, decentralized or hybrid – has it adopted for the management of its e-government systems? What benefits, disadvantages and constraints have been associated with the approach it has taken?

b. Select one area of e-government managerial responsibility. For that specific area, outline the pros and cons of three approaches – centralized, decentralized and hybrid – using real-world case evidence wherever possible. Can you draw any overall conclusion?

Sections 2.1 to 2.4

a. How do tensions between *center* and *periphery* differ in the public as compared to the private sector? How do these differences impact the approach to management of IT-based systems?

Practitioner Exercises

Section 2.1

a. Reflect on the content, potential advantages, constraints and other problems of a centralized approach. Then, in relation to your own organization, note down answers to the following questions:

- To what extent have the various e-government systems responsibilities described been centralized?
- Can you provide instances of the benefits of centralized approaches, such as those described in the main text?
- Can you provide instances of the disadvantages of centralized approaches, such as those described in the main text?
- Can you provide instances of the constraints to centralized approaches, such as those described in the main text?

Note down any conclusions that you may draw from your answers about the relevance of centralized approaches in your organization.

Section 2.2

a. Reflect on the content, potential advantages, constraints and problems of a decentralized approach. Then, in relation to your own organization, note down answers to the following questions:

- To what extent have the various e-government systems responsibilities described been decentralized?
- Can you provide instances of the benefits of decentralized approaches, such as those described in the main text?
- Can you provide instances of the disadvantages of decentralized approaches, such as those described in the main text?

Responsibility	Centralized	Hybrid	Decentralized
Computing and data management architecture			
Systems development			
Procurement			
Training			
Technical support			

- Can you provide instances of the constraints to decentralized approaches, such as those described in the main text?

Note down any conclusions that you may draw from your answers about the relevance of decentralized approaches in your organization.

Section 2.3

a. Reflect on the content, potential advantages and constraints of a hybrid approach and relate these to your own organization. Then, note down answers to the following questions:

- To what extent can your organization be seen as following a hybrid approach in any of the e-government systems areas described in the main text?
- In areas where a hybrid approach is operating, does it seem to offer any additional benefits over a more centralized or more decentralized approach? If so, who mainly receives these additional benefits? If not, why not?
- In areas where a hybrid approach is not operating, would it offer any additional benefits over the current approach? If so, what constraints prevent such an approach from being implemented?

Note down any conclusions that you may draw from your answers about the relevance and implementation of a hybrid approach in your organization.

Section 2.4

a. Reflect on the discussion about approach trends and determinants and relate it to your own organization. Note down answers to the following questions:

- Which of the factors do you recognize within your own organization?
- What approaches have been followed by your organization in the past, and what current trends can you perceive?
- How does this pattern compare to that described by the diagrams in this section, and to the generalizations about 'best' approaches?

Note down any conclusions that you can draw about your organization and the approaches to e-government systems management it may adopt.

NOTES

1. Centralized approaches to data management are discussed in the Online Appendix for Chapter 4.

2. Details of longer group activities are provided in the Online Appendix to this chapter

3

eGovernment Strategy

Key Points

- Increasing numbers of public agencies are developing an e-government strategy.
- Centralized e-government strategic planning is a six-step process that, overall, asks: 'Where are we now?', 'Where do we want to get to?', and 'How do we get there from here?'
- Centralized e-government strategic planning may be fundamentally misconceived, may face severe constraints to its implementation, and may create negative impacts within the public sector.
- A hybrid approach can bring balance between a number of tensions inherent to e-government planning.

An e-government strategy is a plan for e-government systems and their supporting infrastructure which maximizes the ability of management to achieve organizational objectives. Increasing numbers of public agencies are developing an e-government strategy. This chapter therefore looks at this process in some detail, relating it to the theme of hybrid approaches to management.

3.1 AN OVERVIEW OF εGOVERNMENT STRATEGIC PLANNING

Through the influence of the private sector and the strength of discrete public agencies, approaches to e-government systems are typically conceptualized at the level of individual departments or ministries. This chapter will therefore treat e-government strategy mainly as an activity undertaken within a single public sector organization.[1] We begin by focusing on a set of core questions about e-government strategy for public agencies.

Why?

Why are increasing numbers of public agencies trying to develop an e-government strategy? The explanations are various (Holmes, 2001; Grönlund, 2002; Accenture, 2003).

A strong component of explanation comes from the realm of politics:

- The fad/'me too' factor of copying current trends or copying appearances in other organizations.

- The desire of some senior officials to wrest control of e-government from technical staff and/or individual departments.
- The desire for the kudos and resources associated with a major organizational initiative.
- The demand for such strategies from central government agencies.

There are also more rational drivers causing e-government to increasingly be seen as a senior management issue that requires planning at a strategic level:

- The growing contribution of e-government to processes of public sector reform. Reform represents strategic change. If IT is heavily involved in reform, it too must be planned strategically.
- Increasing expenditure on IT for e-government, often with few obvious organizational benefits, makes senior public managers wish first to question and then to control IT budgets from a rational perspective. This is particularly true as more ambitious e-government systems have been proposed, requiring large, long-term investment decisions, and as pressures increase to make senior managers more accountable for the outcomes of these investment decisions.
- The pervasive impacts associated with e-government, which affect working practices and procedures; jobs, skills, and motivation; internal organizational structures; external relationships with clients; overall organizational efficiency and effectiveness; organizational image and political legitimacy; and so on. Given these profound impacts, senior managers are inevitably drawn into e-government issues.
- Very open e-government failures in some public agencies, creating bad publicity

for which senior officials are seen as ultimately responsible. This impels these officials to take more central responsibility for e-government.
- eGovernment failures that stimulate growing recognition of serious organizational constraints on systems development and implementation. Successful introduction of new e-government systems may require major changes in the allocation of resources, including organizational power. Senior managers often realize that they must take charge because only they have the clout to overcome resistance to such changes.

These drivers are enabled by the growing awareness among some senior public managers of information as a corporate resource, and by their own growing ability to use IT.

In addition, the growth of e-government strategies in the public sector is impelled by the potential benefits that a strategy can bring (e.g. OECD, 2003b; Gupta et al., 2004). Some of these are political, such as providing senior management control over organizational systems, accessing central funds that are only available on production of a strategy, and avoiding public reprimands and penalties where strategies are demanded by higher-level bodies.

An e-government strategy is also seen as a key mechanism to produce centralized-approach benefits of the type discussed in Chapter 2, particularly cost savings and a fit between systems and organizational objectives. It promises to allow development of e-government systems that are a high organizational priority to take precedence over other activities; to ensure compatibility of data structures, hardware and software; and to eliminate duplication of effort.

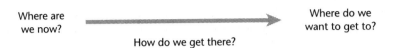

Figure 3.1   Overview of strategic planning

Finally, a successful strategy can develop senior management understanding that e-government systems are information systems not just IT, and build consensus and commitment to a strategic vision for e-government. It permits a fundamental review of the organization's use of information and technology, leading to a comprehensive understanding of information systems requirements. It also provides a detailed plan of action on e-government for the organization.

What?

Like any strategic plan, an e-government strategy seeks to answer three questions, illustrated in Figure 3.1:

- *Where are we now?* (i.e. how are systems working now, and what external factors affect them).
- *Where do we want to get to?* (i.e. in future, how should the organization's e-government systems be or work differently from at present).
- *How do we get there?* (i.e. what actions need to be undertaken to achieve the outcome identified in answering the second question).

When?

In simple terms, the answer is: 'You undertake e-government strategy when the time is right'. In some public agencies, one hears managerial statements such as

- 'We haven't got time to plan strategically, we need this e-government application immediately.'
- 'We have better things to spend our money on than messing about with data structures.'
- 'I'd rather train my staff to use their computers, not to indulge in some planning exercise.'

This is not fertile ground for strategic planning. The attitudes expressed in the statements above can easily sustain over time, given public sector pressures to deliver quick gains from e-government, and given the increasing cost consciousness that public sector reform often brings. They lead to some of the problems with strategy discussed later in the chapter.

In other cases, though, after several years' experience of the problems of a decentralized approach, senior officials and others may come to perceive the costs of this approach more clearly. A head of steam may build up to support a more strategic approach to e-government planning. Some of the danger signs that build such a head of steam are (Destatis, 2002; McCalla, 2003):

- e-government systems being created without consideration for overall organizational objectives;
- outdated systems still in use due to inability to plan alternatives;
- data that cannot be shared between different e-government systems because there are no organization-wide standards;

Box 3.1 Problems of Federal eGovernment Expenditure in the US

The 2003 US federal budget identified 'six chronic problems that limit results from Federal IT spending:

- Agencies have automated existing outdated processes, instead of fixing underlying management problems or simplifying agency procedures to take advantage of new e-business and e-government capabilities.
- Agencies have made unnecessarily duplicative IT investments.
- Inadequate program management – many major IT projects have not met cost, schedule and performance goals.
- Few agencies have had plans demonstrating the linkage between IT capabilities and the business needs of the agency.
- Agencies have built individual capabilities that are not interoperable with one another. Few IT investments significantly improve mission performance.
- Poor IT security – major gaps have existed in agency and Government-wide information and IT-related security.' (US Congress, 2003: 2–3)

- IT being seen as the end rather than the means; in other words, when e-government is seen as an end in itself;
- no clear locus of responsibility for dealing with these problems;
- comparative organizations have a strategy.

Such a head of steam can be clearly seen within the analysis of problems with e-government in the US described in Box 3.1.

eGovernment planning will run into trouble if the head of steam is not present: if it is undertaken before key stakeholders feel the push of the drivers listed above and the pull of the potential benefits. For organizations in which stages of e-government computerization are recognizable (see Figure 2.5), this means that strategy only tends to emerge after Stage 3.

3.2 THE STEPS OF eGOVERNMENT STRATEGIC PLANNING

eGovernment strategic planning is typically conceived as a series of steps that are undertaken systematically over a period of a few weeks or a few months. These steps are summarized in Figure 3.2 (developed from Turban et al., 2001; Chaffey, 2002; Laudon and Laudon, 2004). Once completed, they produce a framework for organizational action that can endure for a number of years. The steps are described below in greater detail.

1. Strategy Foundation: Create eGovernment Planning Structures/Roles

In order to control the process of strategic planning, a special body is usually set up, called something like 'eGovernment Steering Group'. It will typically consist of senior staff or other powerful stakeholders from various parts of the organization, together with some technical advisors. Increasingly this committee is likely to be chaired by a Chief Information Officer (CIO), as in the case of Kentucky state, summarized in Box 3.2.

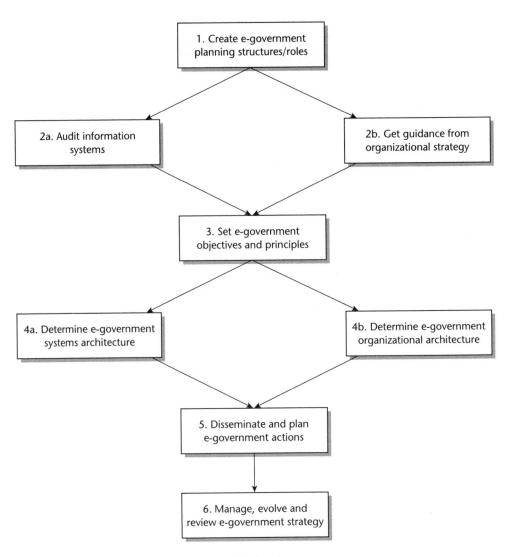

Figure 3.2   The steps of e-government strategic planning

This body normally reports to the very top levels of the organization because of the strategic nature of its work, which includes setting the scope of, and commissioning the e-government strategy; taking necessary strategic decisions relating to e-government systems (such as those presented during strategic planning); communicating the e-government strategy to the rest of the organization; ensuring the necessary resources are in place to achieve strategic objectives, and allocating those resources; and monitoring and controlling the overall development and operation of e-government within the organization, and checking this against stated objectives.

Other organizational groups (which may overlap membership to a greater or lesser degree and which are summarized in Figure 3.3) are likely to be responsible for activities such as:

Box 3.2   Strategy-Making Roles in the Commonwealth of Kentucky

Ultimate responsibility for strategy rests with the state CIO but responsibility for establishing the strategy and adopting it is taken on by the state's CIO Advisory Council, made up from all the lower-level CIOs (or their equivalent) in the state's main departments and agencies. General input on more technical issues – such as the technical architecture for e-government – is provided by the state's Enterprise Architecture and Standards Committee. There are also more specific boards or councils that provide input to the process on issues such as geographic information and telehealth, and an IT Advisory Council that provides an external view from citizens and businesses and public agencies. Implementation of strategic plans is undertaken by two main offices within the Governor's Office of Technology: Infrastructure Services, and Consulting and Project Management.

As is common in many public organizations, some Internet-based elements of e-government are seen as distinct from the totality of public sector use of IT, with the result that a separate body – the Electronic Services Executive Committee – has been created to develop strategy for the narrow sub-set of e-government that focuses on the state's portal. (CoK, 2003; GOT, 2003)

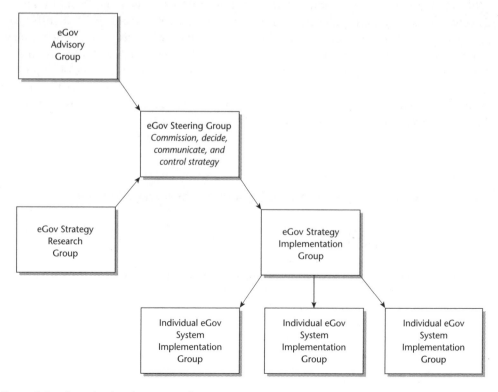

Figure 3.3   Organizational structures for e-government strategy

- researching the strategic plan, developing options for committee decision, and producing the final plan;
- implementing the strategic plan, including managing the development of individual e-government systems; and
- developing and implementing individual e-government systems.

2a. Strategic Analysis: Audit Information Systems

An e-government-specific answer to the question 'Where are we now?' requires a comprehensive understanding of the current state of e-government and other information systems. Note the inclusion of all types of information system, manual or computerized: hence the title 'audit information systems' rather than 'audit e-government'.

Information systems (IS) audit is often conceived in a very narrow sense, just as an inventory of IT within the public agency: all computer applications with their hardware, software, networks, physical location, licensing and ownership; and often just security-related (e.g. GAO, 2001). However such an approach is far too narrow to form an effective analytical base for strategy (TBCS, 2000). It must be expanded in several ways, as described below.

Systems Perspective

Audit must recognize the full information system (see Chapter 1), describing not just the technology resources, but also the information that information systems deliver, the information processes undertaken, and the human resources involved, covering information skills (e.g. data gathering and presentation), IT skills (e.g. hands-on computing), and system development skills (e.g. systems analysis and design).

Issues Perspective

The audit should be more than just a list of resources, but should help identify key issues that will inform and affect subsequent decision making on e-government. These might include a sense of important problems or complaints facing the current information systems, or an assessment of emerging trends.

Box 3.3   Web-Centered eGovernment Stage Models

Review of various e-government stage models can be used to form the following four-stage model (Ebrahim et al., 2003):

- *Information*: Basic publication of information on a static web site.
- *Interaction*: Basic two-way communication is possible between government and site users, for example, filling in a basic application form.
- *Transaction*: Complete government processes can be undertaken online, including payment of fines, accessing benefits, and receiving permits/licenses.
- *Integration*: Back-office processes are altered to allow either vertical integration of different levels of government, or horizontal integration that brings together related functions/services.

Stakeholder Perspective

Both directly and indirectly, information systems affect stakeholders both inside and outside the main public agency. The audit should therefore be external as well as internal. It should understand the technology, skills, needs and issues of client groups. It should also benchmark against similar organizations. A common benchmark, at least for web-based e-government, has been the stage model described in Box 3.3. (Another relevant benchmarking model is shown as Figure 2.5.)[2] However, real benchmarking will need to go deeper than this to look at the types of e-government system actually being employed in other agencies.

Contextual Perspective

This includes the outer two layers of the 'onion-ring' (see Chapter 1) within the audit. It will look at management systems and structures within the public agency. It will look at IT trends and standards within the local environment. It will review financial and other constraints specific to e-government systems change. Perhaps most important, it will incorporate an understanding of relevant policies, guidelines and initiatives that impact on e-government. Policies generally are discussed in Chapter 6. A specific example of overarching policies for the US context is given in Box 3.4.

Box 3.4   The Strategic Context for Federal Public Agency eGovernment Strategy in the US

Federal agencies in the US seeking to create an e-government strategy must locate that strategy within a series of external measures. By 2005, these included:

- The 2003 Federal Enterprise Architecture: A 'business-based framework for Government-wide improvement ... constructed through a collection of interrelated 'reference models' designed to facilitate cross-agency analysis and the identification of duplicative investments, gaps, and opportunities for collaboration within and across federal agencies.' (FEAPMO, 2003)
- The 2002 eGovernment Act: Setting up and supporting a series of e-government projects in many federal agencies.
- The 2002 Federal Information Security Management Act: Requiring security issues to be integrated into IT planning (supported by the 2004 Presidential Directive on Homeland Security).
- The 2001 President's Management Agenda: A 'strategy for improving the management and performance of the Federal Government' (OMB, 2005a) that encompasses five strands: competitive sourcing, strategic management of human capital, improved financial accountability, budget and performance integration, and expanded e-government.
- The 1998 Government Paperwork Elimination Act: Requiring electronic options for transacting business with government.
- The 1996 Clinger-Cohen Act: Requiring capital planning for IT investments to link them to agency objectives and accomplishments.
- The 1996 Electronic Freedom of Information Act amendment: Requiring quality and accessibility of agency data.
- The 1993 Government Performance Results Act: Requiring agencies to link activities (including IT-related activities) to performance outcomes.

With network-based systems, much of the IT can be audited automatically with audit software. However, that covers none of data for the other perspectives identified above. For this, data must be gathered using a mixture of questionnaire, interview, analysis of documentation and physical checks. These are frequently combined with the research work required for completion of subsequent components of strategic planning. The results may be presented in SWOT format: internal e-government strengths and weaknesses; external e-government opportunities and threats.

2b. Strategic Analysis: Get Guidance from Organizational Strategy

The rationality of e-government strategy requires that e-government systems help meet the needs of the public sector organization. An e-government strategy should therefore be firmly rooted in one particular element from the organizational context: the wider organizational or business strategy for the whole agency. Business strategy answers the questions we noted earlier, but in a broader framework than e-government strategy.

It first asks, 'Where are we now?' An answer would include details of the organization's current structure and functions; key client groups; existing problems that need to be addressed; and important current and forthcoming factors – particularly policies and political priorities – within the internal and external environment. As with the IS audit, this quite often includes a SWOT analysis: details of current organizational strengths and weaknesses, external opportunities that may present themselves and threats to its operation, including current constraints.

It next asks, 'Where do we want to get to?' An answer would include details of the organization's objectives, and some vision of the future organization that will enable it to overcome current and forthcoming problems, and to achieve its objectives. Finally, it asks, 'How do we get there?' This would be achieved through a statement of management strategy about major changes to organizational structure and functions in order to reach its future vision. An example of a broader strategy that shapes e-government strategy is given in Box 3.5.

More specifically, two types of organizational function are derived from the organization's wider business strategy and prioritized for further investigation:

Box 3.5   Agency Strategy as a Shaper for eGovernment Strategy

Taking the example of the US Department of the Interior, the context for e-government strategy is shaped by (DOI, 2002):

- Its five goals: To protect the environment, provide recreation for America, manage natural resources, provide science for a changing world, and meet its trust responsibilities.
- Its 'four Cs' vision: Of conservation through cooperation, consultation, and communication.
- Its four key principles of reform strategy: Of customer value, accountability, integration and modernization.

- existing organizational functions that are to be retained in order to meet organizational objectives; and
- new organizational functions that need to be introduced in order to meet organizational objectives.

3. Strategy Framework: Set eGovernment Objectives and Principles

The eGovernment Steering Group may use the data gathered so far to produce a broad statement of the role and objectives of information and of e-government within the organization. This statement may be specific (tying e-government to particular organizational objectives) and/or it may be generic (a general statement of information and IT principles). An example of each is given in Box 3.6.

As well as setting the scope for the e-government strategy exercise at this stage, these objectives and principles can also be used to develop the criteria against which

---

Box 3.6   Strategic Principles for eGovernment

Agency-Specific

eGovernment in the US Department of Housing and Urban Development is intended to:

1. Improve housing opportunities, self-sufficiency, and quality of life for citizens and HUD beneficiaries by leveraging electronic commerce to meet their needs directly;
2. Ensure HUD's business partners have the needed tools to deliver HUD products and services effectively and efficiently in a virtual environment; and
3. Restore the public trust by utilizing technology to operate a productive and responsive enterprise. (HUD, 2001: 11)

Generic Principles

eGovernment strategy should be guided by the following principles, making it:

1. Easy to use, connecting people with federal, state, regional, local, tribal, and international governments according to their preferences and needs.
2. Available to everyone, at home, at work, in schools, in libraries and other convenient community locations.
3. Private and secure, with the appropriate standards for privacy, security, and authentication – generating trust – required for e-government to grow and serve the public.
4. Innovative and results-oriented, emphasizing speed and harnessing the latest advances in technology.
5. Collaborative, with solutions developed collectively and openly among public, private, nonprofit, and research partners, on the basis of their experience and expertise.
6. Cost-effective, through strategic investments that produce significant long-term efficiencies and savings.
7. Transformational, harnessing technology through personal and organizational leadership to change the way government works, rather than merely automate existing practices. (CEG, 2001: 5)

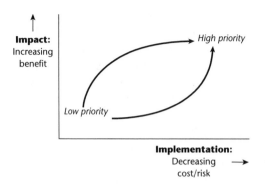

Figure 3.4   eGovernment project prioritization schema

e-government proposals may be evaluated and/or prioritized. This is the essence of 'portfolio' or 'program' management: using criteria to align projects with agency strategy. Typical prioritization criteria are a mix of impact (benefit) and implementation (cost) factors, and are judged from a mix of rational and political standpoints (see Figure 3.4) (developed from Hauschild, 2002; Gupta et al., 2004).

Impact priorities, for example, might be:

- highest savings/financial return on investment;
- highest public visibility/political return on investment;
- highest learning/demonstrator effect;
- strongest focus on existing organizational deficiencies; and/or
- strongest support to key external client services (as opposed to internal administrative activities).

Implementation priorities, for example, might be:

- lowest risk/highest feasibility;
- lowest cost to implement; and/or
- fastest time for completion.

Accenture (2003) uses such criteria to argue that priority should go to systems linking government to business (G2B) rather government to citizen (G2C) because businesses have better infrastructure, stronger incentives, and make greater use of government than citizens. G2B systems are thus more likely to succeed and are more likely to have a positive impact when/if they do succeed. Whether or not governments follow this in practice is another matter. For example, Box 3.7 shows US e-government project criteria that would not necessarily prioritize G2B over G2C. In addition, the criteria list provides no insight into the political considerations that shaped final selection of projects: the scores provided by this rational element were indicative, not binding for final prioritization. In an overall sense, politics may well dictate prioritizing G2C applications since these reach a greater number of voters. Realpolitik may therefore weight political impact over implementation, by contrast with Accenture's more rational approach, which tends to weight implementation over impact.

4a. Strategy Definition: Determine eGovernment Systems Architecture

eGovernment strategy can be seen as needing to lay out the ITPOSMO dimensions for the future (see Chapter 1). The information, technology and process dimensions are together seen as an *e-government systems architecture*: a plan of the e-government systems that the organization will require in future. This architecture forms a major element of 'Where do we want to get to?' for e-government.

The e-government systems architecture can be described in terms of the individual e-government applications with details of data capture, input, processing, storage and output plus links to decision and action processes (CIPSODA: see Chapter 1). It will also consist of a number of different models, including:

Box 3.7 Prioritizing eGovernment Applications in the US

eGovernment projects could score between 10 and 80 using the following scoring system (OMB, 2003). Scores were allocated by teams of subject area experts.

a. Improvement in Service Delivery:

- Convenience/ease of doing business with the government (10 = significant paperwork or similar burden reduction; 1 = little reduction)
- Order of magnitude benefit (two orders of magnitude improvement in program results for citizen = 10; little improvement = 1)
- Number of customers (10 = hundreds of millions; 1 = hundreds of thousands)

b. Doable Category:

- Timeframe for initial deployment of capability with the overall timeframe of 18–24 months (10 = less than 6 months; 8 = 6–12 months; 6 = 12–18 months; 4 = 18–24 months; 2 = 24 months or longer)
- Risk of implementation (10 = key risks are being addressed, project is underway; 5 = the availability of COTS [*commercial off-the-shelf*] or government best practices; 1 = initiatives which required new development and projects where there was significant resistance or failure to-date)

c. Benefits Category:

- Monetary benefit: potential return on investment from consolidating redundant spending on IT or reducing inefficient program administration resources (10 = tens of billions in reduced redundancy; 1 = hundreds of thousands)
- Improvements in operational effectiveness: including response time reduction (10 = high; 1 = low)

d. Resource Requirements:

- Rough order of magnitude investment needed ranging from less than $5 million (scored as 10) to over $100 million (scored as 2)

- A *data model* showing the structure of unified, organization-wide data to which the e-government systems will have access; often illustrated using an entity-relationship diagram (this and the other diagrams mentioned here are described in greater detail in Chapter 8).
- A *process model* showing the key activities of the organization that the e-government systems will either support or undertake; often illustrated using a process diagram.
- A *data/process model* showing the organization-wide connection between business processes and data entities, and the organization-wide movement of data that e-government systems will enable; often illustrated using a data flow diagram.

These strategic models can be developed in various ways, as described in Box 3.8. In all cases, the main organizational model can be supplemented by more detailed models that are specific to particular organizational functions.

Box 3.8   Methods for Determining eGovernment Architecture

A number of top-down methods for identification of process and data requirements are available (Laudon and Laudon, 2004; Jessup and Valacich, 2006). Two common ones are information engineering (IE) and critical success factors (CSFs). Both were developed in the private sector but have been applied to the public sector (Houtari and Wilson, 2001; IES, 2004):

- *Information engineering*: This looks across the whole organization and focuses on what it sees as two key components of organizational functions or 'business areas'. First, *business processes*: the individual activities of the organization that help meet public sector objectives. Second, *data classes*: data entities of relevance to the organization that are made up from individual data elements (or *attributes*). Data and process are principally connected, and therefore principally investigated, through the mechanism of decision making and action. These are therefore identified through a wide survey of those inside or outside the public agency that make decisions or undertake transactions. They are asked about their objectives, activities and the data that they use. This may be supplemented by document analysis and observation. All these techniques will focus both on current good practice and on problems that need to be addressed. From this investigation, the entire organization is analyzed into two long lists of business processes and data entities. These are cross-checked through a process/data matrix that shows which processes create or use which data. The data entities and processes can then be grouped together into clusters of data and processes that represent required e-government systems within the organization.
- *Critical success factors*: This also looks across the whole organization. It starts by asking managers to specify the factors they consider to be critical for the successful performance of particular organizational functions (previously identified as central to the achievement of organizational objectives.) These factors are then analyzed to determine their key decision and action processes. Next, the information required to monitor performance of these processes is identified. This information can then be grouped together into clusters that represent required e-government systems within the organization.

Both techniques are better for analyzing existing rather than proposed organizational functions (Avison and Fitzgerald, 2003; Laudon and Laudon, 2004). By comparison with IE, the CSF method tends to require less effort. It can also be better at highlighting new systems rather than just focusing on development of existing systems, as IE sometimes does. However, it tends to be more effective in relation to internal systems that support the work of managers, whereas IE will also cover basic data systems, and client-oriented systems.

Both of these methods can be combined with further analytical improvement techniques, such as process or data re-engineering that look for ways of removing redundant business processes or data elements. Techniques such as value chain analysis can be used to identify those processes that do, and do not, contribute to the organization's overall outputs. Increasingly, public agencies may be encouraged to spread their hunt for redundancy beyond organizational boundaries, to look at ways in which information needs and business processes can be shared with other public sector organizations.

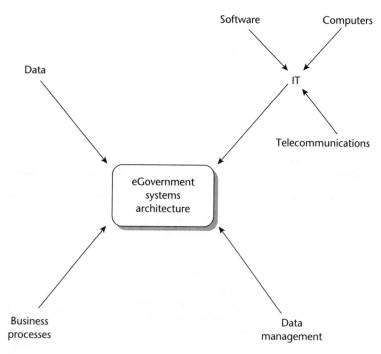

Figure 3.5   Elements of e-government systems architecture

The e-government systems architecture will also consist of organization-wide models for:

- *IT*, showing how computers will be sized and connected within the organization, and an outline of the software to be used;
- *data management*, showing how data capture, input, processing, storage and output functions will be divided across the IT architecture.

A summary of all the elements within the e-government systems architecture is shown in Figure 3.5.

The actual terminology and approach used for the agency's e-government architecture will differ from context to context. In the US central government, for example, there is strong pressure for e-government systems

architectures to fit within the Federal Enterprise Architecture (described in Box 3.4), which has specific components for technology, data and business processes. In some cases, there may also be pressures for at least part of the e-government architecture to be integrated with that of other public agencies, to allow effective sharing of data.

Despite different methods, e-government strategic planning so far often approximates to the stages identified in Figure 3.6, reinforcing the point made in Chapter 1 that e-government systems are information systems consisting of information, technology and processes.

The e-government systems architecture represents a goal rather than a reality so, at this point, the team preparing the strategic plan may present 'How do we get there?' options, with their costs and benefits, for

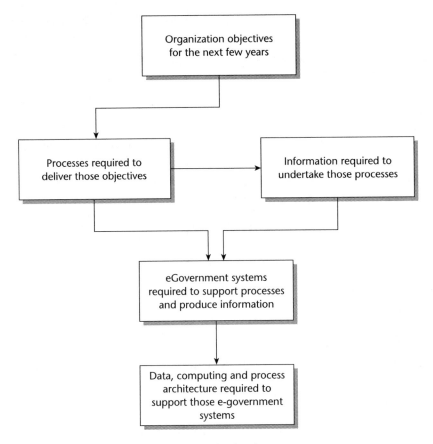

Figure 3.6   Initial stages of e-government strategic planning

the eGovernment Steering Group to decide between. These alternatives can include the different ways of grouping the organization's information and processes into e-government systems and, more likely, different possible computing architectures. Note that, aside from the audit, this is probably the first time that IT has been considered in this strategic planning process. It is the intention that e-government strategy be shaped by organizational objectives and process/information requirements rather than by technology: making sure that it is the *government* rather than the *e* that steers e-government.

Given the organization-wide nature of strategic planning, it is quite likely that data will be structured as a central set of linked, non-duplicated corporate databases. Various functional and cross-functional e-government systems can draw their required data from these databases. It is also quite likely that the computing architecture will be centralized but networked throughout the organization. A sample of such an architecture is shown in Figure 3.7 from 'Bradbury' Training and Enterprise Agency, a UK-based regional organization with responsibilities for supporting the development of local enterprises and the local skills base.[3]

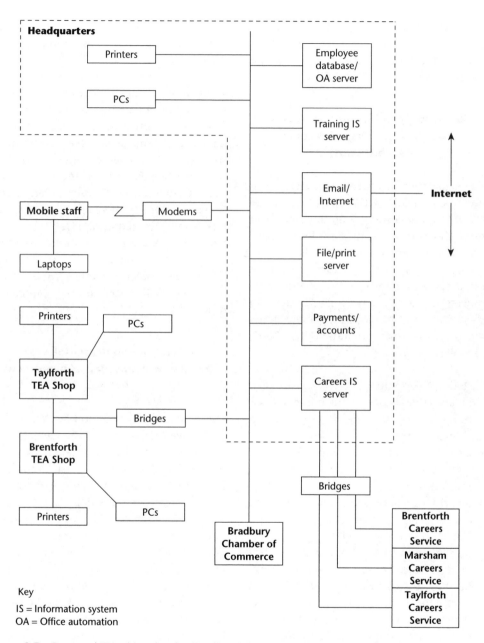

Figure 3.7   Proposed IT architecture for 'Bradbury' Training and Enterprise Agency

The result of all this work should be a comprehensive analysis of future e-government systems requirements, covering data, technology and business processes. The gap between these requirements and what current systems deliver forms the basis for the systems changes that need to take place within the organization. The changes can be divided into improvements to existing systems, and new e-government systems. Each of these can form a potential e-government systems project for the organization.

4b. Strategy Definition: Determine eGovernment Organizational Architecture

The e-government systems architecture just described dealt with the first three ITPOSMO dimensions, but the final four must also be strategically considered: objectives and values, staffing and skills, management systems and structures, and other resources. If not already part of the initial process of placing e-government systems in their wider strategic context, general strategic decisions may include (NIC, 2002; McCalla, 2003):

- stating the approach to management of organizational change, including a determination of the needs for cultural change;
- clearly allocating responsibilities for e-government systems development and management;
- identifying major competency gaps and approaches to closing them through human resource strategies;
- deciding how back-office procedures may be restructured to support e-government;
- locating the e-government/IT function within the wider organizational structure;
- demarcating which services (e.g. systems development, training and systems operation) are to be sourced in-house and outsourced;
- identifying procedures to be used when tendering for and selecting e-government systems products and services;
- specifying standard systems development methodologies and tools to be used; and

- identifying financial approaches to be adopted, such as public–private partnerships.

Many of these issues are discussed further in the chapters of Part 1 of this book.

It will be particularly important to determine the relationship between e-government strategy and budget because the public sector has a golden rule: 'the person who has the gold, makes the rules.' (Barrett and Greene, 2001: 72). In various US states, this link is made by requiring IT/e-government budgetary requests to be linked to some component of strategy and/or by ensuring the annual strategic planning updates are integrated with the annual budgeting process.[4]

5. Strategy Implementation 1: Disseminate and Plan eGovernment Actions

The defined strategy can now be circulated as an 'eGovernment Strategy Statement' and, if appropriate to the organizational culture, discussed and refined. A possible contents list for such a statement is shown in Box 3.9.

Once agreed, the strategy is typically planned in more detail in a matrix format. The columns of the matrix can be a set of e-government project plans, created for improving existing systems and developing new systems. Each plan will typically be presented as a 'business case'. A typical business case for an e-government project might include a statement of project objectives; an estimation of benefits, risks and constraints; and an estimation of resource requirements covering finance, human resources (i.e. jobs and skills), technology, and timescales. Details of project deliverables (i.e. things the e-government projects should produce such as feasibility reports, specification documents,

---

Box 3.9   Typical Content of an eGovernment Strategy Statement

Executive summary

Context

- Organizational strategy
- Context of laws and regulations relating to e-government
- Current status of e-government in organization

Strategy

- Overview of e-government vision, strategy, objectives and success measures
- Strategy component 1: Customer relationship management (management systems and structures, and processes)
- Strategy component 2: Organizational capability (management systems and structures, staffing and skills)
- Strategy component 3: Enterprise architecture (technology and information)
- Strategy component 4: Security and privacy (information and processes)
- Main risk factors

Implementation

- Actions required under the four main strategy component headings

Supporting papers may include more details about the enterprise architecture and its separate elements (e.g. an IT architecture, a data architecture), more details about particular e-government projects and their business cases, and more specific plans of action (e.g. for particular projects). (Adapted from DOL, 2003)

---

and both interim and final versions of the system) and timetables can be approved at this stage. So, too, can mechanisms for reporting back to the eGovernment Steering Group on progress.

The rows of the matrix will be organization-wide resource plans: for personnel training and development, for finance, for technology, etc. There may also be an additional dimension to the matrix – time – showing what is to occur and be paid for within particular financial years.

6. Strategy Implementation 2: Manage, Evolve and Review eGovernment Strategy

Strategic planning is not intended to be a one-time activity but a continuous cycle that needs to be completely revised at the end of the strategic framework period, or earlier if circumstances change or objectives are not attained.

One task of the eGovernment Steering Group is to monitor implementation of the strategic plan. Monitoring gathers information on:

- performance against objectives set for both e-government overall and individual e-government projects;
- benefits accruing to the organization from e-government systems;
- problems related to developing or operating e-government systems, with diagnoses and proposed remedies;
- other impacts associated with e-government systems;
- changes to significant internal and external factors that affect the performance of the organization; and
- resources used and projected for use.

All of this means that the strategy should contain at least some broad sense of milestones or performance indicators of progress.

On the basis of the information gathered, the eGovernment Steering Group may decide to modify the strategy. For example, project priorities may be altered in line with changes in the external environment, or the e-government systems architecture could be revised in the light of emerging organizational functions.

Monitoring is seen as an ongoing activity, but may be incorporated within cyclical reviews of the strategy. These might include two things. First, annual review of progress on e-government projects and the creation of new organization-wide implementation plans for the next 12–18 months that fit with budget cycles. Second, major review every three–five years that starts from first principles (i.e. from a revised business strategy for the organization) and presents a new e-government strategic plan for the organization.

3.3 PROBLEMS AND WAYS FORWARD FOR εGOVERNMENT PLANNING

Misconceptions of eGovernment Strategic Planning

In Chapter 2, potential constraints and potential negative impacts relating to centralized approaches were identified. These often apply to e-government strategic planning (Holmes, 2001; Fountain, 2002). In addition, there may be some misconceptions that undermine the whole basis of strategic planning.

It can be argued that these misconceptions arise because e-government strategic planning is a prescription based on rational models that are more theoretical than empirical. eGovernment strategic planning relies on a number of assumptions that empirical work has shown to be questionable at best and quite invalid at worst (Ballantine and Cunningham, 2001). The questionability of strategy seems particularly strong in the public sector. It may be expected given the private sector origins of strategic planning, which lead it to be based on a set of design assumptions that do not necessarily match public sector realities.

Problematic assumptions include those described below.

That strategy is a large-scale, top-down, proactive exercise in forward planning This vision of what managers do is arguably flawed. Managers seem to undertake very little grand decision making in practice, but tend to focus on incremental steps; partly because they recognize the problems of centralized approaches identified in Chapter 2:

> In contrast to the classical description in which senior managers are thought of as making grand, sweeping decisions ... the

contemporary manager tackles organizational decisions with a purpose, and does
not seek to implement comprehensive, systematic, logical, well-programmed plans.
Systematic, comprehensive plans are generally unable to exploit changes in the environment, and they are just as likely to create
opposition in the organization as they are to
gain support. For this reason, the manager
seeks to implement plans one part at a time.
(Laudon and Laudon, 1998: 124)

One explanation for this step-by-step
approach is that managers are using decisions
in order to make sense of their organization
and its environment. Hence, for those organizations with anything that could be called
a strategy, it more often emerges through re-
interpreting past operational decisions than
through proactive planning. Where some
consistent pattern is found, this is defined as
the organization's strategy: something that
tells the organization more about its past
than its future. IT strategy in the Danish
government has followed this line, as one of
the IT Policy Office advisers explained:

We started off with a vision of using technology for change ... and we didn't know
where we wanted to go. Now we are gradually trying to invent strategy and policies as
we go along. (Skaarup, 1997)

Where public servants are pushed into a
more textbook approach to strategy, they
will often use it for sense-making purposes
in which learning takes precedence over
decision-making (Anttiroiko, 2002).

*That there are known and consistent organiza-
tional objectives to guide strategy formation* It
can be argued that public sector organizations cannot have objectives. They are social
constructs, not living beings, and therefore
there is no such thing as an organizational
objective. Instead, there are the objectives
of individuals within the organization.

These individuals may form coalitions
where they perceive their objectives and
interests to overlap. These coalitions may
conflict with other interest groups (Atkinson
and Leigh, 2003).

This organizational reality has two implications for statements of organizational
objectives. First, these statements face particular problems in the public sector
because their formation will require many
political battles and compromises:

Politicians tend to find the task of setting
clear objectives harder than the boards of
private companies (not that this is easy for
the latter). Again, the exposed and competitive nature of political activity accentuates
the difficulties. Articulating a manageable
number of clear priorities sounds very sensible in the management textbooks, but to a
politician the identification of clear priorities
may lead to loss of support among those
groups who do *not* see themselves as benefiting from those programmes which have
been given pride of place. For the politician,
therefore, it is often easier to say that almost
everything is important ... Senior officials
and managers may be no better equipped
to resolve these conflicts over objectives
which are rooted in competing value systems among the community at large.
(Pollitt and Harrison, 1992: 4)

Statements of objectives are also side-
stepped in order to avoid setting any criterion against which one may later be held
accountable. Thus e-government planners
can often find themselves without any
broader organizational strategy to guide
them (Barrett and Greene, 2001).

Second, where there *is* a statement of
organizational objectives it is often:

• so bland as to be of no guidance value,
  because it has had to please a number of
  different interest groups or because it is
  politically easier to leave objectives very
  vague; or

- intended for external consumption rather than internal ownership (a frequent occurrence where central government has pushed agencies to formulate objectives under performance management initiatives), and thus again of little guidance value since it bears little relation to the actual interests and work of organization staff; or
- representing one powerful individual or group's interests, rather than most of the agency's employees or clients, which is hardly a stable basis for long-term planning of e-government, given the volatility of public sector organizational politics.

That there is sufficient certainty and stability within the organization's internal and external environment to make plans created at one point in time applicable at some future point in time For many public agencies, conditions of stability do not exist. The annual budget cycle alone provides an undercurrent of short-termism within most agencies.[5] Many public organizations also find themselves in situations of constant and largely uncontrollable flux from factors such as (Barrett and Greene, 2001; Doherty and Horne, 2002): changeover in ruling political parties; constant circulation of senior politicians and officials; emergence of new political initiatives and legislation that alter organizational activities, priorities and even structures; sudden imposition of cost-cutting measures; sudden external crises that demand a reaction; changes within the client groups the organizations serve; and changes in IT, IT standards and IT suppliers.

All of these changes mean that the relevance and applicability of any e-government plans in the public sector falls away very rapidly with time.

That those involved will behave in an organizationally rational manner As argued in Chapter 1, politicized or semi-politicized approaches are more often the norm in the public sector than organizational rationality. Any involvement in strategy therefore tends to be rooted in motivations that may conflict with strategy's rational assumptions.

For example, the notion that strategy is being driven by a pursuit of organizationally-rational goals comes unstuck when one examines the real-world drivers found in some public agencies. Typical examples of these were alluded to above. One key driver is the need to respond to external pressures, such as central government's refusal to provide resources until the public agency goes through the motions of creating an e-government strategy. A knock-on of the external political drive for strategy is that it may have to be completed to an unrealistic time-scale. This pushes agency staff to skip over parts of the process, and to repackage old wine in new bottles: trying to rework existing initiatives and documentation to fit the required mould.

Other drivers could be:

- a desire by senior public managers to increase management control over e-government systems in order to gain resources, avoid reprimands for failures, or for internal political purposes;
- a desire by one individual or group to improve their career advancement opportunities by adding 'involvement in e-government strategy formulation' to their CV/resumé.

In the public sector, strategy's assumptions of rationality face other challenges (Ballantine and Cunningham, 2001: 299–301). Strategy 'assumes some monolithic vision of organizations in which the organization's vision, objectives, goals, and critical success factors are unitary and unproblematic'. 'Given the many competing stakeholders and visions' in the public sector, this assumption is not met. Reflecting its drivers, strategy formation can often be a time of intense political competition since strategy seeks to interfere in a significant way with issues of resource flows, power and control. The public agency, then, is anything but unitary. In addition, strategy conceives 'the strategists as independent observers who can exercise judgement by disconnecting themselves from the entangled everyday reality of the organisation ... In practice, this can never be, because strategists are always participants in organisational processes as well as observers.'

The Outcome of eGovernment Strategy

eGovernment strategic planning may be fundamentally misconceived, may face severe constraints to its implementation, and may create negative impacts within the organization. What is the impact of these in the public sector? Four common outcomes are found.

Lack of Strategy

Many public sector organizations have no e-government strategy. For example, a large-scale survey of US local government found 91 percent had no strategic plan to guide e-government (Holden et al., 2003). In some cases, this is because strategy is never started: managers consciously or subconsciously realize the flaws and do not waste resources on a pointless activity. In other cases, strategy is never finished. The organization sets out boldly to follow the type of rational approach outlined above. But, at some point, the initiative collapses under the weight of its own contradictions and constraints.

Underused Strategy

Where strategies are produced by public sector organizations, they may be underused or even unused in various situations that include:

- *When strategy has been about image not content*: For the purposes of either internal or external imagery, strategic planning sometimes takes place but is just window dressing. Those involved just go through the motions of planning, and the content cannot be used largely because it was never really intended for use. There is at least an impression of this given in many publicly available agency e-government strategies. They are jam-packed with 'management-speak' jargon: a strong signal of delusions, illusions and a general lack of connection with reality. The strategies give the impression of box-ticking – doing just enough to meet the demands of external policies and oversight agencies; and often doing that in a hurry – without true internal ownership of, or commitment to, the strategy.
- *When strategy has been hijacked*: When a power culture dominates in public agencies, the e-government strategy may be taken over to serve the requirements of one dominant group within the organization. The skewed content of strategy and its limited ownership mean it may be underused.
- *When strategy is 'strategic concrete'*: Some public sector organizations do struggle through all the constraints to produce a textbook strategy. The misconceptions and disadvantages then come to the fore. The British Army fell into this trap when it produced its first IT strategy. The strategy document took a very long time to produce. It ran to 800 pages and

created a 'strait-jacket of detail' that meant managers 'felt like prisoners of over-rigid procurement methodologies and ... over-rigid IT strategies and management structures' (Hayward, 1997: 36). In practice, the document largely remained on the shelf, unable to cope with local conditions or with environmental changes.

Damaging Strategies

Textbook centralized e-government strategy can work for some public agencies. But this is more by luck than judgment. In other cases, strategy can lead public agencies off in the wrong direction as they are pushed to implement their misconceived plans. Davenport (1997: 23), for example, cites the dangers of the rational-technical methods that produce organization-wide information architectures:

> ... more resources are often thrown after information architectures and plans, and more years wasted. When these technical methods are applied broadly to model information needs, not only do they fail to add value, they also distract from business change.

Alternative Approaches are Used

Some public managers recognize that the rational, centralized approach to e-government planning is both infeasible and undesirable in their organizations. Nonetheless, they wish to proceed with some sort of planning and must adopt an alternative approach. In some cases, this alternative may focus on process not content. This recognizes that the process of trying to create a strategy may be more valuable than the formal deliverables. Value is sought from the informal process deliverables such as: making sense of the past, learning from experience, encouraging dialogue and communication, and making choices (Davenport,

1997; Ballantine and Cunningham, 2001). Alternatives can also be seen as hybrid approaches. These are discussed further in the following sub-section, where we change from a terminology of 'strategy' to 'planning', reflecting some of the issues just raised.

Hybrid Approaches to eGovernment Planning

It seems that a hybrid approach to e-government planning could be beneficial. But what does this mean? Implicit within much that has been written above is a sense that a hybrid approach could bring balance between a number of tensions inherent to e-government planning:

- *Rational and political*: eGovernment planning must recognize and incorporate the political world that public agencies inhabit. However, it must try to balance this against some of the rational organizational purposes that e-government planning is prescribed to address.[6]
- *People and technology*: By defining e-government systems as information systems, and by noting that e-government is made up from 'government' as well as 'e', we try to signal a balance between people and technology.
- *Internal and external*: In the public sector, e-government planning must seek to achieve a balance between the internal needs of the agency, and the external requirements imposed on the one hand by higher-level legislation, policy and agencies, and on the other hand by clients.

Above all, though, a hybrid approach to e-government planning will mean a balance between *central and local*. So, for instance, it could mean that e-government planning is

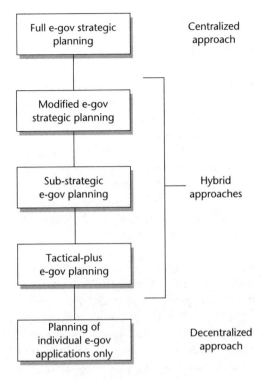

Figure 3.8 Hybrid approaches to e-government planning

Modified eGovernment Strategic Planning

If e-government planning is to proceed largely as described above, with a strong strategic component, then a hybrid approach would involve more active participation of users and local units in the formulation of strategy (Bishop, 2001). The strategy planning process would then involve decisions about other e-government management responsibility areas according to a hybrid framework (see Chapters 2 and 4): balancing the needs of internal and external stakeholders in setting priorities; planning which data items are generic and which are specific; dividing out responsibilities for e-government systems development; and so on.

This modified approach would also encompass the more flexible notion of strategy as guidelines rather than blueprint, 'allowing for revisions based on experiences from the ongoing process of change.' (Nilsson and Ranerup, 2002: 313).

Sub-Strategic eGovernment Planning

Given the many constraints to strategic planning, it may be more feasible to plan at what might be termed the 'sub-strategic' level. This pares back what planning hopes to achieve until the intention matches what can be achieved in the organization.

For example, it may not be possible to drive the planning process in terms of organizational objectives. In this case, plans could be based on an external and internal survey of information-related needs and problems. The sub-strategy would aim to prioritize and then address these over the short to medium term. It might not necessarily involve all of the steps and techniques described, instead selecting only those that can be implemented. It would focus on general tools (SWOT, benchmarking, value chain analysis) rather than the

seen as incremental, as participative, as limited in scope: guiding more than dictating.

The successor to the UK Army's 800-page strategy document, cited above, took a hybrid approach and was only 30 pages long. It provided a guiding framework, allowing for some local flexibility and initiative. By setting out general principles rather than specific details, it also provided the flexibility to deal with subsequent organizational and environmental changes. This approach is sometimes referred to as 'picking a course and steering it': being adaptable to new constraints and new circumstances as they arise rather than imagining that the strategy is cast in 'tablets of stone'.

Taking this approach, public agencies can proceed in one of three main ways, as illustrated in Figure 3.8.

great detail of IE, or it would use CSFs in a generic way rather than pushing them down to the level of specific data/process detail.

Alternatively, the strategy could be pared back so that it focused quite specifically. Davenport (1997), for example, suggests focusing on just:

- one particular type of data to improve, for example, personnel or service or finance;
- sharing information, since this is often so poor in public sector organizations;
- information tasks: looking at each of the CIPSODA tasks (see Chapter 1) in turn for major service delivery processes in the agency to see how those tasks could be improved.

Tactical-Plus eGovernment Planning

If more strategic approaches fail, there may just be a focus on individual e-government systems, with an attempt to broaden the scope of planning to place such systems in their organizational context. This is planning at what can be termed the 'tactical-plus' level. It might include:

- pushing the objectives of an individual e-government system 'upstream' to think how it contributes to the overall work of the organization;
- assessing the opportunity costs of going ahead with this particular e-government system rather than others; and/or
- assessing whether there should be compatibilities between this and other existing or planned systems.

Into this category, one can also place the notion of emergent strategy. This is the way in which higher-level 'strategic' ideas emerge from the tactical decisions taken with individual systems. For example, one UK police force – while maintaining the empty façade of a formal, forward-planning strategy – only developed any true notion of higher-level planning for e-government through its work on one specific system (Horton and Dewar, 2001).

ACTIVITIES

Shorter In-Class Activities[7]

Section 3.1

a. 'You don't need a strategy for e-government. You just get on and do it.' Discuss in pairs then plenary.

b. Concerns about security of e-government systems are tending to grow. Discuss what implications this has for e-government strategy.

Section 3.2

a. Does it make sense to divide off structures for Internet-based e-government from structures for other e-government systems, as described in Box 3.2?

b. Look at Box 3.5 and pick any two of the 13 goals, vision elements, or reform principles. How could e-government help deliver on the two aspects you have chosen?

c. Compare the e-government principles listed in Box 3.6. Discuss which you find more useful: the agency-specific, or the generic principles.

d. Pick an identified public sector orga-nization. In pairs, imagine you are the e-government strategy team leaders for that organization. Pick a maximum of three criteria that you will use to prioritize e-government projects for the organiza-tion. Be prepared to justify your selection.

e. Do the criteria in Box 3.7 give greater weight to implementation or impact? How politically realistic are these criteria?

f. Circulate a copy of a public sector e-government strategy. Identify how many of the elements in Box 3.9 are covered. Is anything important missing from either the strategy or Box 3.9?

Section 3.3

a. 'Politics determines everything in the public sector. There is no place for rational textbook ideas like e-government strat-egy.' Discuss in pairs then plenary.

b. Get class members to provide theoretical or real-world examples for each cell in the matrix shown below.

c. Give examples of the main ways in which e-government planning can be 'hybrid'.

Responsibility	Centralized	Hybrid	Decentralized
eGovernment Planning			

Assignment Questions

Sections 3.1 to 3.3

a. Obtain an e-government strategy docu-ment from a public sector organization. Evaluate it using the following questions:

- Does it indicate where the organization is now?
- Does it indicate where the organization wants to get to?
- Does it indicate how the organization gets from where it is now to where it wants to get to?
- How and how well does it do these three things?
- Is there a clear statement of expected benefits from/intended rationale behind the strategy?

- Is there a clear indication of who is responsible for creating and implement-ing the strategy?
- Is the planning and prioritization of e-government systems clearly driven by high-level organizational objectives?
- Is an organizational e-government systems architecture laid out? What does it consist of?
- How many of the strategic decisions iden-tified in Step 4b have been made in the document?
- Is there a clear implementation plan?
- Is there a mechanism for monitoring and evolving the strategy?
- Where would you place it in Figure 3.8?

Section 3.3

a. Which can better explain the reality of strategic planning in the public sector:

rational or political models? What are the implications of your answer for e-government strategy?

Practitioner Exercises

Sections 3.1 to 3.2

a. eGovernment strategic planning must be seen as an in-depth, group activity. The exercises listed here are, therefore, just introductory overviews to the initial steps of that strategic planning process.

Overview activities: What rationale is there for introducing e-government strategic planning in your organization? What are the drivers and what are the intended benefits? Is it an appropriate time for your organization to enter into e-government strategic planning?

Step 1 planning: What organizational structures would need to be created to plan and implement an e-government strategy in your organization? Who would be the members of those structures? What would the remit of those structures be?

Step 2a planning: Would your organization need an IS audit? If so, what would be the scope of the audit? From whom would you need permission to conduct the audit? How would you carry out the audit: both gathering data and recording data? Who would be involved in the audit?

Step 2b planning: Does your organization have accepted objectives? If so, what are they? If not, why not?

Step 2 overview:

The Organization
Objectives: Write down your organization's objectives. Even if these have not been formally stated, think what – in broad terms – the organization should be achieving.

External stakeholders: Draw a diagram of the main external individuals, groups and institutions with which your organization interacts. Ensure that both suppliers and clients are included.

Internal stakeholders: Draw a diagram of the main internal groupings within your organization; this might relate to job categories, functional divisions and/or informal groupings.

From both diagrams, you can now identify those who should be involved in strategy and other planning. The diagram may also help you identify those involved with key organizational processes, and those who may drive e-government project prioritization.

Major external processes: List the main activities of your organization that relate to the 'outside world'. Indicate which stakeholders are involved in those processes.

Major internal processes: List the main activities of your organization that relate to its own administration (e.g. personnel, finance/accounting, etc.). Indicate which stakeholders are involved in those processes.

From both diagrams, you can identify gaps between what the organization *is* doing and what it *should be* doing. You will also see the intended processes as the site for the organization's major e-government systems.

Weaknesses and threats: List the main internal weaknesses/problems of the organization, and the main external threats to its operations.

Strengths, opportunities and vision: List the main internal strengths of the organization, the main external opportunities that the organization could take advantage of, and detail any future vision that may exist for the achievement of organizational objectives. The latter should include contextual elements like policies, guidelines or targets for e-government.

This analysis will highlight main areas for change and, possibly, priorities for new e-government systems.

Overall, your e-government strategy should seek to address identified weaknesses, counter identified threats, sustain identified strengths, grasp identified opportunities, and fulfill identified vision.

eGovernment Systems as Information Systems
Information systems: List the organization's current information systems (manual and informal as well as computerized and formal).

IT: List the main computerized applications (i.e. e-government) currently used in your organization.

Information systems and stakeholders/ processes: Review the stakeholders and processes identified above. Which of these are supported by a formal information system? Which of these are not yet supported by a formal information system? On this basis, can you identify any new e-government systems or information systems improvements that are needed?

Systems problems: List the main current problems with information and information systems in your organization. Cross-check with the organizational weaknesses and threats already identified to see if they contain other information/IS-related problems.

Systems opportunities: List any opportunities that may exist in relation to e-government systems, particularly deriving from advances in IT. Cross-check with examples of leading-edge practice in similar public agencies. Cross-check also with the organizational strengths, opportunities and vision already identified to see if they contain any related opportunities.

Your e-government strategy should seek to address systems problems and grasp systems opportunities. On this basis, can you identify any new e-government systems or information systems improvements that are needed?

Systems constraints: List the main constraints to e-government systems change in the organization. You can use ITPOSMOO as a checklist.

Systems priorities: List the criteria that should be used for prioritizing e-government systems projects within the organization.

Step 3 overview: On the basis of the foregoing analysis, review the main rationale, objectives and principles behind e-government within the organization. Include prioritization criteria against which to judge individual e-government projects.

Step 4a overview:

IE: From the process lists constructed for step 2 above, identify two to three main activities that your organization undertakes to help meet its objectives/remit. List two or three major items of data used across your organization that support those activities.

CSF: On the basis of the SWOT/vision analysis undertaken for step 2 above, identify two or three factors you consider critical for the successful performance of your organization. What decisions and processes are needed in order to produce those factors? What data is needed in order to support those decisions and processes?

Using the components identified for an e-government systems architecture, outline the current systems architecture for your organization.

Section 3.2

a. Apply the scoring scheme in Box 3.7 to two or three of your current e-government applications. Do the scores provide any useful insights into the value of those applications?

Section 3.3

a. Think about how the misconceptions described in the main text might apply to your own organization, and note down answers to the following questions:

- Do managers plan in the large-scale, top-down, proactive manner of the rational model or in the more incremental/retrospective manner described by other models?

- Does your organization have 'organizational objectives'? If so, do these form a credible basis for strategic planning? If not, why is this?
- Is there sufficient certainty and stability for your organization to make planning possible?
- Do managers in your organization behave more according to models of organizational rationality or personal politics?

Note down any implications of your answers for the applicability of e-government strategic planning in your organization.

b. Building on answers to the previous exercise, identify what practical difficulties (arising from constraints (refer also to Chapter 2) and misconceptions) you might face in undertaking a centralized e-government strategic planning exercise in your organization. Are there ways in which these difficulties could be addressed in order to proceed with a centralized strategy? If not, is there a hybrid approach to e-government planning (modified strategic, sub-strategic, or tactical-plus) that could be more appropriate to your organization? In either case, what would be your actual first steps in getting an e-government planning exercise started?

NOTES

1. Discussion of e-government strategy at higher levels can be found in the Online Appendix for this chapter.

2. There are further benchmarking/stage models in the Online Appendices for this chapter and for Chapter 6.

3. There is more discussion about planning the network architecture for a public agency in the Online Appendix for this chapter.

4. Budget issues are taken up further in the Online Appendix for this chapter.

5. An issue discussed further in the Online Appendix for this chapter.

6. The issue of the rational and the political is discussed further in the Online Appendix for this chapter.

7. Details of longer group activities are provided in the Online Appendix to this chapter.

4

Managing Public Data

Key Points

- Data quality problems can and do undermine e-government.
- Data quality can be measured using the CARTA checklist.
- Data quality is typically addressed through general controls, which affect all e-government systems in an agency, and application controls, which relate to individual e-government systems.
- Hard solutions to public data quality problems are technology-based and fairly easy to introduce.
- Soft solutions are more difficult to implement but address more fundamental issues of human perceptions and motivations.
- Hybrid solutions combine both hard–soft and central–local components.

As argued in Chapter 1, e-government systems are information systems. The data in e-government systems is therefore fundamental to the functioning of the public sector. It is too easy to assume that all is well with this data. Yet most e-government systems have data quality problems; sometimes so bad that they undermine the whole edifice of government functioning (Milner, 2000). For example:

- An audit of Hawaii's welfare claimant data found one-third of data records to be incomplete (State of Hawaii, 2001).
- Sixty-five percent of the data on the UK Police National Computer needs updating (*Computing*, 2002).
- The average UK central government web site contains 2000 errors (E-Government Bulletin, 2002a).

- A study in the Swedish Post Office found it was losing around US$20 million per year because of poor data quality in its address registers (Bygrave, 2003).

In looking at the management of public data, this chapter therefore has a central focus on management techniques to improve data quality. These techniques are divided into two main groups. The first group is a detailed and comprehensive set of hard, rational, technical guidelines that address data gathering and data input. The second group builds from a soft analysis of personal motivations and their (often negative) impact on data quality.

The chapter will also consider what it means to adopt a hybrid approach to public data management. This can be seen to involve not just an accommodation between the hard and soft approaches introduced in Chapter 1; but also accommodation between the centralized and decentralized approaches discussed in Chapter 2. Having said this, there is an increasing emphasis on centralized approaches to public data management as the importance of, and legislative framework surrounding, policies for public data grows. This will be discussed further in Chapter 6.

Although many of the techniques presented can be difficult to implement, the chapter nonetheless provides some valuable tools to address data issues in the public sector.

4.1 PROBLEMS WITH PUBLIC DATA QUALITY

Data quality issues in e-government systems are introduced in the case study in Box 4.1.

Box 4.1   Data Quality and the Shooting Down of Iran Air Flight 655

On 3 July 1988, the US Navy Cruiser USS *Vincennes* fired two missiles at an aircraft it believed to be a hostile military jet in attack mode. ... [The aircraft was misidentified] ... resulting in the destruction of an Iranian Passenger Airbus (Iran Flight 655). Data-quality problems may have contributed to the decision that brought 290 people to their deaths. ... The USS *Vincennes* is one of the US Navy's newest and most technically advanced ships, an anti-air warfare (AAW) cruiser equipped with the world's finest battle management system [*Aegis*]. Aegis is capable of simultaneously processing and displaying several hundred surface and air radar tracks. Its great tactical advantage is the speed with which it determines course, speed and altitude... .

Research has shown that the Aegis System did not make errors in identification, but that errors manifested themselves in the socio-technical seam of the overall system. A management information system (MIS) includes the interfaces and people that use those interfaces. When looked at from this perspective, data-quality problems become apparent, and knowledge of them might have prevented the disaster ...

Data quality was a major factor in the USS *Vincennes'* decision-making process. Problems were manifested in the use of wrong target identifiers, incomplete information, conflicting information, voice-communication problems, and information overload. In addition, there may have been interactions with experience level, time pressure, and information overload.

When multiple USS ships simultaneously identify an aircraft, multiple track numbers are initially assigned to the entity. The Aegis System resolves these duplicate numbers to a single, unique track number, TN*xxxx*. However, the system recycled the numbers that had been assigned initially; this reuse of the identifiers was at the heart of the disaster. An *inconsistency* error occurred at the socio-technical seam, the interface. Human users may see the initial number and not realize that the computer has replaced it with another; there was no system alert to notify users of the system's reuse of the number. In the example, a target identifier, TN4474, was used twice – once to identify Flight 655, and then (later) to identify a fighter plane that was 110 miles away. The identifier used to track Flight 655 changed from TN4474 to TN4131. Seconds before firing, the *Vincennes* Captain asked for the status of TN4474 and was told it was a fighter, descending and increasing in speed. He and his crew had been discussing and tracking the radar blip of Flight 655, and then confused its tracking number, TN4131, with the fighter's number, TN4474. When the Captain gave the order to fire, the *Vincennes* shot down TN4131 rather than TN4474. If the duplication of identifiers had been recognized, the involved parties could have avoided the disaster ...

Incomplete information resulted from the computer-generated displays, large display consoles (LDCs), displaying objects as white dots in half-diamonds for hostile aircraft or in half-circles for friendly aircraft. The relative length of the white lines projecting from the dots indicates course and speed. The use of relative length for speed restricts the use of relative length for size, and this deprived the *Vincennes'* officers of another visual check. A commercial airbus is much larger than a fighter and a size symbol linked to the air contact would have let the *Vincennes'* crew note that the Flight 655 contact was too large to be a fighter.

Information *inconsistencies* also complicated the decision-making process. Captain Rogers explained '... we had indications from several consoles, including the IDS [Identification System] operator, that the contact's IFF [Identification Friend or Foe] readout showed a mode III [civilian] squawk but more significantly to me, a mode II [military] squawk ... previously identified with Iranian F-14s was also displayed'.

Another discrepancy was between the Aegis System's tapes and five crewmembers' reports (*accuracy*). The Aegis System's tapes and system data indicated that Flight 655 was in ascending mode; five crewmen operating separate consoles reported that the aircraft was descending. Captain Rogers stated that the aircraft was at an altitude of between 7000 and 9000 ft at the time of the shooting. Data captured from the system indicated that the aircraft was at an altitude of 13,500 ft. Captain Rogers explained that, 'It looks like the system worked the way it's supposed to ... However, there are problems with the way the consoles are designed, the displays are presented, and the communication nets work ... (*fitness for use*) (Fisher and Kingma, 2001: 113–14).

This case presents an extreme example of the importance of data quality in e-government systems.

We can use this case and others to define data quality in terms of five 'CARTA' indicators:

- *Completeness*: The degree to which all the data required by users is present in the e-government system.
- *Accuracy*: The level of errors/incorrect data within the overall system data.
- *Relevance*: The degree to which data is necessary in order to complete particular user decisions and actions.

- *Timeliness*: The degree to which data can be delivered by the e-government system within a required timeframe.
- *Appropriateness of presentation*: The degree to which data produced by the e-government system is accessible and intelligible to the recipient.

The more CARTA the data, the higher its quality; the less CARTA the data, the lower its quality.

We can also use other information systems models to identify the causes of data quality problems in e-government. For example, thinking of the CIPSO model

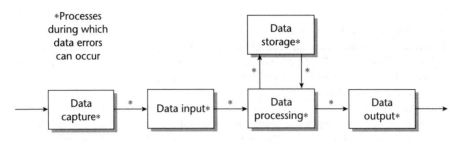

Figure 4.1   Potential data error points in the e-government system cycle

from Chapter 1, it is estimated that around 80 percent of system data errors arise during the human elements of the process (TDWI, 2002). Historically, this has occurred mainly during capture and input, because these were traditionally human-intensive tasks with errors arising from misreading, mistyping, and lost or omitted inputs. It has also occurred after output, also because of misreading or misunderstanding, both of which were evident in the Box 4.1 case.

But data errors can occur at any stage in the information cycle, for example, during processing, storage, output or transmission between those stages, as illustrated in Figure 4.1.

In all cases, the data output will not be accurate or reliable. These deficiencies will then feed through the whole system, like the Biblical story of the house built on sand. eGovernment systems with poor data will similarly be prone to collapse as the poor data foundation undermines decision making and action, as summarized in Figure 4.2.

More succinctly, this is often described as *garbage in, garbage out (GIGO)*: what you get out from your e-government systems can only ever be as good as what you put in, and if you put in garbage, you get out garbage.[1]

This is an issue for all organizations, but it is particularly an issue for the public sector and e-government (Heeks, 2000a; Fletcher, 2000):

- The public sector is especially information-intensive, and therefore relies heavily on data in order to undertake its functions.
- The public sector often has responsibility for decisions that are critical to an individual's, a region's or a nation's welfare. Public data quality can, therefore, be truly a matter of life and death as it was in the Box 4.1 case.
- The public sector has legal obligations relating to data quality and accessibility, for example in relation to freedom of information. It therefore faces a significant threat of litigation if data quality is poor.

The public sector may also face additional constraints – on skills, on technology, related to the large size of its data sets – that increase the risks of data quality problems.

Causes of Public Data Quality Problems

What causes data quality problems? If we look at the onion-ring diagram (see Figure 1.2), almost any item in the diagram could have a negative impact on data quality. However, we can divide out arguments about causes into two main camps: hard and soft. These arguments contrast hard, technical causes of data quality problems against soft, human causes.

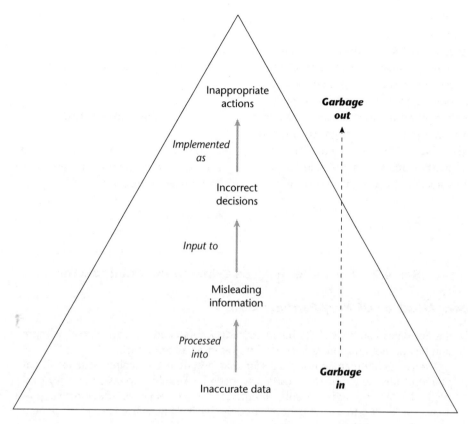

Figure 4.2   Impact of inaccurate data

Looking first at the hard side of the coin, one can see that public managers love to blame data glitches on 'computer errors', and that some technical problems do arise which affect the data held by IT:

- *Environmental hazards*: High temperatures and high humidity can cause hardware components to break down, thus corrupting data. Static electricity can damage both electro-magnetic components and corrupt data. Dust and smoke can short out components and make moving parts stick, especially damaging disk drives and the data on them. Fire, flood and lightning have a fairly obvious

and catastrophic effect on IT-based systems.

- *Electrical problems*: Power spikes or surges (increases in voltage), and *brownouts* (decreases in voltage) can corrupt disk-held data and damage internal components. Power cuts cause an inability to work, and a loss of all data in memory.
- *Equipment breakdown*: This can prevent data being exchanged or accessed.
- *Software errors*: The presence of *bugs* (programming errors) in the software of an e-government system can have any number of effects. These include overt or, worse, undetected corruption of data.

But to what extent can these truly be classified as 'computer errors' or technical problems? The presence of bugs should be seen mainly as a problem of human, rather than technical, origin relating to the management of systems development. Even the actions of environmental or power hazards can often be traced to human inputs in the design, construction or operation of IT-based systems. This must put a question mark over the value of some hard approaches to public data quality.

We can reinforce this point by looking at another way in which technology could be blamed for inducing a further vulnerability and danger to data accuracy: the threat of computer crime.

Computer Crime

We start by looking at a couple of examples of computer crime in the public sector, summarized in Box 4.2.

Box 4.2   Computer-Related Crime in the Public Sector

Hack Attack on US Navy Purchase Cards

> The Navy has canceled all its purchase card accounts after discovering that more than half of them may have been compromised by a hack attack.
>
> Defense Department officials ... said that a system containing data for about 13,000 of the Navy's purchase cards had been hacked. In response, the Navy canceled all purchase card accounts, about 22,000, to 'minimize unauthorized purchases,' according to a statement released by the DOD Purchase Card Management Office. (French, 2003a)

The hackers gained access after several weeks of probing a Defense Logistics Agency web site. It is believed that there were no unauthorized purchases made with the cards, but details of billing records were accessed. The General Accounting Office (as then-named) had already criticized weak controls with the DOD's purchase card system, which 'have been used by federal employees to buy, among other things, prostitutes, breast implants and sports tickets' (French, 2003b).

'Cyber-warfare': Politically-Motivated Hacking

India and Pakistan have had a long-running disagreement over the state of Kashmir. In the real world, this has generally been expressed through low-level fighting: minor artillery barrages and other small-scale skirmishing that flares up from time to time. The growth of e-government has enabled a second front to be opened up, in the virtual world. For example, hundreds of Indian web sites are defaced each year by pro-Pakistan hackers. Sites hit include those of the Indian Parliament and Department of Customs and Central Excise, as well as those of leading public sector institutions such as the Indian Institute of Science and the Bhabha Atomic Research Center. Pakistani sites have equally been hacked by pro-India hackers. (Adapted from Gupta et al., 2004)

Computer crime is a major problem for the public sector: internally, public employees are a significant source of such crime (Smith, 1999); externally, threats seem to be growing: the UK's key government departments are each targeted around 100 times per week by hackers (McCue, 2002), and cyber-security has risen sharply up the agenda in many countries as a result of the terror attacks of the early 21st-century.

As well as entry of inaccurate data onto computer systems for personal gain, computer crime also includes:

- *Alteration of existing data*: For example, a worker increasing the rate of pay recorded for them in the payroll system, or the defacing noted in Box 4.2.
- *Unauthorized access to existing data*: Such as that described in Box 4.2 for the US Navy system.
- *Deliberate destruction of data*: For example, removing part of the organization's financial records just for the hell of it or introducing a computer virus.

Computer crime also covers physical theft of computer hardware or software (*software piracy*). Some public agencies even include personal use of organizational IT, such as typing and printing a personal letter or buying goods on the web from your office PC.

In the cases in Box 4.2, and in the other examples just given, we can see the relationship between the hard and the soft. The frauds and other misdeeds are enabled by IT, but they are driven by human motivations – nosiness, power, fame, greed, revenge, political enmity, etc.

This all suggests distinct limitations if we adopt only a hard, technical approach to data quality. Some soft, human considerations must be included. These could form a hybrid approach if used in combination with a necessary understanding of the technology. Each of these approaches will now be described in turn.

4.2 HARD SOLUTIONS TO PUBLIC DATA QUALITY PROBLEMS

Despite the caveat just issued, we will start by considering the main hard, technical response to problems of data accuracy, including computer crime: the imposition of various controls. These can be divided into two groups: *general controls*, which affect all e-government systems and which are discussed next; and *application controls*, which relate to one particular e-government system and which are discussed in the following subsection. The importance of such controls in the public sector can be illustrated, as in Boxes 4.3 and 4.4, by what happens when they are absent.

General Controls

The importance of general controls is illustrated by the cases in Box 4.3. General controls can be divided into three main types:[2]

- *Access controls*: Used to control user access to physical or digital components of an e-government system. Examples include security guards and passwords.
- *Communications controls*: Used to control user access over computer networks. Examples include encryption and firewalls.
- *Other technology controls*: Such as controls to address virus, fire or power issues.

**Box 4.3   When Hard General Controls are Missing in
the Public Sector**

Inadequate Access Controls

In 2000, the UK government set up an Individual Learning Accounts scheme that provided subsidized training for adults. Unscrupulous training providers managed to get access to the personal details of trainees who had enrolled onto the scheme. They then used these details in their own training records submitted to government, claiming money for people they had never trained. Because of the deficient controls over access to data, the whole US$400m project had to be abandoned at the end of 2001. (Government Computing, 2002)

Inadequate Technology Controls

When the Love Bug virus hit the US government in 2000, 'the federal Department of Health and Human Services was swamped with three million I LOVE YOU messages, resulting in email disruptions lasting up to six days. Social Security needed five days to remove the virus from its computers and become fully functional again. The Pentagon pulled military personnel away from other work to deal with the attack' (Holmes, 2001: 206).

Box 4.4   When Application Controls are Missing in the Public Sector

At the California Environmental Protection Agency, employees accidentally inserted hundreds of thousands of documents with duplicate identification numbers into a database used to track the movement of hazardous wastes. The resulting output was so unreliable that it became difficult, if not impossible, to find out when toxic waste was being transported or dumped, or to prosecute the perpetrators of hazardous-waste violations. (James, 1997)

Application Controls

To prevent the kind of problem identified in Box 4.4, many public agencies use application controls. The most important of these are input controls; that is, controls on the process of data entry that can be built into the e-government system. In many cases, if the control is violated, a customized message will appear providing guidance on the problem, and the new record will not be accepted until the error is corrected.

Typically, the controls operate on each field within a database record and are stored as rules associated with that field.[3]

Assessing Technology's Contribution to Public Data Quality

Many of the hard controls described above – especially the application controls – are the automation of manual processes by IT. They encapsulate IT's main potential positive contribution to data quality, with its greater reliability compared to humans for almost all elements of the information systems cycle, from capture and input, through processing and storage, to output. This contrasts with the earlier description of technical problems that IT may enable.

Looking at both sides, we can now summarize the role of IT in public data quality using the CARTA indicators. These suggest a relatively limited role for the technology:

- *Completeness*: Completeness depends mainly on the source data and the process of designing data capture, on which IT has little impact.
- *Accuracy*: IT can help make the processing and output of information more accurate. To some extent, IT can help improve the accuracy of data input thanks to the controls it imposes. However, IT does have the appearance of giving with one hand but taking away with the other. It may help improve data accuracy by providing tighter controls, but it helps reduce data accuracy by increasing opportunities for data manipulation and introducing new vulnerabilities. Over and above this, IT cannot do much about the fundamental accuracy of source data or of the data capture process in most e-government applications.
- *Relevance*: IT makes little difference to this, since it depends on contextual issues that the technology does not affect.
- *Timeliness*: IT can increase the speed with which data is input, processed and output.
- *Appropriate presentation*: IT can improve presentation, for example, with more varied output possibilities. Its impact on accessibility is more balanced. The inaccessibility of data is a central constraint to its effective use. For example, papers and files lying in huge, disorganized, crumbling piles are a familiar sight in some public agencies. These files contain data that

could be useful, but which it is virtually impossible to access. IT can help. By improving the processes of both storage and retrieval, it can allow data to be accessed more quickly and more widely than before. It may also help to save space. However, this only applies (a) for those who themselves have access to and can use IT, and (b) if the electronic data formats are still readable by present-day technologies. It can also increase accessibility to those who want to use public sector information for nefarious purposes.

In sum, there is no simple relationship between IT and public sector data quality. In some cases, IT will be an important part of an improvement strategy, but this should not be taken for granted. An equal – perhaps greater – eye must be kept on the soft, human aspects of data quality; an issue to which this chapter now turns.

4.3 SOFT SOLUTIONS TO PUBLIC DATA QUALITY PROBLEMS

Understanding Public Data Quality from a Soft Perspective

The responses to data quality problems described thus far fall quite firmly into the camp of the hard and the technical. Yet, the contextual framework presented in Chapter 1, and discussions earlier in this chapter should have alerted you to the fact that there are wider issues of data quality; issues particularly that relate to soft, human elements in public data systems. Taking a softer perspective may help us to understand why the hard controls described above have often not been implemented, or have been implemented but have failed to produce the intended improvements in data quality for e-government. Box 4.5 presents three examples that inspect public data quality from a soft perspective.

Box 4.5   People and Data Quality in Public Sector Information Systems

Case 1: Data Problems in US State eGovernment Projects

This was a set of e-government projects in a US state that went badly wrong. In part, poor monitoring of the projects and poor data quality for monitoring were the root cause of the trouble. What contributed, in turn, to these problems?

At one level it was fairly simple things, like the lack of enough staff to develop a decent monitoring system that would have clarified what was going on in the e-government projects.

It also related to that old question – is making software an art or a science? The managers of the e-government projects would have tended to answer 'an art'. Therefore, they saw little value in developing objective monitoring data about the projects, because they did not intend to use such data in their decision making. Instead, they put a lot of emphasis on informal and more subjective methods – watching the programmers at work and (relatively unsuccessfully) trying to have chats or meetings with them.

Managing those programmers was not easy. They had relatively little regard for the project managers, who were not IT or e-government professionals. Indeed, the programmers cared little about the projects, which they felt were not stretching them as IT professionals. Their commitment was poor, and their interaction with managers as limited as possible.

While the programmers had a rich pool of data about progress with the projects, they were themselves given no responsibility for collating it or passing it on. This was particularly the case when problems began to arise on early projects: the programmers were not keen to convey this news.

But the managers themselves must also take a lot of responsibility for the problems because of their attitude to the state's IT project oversight function. They felt that the delivery of monitoring data on the projects to the project oversight committee would have a damaging rather than beneficial effect on the projects. They worried that the committee would see the problems, and then have the funding for the projects terminated and perhaps reprimand the managers as it became clear that targets and goals remained unmet. So they felt, instead, it was better just to keep quiet. (Unsourced)

Case 2: Data Poverty in Russia

Since the collapse of the Soviet regime, there is less secrecy in public data gathering, and biases are more evident, but under Goskomstat (the State Committee of the Russian Federation on Statistics), data collection has not improved and may even be seen as having deteriorated (Aslund, 1995). There are many reasons behind this deterioration but three issues stand out – the introduction of taxation; the volatility of business induced by the introduction of markets; and the growth in corruption. ...

A good example of the 'new times' has been seen in the aftermath of privatization. After state enterprises were auctioned, data became more, not less, inaccurate as businesses split up, declared bankruptcy, changed their names, hid production, and changed locations frequently to avoid taxation (Whalen and Bahree, 2000). Contemporary businesses still prefer to release minimal data, even to allies, and Russian entrepreneurs maintain minimal accounting data because of what they perceive to be exorbitant and shifting taxes and fees. ...

The various information-related shortcomings at the enterprise level have a significant impact on national statistics gathered by bodies such as Goskomstat. Authorities know that private production is underreported for tax-avoidance and that many enterprises fail to register with national and local authorities to avoid taxes; as many as 50% of private enterprises may have been unregistered by the mid-1990s. ... In addition, foreign trade statistics are unreliable because of widespread smuggling, bribery, and irregular registration procedures. (Chepaitis, 2002)

Case 3: How Powerful Bureaucrats Are Deceived

Lowers [*the relatively weak data sources, capturers and inputters for public sector information systems*] often accept the imprint of the dominant reality of the uppers [*the relatively powerful bureaucrats who are data users*]. ... Some lowers construct or reflect back realities to be acceptable to uppers. When enumerators in questionnaire surveys avoid the inconvenience of actually asking questions, but instead make up the responses, they are concerned above all that their concoctions be credible. They, as lowers, therefore go to pains to ensure that their entries will correspond with what they believe to be their superiors' expectations. ... In (lower) consultants' reports to their (upper) sponsors, there is a gradation from cautious choice of language ('toned down') through self-censorship to exaggeration, being economical with the truth, and outright fabrication and lies.

Lowers also protect themselves by withholding information which if presented would be damaging for them. ... The behaviour of lowers in reflecting back the reality of uppers or in distorting or filtering information passed upwards can be described variously as reverent, respectful, courteous, polite, prudent, self-seeking, dissembling, deceiving and lying.

For bureaucratic organizations ... [*Figure 4.3*] presents the theory and practice of feedback. The motives are varied, and often combine fear of penalties, hope of rewards, and a desire to present the self favourably. Whatever the motives, the powerful uppers are deceived. (Chambers, 1994; 1997)

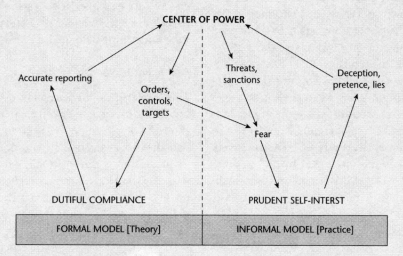

Figure 4.3   Power and information in bureaucracies

Figure 4.4   Different data roles played by people in public data systems

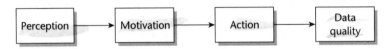

Figure 4.5   A soft perspective on data quality

From these and other cases, we can see various different data roles that humans can take in relation to public data systems. We could identify a different role for each one of the CIPSODA elements of an information system. However, that model can be simplified somewhat to produce the summary shown in Figure 4.4. This removes the roles of storage and output (because technology normally fulfils those roles) and merges the roles of decision maker and actor into the term 'user'.

The people occupying each one of these roles will have a different perspective on data, and we can develop a simple model of this, shown in Figure 4.5. The model sees perceptions about how data is or is not used as shaping the motivations of each stakeholder which, in turn will shape their actions which, in turn will have an impact on data quality (Te'eni, 1993; Klein et al., 1997).

The soft perspective therefore argues that one of the keys to data quality, or lack of it, lies in the motivations of those involved. Where they are motivated to do so, those involved will help data quality to be high. Where they are motivated to do otherwise, data quality is likely to suffer.

Some examples of perceptions – and their related motivations – will illustrate (developed from Cain, 2001 and Bygrave, 2003).

Perception of Data Irrelevance

Sources in public data systems, such as those asked to take part in a census or other survey, are often asked to provide data that is for the use of someone other than themselves. Similarly, those capturing, entering and processing data are often treated as clerical automata, merely transmitting data to be used by some senior official. In such situations, the humans involved see the data as largely irrelevant to their own work and their own lives, because they never use it. As a result, they have limited motivation to worry about data quality, and their actions – for example, lack of care in response, or lack of concern about data entry errors – may undermine data quality.

Perceptions of Non-Use

This is related to the perception of data irrelevance. In some e-government systems, those involved know (or believe) that the data they are giving or collecting or inputting or processing is never actually going to be used. This will have a knock-on effect on data quality. Within the politicized context of the public sector, for example, data entry staff may know that the data they type in is not used; perhaps because senior officials make decisions using informal, political data rather than rational data from the computerized e-government system. In that case, perfectly logically, the data entry staff will not be motivated to care about ensuring accuracy of the data they type in. Alternatively, take the case of residents asked to provide input to the planning of a community policing strategy. Having once taken the trouble to provide data, they might feel that their efforts have produced no discernible result if no sensible strategy emerges. Feeling their data was not going to be used they might, in future, be motivated to refuse to provide further data to the police service.

Perceptions of Data-Related Punishment

The cases in Box 4.5 are strong examples of people perceiving that – if they provide data for a government information system – this will lead to some negative consequence. This problem, for instance, affects all tax and revenue services worldwide. Citizens and businesses perceive that providing accurate financial data will lead to a punishment: their having to pay tax. They are therefore motivated to withhold data (by not providing a tax return, or not providing a full tax return); or to distort data (e.g. to underestimate their income/profit or overestimate their expenditure/losses). Any situation in which information is felt to have a political value may also lead to it being withheld on grounds of the old adage 'information is power'.

Perceptions of Other Data-Related Rewards

Where performance-related pay has been instituted in the public sector, staff will rightly perceive that the provision of certain performance data (i.e. apparent performance above target) to their managers will lead to some personal reward (i.e. a pay bonus). In this situation they will be motivated to hide negative performance data and

to inflate or make up positive performance data, thoroughly undermining the performance management system. Conversely, political leaders may be motivated to paint a falsely negative picture of difficulties in their district if they believe this will trigger a flow of assistance and development resources from federal or international funds.

These reward and punishment perceptions particularly affect the public sector and its clients (to whom it will often be providing money, services or other resource rewards), and compliers (whom it will often be 'punishing' via a gamut from tax bills through fines or license revocation up to imprisonment). In all these cases, the citizen's self-interest dictates that they will not be motivated to not present or handle data accurately. To paraphrase text from Box 4.5, their actions may run anywhere on a continuum from omitting certain facts, to misrepresentation, to downright lying. Given the power of our perceptions on our actions, there is really no such thing as objective data in the public sector. All data has been shaped by those who provide, handle and use it.

All this assumes that those involved do have some perceptions, but there may be situations in which there is a lack of perception; for example, where sources do not know why data is being sought from them. They will try to work this out from situational clues, but they may guess wrong and accordingly skew the data they provide wrongly. Equally, there can be cases of lack of knowledge; for example, where sources feel motivated to provide data even though they do not have that data. In other words, they will make up answers which have no basis in reality, perhaps to please the data gatherer.

We have reviewed a wide range of possible influences on the data stakeholders. One consequent problem is that so many people can be involved in the data cycle from source to use. It only needs one link in this chain to be demotivated or motivated by factors other than the interest of the organization, for problems to arise. The end result will be data of limited value to the public sector, regardless of the efforts of others.

This, in turn, may lead to a vicious circle of mutually negative reinforcement:

- of sources who see data is not used, so do not try to provide accurate data;
- of data handlers who see data is not used, so do not try to record or enter or process data accurately; and
- of data users who see that data is inaccurate, so do not use it.

Such a vicious circle characterizes a depressing number of e-government systems.

Improving Public Data Quality

In situations like those described, what would the soft approach advocate as a way to address data quality problems in e-government systems? The key will be the perceptions and motivations of all those involved in the chain. In particular, the public agency needs to find ways to align perceptions and personal motivations with formal organizational objectives.

What mechanisms exist for doing this? Some suggestions follow, summarized in Figure 4.6.

- *Ensure there is a user*: Perception of data non-use is a major demotivator. Matters can be improved if the e-government system is redesigned to ensure that the data being gathered is actually used for decisions and actions. This may involve changing the content of data gathered to match the true information needs of users.

- *Merge stakeholder roles*: The greater the number of stakeholders in the chain, the greater the chance of motivational problems. Merging roles will reduce this danger. Those who capture the data can also be those who input the data. For example, where a survey was being undertaken, role merger could mean the use of handheld devices that can accept data input in the field. Going further, data sources can themselves capture and input data. Where the consumers of public services themselves become producers of their own data, this process has been named 'prosumption' (Bellamy and Taylor, 1998). The use of web-based electronic forms enables this.

- *Make early stakeholders into data users*: Sources, capturers and inputters typically do not use the data that depends on them. If they are turned into users, they have a much greater motivation to ensure the quality of system data. In Nicaragua, for instance, health data was traditionally gathered from each village by local health workers (Horejs, 1996). It was then passed up to district, then state, then national level, in what can be seen as a variant on the source–user data chain. Villagers (the data sources) and local health workers (the data capturers) never saw their data again, and had no motivation to improve its quality. Following a change of government, data and resources were fed back from higher levels to lower levels. Villagers and their health workers were then able to make comparisons with other villages and were able to use 'their data' to make decisions about local health priorities. Data sources and capturers therefore became users too, and data quality improved.

Turning this around somewhat, one can look at the data that early stakeholders (primarily the sources) already use, and

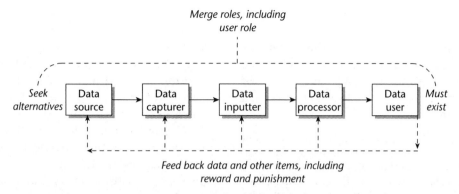

Figure 4.6   Soft approaches to improving data quality

reuse that for other purposes; that is, find the ways in which sources are already users.

- *Other feedback to early stakeholders*: Even if early stakeholders do not become data users, other types of feedback can motivate them. This can be as little as a simple word of thanks from the user, or an explanation of why and how the data is being used. One state agricultural office was frustrated at the poor response from districts that were asked to submit crop output data. The office then created a monthly newsletter the centerpoint of which was a set of summary crop data. Blank entries were recorded against those districts that had failed to submit data on time. The embarrassment motivated districts to improve that data delivery.
- *Other reward and punishment techniques*: Giving money to data sources and higher pay to data capturers, inputters and processors is one motivational technique, but money is not the only motivator. In the US state of Maine, those responsible for an education policy information system, gave important system design responsibilities to data sources (LaPlante, 2000). As a result, they were better motivated to provide good quality data for the system.

Punishment too can play a role, such as realistic threats of fines or imprisonment for those failing to fill or filling inaccurate tax returns, or threat of removal/reduction of budget by an auditor for failure to produce accurate audit figures.

- *Find alternative sources*: Identify alternative sources for the same or similar data, who/which have less self-interest in the use of the data (though they will need to be motivated by other means). For example, get administrative staff to return data on service activities of professionals (e.g. number of clients met) rather than the professionals themselves.

Such changes are not easy to achieve. You can make an e-government system appear to work, but it is much harder to have an impact on the quality of system data. In the Nicaragua case, the new approach was only possible because it occurred in the aftermath of a national popular revolution. The approach ceased with the fall of the Sandinista government. This is but one example of a wider point: that those stakeholders with power (typically the users) are the key to data quality. If they genuinely want and use good quality data, then improvement measures will usually work. If they do not, improvement measures will usually fail.

Some therefore argue that this type of soft solution to data quality will only truly emerge with the type of transformation of power relationships that temporarily occurred in Nicaragua:

> Replace dominance with deference and respect, and reverse positions and roles ... encourage and enable lowers [*those without power*], so that it is they as lowers, not others as uppers [*those with power*], who appraise and analyse their reality. The lesson is to reverse power relations through changing behaviour ... sitting down, listening and learning, facilitating, and having confidence that 'they can do it'. (Chambers, 1994: 24)

Personnel General Controls

The ideas above are drawn from the models of e-government-as-information-system that we have developed. Alternatively, the issue of data quality can be approached in a soft direction from the perspective of human resource management. This provides a set of slightly different ideas; albeit ones that acknowledge the importance of human motivations.

Examples of basic reward and punishment for personnel were discussed above. Other examples of personnel-based general controls (those which affect all e-government systems) are given below (Cain, 2001; Turban et al., 2001):

- *Appropriate employee selection, training and supervision*: Considerations of integrity and competence to implement controls may come into selection, for example. Awareness of penalties for wrongdoing may come into training, as will explanations of the threats and countermeasures described here. Supervision of staff is likely to increase the application of other controls.

- *System accountability*: If there is a clear locus of management responsibility for the operation of a basic data system, this may encourage the implementation of controls. Some departments and ministries will create a post entitled something like 'database administrator'. It is this person's responsibility to implement the various controls described here. Other staff must also know to whom they report viruses, hacks and related problems.

- *Separation of duties*: This means ensuring that the same person cannot both perpetrate and conceal an accidental or deliberate data manipulation on an e-government system. Separations might include those entering data from those checking or authorizing; those entering data about cash from those handling the cash; and/or those entering data onto a system from those developing the system. One problem here is that separation of duties can run counter to the role merger approach suggested above. It will also run counter to the requirements of workflow efficiency and joined-up government, which can encourage an integration of duties within a single public servant.

- *Immediate revocation of access privileges of dismissed, resigned or transferred employees*: This group can be considered high risk in terms of computer crime because their motivations will be significantly misaligned with those of the organization.

4.4 HYBRID APPROACHES TO PUBLIC DATA QUALITY

The hard responses referred to in this chapter are relatively easy to implement, and can all have a role in improving data quality. However, they are likely to produce few or no improvements unless supported by action on soft issues – especially stakeholder motivation and the power relationships underlying motivation.

Why for example, do so many public agencies keep failing to properly implement basic hard general and application controls? Because they are unaware of such controls? No. Because there are insufficient incentives to motivate staff to implement such controls effectively? Yes.

This therefore suggests the need for a hybrid approach to data quality in the public sector. Public managers must adopt not just the easy yet relatively ineffective hard solutions, but also the more difficult yet more fundamental soft solutions. They also need to adopt a set of hybrid solutions that sit at the interface between people and technology: representing the socio-technical component of hybrid approaches.

Examples are given below of this type of socio-technical hybrid initiative: hybrid administrative controls from both the general and the application-specific camps.

Hybrid Administrative General Controls

Controls may include (GAO, 2001; Gupta et al., 2004; Jessup and Valacich, 2006):

- *Policy development and dissemination*: Problems can be reduced by making staff and external clients aware that data accuracy is an issue and that documented procedures exist for data monitoring.
- *Password update*: Because of their vulnerability, passwords should be periodically modified, ideally through regular and automated prompting by the computer system.
- *Data backup*: Data within the system should be regularly *backed up*; that is,

copied onto a separate medium that can be used if there is some error in, or destruction of, the main data. Backup is sometimes done daily for all changes in data (*incremental backup*) and weekly for all data (*full backup*). Recovery procedures to access this data in the event of a problem need also to be developed. This may require copies of data files, operating system and application software to be kept in a fire-proof safe or in a separate location.

- *Repair and maintenance*: Procedures for IT repair and maintenance should be put in place to ensure that access to data is not blocked for long. This might include keeping frequently used spares on hand.
- *Insurance*: This can be purchased organization-wide to cover theft, fire, flood, and so on.
- *Bans*: Many organizations ban eating, drinking and smoking in areas where computers are being used. Some ban the introduction of software or data from outside the organization, though such bans are increasingly difficult to enforce as network systems spread.
- *Careful use of technology*: Staff and clients can be taught basic care of the technology they use: storing disks in boxes, away from heat and electromagnetic sources; tidying away trailing cables; not trying to repair equipment unless they know how; not loading salami slices into their colleagues' DVD drives; and so on.

Many agencies seek to improve data quality on their e-government systems through *data audit*. The size of the audit problem for the public sector is immense: 'data quality across most government departments and agencies is by its nature low: the databases of names and addresses, for instance, are huge, holding millions of records, often including historic data. ... Just checking for duplication can be a huge task, let alone checking the entire database for inaccuracies and correcting them. For example at English Nature a project to clean data for use through a geographic information system took over eight years.' (Mansell-Lewis, 1999: 60).

Because the task is so great, many public sector organizations do only a partial audit; for example, checking a sample of records on a regular basis (Wessmiller, 2002). Such checks can be made against data gathered by other means. The check data may come from manual files, from re-surveying the original data sources, or from interviews with data users. All of that is very time-consuming and more automated methods are being used. Examples include deduplication software and automated tools that match all addresses in the e-government database against a database of all addresses and postal codes in the country; the latter being provided by an increasing number of postal agencies. Such tools can also be used at the point of data input.

Although not suitable for all data, one useful audit method for data about people is to allow those people to access and check their own records; a process that aligns well with the points on motivation made above. Employees or clients, for instance, could be allowed to check their personal details and service histories. As well as adding new material, this and other audit techniques must also focus on the removal of obsolete data: *data purging*.

At a higher level, e-government systems can be subject to *system audit and contingency planning*. This involves identifying, planning and preparing for major system problems, greater than those that simple data backup or equipment repair can cover. It includes identification of likely vulnerabilities in an e-government system – such as computer crime and breakdown, flooding

or burning of the main computer system – and an assessment of the probability and impact of related risks. In some cases, this may involve the auditors trying to access or manipulate data in imitation of a computer criminal.

It then includes (a) recommendation and implementation of short-term remedial or preventive measures, and (b) initial preparation, continuous preparation and planning of contingency procedures to enact if problems arise. Initial preparation covers site planning, such as locating computers above the ground floor to reduce the risk of flood and theft. Continuous preparation activities range from regularly storing copies of key data off-site to having a separate backup computer center – a hot (active) or cold (inactive) site – available for use at any time. Contingency plans spell out who should do what in terms of data, software, hardware and networking if one of the problems occurs. It might also include options for temporary manual operations. At large or organization-critical computer sites, there may be annual mock disaster exercises to practice the contingency plans.

All of this is often wrapped up together into an overall data security policy, sometimes related to certification via international data security standard ISO17799 (UNDESA, 2003a). As discussed in Chapter 6, such policies are increasingly used in government.

Hybrid Administrative Application Controls

These are controls that relate to one specific e-government system. They include (OISC, 1998; Champlain, 2003):

- *Data authorization*: For example, a requirement that all data entry forms have to be signed by an authorizing staff member before (and possibly after) input to the e-government system. This may be done if there is a danger of fraudulent input or of manipulation of data between capture and input. Alternatively the detailed output reports may need to be signed off.

- *Data input guidelines*: In situations where the computer does not control input, guidelines may need to be issued to ensure consistency of input. For example, to ensure that names are entered in the form 'Armanov' rather than all in lower case or all in capitals. Some systems provide a text caption that appears when data is being entered in a particular field to act as a reminder of the consistency guideline.
- *Use of batch processing*: This is used on the assumption that data inputters will be more consistent and less likely to forget important input rules if they type in a large group of entries at one time.
- *Recording data entry*: In the absence of a paper record, some method of separately recording all transactions/data entered into the e-government system may be instituted to provide a manual backup or audit record.
- *Double input*: This is an extreme case of control, where two inputters type in the same material and the system only accepts those items that are typed the same by both staff.
- *Output scans*: This involves getting someone to look through output reports to check for errors or compare with inputs.
- *Output distribution controls*: These aim to ensure that all authorized users, but only authorized users, receive output from the system.
- *Use of codes*: Codes are in widespread use in public sector databases. They can increase accuracy of data input, helping reduce what needs to be input, and providing for unique identifiers. They can

also save data entry time and improve opportunities for data sorting. However, they do have to be learned, they may lack meaning and this can reduce accuracy.[4]
- *Use of well-designed input screens*: Following certain design principles for the input interface – the on-screen design into which data is entered – is found to reduce the number of errors during the process of data entry.[5]
- *Use of well-designed output*: Data quality can fall down because of shortcomings in the way that data is output to human decision makers. Therefore, care should be taken in the design of output, to reduce the likelihood of errors.[6]

Other Hybrid Controls

The focus of most prescriptions in this chapter has been the e-government system from data input onwards. However, data problems often begin earlier than this, before data ever reaches the main system. Such problems may be rooted in poor design of data-gathering exercises leading, for example, to cases in which data is gathered in the wrong places, or in which an adequate level of detail is not gathered. An audit of streetlighting in Connecticut, for instance, found data-gathering errors to partly underlie a difficulty of properly verifying work order costs (CDPUC, 2003).

We can therefore extend the start of the Figure 4.1 model by adding in the processes – and potential error points – that precede data capture. The result is shown in Figure 4.7.

IT has little impact here because it is humans that design data gathering. A hybrid response to improve data gathering will therefore involve human planning and implementation more than technology.[7]

Finally, there are hybrid controls that aim to ensure the development, testing and

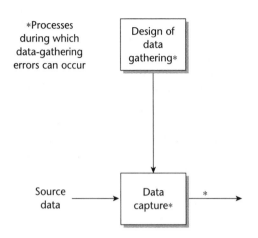

Figure 4.7   Potential error points in data gathering

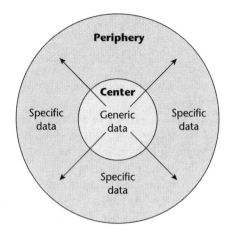

Figure 4.8   A hybrid approach to data management

documentation of new e-government systems is carried out to a high standard. This should reduce the dangers of malfunctioning software leading to data errors. Some of these controls are described in Part 2 of the book.

Other Aspects of Hybrid Public Data Management

This chapter has focused mainly on the hard–soft dimension of data management in the public sector; and specifically on the issue of managing for data quality. One can equally, though, look at data management from the central–local dimension introduced in Chapter 2.[8]

There is no strong overlap between hard–soft and central–local. More plausible is that general controls (hard, soft or hybrid) can be associated more with centralized approaches; application controls (hard or hybrid) can be associated more with decentralized approaches. Even here, though, it is easy to envisage exceptions.

In a decentralized approach, data management is the responsibility of individuals or groups within the public agency. Staff are

free to structure, manipulate and manage data according to their particular needs. While this freedom has obvious advantages, it would be pretty much unthinkable in most public agencies today because of the costs and barriers to effective data management that it would create.

More feasible is a hybrid approach to data management involving a division of responsibilities between center and periphery (Heeks, 2000b). This division is illustrated in Figure 4.8.

This division defines the center's role as being the management of generic data items (i.e. those used across all or most of the organization). Typical *generic* data items would include those about the public agency's clients, employees, finances, projects and services.

The periphery's role would be to make use of generic data; to alter generic data only within certain centrally determined controls; and to control *specific* data items (i.e. those used only by individual staff or work units), for example, those within a database of personal contacts.

Given that users tend to be relatively poor at implementing data security controls, some public agencies take a central role in enforcing, and not just encouraging, these controls on local data systems. Where IT is networked, it is relatively easy, for example, to place anti-virus software onto user computers and to perform automatic backups of user data.

In summary, then, a hybrid approach to public data management will involve both hard–soft and central–local components.

ACTIVITIES

Shorter In-Class Activities[9]

Section 4.1

a. Read through the case study in Box 4.1, and answer the following questions:

1 Is data quality in the public sector an important problem?
2 In CARTA terms, what was wrong with the quality of data?
3 Where in the CIPSO model of e-government systems did a problem exist?
4 Were the data quality difficulties caused mainly by technical or by human components in the system?

b. Consider the US/UK 2003 invasion of Iraq. Discuss how data quality played a role in the arguments for and against justification of this invasion.

Sections 4.2–4.4

a. Review the cases described in Boxes 4.1, 4.2, 4.3, 4.4 and 4.5. Suggest specific hard, soft and hybrid approaches to data quality that might have helped to prevent problems arising in these cases.

Assignment Questions

Section 4.1

a. Public sector organizations face greater data quality problems than private sector organizations. Discuss.

Sections 4.1–4.4

a. Select a case of e-government failure with a data quality component. Answer the following questions about the case:

1 How important was data quality in the failure of the e-government system?
2 In CARTA terms, what was wrong with the quality of data?
3 Where in the CIPSO model of e-government systems did a problem exist?
4 Were the data quality difficulties caused mainly by technical or by human components in the system?
5 Based on what you have learned from this chapter, what recommendations would you make to address the data quality problems you have identified?

Section 4.3

a. Select a real-world e-government system with data quality problems. Identify the main stakeholder groups, and then identify which one or more of the following roles each stakeholder group has:

• Source: initial provider of the data.
• Capturer: who initially gets the data from the source.
• Inputter: who inputs the data into the e-government system.
• Processor: who changes the data into processed data.
• User: who gets output from the e-government system and uses it for decisions and actions.

The stakeholders are motivated by their perception of how data will be used. What is that perception? For each stakeholder group, identify what they think the data will be used for, and hypothesize how this will affect their data-related motivations and actions. What is the likely overall effect on data quality in the e-government system? How could any negative effects be addressed?

Section 4.4

a. What constitutes a hybrid approach to data management in the public sector?

Practitioner Exercises

Section 4.1

a. Review data accuracy issues in your organization by making notes on the following questions:

- How serious would you estimate data accuracy (including computer crime) problems to be in your organization?
- In CARTA terms, what is mainly wrong with the quality of data?
- Where in the CIPSO model of e-government systems do problems mainly exist?
- Are the data quality difficulties caused mainly by technical or by human components in the system?

Your answers may give some sense of the extent and causes of problems that the controls described in the main text try to address. However, you should remember the large potential for data problems and crime to remain undetected.

Sections 4.2–4.4

a. Choosing one or more of your organization's e-government systems, investigate

the general controls that exist by making notes on the following questions:

- Running through each of the general controls listed in the main text and Online Appendix (hard, soft and hybrid) which of them is being used in theory, and which is not?
- Of those being used in theory, which are actually being used in practice? If you identify a gap between theory and practice, why does this arise?
- Of the general controls that are not being used, are there any that should, in theory, and could, in practice, be introduced into your organization's e-government systems?
- What barriers exist to the successful implementation of these general controls?

Sections 4.2 and 4.4

a. As with the previous exercise, choose one or more of your organization's e-government systems. Investigate the application controls that exist by making notes on the following questions:

- Running through each of the application controls listed in the main text and Online Appendix (hard and hybrid), which of them is being used in theory, and which is not?
- Of those being used in theory, which are actually being used in practice?
- If you identify a gap between theory and practice, why does this arise?
- Of the application controls that are not being used, are there any that should, in theory, and could, in practice, be introduced into your organization's e-government systems?
- What barriers exist to the successful implementation of these application controls?

Perceptions/ Motivations	Sources	Gatherers	Inputters	Processors	Data users	Other stake-holders
Perception of data irrelevance						
Perceptions of data non-use						
Perceptions of data-related punishment						
Perceptions of data-related reward						
Other influential perceptions or motivations						

Section 4.3

a. Reflect on one or more of the main e-government systems in your organization. For each system, identify the main data stakeholders involved: sources, gatherers, inputters, processors, data users and other stakeholders. For each of these, run through the checklist of possible perceptions and motivations to see which, if any, may apply to those stakeholders. You can fill in a copy of the table shown for each system.

If you do identify negative perceptions or motivations, note down the likely impact on the data quality and functioning of the e-government system. Now look through the list of techniques for improving stakeholder motivation. Which, if any, might be applicable to the system you are analyzing?

NOTES

1. A more trenchant variant is *garbage in, gospel out* – a reminder that, however poor the data entering the system, users often believe wholeheartedly in what emerges from their e-government systems.

2. Each of these is explained in greater detail in the Online Appendix for this chapter.

3. More details on such input controls are provided in the Online Appendix for this chapter.

4. Further details about codes and coding are provided in the Online Appendix for this chapter.

5. These design principles are discussed further in the Online Appendix for this chapter.

6. Design principles for data output are discussed further in the Online Appendix for this chapter.

7. Details of good practice in data-gathering design are provided in the Online Appendix for this chapter.

8. There is further discussion of the centralized approach to public data management in the Online Appendix for this chapter.

9. Details of longer group activities are provided in the Online Appendix to this chapter.

5

Core Management
Issues for eGovernment

Key Points

- IT units for e-government can be in decentralized, centralized or hybrid locations, or can be outsourced under either centralized or hybrid approaches.
- Human competencies (skills, knowledge and attitudes) are crucial to e-government but can be undermined without use of effective recruitment and retention practices.
- The golden rule of government ('whoever has the gold sets the rules') reflects the importance of e-government financing, where new hybrid approaches are emerging that attempt to combine private sector ideas with public sector values.
- Hard, rational 'best practice' in e-government project management does not seem to deliver, and needs to be tempered with a softer, more behavioral approach.
- Politics is more important than technology in e-government systems, and e-government players should focus their personal development accordingly.

The previous three chapters in Part 1 presented details of a number of specific responsibilities that are faced in the management of e-government systems. This chapter and the next discuss a set of more cross-cutting management issues that arise in relation to e-government. For better or worse, the issues have been tortured until they all begin with the letter 'P'.

This chapter deals with core issues – those that managers in the public sector have always faced:

- *position* (the location of the IT function within public sector organizations);
- *people* (recruitment and retention of staff involved with e-government);

- *pelf* (dealing with the financial aspects of e-government);
- *projects* (the ways in which e-government projects are managed);
- *politics* (the role of organizational power and politics in e-government).

Chapter 6 deals with so-called emerging issues: those that have come to prominence in the past decade or so. However, in reality, the division between core and emerging is somewhat arbitrary.

5.1 POSITION

Where in the organization is the IT function to be located? There are various different possibilities, discussed below. The term 'IT unit' will be used here, reflecting its widespread employment in the public sector. Building from Chapter 1, though, 'IT' is seen to be an unhelpful label: it places too much emphasis on technology, and it fails to signal the need for e-government to be managed as complete information systems.

Decentralized Location

At the extreme, responsibilities for e-government may be so decentralized that no organizational IT structures, staff or budgets exist: everything is left up to individual staff. One stage up from this is the situation in which one member of staff in each section is identified as the computer 'whizz-kid'. While continuing to perform their usual managerial or clerical role, they informally take on an IT support role. One stage further up, some or all of the organization's departments have their own IT staff and/or IT unit and a specific departmental IT budget. These resources are focused on serving the needs of the individual departments.

Centralized Location

At the other extreme is the centralized IT unit. Such units are normally funded from a central budget. They are naturally larger than their decentralized counterparts. They may therefore be divided internally into a number of sub-units covering specialisms such as computer and network operations, systems development, data management, and strategic planning.

The location of the IT unit within the overall structure of the organization reflects attitudes to e-government in the organization, and also partly determines what the unit can and cannot achieve within the organization. The unit's location plus its reporting structure, the involvement of senior managers in e-government issues, and the size of the IT budget all send powerful messages to the rest of the organization about e-government. Partly because of this, the IT unit's location is likely to change over time as the case in Box 5.1 shows.

Box 5.1   Changing Location of the IT Function in the City of Birmingham, UK

The City of Birmingham was a pioneer in the use of computers in the 1950s and 1960s. By the 1980s it had developed over 40 major systems including city accounts, rates and housing allocation ... In 1983, Birmingham decided that it needed a strategy for managing the development of IT, not only because the acquisition of hardware and software was piecemeal, but also because the use of the technology was too narrowly conceived. In an attempt to rationalize the use and acquisition of equipment, an Information and Services Division (ISSD) was created as a section of the Treasurer's Department. ... (Isaac-Henry, 1997: 148–50)

The strategy of 1987 separated users from providers ... IT planning and strategy development was now the responsibility of the Management Information Systems Division ... now attached to the Chief Executive's Department and not to the Treasurer's.

(Continued)

Box 5.1   **Continued**

In 1989 the City was again in the throes of modifying its IT strategy. It was argued that the pressures from Government legislation ... and other sources, meant that the City could not guarantee the level of investment needed to sustain existing IT resources, that it was also difficult to retain highly skilled staff and that their rapid turnover meant fluctuating workload and difficulties in achieving objectives. ... The City reluctantly turned to the private sector for the solution, outsourcing the provision of IT in the authority. (Isaac–Henry, 1997: 148–50)

During the 1990s, therefore, there was a steady growth in outsourcing, on a relatively piecemeal basis, involving individual contracts and e-government projects or services. By the 21st-century, the piecemeal approach and the short-term nature of outsourcing deals was seen as too high-cost. In 2004, Birmingham consolidated all outsourced IT infrastructure/services into a single, 15-year contract worth nearly US$1 billion, based around a strong, long-term partnership with a private sector provider. It also continued a mixed policy of retaining some elements of e-government work for in-house staff. (Adapted from Morgan, 2004)

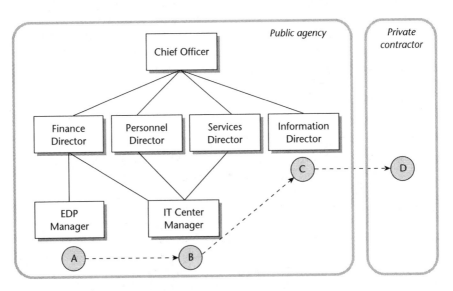

Figure 5.1   Chronology of central IT unit location

There are three typical locations for the central IT unit and main IT manager within public sector organizations. These sometimes follow a chronological pattern, as they did in Birmingham. This pattern is illustrated in Figure 5.1 as the move from location A to B to C to D. Each of these will now be described in more detail.

Situation A: Departmental Location

In situation A, the organization's central IT unit is located within one functional department of the organization, with the IT manager reporting to the head of that functional department. The department is often finance/accounts – called the 'Treasurer's Department' within the Box 5.1 case. Historically, the IT units of many public sector organizations began here because payroll and accounts were the first large-scale computerizations. Unit and managerial titles were often oriented towards IT ('The IT Section') or the now-defunct electronic data processing ('The EDP Manager').

The advantages of such a location can include:

- the heavy use of computerized systems by the controlling department, allowing a close relationship to build up between users and IT unit staff;
- the strong organizational position of the finance department which would allow it to defend the IT unit;
- the possibility of easier access to financial resources for IT projects than might be the case if the unit lay outside the finance department.

The disadvantages of such a location can be that computing staff give a higher priority to, and have a much better understanding of, finance rather than other organizational systems. Having a relatively low and dependent position in the organizational hierarchy can also make it difficult to adopt an organization-wide approach to the planning of information/e-government systems; let alone an approach that properly considers the needs of external clients.

Situation B: Low-Level Independence

In this situation, the organization's central IT unit is independent of any individual department of the organization, with the IT manager reporting to a neutral senior manager or to a senior management committee. Unit and managerial titles may now focus on 'information systems', reflecting a growing understanding that technology is only one part of e-government.

Historically, public sector IT units often change to this location once the close association of IT with one department becomes strongly detrimental to the rest of the organization. In Birmingham City Council's case, the unit skipped this location.

The advantages of such a location can include greater equality of priorities across the whole organization, making the unit a true organization-wide service center.

The disadvantages of such a location can include:

- probable lack of any particular organizational champion to help win resources for the IT unit;
- possible lack of clarity in reporting routes;
- continued difficulty in adopting an organization-wide approach to information/e-government systems planning;
- dangers of 'decibel planning', where the departments which make the most noise are those that receive most IT resources.

Situation C: High-Level Independence

Here, the organization's central IT unit is independent of any individual department of the organization, with the IT manager reporting direct to the head of the organization.

Information is now on a par with finance and human resources, and unit and managerial titles may focus on this. Managers, for instance, might be called 'Information Director' or 'Chief Information Officer'.

Historically, public sector IT units change to this location once information starts to be recognized as a strategic organizational resource. As in Birmingham's case, this is often when a new structural division arises within the IT function. The unit may be split into a *user* division, responsible for planning systems, and a *provider* division, responsible for supplying the required systems. This division is a necessary prelude to the outsourcing that forms situation D.

The advantages of such a location can include:

- greater organizational status and power that enable the IT unit to argue strongly for resource allocations;
- the ability to adopt an organization-wide approach to information/e-government systems planning;
- the independence to enable greater consideration of external stakeholders;
- greater recognition and motivation for IT staff.

In general, all three centralized structures described here are better than decentralized ones for IT staff since they provide a clearer career path and greater opportunities for advancement. It may therefore be easier to attract, manage and retain such staff with a centralized approach. However, two other potential outcomes of situation C can be read as a mixed blessing that might benefit the overall organization, but not individual IT staff. There can be greater visibility for the IT unit, leading to increased pressures to help meet organizational objectives. There may also be a greater likelihood of value-for-money investigations

of e-government systems that can lead to outsourcing.

The move to the C-type of structure should be associated with increasing integration of the IT function into the organizational mainstream. This may mean greater shaping of the IT function by the business needs of the organization rather than, say, technical requirements; and greater involvement of senior mainstream managers in e-government decisions. However, there is a continuing danger that information management is still seen as specialist activity separate from the mainstream of managerial activity.

Situation D: Outsourcing

Outsourcing is the use of an external organization to provide a service that might otherwise be provided in-house. As such, outsourcing can cover a wide variety of e-government systems activities, including:

- analysis and design, for example, feasibility study or process redesign;
- construction, for example, procurement advice or programming;
- implementation, for example, training or data conversion;
- operation, for example, running the computer system or providing maintenance.

It can also include ownership of the IT facilities used to run e-government systems. Thus, outsourcing can cover many of the IT functions, but it would be rare for the entire central IT unit to be outsourced: a rump of strategic planners and contract managers is usually left inside the public agency, typically in position C.

One of the main intentions behind IT outsourcing by public sector organizations is to cut costs, and thereby achieve more within existing financial constraints. For example, the US city governments in Indianapolis and Minneapolis both outsourced their entire IT infrastructure, and claim they are achieving cost savings of around US$3 million per annum (Eggers, 2003).

An equal, if not greater drive to outsourcing is to address human resource constraints by accessing staff, skills and ideas that are not available in-house. Other perceived benefits of outsourcing include the provision of a higher quality of service; greater certainty about costs; greater flexibility, especially of labor since it is easier to hire and fire external staff; access to advanced technology; and greater ability to focus management on the core deliverables of the public sector (Chen and Perry, 2003; Gupta et al., 2004; Boddy et al., 2005).

Of course, if these benefits are to be realized, one pre-condition must be the presence of sub-contractors who are willing and able to take on outsourcing contracts.

Even if outsourcing can proceed, benefits do not come automatically: the relationship with the sub-contractor must be well planned and well managed.[1] Yet, sometimes, outsourcing proceeds without sufficient in-house project management and contracting skills to coordinate and continuously monitor the outsourcing process. Even if these skills are present, evidence of cost savings compared to use of in-house staff is not always found: one comprehensive study of public sector outsourcing found costs for outsourcing the total IT service were higher compared to the in-house option (Hill, 2004). In part this arises because the costs of managing the relationship are often higher than expected and there can be other problems with the position D approach (Bishop, 2001; Kieley et al., 2002):

- a clash of work cultures and understanding between the public sector client and the private sector sub-contractor;
- a loss of control over the service being provided, with the sub-contractor starting to dictate to a dependent client;

- a loss of core e-government competencies to the sub-contractor, such as controls over security.

As a result, there have been concerns that outsourcing is not the most effective approach to delivery of e-government. For example, when the US General Services Administration launched an outsourcing initiative for IT infrastructure in federal agencies, less than one-sixth of IT managers responded positively, and well over one-third emphatically ruled out use of outsourcing because of its direct and indirect costs (Holmes, 2001).

Given this evidence of both costs and benefits, rationality would require that outsourcing only proceed if the following three conditions are satisfied:

- total costs of outsourcing are lower than the in-house option;
- total costs of outsourcing are lower than hiring new staff or training existing ones to cover any missing skills; and
- there are no problems associated with data confidentiality, security, and so on.

Given the evidence of cost and other problems with outsourcing, one might expect it to be on the decrease. However, in practice, decision making about outsourcing in the public sector has only partly been driven by organizational rationality. It has also been driven by behavioral/political factors (Peled, 2000a). Managers are found to outsource e-government work because they:

- have been naive in their assumptions about the benefits that will ensue;
- believe association with such an initiative will be good for their careers;
- wish to 'clip the wings' of the in-house IT unit;
- stand to gain financially thanks to the covert generosity of the sub-contractor.

Public sector outsourcing has particularly grown in several countries because of legislative requirements and other central pressures.

Because of these political drivers, overall outsourcing of e-government activities is on the increase, even though the rhetoric and dogma of outsourcing may have receded slightly from their high water mark in some governments, and even though many rational shortcomings of outsourcing have emerged. In the UK, the value of central government IT outsourcing contracts for initiation during 2003–2005 was US$20 billion, compared to US$7.5 billion-worth during 1997–2002 (Arnott, 2003). Similarly, IT is the number one outsourced area in US government with the value of contracts doubling between 2002 and 2005, and likely to reach around US$15 billion by 2007 (Chen and Perry, 2003; Eggers, 2003; Martin and Singh, 2004). However, as noted next, growth has also been associated with hybridization.

Hybrid Approaches to IT Location

Looking within the public agency, a hybrid location can mean either a separation or integration of central and local responsibilities. For example, there could be a hybrid management structure for the IT unit, with a management group that involves internal users and senior officials as well as IT staff. Alternatively, a hybrid structure for the IT unit could mean that it reflects the wider structure of the public agency. Thus, for example, a unit supporting a local government could have a team covering housing, another team covering public works, another covering environment, and so on.

A broader interpretation would be a hybrid philosophy and structure for the IT unit that regards internal users as its customers and thus creates a 'user support center'. This may go under a variety of different names – such as 'information

center' – but it is essentially an internal extension/outreach unit.[2] It reaches out from the center to support staff within individual sections, and it helps them make best use of their e-government systems and technology. This is classically hybrid, being an emanation of the center that is located in, and focused on the needs of, the periphery.

A variant on this is the 'dual support' system, with front-line support located in user departments, and more specialist backup located at the center. Within Hull City Council, in the UK, each department has a local 'e-leader' who can take responsibility for basic training, troubleshooting and day-to-day support (Say, 2002a). Staff in the central IT unit provide help desk facilities for more complex support and also install, configure and support cross-Council systems.

A hybrid approach is also emerging in relation to outsourcing for e-government. First, there is evidence of a need to move away from the total outsourcing model to a more selective mix of in-house and outsourced e-government functions (Hill, 2004). Second, the sharp divisions of the 1980s and 1990s are giving way to a more hybrid partnership-based model of supporting IT for e-government:

> the primary idea is a contractual arrangement where each brings something to the table, where private-sector enterprise and innovation are combined with public-sector experience and values, and where there is a shared approach to the provision of services and to the risks and rewards involved. (Holmes, 2001: 46)

Hybridization of this sort was forced on the US Department of Housing and Urban Development when its outsourcing contract with DynCorp had to be suspended because of the uneven nature of the relationship. It only restarted once that relationship was reconstructed as a proper two-way partnership with regular joint team working, and with the private partner willing to listen as well as speak.[3]

One final hybrid locational innovation is that undertaken by San Diego city in the US. It created its own 'city-owned, independent nonprofit corporation that sells a variety of IT services to the city via an operating agreement' (Barrett and Greene, 2001: 91). This has also helped solve some of the people and politics problems discussed below.

5.2 PEOPLE

Technology is important to e-government systems. But people are more important. eGovernment managers must therefore spend much of their time dealing with people-related issues. A number of these issues are investigated below, but we start by understanding the people-related needs that new e-government applications create.

The planning, development and operation of any new e-government system is likely to require new competencies, thus creating a gap between the competencies staff currently hold and those they need. Competencies can be understood in relation to three domains (Mundy et al., 2001):

- *Skills*: All of the stages and techniques of systems development and operation require skills in order to put them into practice. Organizations may therefore find a skills gap in anything from spotting opportunities for new e-government systems, to analyzing current use of information, to process redesign, to software programming, to system installation and use. In addition, there can be 'meta-level' development skill requirements relating to project and change management, communication and negotiation, problem solving, and so on.
- *Knowledge*: eGovernment systems development and operation requires knowledge.

Organizations may therefore find a knowledge gap where staff do not know about systems development methods, or about the nature and role of information and information systems, or about organizational systems and processes, or about the basics of IT, or about the design options that could be applied to the new e-government system, or about why the new system should be operated in a particular way.

- *Attitudes*: Where different stakeholders have different attitudes to the new e-government system, one could talk of an 'attitude gap'. In many ways this reflects the different values and objectives of different stakeholders.

The impact of competency deficiencies is a continuous theme in e-government, with lack of competencies appearing on virtually every list of challenges and constraints. The dearth of competencies is a major brake on the spread of e-government and a major cause of system delays and failures.

Public managers face two main options in filling these competency gaps that new e-government systems create. They can train existing staff, or they can recruit new staff. Each of these will now be discussed.

Training

Examples of training aimed at closing e-government skills and knowledge gaps are fairly straightforward, covering mainly project management, change management, IS and IT issues. Some aspects of this are discussed in Chapter 11. More sophisticated training would aim to develop the hybrid manager skills and knowledge described throughout this book and summarized in Chapter 12.

Training to change attitudes is less widely used, more varied and harder to implement successfully. But, it is arguably more important given that it addresses resistance to change. Central to resistance and acceptance is the issue of motivation, which arises for all those involved with e-government, as they ask, 'Why should I: what's in it for me?' Training content can therefore benefit from including attitude-related material that speaks to three things:

The rational mind This can be addressed through arguments about the ways in which IT cuts costs, improves effectiveness of decision making and service delivery, and so on.

The political mind This can be addressed through arguments that go to the roots of self-interest. Individual self-interests differ and these need to be identified for each individual stakeholder before they can be addressed. Having said this, political leaders – for example – typically want:

- to respond to their need for stronger control over the mechanisms of government;
- to respond to national political pressures from other politicians, institutions of civil society (the media, lobby/pressure groups, unions, chambers of commerce, etc.) and – to some extent – from citizens;
- to respond to global threats or opportunities such as criticism in the foreign media or availability of foreign investments.

Demonstrating ways in which IT can help deliver these responses will help align leaders' self-interest with e-government.

The heart This can be addressed through stories, particularly of those implementing or benefiting from e-government, that resonate at an emotional level. Examples might be innovative officials overcoming the odds to deliver e-government, or of disadvantaged clients benefiting from e-government.

Training for e-government currently focuses too much on speaking to the rational mind;

it needs to do more to speak to two more powerful organs: the political mind and the heart. Greater use of case studies of e-government failure and/or best practice will likely be a move in the right direction (Parrado, 2002). Cases can persuade stakeholders, for instance, of the dangers of ignoring basic systems development practice, or of the importance of understanding the organizational and human context of e-government systems. It was this kind of approach that was adopted by Jacksonville, in Florida, when it set out to change attitudes towards ethical practice in an era of e-government that has brought ethics even more to the fore in the public sector (Robb, 2000).[4]

Alternatively, demonstrations of functioning e-government systems can be used to highlight system benefits; these might persuade users to become involved in systems development when they would otherwise be reluctant. There are also more active approaches such as story-telling or role-play exercises; for example, to highlight the gap between users and IT staff. These may convince staff of the need to improve communications and build consensus. Similarly, group-forming activities for key stakeholders are used to help build a sense of unity to assist the formation of consensus on major reform issues.

Staff Recruitment

Alongside training, public agencies can seek to boost their e-government-related competencies through recruitment. Examples of recruitment techniques are given below (drawn from Heeks, 1997; Berman et al., 2001; Johnson, 2001; Devlin, 2003). These are hybridized ideas that draw on private sector experience but inject public sector values and realities.

Emphasize job security and public service job content   Public agencies need to work harder to promote a better image of e-government work. 'One main component of this image ... is a work purpose that allows employees to identify with an altruistic goal of providing benefits to citizens through improved and more effective information systems for decision making and service delivery, instead of feeding the bottom line for anonymous corporate shareholders.' (Johnson, 2001: 354). Another component will be to actively contrast the greater job security of public jobs with the private sector's 'slash and burn' mentality. A third component will be a greater emphasis on the innovative e-government work that is going on. IT staff in the public sector always cite these as important motivators, but those yet to join must be made more aware of them.

Cut back on recruitment bureaucracy   Potential IT recruits often apply for several jobs at once. Public sector recruitment and offer procedures are often so slow that candidates have already accepted other appointments before the public agency contacts them (Cohen and Eimicke, 2002).

Develop short-term assignments for outsiders Professionals in private firms, non-profits, academe, and other public agencies can welcome the opportunity to work on a temporary secondment basis in the public sector. Collaboration with education and training institutions – as well as raising awareness – can also develop internships for those institutions' students.

Use up-to-date recruitment techniques   The traditional badly-designed advertisement in a local newspaper needs to be replaced by well-designed national advertising, Internet-based adverts, job fairs, use of recruitment agents, and other up-to-date techniques. 'Public sector IS managers also need to be actively involved in professional information systems societies in order to expand their network of potential recruits.' (Johnson, 2001: 356). This illustrates the point that being a hybrid e-government manager means accepting that one can learn from the best of private sector practices, even if they are not slavishly copied.

Offer recruitment bonuses   The private sector offers referral bonuses to existing staff who identify new IT recruits, and signing-on bonuses to those recruits. The public sector may struggle to pay such bonuses in cash but can use cash proxies such as additional vacation days or additional training opportunities.

Recruit non-IT staff   Reflecting the hard–soft dimension of hybrids, there is a growing emphasis on the non-technical aspects of e-government jobs. It can therefore make more sense to take on non-IT recruits (from both inside and outside the organization) and train them in the IT/IS skills required, rather than taking on scarce IT recruits.

Staff Retention

Training and recruitment are valuable tools in the e-government manager's arsenal. However, they will be greatly undermined if those trained or those recruited leave the organization. Unfortunately, this is exactly the problem that faces public agencies, especially for staff with specific IT/IS competencies. There is general agreement that there are important IT staff shortages in the public sector and that problems lie ahead due to an ageing staff profile, but estimates of turnover rates vary quite wildly from 1 percent up to 45 percent per annum, though with common averages between 10 percent and 20 percent (*Computer Weekly*, 1999; Bhambhani, 2002; Walker, 2003). Much of the variation can be explained by the broader socio-economic context: turnover rates typically fall when the general economy is doing badly; they also tend to fall in the aftermath of national crises when public service is valued more highly. Turnover figures should also be benchmarked against the fact that IT staff turnover rates tend to be fairly high in the private sector itself (Nicolle, 2000).

Even if it were just 10 percent per year, IT staff turnover has serious implications for the public sector. Turnover is costly, with the cost of replacing an e-government professional 'estimated to be between 65 percent and 120 percent of annual salary' (Johnson, 2001: 357). Turnover also reduces morale of remaining staff and it feeds an ongoing competency deficit. The impact of this is delay and failure of e-government.

Pay is one factor in the bleed of IT staff from public to private sector, with estimates that public sector IT managers are paid, on average, 25 percent less than those in the private sector (NCC, 2001). However, pay is not the only factor. A good hybrid manager will recognize that psychological factors play a role: autonomy, challenge, recognition and the opportunity for career advancement. Direct work content factors are also important, such as training opportunities, flexibility of work schedule and clarity of task specification. All of these need to be taken into account and they suggest improved retention techniques that include (Heeks, 1997; Holmes, 2001; Johnson, 2001; Devlin, 2003) those described below.

Articulate and promote a clear development path for IT staff   IT staff may be more loyal if they see how their careers will progress: into IT management, mainstream management, training or some other path. In particular, HR (human resource) departments need to be open to a dual-track approach that projects a path ahead either on the technical side or on the management side. Such paths may be expanded to encompass inter- as well as intra-agency trajectories. On a shorter-term basis, responsibility for a personal development plan can be shifted to the employees, and used as part of the annual performance review.

Improve the handling of training opportunities Training is critical to retention of IT staff – they need it to keep abreast of the skills and knowledge to do their current job, and they need it to feed their personal development requirements. Providing training opportunities is therefore an important element in retention, with provision made by verbal encouragement, payment of training fees, and creating learning resources on-site. Fears about loss of investment are covered in some public organizations by asking for fees, or a proportion of fees, to be repaid if staff leave within a certain time.

Skills/knowledge development of IT staff must also be recognized. This can be done by their manager personally and in public via newsletters and the like. It should also be done more formally in relation to personal and career development plans and appraisals. Formal recognition can make use of the continuing professional development programs of most IT/IS professional associations. Kansas State, in the US, for example, has made use of professional certification in project management to help train and retain its middle- and senior-level e-government staff (Barrett and Greene, 2001).

Focus on innovative approaches to competency-building The traditional training course is now recognized as just one small part of the continuing professional development portfolio. Staff need to take more responsibility through self-directed learning, but can be guided in this by active mentoring from a more senior member of staff. Other ideas

---

Box 5.2   New Approaches to Public Sector Learning

Ways to improve learning by public servants other than training programs include:

- learning sets (groups of staff from different units or organizations sharing learning experiences);
- reflective team working;
- job swaps including work shadowing, deputizing, and secondments to other organizations;
- internal consulting;
- use of external consultants as learning partners;
- learning diaries;
- attending seminars and exhibitions. (Adapted from Doherty and Horne, 2002)

---

about ways to improve learning are included in Box 5.2.

Provide challenging projects and other non-financial incentives   Public sector organizations can address the other psychological and job content factors listed above by techniques that include:

- empowering IT staff both as individuals and in groups;
- providing IT staff with challenging and interesting projects (possibly via short-term mobility assignments to other public agencies);
- outsourcing the 'grunt work' such as systems maintenance;
- investing heavily in the latest IT;
- giving IT staff a large office or high status job title; and
- providing help with childcare and/or flexi-time/telecommuting options.

One final part of the jigsaw is recognition from management. Where IT staff feel they are valued and listened to by a good manager who supports them, they are far more likely to stay. Where IT staff have bad management,

they are likely to leave whatever the other inducements.

Such techniques can also assist recruitment. In Florida State's Department of Management Services, flexible and supportive management combined with a commitment to e-government to build a substantial IT staff. The department 'was able to attract such talent even with relatively low-paying state jobs by giving them the opportunity to shape major applications, an opportunity rarely available to young employees in the private sector.' (Coursey and Killingsworth, 2000: 333). During the early part of the 21st-century, this was a continuing theme – of staff quitting shelved or moribund projects in the private sector in order to work on more interesting e-government projects.

Combined Recruitment/Retention Techniques

Some staff management techniques can have a combined effect on both recruitment and retention:

Improve remuneration   There is conflicting evidence on pay. In the 1990s, during a time of private sector expansion, surveys cited pay as the public sector's top recruitment and retention problem (PWC, 1999; Smith, 1999). By the 2000s, with many e-business projects stalled while e-government continued to be funded, pay had been leapfrogged by issues such as stimulating work content and job security (Mortleman and Thomas, 2004). Wherever its place, though, pay is always an important factor underlying low recruitment and/or high turnover in the public sector.

In some public agencies, the financial, political or bureaucratic barriers to addressing this issue are high. However, far more public sector organizations could take action than do take action. In some cases, this requires the creation of new IT staff pay scales. This, in turn, may require new job classification schemes based on actual value of contribution rather than traditional measures like size of budget or staff managed. Ontario's provincial government grasped this nettle: 'the changes mean huge increases for technical staff, changes that could see the provincial Chief Information Officer (CIO) earn twice as much as the Premier' (Paquet and Roy, 2000: 62).

An alternative used by some agencies is to allow IT staff to contribute a three-/four-day week at work and then have the other day(s) for private work.

Job swaps and secondments US legislation in 2002 introduced the idea of the 'Tech Corps' – legislated as the IT Exchange Program – a program that allows mid-level IT managers in federal government agencies to be loaned to an equivalent post in a private firm for between three months and two years (Harris, 2002). The program also allows for movement in the opposite direction, or even direct job swaps. The incoming private sector staff are intended to bring fresh ideas and expertise; the outgoing public sector staff

will pick up new skills; both sets should benefit from the challenge of change and mutual sectoral understanding. Unfortunately, such programs can promote a continuing message that e-government is inferior to e-business because of their implicit asymmetry: whichever direction staff move, the assumed flow of competencies is from the private to the public.

Use consultants and outsourcing When work is sub-contracted to consultants or vendors, it makes staff recruitment and retention mainly the sub-contractor's problem, and may make turnover less likely since sub-contractor staff are characteristically rewarded according to private sector norms.[5]

Israeli ministries use a hybrid version of this that combines public and private sector elements: the 'Gulgalot' system (Hebrew for 'human skulls'). IT recruits are interviewed by ministerial MIS directors. If they match needs, they are instructed to approach one of the main private sector software firms which will employ them. 'The new employee receives a private sector compensation package and is immediately transferred to the Ministry's MIS department to work on a specific project.' (Peled, 2000b: 55). Most stay with the public sector for many years.

Strengthen HR practices Many public agencies will benefit from reviewing their HR practices. For some, it will mean ensuring that job and person specifications are written specifically for the e-government area, that recruitment interviews and assessment procedures are planned, and that annual performance appraisal/staff development interviews are conducted. For others, though, it will mean a lighter rather than heavier touch. In the Canadian public sector, for example, a review of HR practice in relation to IT staff found it to be 'so broken that we need to start over' with a need for fewer rules, greater delegation and flexibility, and broader, more competency-focused grading levels (Latta, 2002).

5.3 PELF

Money matters loom large in e-government projects. For example, e-government has to work within the confines of public sector budgeting procedures.[6] Related to this, e-government also has to work within the confines of available finance. If it is to be sustainable, the lifetime costs of any e-government system must be less than or equal to the financial resources available. Changing the reality of the finance available is not easy, but successful hybrid approaches to finance are now combining private sector ideas with public sector values.

More internal finance can be directed towards e-government if senior managers can be persuaded but such sources tend to be relatively constrained. So, too, does the practice of selling public information in order to raise funds: a public–private hybrid that – as discussed in Chapter 6 – often runs into a minefield of both privacy and legal issues. A longer-term approach focuses e-government systems development on revenue maximization (Eggers, 2003). In Massachusetts state government, for example, investments were made in a new state-wide billing and accounts receivable system. Among other things, this stopped government paying someone who owed it money. In all, US$10–20 million extra receivables were generated per year, every year, as a result. This was intended to release additional funds for investment in e-government projects.

External finance from central government or international agency initiatives is hard to control and sometimes comes and goes in

cycles of 'feast and famine' that make it difficult to plan sustainable e-government systems. Nevertheless, centralized funds to support e-government initiatives exist in an increasing number of countries and regions; from the US$ hundreds of millions made available in the UK, for example, to a much smaller fund created in the US.

Where regulations allow, some public sector organizations are adopting a hybrid public–private approach by turning to private sector sources of finance. Some public agencies, for example, can take out loans from private finance institutions, which can be used to fund e-government. In other cases, up-front finance comes from the private sector, which is repaid by government through an annual or service-level fee. This was one element of the UK's controversial Private Finance Initiative approach to e-government, and was also used for Hong Kong's one-stop electronic service delivery portal: 'The private sector operator is responsible for developing, financing, operating and maintaining the system, and the Government starts to pay transaction fees to the operator after the accumulated transaction volume has reached a pre-agreed level' (UNDESA, 2003a: 38).

Such arrangements have been used particularly for relatively large, complex, changeable projects and they will only tend to work if the new e-government application provides clear cost savings that can be funneled into payments or – less typically for the public sector – if it provides some income generation. Such arrangements, of course, only work if the private sector is willing and able to bear the financial risks of e-government projects. In many cases it is not, and there has been severe criticism of such projects where the costs of failure have been thrown back on to government, and not borne by the private firms involved (Foot, 2004).

Governments have even gone into joint venture arrangements with private firms. The government of Andhra Pradesh has been India's leading exponent of e-government (Gupta et al., 2004). Serving a largely poor population, it has lacked sufficient financial capital to initiate all of its hoped-for projects. One solution – used for the main government portal – has been the creation of a new joint venture entity between government and India's main IT services firm, Tata Consultancy Services. Not only has it benefited from an initial injection of capital from the private sector, it has also sought to win further funding through its own business activities.

A related approach to raising finance from the private sector has been charging business users of e-government services. The Information Network of Kansas is an example. Its main operational face is the AccessKansas web site run by the Kansas state government (INK, 2005). This includes a wide variety of informational and transactional services. Services oriented to businesses (registrations, property or other records searches, etc.) attract a fee, though costs can be reduced when businesses pay an annual subscription. The income from this cross-subsidizes free access to more citizen-oriented information and services (from road reports to fishing licenses).

More innovative still has been the approach of those private firms whose finance model ensures governments are charged nothing. In some cases, the finance is raised from charges levied on citizen- or business-users of the e-government service that the private firms host on behalf of government. Even more contentious have been models that find other ways of extracting private value from hosting e-government systems. National Information Consortium, for instance, provides free portal services for US state governments, and charges citizens nothing for most transactions. It makes its money from resale of citizen data (Grönlund, 2002).

Overall, though, changing public sector reality by increasing the finance available seems harder than 'cutting your coat according to your cloth'; that is, by reducing the costs of e-government plans until they meet available resources. This would typically involve scaling down the ambitions of such plans by, for example, postponing the achievement of some objectives. However, there are alternatives.

Government's bargaining power and scale economies are often used to drive down costs by purchasing for groups of public sector organizations. At central government level, for example, the US General Services Administration and the UK's Office of Government Commerce both make use of this approach, essentially providing public agencies with a shopping list of discounted items via central framework agreements or 'master contracts'. Such agreements typically begin by covering hardware items, but then extend their range to incorporate government-wide software licenses and then services such as e-government consulting. The UK agency claims to have saved over US$150 million on just one licensing deal negotiated with Microsoft (*Computing*, 2002).

The old cost reduction model – often disliked by agencies – was compulsory centralized control of all or many IT purchases. This still exists to some extent in many countries at national, state and local level, with some governments still undertaking most purchases through a central purchasing agency (McCue, 2001; BVPL, 2003). However, the norm has been some hybrid mix of central and local, such as an opt-in model that allows agencies to use these channels if they wish.

A related mechanism is the standard contract, where a contract negotiated by one public agency or ministry is used by other public sector organizations, rather than starting from scratch with a vendor. Not only does this save on administrative costs, it also helps close time gaps by speeding the process of procurement (ANAO, 2003).

Inter-agency collaborations can go further than sharing contracts. Neighbors from the level of countries down to the smallest units of local government can work together and save money on infrastructural projects, on bulk purchase of consumables, on shared data centers, on common e-government systems, and so on. Important savings have been achieved from just such a collaboration between five German municipal governments around Nürnberg (SOCITM and IDEA, 2002). This has developed a set of sharable infrastructure, service delivery systems, and public–private partnerships.

Costs can be reduced in more innovative ways by acting in concert with the private sector. In Texas, the state government collaborated with a private sector utility company to convert the latter's digitized address database into the basis for a geographic information system (GIS). Both government and company shared the resulting data and both saved costs in creation of their GIS base (TGIC, 2002). Costs were also saved on this project through the collaboration of various public agencies, all of whom made use of the GIS, thus reaping scale economies for government.

Vendors may occasionally donate equipment to the public sector if close personal relationships are involved or if there is a payoff from good publicity or goodwill generated. In the Czech Republic, Microsoft donated both hardware and software to the government's PCs Against Barriers project, which has provided hundreds of unemployed disabled citizens with job-relevant IT skills (Holmes, 2001). Vendors may also agree to develop an e-government application at low cost as a loss leader if it is a leading-edge application that can then be sold to other public sector sites.

Finally, use of project management techniques may help avoid project overruns and other wasteful use of resources, thus reducing unnecessary expenditure. Several governments have therefore developed their own generic approaches to project management. However, such approaches are not without their problems, as the next section explains.

5.4 PROJECTS

Arguably, the overriding management issue for e-government projects should be the challenge of failure. Categories and extent of failure were discussed in Chapter 1. Here we will just note one more partial failure with the archetypal project problems of overpromising and underdelivering on time, budget and functionality. The US Federal Aviation Authority's Advanced Automation System (AAS) lay at the heart of its plans to modernize air traffic control systems. When first contracted in 1988 (taking a mere seven years to go through the contracting process), it was due to be implemented in July 1992 at a cost of US$3.5 billion (Wolfe, 2001). By the late 1990s, much of that had been spent, yet parts of AAS had been canceled, and the core components had not been delivered. At the time of writing, the story continued. Taking just one part of the original AAS plan – the Standard Terminal Automation Replacement System – a US General Accounting Office study found it had doubled in cost to roughly US$2 billion and was seven years behind schedule (Mosquera, 2004).

The impact of this and many of the other failures has been a steady stream of analyses and reports. Many of these come from audit/comptroller offices and increasingly bear the hallmark of a weary parent chastising its wayward children for yet again failing to follow house rules. These house rules

---

Box 5.3   Analyzing eGovernment Project Failures

Generally there had been inadequate planning at a high enough level in the early stages. ... [*Many projects*] had been too optimistic and over-ambitious. They had underestimated, in some cases seriously, the systems and programming effort needed to implement a project, and very often the computer capacity required to undertake the intended task. Costing had been inadequate and forecast savings had not been realised. There had been a tendency, difficult to resist in the first flush of enthusiasm, to try to build too many refinements and subtleties into the system. This over-extended their limited and often inexperienced resources, and caused delay. (CSD, 1971: 12)

---

are typically reiterated in each report. Each failed project (at least those that are not hushed-up) produces a very similar report with too little analysis of why public project managers won't or can't use report recommendations, and too much empty exhortation to behave better next time.

The example in Box 5.3 is more than 30 years old; yet modern reports sound very similar. There is a strong sense of going round in circles and of the oft-quoted lines from Winnie-the-Pooh:

> Here is Edward Bear, coming downstairs now, bump, bump, bump, on the back of his head, behind Christopher Robin. It is, as far as he knows, the only way of coming downstairs, but sometimes he feels there really is another way, if only he could stop bumping for a moment and think of it. (Milne, 1926: 1)

Why has the public sector been so bad at thinking up 'another way'? Partly because, like Winnie-the-Pooh, it keeps bumping into project failures so often it hasn't the time to step back and think. But also because project management inhabits the front line in the battle between rational and behavioral, between hard and soft.

Rational Approaches to Project Management

Most of the reports, most of the models, most of the supposed best practices of e-government project management follow a hard, rational approach. In terms of the ITPOSMO checklist presented in Chapter 1, they focus on data (not information), technology, processes, management structures, and time/money. Where staff are considered, they are one more project resource, not human beings.

Why should this be? It relates partly to the roots of project management in engineering, where the physical resources dominated and where scientific principles were needed in order to successfully implement projects. This idea continues to run through project management. It also relates partly to the dominant image of e-government systems being the image of IT, and the dominant language being the jargon of IT. With these roots in engineering and in technology, projects are seen as rational enterprises to be managed with numbers, controls and rigid rules (Avison and Fitzgerald, 2003).

It is this way of thinking that has led to the development of comprehensive project management methodologies (PMM). Working within this paradigm, the reaction to project failure is: 'The project failed because it was not rational enough.' The identified cracks in the PMM are cemented up with more measurement, more control and more rules (Gupta et al., 2004); hence the calls in US and other governments for

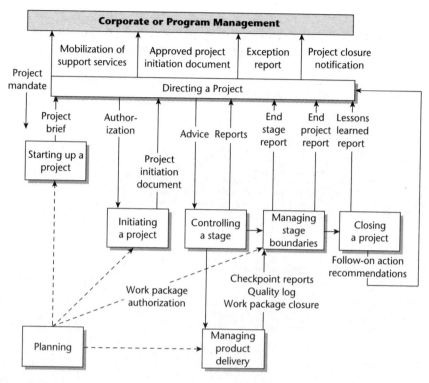

Figure 5.2   Rational project processes – PRINCE 2 overview

use in e-government projects of more planning, more measurement, and more use of hard methodology (GSA, 2003).

We will now look at the hard approach in more detail. The content of an IT project may vary: one typical set of stages is that discussed in Part 2 – assessment; analysis; design; construction; implementation, and beyond. Here, though, the focus is on the management superstructure that fits around the project content.

One such superstructure is PRINCE 2 (PRojects IN Controlled Environments), described as 'a structured method providing organisations with a standard approach to the management of projects.' (APM, 2005). This was developed by the UK government's Central Computer and Telecommunications Agency (later subsumed into the Office of Government Commerce), and its use has been strongly encouraged in

UK e-government projects. It is also used by a number of other governments worldwide. State and federal agencies in the US and other countries use very similar approaches, based on outputs from organizations such as the Project Management Institute.

Component parts of these types of rational approach are shown in Figure 5.2 (CCTA, 1997: 13).

Some key elements of a rational approach to project management will now be discussed in more detail.

Project Organization

Projects require organizational roles and structures to be put in place if they are to be properly managed. There are endless permutations of these. One example is given in Box 5.4.

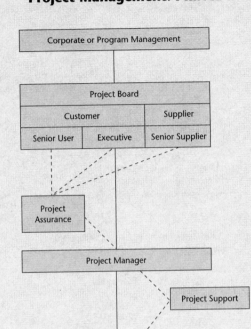

Box 5.4   Formal Roles and Structures for eGovernment Project Management: PRINCE 2

Figure 5.3   Formal e-government project roles

The roles indicated in Figure 5.3 are explained as follows (Bentley, 2002):

- *Corporate/Program Management*: Typically a body like the eGovernment Steering Group described in Chapter 3.
- *Project Board*: The group that is accountable for the project, and makes the major project decisions.
- *Executive*: The individual ultimately accountable for the project, who represents the 'business interests' on the project.
- *Senior User*: Ensures that the e-government system is fit for purpose and meets users' needs.
- *Senior Supplier*: Represents the technical/IT side: the designers, programmers, operators, and so on from inside or outside the organization.
- *Project Manager*: Manages the project on a day-to-day basis.
- *Team Manager*: Manages part of the project if it is large.
- *Project Assurance*: Independently monitors project progress on behalf of the Project Board.
- *Project Support*: For some projects, provides generic project assistance such as 'project management tools, guidance and administrative services'; may also help with configuration management and change control.

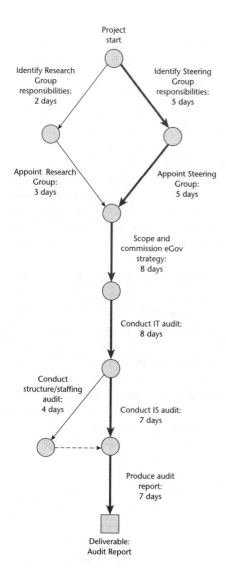

Figure 5.4   Critical path diagram

Project Planning

Project planning typically involves the production of diagrams such as Gantt charts. These plans are made by breaking down the e-government project into a set of tasks and sub-tasks with the key resources of time, people and money being allocated against each task/sub-task. Many of the tasks have defined *deliverables*: tangible outputs such

as a requirements specification document, an installed set of network cabling, a software prototype, and so on.

Having identified tasks and deliverables, project managers must estimate the resourcing necessary to complete the project, the tasks and sub-tasks. Typical methods of estimation include (Yeates and Cadle, 2002):

- *Analogy*: Finding an e-government project similar to the current one and using its resource requirements, adjusted for dissimilarities.
- *Delphi*: This uses an iterative, group approach. A group of estimators each individually produce a breakdown of project tasks and estimates; these are summarized anonymously and then the summary is sent round to the group for further reconsideration and revision. This can continue for several rounds until 'a reasonable consensus' is reached.
- *Function point analysis*: This looks at the project overall and gives a function point score based on the content, complexity, performance and other features of the e-government system. Based on the software being used and incorporating consideration of risk factors, an overall resource estimate can be made.

In all cases, we can differentiate the total amount of person-hours required by all tasks, and the total elapsed time from start to finish. The latter will be far smaller because many people will be working on parallel project tasks at the same time. Working out which tasks can go in parallel and which cannot involves further planning to see which tasks depend on which other tasks. The result is typically set out in a critical path diagram; the critical path being that set of tasks that will affect the overall project timing if they are delayed. An example is shown in Figure 5.4 taking part of a project to develop an e-government strategy, with the critical path shown in bold.

Plans must be far more than just a critical path; they must include deliverables, resource requirements, and reporting arrangements. Over time, the number of elements that must be planned has grown, typically in response to perceived problems with past projects. What was once just a 'project plan' has now been broken down; for example into: a scope management plan, a resource plan, a risk management plan, a procurement plan, a quality plan, a communication plan, a security plan, a change management plan, and a cost management plan (AOIT, 2003).

To take just one example, a risk management plan must identify what risks may arise during implementation of the new e-government system. Project staff must then analyze the likelihood and impact of each risk. They must determine what actions should be taken both to mitigate the risk and if the risk arises. They must also incorporate a risk management strategy that covers 'who is responsible for managing various areas of risk, how risk will be tracked throughout the project, how contingency plans will be implemented, and how project reserves will be allocated to handle risks.' (AOIT, 2003: 13).

Project Monitoring and Control

The framework rational models for project monitoring and control will be similar to those used in standard MIS (Heeks, 1999a). The body allocated to deal with project monitoring will monitor key deliverables (the outputs) and compare them against either best practice standards (for example in the case of project documentation) or against project plans (for example in the case of installation of the e-government system). They will also receive exception reports which identify actual or potential deviations from plan, and will authorize control actions to bring the project performance back within acceptable tolerances.

This 'regular' monitoring and control approach may be strengthened by formal quality management approaches to IT projects. One of the main relevant international standards is ISO 9001:2000, which applies the International Organization for Standardization's generic quality standards to a variety of fields, including the development of software. The ISO approach supports development of an overall quality system, a quality records system, a statistical system for analyzing software processes and product, and procedures for tracking, controlling, testing and correcting software.

As well as internal monitoring and control, e-government projects are sometimes subject to external oversight. This can take a number of forms. At one end of the spectrum are the formal, fully external audits, such as those undertaken by the Government Accountability Office in the US Federal Government. At the other end are peer reviews, which typically involve IT project managers from other departments, but also potentially some staff from within the same organization. The emphasis here tends to be more on guidance and assistance, and also on helping the peer group to learn. By contrast, audit tends to operate in wholly rational mode to look for deviation from rational best practice.

The value of rational oversight remains subject to debate. As noted, post hoc audit reports seem to appear with monotonous regularity in many governments without any particularly discernible impact on the rate of e-government project failures. On the other hand, oversight actions launched during a project can be of some help. Those relating to the Federal Aviation Administration's AAS, described above, 'did not cure AAS of all its ills, nor did they turn it into a model project. ... Instead, the oversight actions changed a project with no probability of success into one where some level of success was possible' (Wolfe, 2001: 247).

Peer review – a hybrid rather than rational project technique – seems to have a better record, and has now been adopted by a number of governments as a best practice. The US government's 1996 Clinger-Cohen Act set up the IT Resources Board for this specific purpose, to act as a pool of peers for project review.

Behavioral Approaches to Project Management

Some, though not all, PMMs do include statements to the effect that they can be tailored to project circumstances. However, message given and message received are two different things. The subliminal message that radiates from methodologies is 'here's the answer from A to Z, just follow my steps to be OK'. 'Must' and 'require' take top billing. By contrast, customization messages are often hidden away and they fall some way short of encouragement to be flexible and to pick and choose. Adding to which, it is only staff with considerable project skills and expertise who will feel confident to pick and choose (CITU, 2000). Yet those staff are in very short supply in the public sector.

Where there has been some 'top-down customization' in most PMMs is in relation to project scope and size. Those writing methodologies have recognized that the leviathans they create are wholly inappropriate in some situations. Smaller projects can drop some project management deliverables, or reduce their detail. For example, small projects in Arkansas state need only deliver a project charter (citing scope, authority and critical success factors);

a scope statement; a project schedule; a list of identified risks; and a set of budget estimates – no feasibility analysis, no cost analysis, no risk management plan, and so on. (AOIT, 2003).

What constitutes size/scope will vary from situation to situation. A typical categorization for a federal agency is (DOL, 2002):

- minor: cost less than US$100,000;
- medium: cost greater than US$100,000 but less than US$5 million;
- major: involves modification to IT infrastructure;
- very major: 'initiatives that cost more than $5m per year, OR impact more than one DOL agency, OR involve highly visible/sensitive systems, OR set a new technological direction, OR impact a financial system'.

While issues of size/scope can be handled by modifying the rational model, there are deeper problems for rational PMMs. As we have seen time and again in this book, the rational model fails to fully explain or predict what happens in the public sector. It also fails to fully guide real-world best practice, leading e-government practitioners to criticize PMMs for their inflexibility (*Government Computing*, 2003a). Indeed, some who study the realities of projects see the rational approach as potentially guiding worst practice:

Applying this technical approach to IT projects builds into those projects their own seeds of destruction. Because this approach builds into projects, which are about people more than technology, assumptions about certainty which will inevitably be proved incorrect. It will constrain people sufficiently to make conflict and problems inevitable. And it will create a project culture of linear thinking which will make problem solving, during the inevitable crises, unimaginative and ineffective. ...

IT projects die by their own hand. The more they are bound by lists, rules, checks, restrictions, regulations, and so on, the more they drive out the human spirit of creativity, of innovation, of dealing with ambiguity, and of fun. People brought up in technical environments may not see the horror of this kind of approach. Many business users see it all too clearly. And they keep well away. (Patching and Chatham, 2000: 41–2)

Their solution?

Throw away the rule book. For your next project, think about breaking each and every rule you have held dear in the past. Think of a project as being about people and behaviour, rather than about plans, technology and reports. Be radical, revolutionary, and bold. Be human. (Patching and Chatham, 2000: 42)

Enticing though this may sound, it is unlikely to take hold in e-government projects, bound as they are by their twin roots of technology and bureaucracy. Fortunately, behavioral analysis of e-government projects does offer more specific guidance for action:

An organization that slavishly follows a standard project management manual is likely to get into big trouble. At a minimum, projects with organizational complexity require substantially more executive direction. Many of the decisions are political, not technical. (Reeder, 1998)

Yet, as noted, the 'techie' image and approach of e-government projects encourage senior officials to stay away and leave things up to IT staff. Surveys show that – behind the public relations image – only a minority of projects have consistent involvement or support from politicians or non-IT senior officials (ibid.; *E-Government Bulletin*, 2002b).

To plug this gap, and ensure that a more behavioral approach and more behavioral expertise are introduced, some governments are mandating the involvement of senior non-IT officials. The Canadian government,

for example, defines a formal requirement on e-government projects for two things (OECD, 2001). First, a project sponsor who is responsible for the business function, and who has solely behavioral-side competencies (judgment, leadership, communication, organizational awareness). Second, a project leader who is a senior departmental official with, again, largely behavioral-side competencies and only cursory IT management skills at best. Similarly, the UK government's analysis of e-government project failures concluded with the requirement for projects to have a 'senior responsible officer' (CITU, 2000). The officer would be drawn from the business not the IT side of the organization.

More generally, behavioral approaches are good at addressing the middle O dimension of ITPOSMO: objectives and values. For example, they recognize that you have to sell an IT project if it is to succeed. Box 5.5 presents a cursory introduction to this, discussed in greater detail below.

Selling an e-government project means first identifying the potential buyers, that is, the project stakeholders. Key among these will be (Yeates and Cadle, 2002: 276):

- *decision makers*: those who make major project-related decisions, such as whether or not to proceed with the project;
- *gatekeepers*: those who control access to higher authorities;
- *influencers*: those who advise decision makers or whom decision makers take note of;
- *end users*: those who will directly use the output from the e-government system and/or from the business function it supports;
- *champions*: those who will support and muster resources for the project.

For a project to be sold to any of these stakeholders, they must want to buy. They will

---

Box 5.5   eGovernment Project Selection as a Political Campaign

1   Select a candidate (the e-government project you wish to be implemented).
2a   Work the 'smoke-filled rooms' to establish support (work with a wide range of individual stakeholders and small groups to get their support; accept some compromises if necessary in what you seek to achieve; be seen to be listening and reacting).
2b   Give the candidate a media campaign to establish support (in public meetings use simple slogans and focus on project benefits).
3   Hold an election (present the project proposal to the individual or group with the power to sanction it).
4   Take office (implement the project). (Adapted from Turban et al., 1996: 415)

---

only want to buy if the project meets a need that they have: that is if it fits with one or more of their personal objectives and answers the key question already noted in Section 5.2: 'Why should I: what's in it for me?'. Those trying to answer by selling the system must learn to distinguish between selling features ('This e-government application automates the procurement process') and selling benefits ('This e-government application will allow you to buy things more quickly and easily'). IT staff particularly tend to focus on features. But most stakeholders are not interested in features. They are interested in benefits. Yet you can only know what the benefits are for an individual if you know their personal objectives.

Getting through to understand these objectives is the key to successful selling (indeed, to playing the game of organizational politics more generally). The problem is the pressure in public sector organizations for a 'discourse of rationality': holding discussions in the 'language' of rationality, with the pretence that everyone in the organization behaves rationally.

Smart behavioral players work to break through the rationality barrier to get to the real objectives and values underneath. They do this in a number of ways, but particularly (Yeates and Cadle, 2002: 271–5):

- by understanding that professional relationships have different bases and require different techniques from those adopted with social relationships;
- by establishing rapport with the other person: looking for common ground; developing on their areas of interest; even mirroring their speech and body language in order to 'tune in';
- by active listening that involves really concentrating and asking questions to get to the root of issues, beliefs, problems, needs, and so on;
- by tailoring communication to the needs of the recipient (see Box 5.6).

The same approach needs to be taken in relation to any formal negotiations that may take place within the project context. Here, the politics within public sector organizations comes to the fore, with the various parties using their power in the form of influencing and negotiating techniques. Categories of power and specific techniques are discussed below in Section 5.5, but here we can provide an overview. A systematic application of techniques to negotiation might take the following steps, building on the behavioral techniques just listed (Fowler, 1998; Armstrong, 2003):

Box 5.6   Tailoring your Message

A behavioral approach to e-government projects means understanding the different individuals that have to be dealt with, and tailoring messages accordingly. At a simple and formal level, this could mean emphasizing the financial aspects when talking to an accountant, and emphasizing the personnel aspects when talking to an HR manager.

However, tailoring can become a lot more subtle. For example, one can use simple psychological methods to characterize stakeholders and to customize communication to fit individual characteristics. A simple version of this is presented by Patching and Chatham (2000: 195), dividing individuals into four types and providing their preferred communication style and content:

The sociable ones:	The idealistic ones:
• Be clear and explicit, don't just imply. • Show me how people will benefit. • Demonstrate immediate and practical results. • Show me respect.	• Engage with my personal values. • Paint pictures and draw analogies that have meaning. • Be passionate and engage my imagination. • Show how it will contribute to the greater good of human kind.
The theoretical ones:	The down to earth ones:
• Show how it fits into the bigger picture. • Ensure the theoretical base is sound. • Appeal to my intellect and imagination. • Be a credible source of information.	• Be organized and structured. • Be practical and realistic. • Work logically and systematically through your analysis. • Offer proof and evidence.

Rather more complex use of individual difference is seen in the emergence of neuro-linguistic programming (NLP) as a popular behavioral tool. NLP cues in to those differences and uses words and behaviors relevant to the recipient to build rapport and transmit a relevant message (Knight, 2001).

Whatever the delivery techniques used, though, content must always bear in mind the individual's personal objectives and values.

1 *Preparation*: Getting as much information as possible not just in relation to the topic under discussion but also in relation to the objectives and values of other parties; being clear about one's own 'bottom line'.

2 *Initial exchange*: Drawing out other individuals and probing with questions to develop a better sense of their objectives and values; weighing up relative bargaining powers.

3 *Negotiation*: being assertive; using and observing body language; identifying issues that can easily be agreed and issues that are low-cost to one side but high benefit to the other; being creative

about what can be traded; exploring possible compromises.

4 *Agreement*: summarizing the discussion; avoiding/dealing with last minute conditions.

5 *Implementation*: setting out a clear schedule of tasks and responsibilities.

The acquisition of negotiating skills and the ability to apply the techniques just described is becoming increasingly integral to e-government project management (IDLO, 2002; Chen and Perry, 2003).

Hybrid Approaches to Project Management

Hybrid approaches recognize that successful e-government projects handle the whole gamut of ITPOSMO: the hard components (information as data, technology, processes, people as resources, management structures, other resources of time and money); the soft components (objectives and values, people as humans); and the in-between components (information and knowledge, skills, management systems). They see that projects need both head and heart; that projects are both logistical operations and political campaigns (see Box 5.7).

Some public sector organizations are developing such a hybrid approach. In the US state of Massachusetts, for example, there is a combined rational and behavioral approach to e-government projects (OSC, 1997). For the rational part, the emphasis is on getting the basics right and allowing for flexibility without an overwhelming pressure of depth and detail that obscures the big picture. To assist this, project task orders are used; documents of just a few pages' length which cover:

Box 5.7   What Makes for a Successful eGovernment Project?

Although skewed towards the rational end of the spectrum, Washington state government's analysis of the profile of a successful e-government project, based on its own experience, does highlight the need to encompass all the ITPOSMO components and the need for a flexible methodology:

> The profile of a successful IT project tends to look like this: The project is tightly focused, thereby resisting scope creep and lending itself to scaleable and incremental development. It has a strong organizational structure behind it. Supported by a pro-active executive sponsor, the project managers have the expertise to do the job and are entrusted with the latitude to adapt to the inevitable changes that come along during the process. The project team studies the external landscape, learning from the experience of other jurisdictions in attempting to develop similar projects. In developing a detailed timeline at the beginning of the process, the project team builds in generous contingencies for delays at each stage, recognizing that complex processes often thwart best case scenarios. ...
>
> Successful projects are also characterized by project managers and contractors who are able to communicate effectively within the organization, thereby fostering broadly-based participation by the people who will be using the new systems – and with external stakeholders who must be convinced of the project's merits on the basis of service delivery, economic and political justifications. (DIS, 1995)

- *business problem and scope of work*: the problem being addressed; the rationale for the e-government project; and the major tasks to be undertaken;
- *workplan and time schedule*: a Gantt chart 'not intended to be a project log of each and every small detail, but rather a comprehensive plan of tasks, team resources and timelines';
- *management approach and personnel*: for both the steering committee and project implementation team;
- *acceptance criteria and deliverables*: the key outputs from the project and criteria that will be used to judge whether or not that output is acceptable;
- *task order budget*;
- *signatures*: of all the key 'business partners'.

For the behavioral part, the emphasis is on getting non-IT support and guidance;

recognizing some of the human and political issues that arise in e-government. Crossing the two are hybrid structures and systems of supportive external input. For example, there are coordination groups and steering committees that will ensure the necessary communication, support and oversight for projects. It is an intention of the hybrid approach that such structures will allow (a) early identification of failures; and (b) mechanisms to disperse learning about both success and failure. However, this still seems easier to achieve in the private sector than in the public sector.

5.5 POLITICS

eGovernment is all about technology, isn't it? Box 5.8 provides some real-world insights into what e-government is all about.

Box 5.8   Politicking over eGovernment Systems in the Israeli Government

The Internet

At the end of 1996, two visionary, energetic, and politically influential officials simultaneously launched parallel campaigns to propel the government into the Internet age. The first was Michael Eytan, a Knesset (parliament) member, who mobilized 70 lawyers, business leaders, technologists, scholars, politicians, and civil servants who jointly prepared a document recommending specific steps the government had to take to ensure its preparedness for the information age. After six months of bitter budgetary struggle, Eytan acquired funding to establish a new unit titled HILA within the Prime Minister's Office whose mandate was to spearhead the government into a new electronic era. The second official was a senior MoF [*Ministry of Finance*] bureaucrat who established a 'Government Internet Committee' whose mandate too was to promote Internet use in the public sector. The two Internet units fiercely battled over every conceivable topic ... For example, when in January 1998, MoF published a detailed public tender inviting vendors to build Internet applications and host them on its [*MoF's*] servers, Eytan's ministerial committee published a decree instructing vendors to host such applications on their own computers and then sell services directly to individual ministries. The MoF unit published budget ordinances and the Prime Minister's Office unit retaliated by publishing ministerial decrees, each seeking to enforce its standards on other ministries. After two years of bitter 'Internet wars', the MoF unit emerged victorious. (Peled, 2000b: 52–3)

Office Automation

Large entities that they are, most Israeli ministries require some kind of 'group-ware' solution to allow thousands of employees to store, share and retrieve their electronic communications. In 1991, MoF launched an 'automated office' software development project dubbed 'Maor'. Around the same time, several other ministries launched similar projects. MoF then decided to develop a second version dubbed 'Maor 2000' and to compel other ministries to adopt this new version ... .

In retaliation, several other ministries doubled their efforts to build different automated office solutions that were completely incompatible with 'Maor 2000'. For example, the MIS director of the Tourism Ministry used 'guerilla marketing tactics' to convert his own 'Tiuk Kal' (Hebrew for 'Easy Filing') software into the de-facto automated software standard in the Government. He gave the software free of charge to the Ministry of Commerce and Trade. MoF officials stopped him in the nick of time before he gave this software to several other ministries. Similarly, the PMIS director of the Transportation Ministry was determined to build her own automated office solution based on Microsoft 2000 technology. She launched her own automated office project *after* MOF instructed other ministries to use 'Maor 2000'. (Peled, 2000b: 54)

Retaliation? Guerilla tactics? Wars? The language used in the Box 5.8 cases seems more at home on the battlefield than the world of e-government. Yet it is actually just one representation of the point made repeatedly in this chapter and in this book: e-government is far more about people and politics than it is about technology and rationality:

Sometimes, IT projects fail because of economic reasons; rarely, if ever, because of technological factors. Most usually, the failures are political in nature. ... Instead of studying the manuals for the next release of Java, C++ or Lotus Notes, read Machiavelli's *The Prince*. (Strassmann, 1997: 82)

Why should there be so much politicking around e-government? In short, because two pre-conditions of politicking are met. First, there are interdependent groups that have different objectives and values. This is clearly the case in public sector organizations. The 'interdependent but different'

perspective applies to the formal functional divisions within public agencies. It also applies particularly to e-government systems, as was illustrated by the IT square (Figure 2.2). All four groups shown in the square – senior public managers, politicians, IT professionals, mainstream staff – have to be involved together in e-government implementation, but they have very different perspectives.

Second, there are important but scarce resources involved. Peled (2000b: 47) explains how this applies to e-government:

First, the information contained inside computers often determines which organizational factions will gain or lose power relative to others. Second, computing infrastructure is expensive and therefore those who are in control of it control a large portion of the organization's capital investments. Finally, many people perceive those who are engaged in computers to be advanced, sophisticated, and professional.

So e-government brings together in large amounts both critical tangible resources – people, money and equipment – and critical intangible resources – information, power and kudos. They therefore form a key locus for organizational politics.

Power and Influence

What does 'organizational politics' mean? We can divide it into two related factors: power and influence:

> Influence is the process whereby A seeks to modify the attitudes or behaviour of B. Power is what which enables him [sic] to do it. ... If we are to understand organizations we must understand the nature of power and influence for they are the means by which the people of the organization are linked to its purpose. (Handy, 1992: 123)

Analyses of e-government systems from a power and influence/personal politics perspective are few and far between. Yet these issues are obviously critical to the management of those systems. All of the fine ideas elsewhere in this book – about balancing center and local, on best practice for staff recruitment/retention, about methods for e-government implementation, on the qualities needed for an e-government leader – are largely irrelevant to any individual actor unless they have the power and influence to introduce those ideas. To understand these issues further, we first look at power.

Power is notoriously tricky to define: 'We may say about it (power) in general only what St. Augustine said about time, that we all know perfectly well what it is – until somebody asks us' (Bierstedt, 1950: 750, cited in Bannister, 2003). One approach to definition identifies different types of power (from Buchanan and Huczynski, 2004, with adaptations from Blair and Meadows, 1996 and Mullins, 2002):

- *Reward power*: The ability to distribute valued resources as rewards. Such resources may include promotion, money, praise, office space, information, and so on.
- *Coercive power*: The ability to punish. This comes from the ability to instigate either formal or informal punishments. It can also be associated with the 'negative power' to prevent or delay things happening, which is a form of punishment. It is the threat of punishment rather than punishment itself that is used in many cases.
- *Legitimate power*: The power that comes from one's formal position of authority within an organization. Often that power relates to the rewards, punishments, information (i.e. the other components of power) that go with the formal position/role. It also, though, relates to the symbolic power of a role and the rights within a position to access others, to take decisions, and to make and implement rules.
- *Expert power*: Power that comes from expertise that is acknowledged and valued by others. This partly relates to a real track record of suggested courses of actions that worked (and a lack of those that failed). However, it also related to imagery; to making oneself appear to be an expert.
- *Personal (referent) power*: The ability to influence others due to one's personal characteristics. This relates to a range of often hard-to-define factors that include charisma, confidence, empathy and competence. As with expertise, these relate as much to a projection as to real ownership of a characteristic.

These five types, to a certain degree, can be related to the individual as they are; there are also sources of power that derive from the individual's position in a network, including:

- *Information power*: The ability to gain valuable information and the ability to use it in decision making or communication. Such information typically comes from being well-placed in an organizational network. This means having: betweenness (being between others so you can control information flows between them); connectedness (being linked to many others inside and outside the organization); closeness (being close to others so you have direct access to them).
- *Affiliation power*: Power derived from one's association with other powerful figures or groups. This, like other sources but even more so, relates to perceptions as much as realities. It is also a reminder, though, of the contribution of social capital to all types of power: that which allows one to draw on resources from other members of a personal network.

Techniques of Influence

When an e-government system is being introduced, all stakeholders involved will have the bases of power described above in different mixes and to greater and lesser extents. The way they seek to use their power to alter the course of the introduction will be through various techniques of influence (adapted from Buchanan and Huczynski (2004: 840–1) partly citing Kipnis et al. (1984)):

- *Reason*: 'Relies on the presentation of data and information as the basis for a logical argument that supports a request.' Reason is typically a first choice for influencing a boss or subordinate, and it often relates to a base of expert or information power.
- *Friendliness*: 'Depends on the influencee thinking well of the influencer.' It is often used with co-workers, but may also be used with subordinates and superiors. It often relates to a base of personal power.
- *Coalition*: 'Mobilizing other people in the organization to support you, and thereby strengthening your request.' It depends on the size and strength of the influencer's personal network, and so relates to affiliation power particularly.
- *Bargaining*: 'Negotiating and exchanging benefits based upon the social norms of obligation and reciprocity.' The resources traded are very varied but can include assistance, support and information. It often relates to a base of reward power.
- *Assertiveness*: Uses continuous reminders via an insistent and forceful manner. It is often used with subordinates and relates to a base of legitimate power.
- *Higher authority*: 'Uses the chain of command and outside sources of power to influence the target person.' This can be the threat or promise of involving the influencee's boss, or invoking that boss' own priorities. It can also involve an appeal to higher ethical or cultural values within the organization. It may involve recourse to outside 'experts', such as consultants, or to the media. A variation, much found in e-government, is to blame the technology or the data, though this may fall under the heading of manipulation. Its strength relies particularly on affiliation power.
- *Sanctions*: Influence through the promise of reward or threat of punishments. In its negative form, this may encompass all formal disciplinary procedures up to dismissal. It may encompass informal actions: blame, bad-mouthing, bullying. It may also encompass the removal of rewards (e.g. transfer, demotion). Sanctions often relate to a base of legitimate or coercive power.

- *Manipulation*: Influence by controlling the framing of discussions, or the claimed rules for discussion, or the information that is allowing into a negotiation. Part of this process will be the manipulation of the public discussions and public relations that set much of the agenda for government. This type of approach may also include undermining others involved.
- *Withdrawal*: Influence through disengagement or non-compliance.

A number of these tactics can be found in virtually all e-government projects, except that they are generally kept well hidden from outside view. An example of their use is given in Box 5.9.

A key failing of those involved with e-government systems, particularly IT professionals, has been their denial of the importance of – and withdrawal from

involvement with – power, influence and politicking:

> IT managers are often politically naïve. They perceive political behaviour as manipulative and unscrupulous, and many therefore engage in avoidance tactics. (Patching and Chatham, 2000: xxxiii)

From what has been presented above, though, it is clear that issues of power and influence are critical. Time and again, middle managers in public sector organizations have good ideas for new or redesigned e-government systems. Yet they cannot get those ideas implemented. They blame their bosses, or the IT staff, or politicians, and so on. In many cases, though, they should blame themselves for failing to recognize their own need for better communication, negotiation and, above all, influencing skills. All these items need to be added to the portfolio of any aspiring e-government hybrid, as summarized in Box 5.10.

Box 5.9   Games Playing in Ireland's Penalty Points Systems

In 1997, an e-government project was announced to implement a penalty points system for traffic offences in Ireland (Bannister, 2003): 'This system finally stuttered into life in early 2003 with just one of the 68 listed offences (speeding) being operational' (p. 35). The main reason for delay was politicking by the four main agencies involved – the Department of the Environment and Local Government (with ultimate responsibility for licensing), local authorities (which issue driving licenses), the police, and the judicial system.

The police needed their computing systems to be upgraded, and sought to create an unstoppable momentum for this by issuing a tender. Using its legitimate power, their parent Department of Justice refused the required funding to fulfill this tender. Through a well-timed leak to national newspapers blaming the DoJ for delays to the penalty points system, the higher authorities of the media, citizenry and, hence, more senior politicians were enlisted on the side of the police, who showed good mastery of two techniques: (a) selective release of information; (b) using public forums to pressurize other players.

The courts, meanwhile, wanted nothing to do with the new system because they already had more than enough on their plate, 'being in the middle of a major system upgrade'. They opted for a tactic of withdrawal.

Box 5.10   Being a Political Player in eGovernment Projects

- *Play politics*: Public sector projects – including e-government – are all about politics. So, be realistic, and join in the game. Identify your sources of power. Develop your persuading, influencing and negotiating skills. Then use them.
- *Play chess*: Picture the e-government project as a chess game. Ask yourself – what piece am I? Are you the all-powerful queen, a middle-ranking bishop, or just a lowly pawn? If you are one of the lesser pieces in the game, you will face problems unless you can find a powerful ally: the equivalent of a rook or queen in chess. If you have trouble from middle-ranking stakeholders, ask yourself if there's a more powerful player that you can bring in – a senior official, a politician, an external agency, the media, and so on.
- *Play in public*: Saying something in public often encourages stakeholders to make that thing happen – they will be embarrassed if they fail to match up to public pronouncements. Effective change agents use statements at internal and external public meetings to maintain momentum and motivation on e-government projects. (Adapted from Heeks, 2003a)

ACTIVITIES

Shorter In-Class Activities[7]

Section 5.1

a. According to Bretschneider (1990), the IT unit tends to be placed further down the organizational hierarchy in the public sector compared to the private sector. Discuss whether this is still true and reasons behind your argument in pairs then plenary.

b. Read through the Box 5.1 case study and identify where the pressures for change of IT function location come from. Are the pressures mainly internal or external? How typical do you think that is?

Section 5.2

a. Get class members to provide theoretical or real-world examples for each cell in the matrix shown below.

b. Despite a continuous stream of good ideas on personnel management, the public sector seems to continuously suffer from a shortage of e-government staff. Is outsourcing the only answer? Discuss in pairs then plenary.

Section 5.3

a. You are a bank manager and have been approached by a public agency for a loan

Responsibility	Centralized	Hybrid	Decentralized
IT structures and staffing			

to develop an e-government application. Would you regard that as a high- or low-risk loan? How could the money be repaid?

Section 5.4

a. Identify at least two reasons why e-government project managers seem to keep repeating mistakes commonly highlighted by audit/oversight reports.

b. Discuss your reaction to the rational project processes and structures shown in Figure 5.2 and Box 5.4. Are you attracted or repelled by them? Are you convinced or skeptical about them? What are the implications for the kind of project management approach you would work best with?

c. The approach described in Box 5.7 is claimed to encompass all the ITPOSMO components. Which of the seven dimensions can you explicitly identify?

Section 5.5

a. Imagine you are a senior public servant caught up in the situations described in Box 5.8. What would be your best course of action?

b. Imagine that you are a middle manager in a public agency with a good idea for a new e-government system. How will you convince your boss to support that idea? Identify your likely sources of power (using the seven different types listed in the main text) and identify the influence techniques you would use.

c. If you were working for the Department of Justice in the Box 5.9 case, how would you respond to the police department's tactics?

Assignment Questions

Section 5.1

a. 'A hybrid location is better than either a decentralized or centralized location for the IT function in public agencies.' Discuss.

Section 5.2

a. From the literature, identify a set of current best practices for staff recruitment and retention in the private sector. Which, if any, of these could be applied specifically to IT staff in the public sector?

Section 5.3

a. Can private funding of e-government projects really work, or are the financial interests of public and private sectors too divergent?

Section 5.4

a. Given limited time, are e-government project managers better advised to focus more on technical or more on human issues?

Section 5.5

a. 'All you need to know about managing e-government can be found in Machiavelli's *The Prince*'. Discuss.

Practitioner Exercises

Section 5.1

a. Reflect on the pros and cons of the different organizational locations described and then note down an answer to the following question:

- Where is the central IT unit in your organization located, and to whom does the IT unit manager report?

Note down any implications for your organization, such as those that relate to the identified advantages and disadvantages. Are there any recommendations for change that you would make?

Section 5.2

a. What are the current IT/IS staff recruitment and retention practices in your organization? Could they be improved using either the techniques identified above or other techniques? If so, what would the priorities be and how might they be introduced?

Section 5.3

a. Review the methods of raising finance (or reducing costs) identified in this chapter. Could any of them usefully be applied in your own organization to help e-government?

Section 5.4

a. When e-government projects in your organization are being managed, which gets managed most: hard or soft factors? When e-government projects go wrong in your organization, which does any formal analysis of failure highlight: hard or soft factors? Based on this analysis and on your own opinion, do you think your organization should be moving towards a more rational, a more behavioral or a more hybrid approach to project management? What specific improvements to project management practice does your answer imply? How could these implemented?

b. Identify a recent or current e-government project. Who were/are the key project stakeholders? What were/are their personal objectives and values? How could an understanding of these be used to sell benefits? How could messages be tailored to those stakeholders?

Section 5.5

a. What politicking goes on in your organization around e-government? Identify a particular e-government issue in which you have been involved. What categories of power (use the seven different types listed in the main text) did you have – or could you have had – relating to that issue? What techniques of influence did you use – or could you have used – relating to that issue? Do you need to improve your awareness of power and your use of influence? If so, how will you do that?

NOTES

1. The issue of relations with the subcontractor is taken up in further detail in this chapter's Online Appendix.

2. Further detail about information centers is provided in this chapter's Online Appendix.

3. More details on partnerships with outsourcing vendors can be found in this chapter's Online Appendix.

4. See the Online Appendix for Chapter 6 for more details about e-government and ethics.

5. More detail about pros, cons and best practices in use of consultants is presented in this chapter's Online Appendix.

6. The issue of public sector budgeting is taken up in the Online Appendix to Chapter 3.

7. Details of longer group activities are provided in the Online Appendix to this chapter.

6

Emerging Management
Issues for eGovernment

Key Points

- Performance management for e-government is a private sector tool in a public sector environment, and a rational tool in a politicized environment that must be customized if it is to work.
- Most e-government performance evaluations miss the key indicator: public value.
- Managers developing data policies for e-government must try to balance an uneasy tension between access, privacy, income and security.
- In developing policies on disability/accessibility, ergonomics, and Internet usage, e-government managers have to steer the line between external pressures and local priorities.

Chapter 5 presented a set of e-government management issues that – somewhat arbitrarily – were identified as 'core': ones that managers have faced for many years. In this chapter, we look at management issues that have come to prominence more in recent years. Once again, the device of the 'Ps' has been used, to highlight two key issues:[1]

- *performance* (the measurement of e-government-related performance);
- *policies* (the organizational policies that e-government managers have to develop and promote); these are divided into policies on public data, and policies on other issues.

6.1 PERFORMANCE

Performance management is a component of public sector reform. It is a technique originating in the private sector that is now being promoted in the public sector. As with most such techniques, issues arise because some of the assumptions underlying performance management do not apply, or apply differently, in the public sector. We will investigate this by looking at IT staff, IS/IT function and e-government performance.

Staff Performance

Performance management in the public sector follows a standard pattern of target setting, measurement, evaluation and control, as shown in Figure 6.1.

In reference to IT staff management, this would involve working first on a clear job specification and then tying the major items of content (ideally those that are output related) down to measurable performance indicators and targets. Actual

Inputs   Outcomes

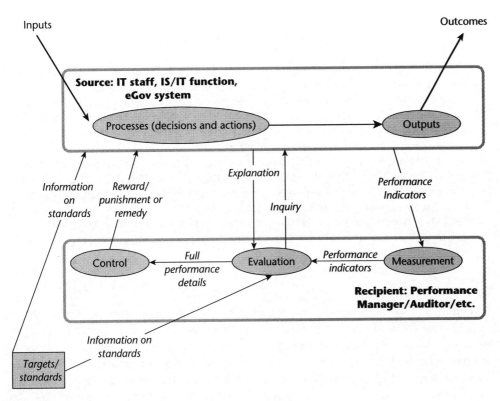

Figure 6.1   Performance management in e-government

measures of performance would typically be discussed as part of regular staff–manager meetings with reasons for under- and over-achievement discussed. Rewards would be instituted for achievement/over-achievement and remedial measures for under-achievement.

We can now look at these in greater detail, starting with the job description, an example of which is given in Box 6.1.

Box 6.1   Job Description for IT Support Officer in Small Public Agency within Larger Department

Principal functions of the IT support officer post are:

- Provide IT-related support and assistance to agency staff.
- Provide the main focus for support, maintenance, development and related documentation of in-house e-government systems.
- Install, manage and document new applications and new hardware. This is likely to include transfer of applications from old to new environments, installation of new network connections, and hardware upgrades.

(Continued)

Box 6.1 Continued

- Maintain up-to-date inventory and insurance-related details of existing agency hardware, software, network-related and other electrical equipment.
- Advise section managers on purchase, selection and use of appropriate new hardware and software. Order IT- and related equipment as requested by budget holders. Maintain a proper record of orders and purchases to provide adequate information and controls for budget holders.
- Investigate, locate and, whenever possible, correct software-, hardware- and network-related faults. Maintain and repair agency equipment and/or liaise with external service suppliers. Proactively use and promote anti-virus, backup and other computer security measures to minimize security incidents.
- Provide software, hardware and related training sessions for staff as required.
- Liaise with departmental IT staff on both operational and tactical issues.

The difficulty with the items listed in Box 6.1 is that there are few clearly measurable components. The danger is that one then has to fall back on subjective, qualitative assessments. At worst, one is left with two, possibly conflicting, assessments – one from the staff member, and one from the performance manager. This can be improved somewhat to the level of inter-subjectivity by polling clients and peers for their assessment of staff performance against stated functions.

An alternative could be to make job description items more detailed and linked to specific criteria. For example, a job component of 'monitor performance against agreed service levels' could be broken down into the following criteria (Yeates and Cadle, 2002: 318):

- Performance statistics, activity logs and fault logs are regularly collected and analysed.
- Performance degradation of the system is recognised and possible solutions are researched and actioned.
- Unreliable or outdated components are replaced.
- Need to enhance or upgrade the system is recognised and reported to management.

The greater specificity of these criteria allows somewhat less room for disagreement, but they still fall short of being objective and quantifiable performance indicators. The difficulty here – one that applies to most public sector staff and structures – is that most IT staff are providing a service, not making a product. Quantification and objectivity can therefore be difficult. Attempts to measure include time to perform a service, number of workstations or users supported per IT staff member, number of complaints, and client satisfaction ratings (SOCITM, 2002).

Great care must be taken that measures are valid (i.e. that they do measure what they seek to measure), relevant (i.e. that they measure something on which the employee's actions have an effect) and valuable (i.e. that they measure what is organizationally important about the job). IT staff behavior will be skewed by performance measurement towards the measured components of the job and away from the non-measured. Only careful selection of indicators will ensure that this skewing is beneficial for the organization.

Even if valid, relevant and valuable performance indicators can be identified and measured, there is still the issue of control to face. Essentially this looks at ways to reward good performance and punish or rectify sub-standard performance. Increasing numbers of public agencies are using performance-related pay ('merit pay') as a key control measure. However, this faces continuous criticism, both as a mechanism per se and particularly as a mechanism for the public sector, where its use has been marked by 'technical, financial, managerial and cultural problems.' (Emery, 2004):

> Performance-based pay reforms ... have yielded no clear improvement in perfor-mance and have failed to create a more flex-ible or more satisfactory evaluation and compensation system. (Laegreid, 2002: 147)

A review of performance management in the public sector therefore includes the fol-lowing public–private hybrid recommenda-tions as alternatives to the standard private sector model of individual performance-related pay (Osborne and Plastrik, 1997; Berman et al., 2001; Emery, 2004):

- Use financial alternatives, such as one-off payments for achieving particular targets, or gainsharing (where all staff share in any financial savings the organization achieves), or skill pay (where staff are paid on the basis of new competencies that are learned and effectively employed).
- Use non-financial rewards, such as per-formance awards, personal recognition from senior staff, career development opportunities, or *psychic pay*: quasi-financial incentives such as paid time off or new equipment. In some surveys, public servants rate these above money as preferred rewards.
- Use group incentives since individual rewards can demotivate other team members, whereas group rewards tend to encourage collaboration. Gainsharing can also fit into this category.

- Use punishment, but with great care. Avoid financial penalties and do not punish occasional mistakes, only chronic poor performance. Use progressive discipline but also use training and peer pressure.

Some public organizations, though, have shifted away from employee performance management because of its practical limita-tions. The shift is away from a focus on the employee, towards a recognition that per-formance depends more on the systems within which the employee works (Cohen and Eimicke, 1998). IT staff and managers work together to identify ways in which performance of e-government processes and systems can be improved. This removes much of the subjective, divisive and judg-mental shortcomings of individual perfor-mance management.

IS/IT Function Performance

Some points already made above apply to performance management of the IS/IT func-tion. They will not be reiterated in great detail but merely summarized either as being a clash between the private sector origins of performance management and different sectoral realities in government, or as being a clash between the organization-ally rational origins of performance man-agement and different behavioral realities. These are reflected in the problems noted about data quality or the skewing of indi-vidual behavior.

Here, the focus will be on three main com-ponents of IS/IT function performance drawn from Figure 6.1 but categorized in Figure 6.2.

The initial points on these axes – no indi-cator, no measurement and no control – are still quite widely found in the public sector in relation to e-government. However, the discussion that follows concentrates on other points on the axes.

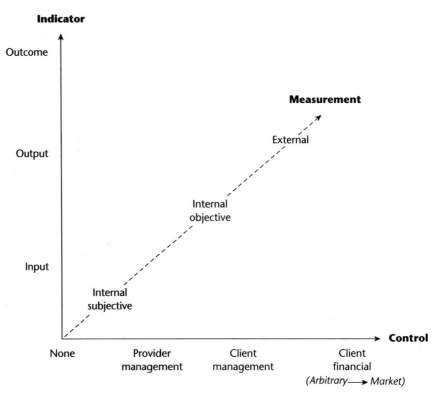

Figure 6.2   Three dimensions of IS/IT performance management

Performance Indicators

Three main focal points for performance indicators can be applied to the IS/IT function:

- *Input*: These are typically seen as *IT* measures that are independent of client involvement. Examples would be up-time for the main computer systems or processor response time.
- *Output*: These are typically seen as *IS* or *information services* measures, since they relate to the service as it is received and used by public sector clients. Examples would be customer satisfaction ratings, response time for help desk services, or volume of transactions processed.

- *Outcome*: These are typically seen as *business process* measures, since they relate to client processes that the IS/IT function supports. Examples would be response time of clients of the IS/IT service to *their* clients or take-up levels of the service the IS/IT users are themselves providing.

As might be expected, input measures are the easiest to develop – they are used by more than 80 percent of UK local governments (SOCITM and IDEA, 2002). However, they are probably the least useful since they bear only a limited direct relationship to clients and what those clients are seeking to achieve. Over time these are being replaced by output measures, such as those described in Box 6.2.

Box 6.2   Output Measures in IS/IT Service Level Agreements

Examples of output measures within IS/IT service level agreements include the following (PTI, 2004):

- More than 75 percent of agency staff report they are satisfied with the service provided by the IT help desk (City of Seattle, Washington).
- A maximum of 15 minutes to elapse between network component failure and IS Division staff response (City of Mesa, Arizona).
- Settlement of credit card transactions recorded on the e-government site to be settled each day with relevant financial institutions by 3am (City of Seattle, Washington).

Yet such measures, while they are outputs from the IS/IT function, still represent only inputs to the main work of public sector organizations. As a result, some public agencies are now moving on to outcome measures. For example, the UK Employment Service negotiated a service contract with private firm EDS related to the provision of 'Employment Service Direct', a new call center-based initiative to help jobseekers, later renamed 'Jobseeker Direct' (GHK, 2002). The contract moved from a measure based on the number of jobseeker records held or processed to a measure based on the number of jobseekers who were put into work by the new initiative (see Figure 6.3). This gave both EDS and the Employment Service a single, clear, common objective that greatly helped contract performance.

Measurement of Performance

How are the performance indicators described above actually measured? In most cases the measurement procedure will be clear within the indicator definition.

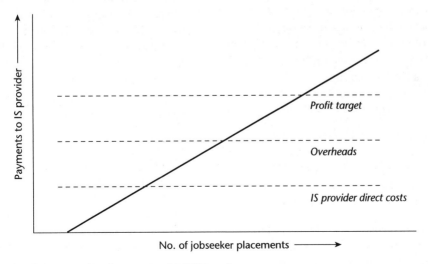

Figure 6.3   Outcome-related payments for IS/IT services

A progression can be seen here too, divided into three categories:

- *Internal subjective*: The measures are based on the judgment of internal clients, such as customer satisfaction rating scales.
- *Internal objective*: The measures are based on objective quantification within the organization, such as the jobseeker placement measure.
- *External*: The measures are based on quantification from outside the organization. This tends to take two main forms. The first is external audit, which may be a required component of IS/IT function provision in some governments. The second is benchmarking, involving the comparison of the IS/IT function used by the organization with others in the public or private sector.

There has been a tendency to move up the scale over time, with a growth in external measures. In the UK, for example, there has been increased use of 'price testing' (comparing the internal costs of a service with the estimated cost/price of external providers) and benchmarking (which includes a broader set of performance measures) (Flynn, 2002). These can be powerful tools to lever reorganization of the internal function, with the threat of moving on to the next step – outsourcing with or without an internal bid – if performance does not improve.

Control of Performance

Once performance has been measured against targets, there must be some means of affecting that performance through control measures. Yet again, these have seen a progression and yet again there are three categories:

- *Provider management control*: Managers within the IS/IT service provider are responsible for managerial rewards and remedial measures.

- *Client management control*: Managers within the IS/IT service client are responsible for managerial rewards and remedial measures.
- *Client financial control*: Managers within the IS/IT service client are responsible for financial rewards and remedial measures.

Moving up the scale tends to be associated with separation of client and provider, and with the introduction of more formalized relationships between client and provider such as service level agreements or, more formally still, binding contracts. Where financial payments are involved, the relationship between the amount paid by the user department and the IS/IT service provided can vary considerably along a continuum (Robson, 1997):

- *Arbitrary basis*: The sum paid does not relate to service use but to some relatively arbitrary measure such as the size of the user department. The lack of linkage creates limited financial control on performance; arguably less than that available via a managed service level agreement.
- *Cost basis*: The sum paid represents the cost of providing the IS/IT service. This could either be the direct cost or the total cost (direct costs plus overheads). There can be a difficulty here in calculating the costs; and calculation can in itself be costly.
- *Price basis*: The sum paid represents a price for provision of the IS/IT service. This could be less than cost if the public agency wishes to encourage use of the IS/IT service. Alternatively, it could allow for pricing above cost if the IS/IT unit was being turned from a cost center into a more autonomous profit center.
- *Market basis*: The sum paid represents a contractually agreed amount set in advance of provision of the IS/IT service. This is the method used for outsourcing arrangements, and it the method that puts greatest control into the hands of the user/client.

These approaches have been designed for the private sector, and one always needs to question their relevance and applicability to the public sector. Other more hybrid financial control arrangements that may apply in public agencies are noted in Box 6.3.

eGovernment

eGovernment performance can be – and is – assessed by public agencies using any of the approaches discussed above for the IS/IT function. There can also be performance measures for individual e-government systems: these are discussed in the section on evaluation in Chapter 11. In addition, there are independent, international performance evaluation studies.[2]

In this sub-section, though, we look at top-down approaches to e-government performance measurement used by individual governments. These have seen many governments adopting a similar benchmarking type of approach that has produced a slew of national targets and comparative rankings.[3] Many of them illustrate the performance management issues identified above:

problems of using private sector tools in the public sector, and problems of using rational tools in a politicized environment.

For example, there was a clear international and political undercurrent to e-government targets: 'A spate of targets swept across governments, with each leadership publicly vying to out-do their neighbouring counterpart.' (Curthoys and Crabtree, 2003: 17). Not surprisingly, then, there are various criticisms that can be leveled at these measures. First, a number of them have political get-out clauses; i.e. they speak of electronic availability of all services that are 'appropriate' (Australia) or 'key' (Canada) or that 'lend themselves to electronic service delivery' (Germany) (Westholm and Aichholzer, 2003). This introduces an element of subjectivity into the performance measures.

Second, these measures focus on intermediate outputs (availability of services) not on final outputs or outcomes (actual use and its impact). Put another way, they focus on supply not demand – most countries can meet their e-government performance targets without a single person actually using

---

Box 6.3   Financial Control Mechanisms for Public Agencies

A number of financial control ideas from the private sector have been hybridized for use in the public sector to good effect. They attempt to combine the original private sector entrepreneurial motivation effect with public sector values (Osborne and Plastrik, 1997; Cohen and Eimicke, 2002). Applications for the in-house IS/IT function include:

- *Gainsharing*: Allows the IT unit to keep a portion of the funds they save during the fiscal year (or biennium) to use in the future. It creates an organizational incentive to save money.
- *Efficiency dividends*: Reduces the IT unit's administrative budgets a small percentage each year but requires the unit to maintain its output level. This forces the unit to achieve productivity gains that at least offset the lost revenues. Because reductions occur every year, the pressure for productivity improvements is constant.
- *Performance budgeting*: Inserts required performance levels into budget documents. When the executive prepares a budget for the IT unit and the legislature passes it, they specify the outputs and outcomes they intend to buy with their money.

**Box 6.4   eGovernment Performance Criteria for
US Federal Agencies**

Agencies in the US federal government have to meet the following e-government
criteria to get a 'green' rating (OMB, 2003):

- Agency must have a 'modernization blueprint' that focuses IT investment on key
  functions and defines how those functions will be measurably improved.
- All major IT systems must have an acceptable business case.
- All major IT projects must average a less than 10 percent cost/schedule overrun and
  a less than 10 percent performance shortfall.
- There must be a verified IT security plan of action.
- Ninety percent of major IT systems must be properly secured.
- The agency must contribute to three of the following four e-government initiatives:

  o one-stop service delivery through FirstGov.gov or other cross-agency centers;
  o minimizing burdens on business through re-using data;
  o intergovernmental deployment of E-Grants or Geospatial One-Stop;
  o obtaining productivity improvements.

---

e-government systems (for example, see Box 6.4). The very few performance measures that are demand focused tell a disappointing story: although there are a few high-performing individual nations (such as Canada and the Scandinavian countries), on average less than half of all Internet users access e-government data and less than 20 percent undertake online transactions (UNDESA, 2003a; Westholm and Aichholzer, 2003; Reddick, 2005). In Europe, for example, a decade of frenetic, costly and much-hyped activity on Internet-based e-government has culminated in just 6 percent of the total population using e-government services (*Government Computing,* 2004). This has led to a re-focusing towards demand and towards marketing of e-government (see Chapter 11).

As illustrated in Box 6.4, one of the common management control techniques used in recent years has been the traffic light system of rating agencies either red, yellow or green for their performance against centrally set e-government targets. These may or may not be linked to explicit rewards, but are certainly linked to strong political pressures to move up the scale towards green. Indeed, e-government performance targets are seen as one of the main drivers behind the growth of e-government (Accenture, 2003).

However, what they truly achieve in terms of public value will be limited by the nature of the underlying performance measures. The criteria listed in Box 6.4, for example, focus almost entirely on inputs, processes and intermediate outputs on the supply side. The central thrust is that agencies must be good at writing documents and at managing projects. It would thus be possible to score a 'green' without producing anything that had actually made life better for citizens and other agency clients.

6.2 POLICIES ON PUBLIC DATA

Public agencies operate in a sea of government laws, orders, policies and regulations. These external drivers pressurize agency e-government managers to develop and

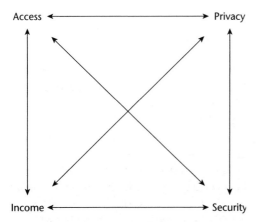

Figure 6.4   Data conflicts in the public
sector

implement their own internal policies on
a wide variety of issues. Some of these –
discussed in this section – relate to the management of public data, including issues of
data security, access and privacy. Some other
policy issues are discussed in Section 6.3.

Data policies must grapple with a four-
way data conflict faced by public agencies,
summarized in Figure 6.4.

Take the income–access tension: 'Open
government encourages making access easier
and cheaper, while financial pressures on
Departments and Agencies to recover costs
and maximise returns on their information
"assets" lead to controls and charging'
(POST, 1998: 31). The more the government
charges for its data, the greater the barriers
to access become. Yet the wider it allows
access, the less it can earn from data sales.

In 1999, a California bill was sponsored
seeking to give electronic access to public
records for the cost of duplicating a record.
The bill was vetoed by the Governor, claiming technical problems but also dangers of
violating the confidentiality of personal
information. The bill's sponsor claimed,
rather, that 'the true opposition to the bill
came from state agencies currently making a

profit by selling the information covered
under the bill' (*Government Technology,* 1999).

The sponsor highlighted the conflict
between income and access. The Governor,
however, invoked the conflict between
privacy and access, something that chimes
with voters, who want e-government to go
slow because of concerns about privacy
(McGinnis, 2003). The privacy–access conflict has been played out in US legislation
which has begun to re-assert the right to
privacy over the right to access. One example is the 1997 Drivers' Privacy Protection
Act which greatly reduced access to state
motor vehicle records (while avoiding
income conflict by allowing states to continue selling those records in bulk for commercial gain) (Hammitt, 2000).

That same conflict is coming to the fore
over other public records and documents.
For example, in the US, court documents
are held in the public domain. As those
documents are increasingly digitized, there
is a step-functional change in accessibility:

> When court records were kept as reams and
> reams of paper in huge record books, and
> viewing them required a day trip to the
> courthouse, the information was only
> accessed in extreme cases. Now though,
> what if it ticks off your neighbor when your
> dog pees on his lawn? He can hop on the
> Internet and dig up everything about you
> that is in those records – accusations, sensi-
> tive financial data, the bank you use – you
> name it. (Dussault, 1999)

States then began struggling to legislate on
this threat to privacy and avoid an electronic free-for-all. A variety of different
strategies was adopted, including keeping
some documentation non-electronic. There
has been gradual diffusion of Judicial
Conference guidelines that recommended
modifying identifiers on civil and bankruptcy case e-documents to reduce privacy
invasion, and not allowing electronic access
to most criminal and social security case

documents: just providing 'skeleton case' details such as court docket and case numbers unless there were exceptional circumstances such as high-profile cases (US Courts, 2001).

CIOs and data managers in public agencies face similar pressures to create data-related policies; partly to steer the chosen strategic line within the data conflict square shown in Figure 6.4, but also as a requirement of external legislative pressures. Here we will focus particularly on some of the central policies that relate to access, privacy and security.[4]

Access Policies for Management of Data Records

Digital information lasts forever or five years – whichever comes first. (Jeff Rothenberg, quoted in *Computing*, 1998: 48)

In the UK Public Records Office (PRO), the oldest government data is William the Conqueror's Domesday Book that records England's national assets in the years running up to its publication in 1086. It is more than 900 years old, yet it can still be accessed today (and understood so long as you can read Latin).

When government worked with paper, archiving was a task that was big but straightforward:

Government departments have been keeping their information in neat, numbered, Treasury-tagged paper files for centuries. Drafts were handwritten or typed; comments were scribbled in the margin or between the lines; final versions were initialled by ministers. By law officials have to save these records. The files ... are stored in the departments for a long period before going through a process of weeding. Eventually most – the irrelevant, perhaps the awkward – are destroyed and the surviving 1% are shipped to [*the PRO*]. When they're 30 years old, they are added to the

PRO's 100 miles of shelves – at the rate of a mile a year – and are opened up to the public. (Burkitt-Gray, 1998: 18)

But, as governments move into the information age, how much of the data being created today will be accessible in nine years time, let alone 900? There are two main issues that public CIOs face in creating policies for data access: storage and retrieval.

As regards storage, public servants have to be persuaded to treat digital data – from email messages to web sites – in the same way that they treat paper: 'there has to be an audit trail, with version numbers for documents, which should be archived in read-only files so that they can't be tampered with.' (ibid.: 18). Those electronic files must then be held securely and passed over to the archivists at the appropriate time. The US National Archives also insist on technical documentation describing how the records were created. While all very well in theory, the problem is that public servants are not yet attuned to this concept of *electronic records management* (ERM) and are engaged in wholesale deletion or over-writing of government records (Meijer, 2003). The 'here today, gone tomorrow' philosophy of the Internet sits uneasily with the legal and social obligations of government to preserve its data, and effective implementation of ERM policies such as those outlined in Box 6.5 are a pressing requirement.

The second problem arises with retrieval. Visit the office of almost anyone with more than decade's experience with IT and there, in a dusty corner, you'll invariably find a box or two of 5 1/4-inch diskettes holding files written in some long-dead word processing package. That data might be but a few years' old, but retrieving it – finding a connected 5 1/4-inch disk drive and then finding the software to access it – will be no easy task. The further back you go – 8-inch disks, magnetic tape, magnetic drums – the

---

Box 6.5   Electronic Records Management for eGovernment

The following elements are advised for electronic records management (ERM) (NECCC, 2002):

- Identify the risks of ERM: to the electronic system (e.g. retrieval issues); to the transactions recorded (e.g. damaging stakeholder relations); and to the records themselves (e.g. loss of evidentiary value).
- Identify and document the generic costs (both tangible and intangible) and potential benefits (increased speed and efficiency) of ERM.
- Identify the legal and agency policy requirements that apply to record keeping.
- Identify the content, structure and context of the actual records to be kept in order to understand the records system requirements.
- Identify the specific value of records to the public agency in order to ensure that time and financial costs are appropriate to the value. Value could be administrative (necessary to the agency's ongoing activity); fiscal (necessary to document financial transactions); legal (necessary due to statute or regulation); or archival (important to provide a contextual history of the agency).
- Ensure ERM system design is consistent with identified requirements and values, and that it can maintain some key elements of security: the authenticity of the record, the confidentiality of the record, the integrity of the record, and the accessibility of the record.
- Ensure ERM processes are designed that allow for final disposition: disposal or transfer to a more general archiving system.

---

harder it gets, yet none of this data is more than 50 years old. Worse, both magnetic and optical media can decay and lose its data.

> Up to a fifth of the information carefully collected during Nasa's 1976 Viking mission to Mars has been lost. Some prisoner-of-war and missing-in-action records and casualty counts from the Vietnam war, stored on US Defense Department computers, can no longer be read. And at Pennsylvania State University, some 3,000 computer files containing student records and school history are no longer accessible because of missing or outmoded software. (*Computing*, 1998: 48)

Records managers and archivists are therefore facing a predicament (Smith, 2004). Data on paper, if stored well, will survive for centuries and can easily be read. National archives in some European states have therefore been reluctant to accept anything other than paper-based records. Archivists who do accept electronic records must either maintain large quantities of increasingly obsolete equipment, or must copy and recopy ever-larger amounts of data onto new formats. As the pace of technological change and the use of IT in government increase, this problem will only grow.

Access Policies for Freedom of Information

In a bid to ensure access to data across the public sector (and beyond) some governments have introduced *freedom of information* (FOI) legislation. In the US, for example the Freedom of Information Act was introduced in 1966 and amended in 1996 by the Electronic Freedom of Information Act, which guarantees public access to most federal government data electronically

(Lewis, 2000). This has resulted in about 400,000 requests for access per year. To help with this access, government information locator services have been set up that identify, describe and assure access to such data.

Although proceeding relatively slowly over time, the enactment of FOI legislation has required the development of in-house policies by public agencies within its purview. Typical issues to be dealt with include (DOI, 2002):

- *Terminology*: Explicitly defining what is meant by terms such as records and requests; and classification of different types of data held by the agency.
- *Procedures*: Clarifying how citizens/ businesses can obtain data direct without requests; how information requests are to be made; and the means by which those requests will be responded to.
- *Data management*: Ensuring that the type of back-office, records and data management procedures described elsewhere in this chapter are followed so that data and records can be located in a timely and cost-efficient manner.
- *Performance measures*: Setting out performance indicators (typically time taken) for the FOI response service.
- *Charges*: Determining a reasonable level of charges to be levied for searches and copying; determining policy on any fee waivers; putting a billing and payment system in place.
- *Handling variations*: Determining procedures in the case of various types of data/records such as those not held by the agency; those held by other public agencies; those deemed sensitive or covered by privacy legislation; those held by other non-public agencies.
- *Appeals*: Setting in place an appeals procedure to appeal against problems with performance, charges or denial of access.

- *Responsibilities*: Designating specific officers as responsible for FOI implementation, and for appeals.
- *Update*: Putting in place a mechanism for review and update of FOI procedures (e.g. in response to new technology, case law, organizational changes, new orders, or FOI response performance and feedback).

In some countries, access is further supported by 'whistleblower' legislation. In the UK, the 1999 Public Interest Disclosure Act provides potentially unlimited compensation for those who are victimized or sacked when they try to 'raise genuine concerns about financial malpractice, breach of contract, abuse in care, dangers to health and safety, risks to the environment, and cover-ups.'

Access Policies and the Digital Divide

IT is very much a two-edged sword as regards access to government data. On the one hand it reduces barriers. Compare downloading a government report via the Internet with going out to buy a paper version. IT has made it far cheaper, quicker and easier to access that data. As noted above in relation to US courts, a wealth of data that, because of the barriers, was essentially inaccessible in paper form becomes accessible when it turns digital. Citizens can also reuse the data more easily because it arrives in electronic form.

The foregoing represents the technological good news. On the downside, IT raises barriers and has created a *digital divide* across which one group reaps the benefits of IT-enabled accessibility and one group cannot. The skills required for accessing manually held information are little more than literacy (though even in rich countries this is an issue, with estimates that around

20 percent of citizens are functionally illiterate (Longford, 2002)). For IT-based data, computer literacy must also be added and not everyone has those skills. Just as important are the issues of cost and ownership. Accessing individual items may be cheaper with IT, but to get that far you need an IT infrastructure in place first – a computer, a network connection, software, and so on. That all costs money whereas, by comparison, actually reading paper-based materials costs nothing.

Because of those costs, there is an uneven profile of those who own and use IT: the rich not the poor; the graduate not the school leaver; the ethnic majority not the ethnic minority; the urban not the rural citizen; the young not the old; men not women. In the mid-1990s, for example, of more than 100,000 daily recipients of White House electronic documents, 85 percent were under 50, 80 percent were male, and 50 percent had a postgraduate qualification (*Infosys*, 1994).

Since that time, general access levels have increased markedly. In North America, for example, the Internet has a penetration rate of two-thirds of the total population (Internetworldstats, 2005). Within this overall increase, the number of women, seniors, ethnic minority members, and so on has also increased. This is all to be expected. The penetration curves for IT are following very similar – albeit faster and steeper – patterns to those carved out by earlier technologies like the telephone and television (Chaffey, 2002).

However, while absolute numbers of previously excluded groups are rising, inequalities persist and one must constantly push behind the averages to find the realities of access. Half the world's population has yet to make a phone call 125 years after the invention of the telephone. Even in western nations, one-quarter of the poorest

20 percent of households does not have a phone (Taylor and Webster, 1996).

Access gaps hold equally for the Internet. The digital divide still runs nationally. In the US, for example (NTIA, 1999):

- High-income urban households are 20 times more likely to have home Internet access than low-income rural households.
- Low-income white families are three times more likely to have home Internet access than equivalent black families; four times more likely than equivalent Hispanic families.
- Those without disabilities are three times more likely to have home Internet access than those with disabilities.

And the digital divide still runs internationally – there are more Internet account holders in London than in the whole of Africa, and many of the latter are rich, white, urban South Africans (Heeks and Wilson, 2000).

Of course, one must equally take care with even these figures. Poor households and poor communities often share technologies in a way that richer ones do not. In Africa, for example, western models of one email/Internet account serving one individual do not hold. Instead, the typical account owner is an intermediary who shares access with an estimated five to ten others through networks of family, friends or colleagues (Heeks, 1999b). However, while moderating the impact of inequality, these modes of operation do not remove an inequality that sees the majority of the world's population cut off from computers and the Internet. If 820 million people worldwide had online access in 2005, that leaves some 5,600 million – around 87 percent of the world's population – who did not (Internetworldstats, 2005).

Governments are generally well aware of the dangers of IT strengthening the social exclusion that prevents some citizen groups from fulfilling their economic and social potential. There is recognition of the major fault-line that can easily run through e-government: those who have greatest need of government data and services are often those who have least access to IT. Pouring resources into e-government can therefore benefit the haves rather than have nots, and increase polarization within society. There are already some signs of this, with evidence that local government electronic service delivery is of poorer quality in areas with lower levels of Internet access (Kuk, 2003).

Governments and agencies are therefore putting in place a variety of access policies that try to overcome the ownership and use inequalities described above. These aim not just to increase access to government data, but also to bring other perceived benefits of access to IT: access to IT-related skills, access to employment information, access to lower-cost online shopping, and so on.

Some initiatives have focused on *increasing ownership*. For example, in 2004, the UK government launched the Home Computing Initiative – a set of tax breaks and other incentives to encourage employers to let staff have computers at home (Pinder, 2004). Other governments have used full payments or subsidies as ways to try to increase the numbers of those who actually own IT.

Ownership initiatives can only go so far and, for many, the costs of personal ownership will remain prohibitive. For these groups, governments may set up initiatives focused on *increasing access* to IT that is government- or community-owned IT. Such IT may be placed in a variety of locations:

- public spaces, such as common areas within shopping malls;
- semi-public spaces, such as libraries or sport facilities;

- dedicated spaces, such as community telecentres housing a room-full of Internet-linked PCs.

Such placement of IT only addresses technology barriers.[5] Here we can mention one other aspect: skill barriers. For some, the skill barriers mean they require the assistance of an *IT intermediary* through whom the citizen indirectly accesses the new IT infrastructure, including electronic public data. Alternatively, they may require an *IT facilitator* who will train them or help them to gain access themselves. These roles may be informal, such as the public librarian who takes time to assist clients, or they may be formal, such as the telecentre worker whose job it is to bring community members online.

Despite all these measures, however, IT inequalities do and will remain. The watchword for government must therefore be 'supplement' not 'supplant'. Provision of public sector data and other services electronically should be seen as an additional weapon in the armory that sits alongside traditional face-to-face and phone-based methods. It should not be seen as a way of replacing those more traditional methods. Unfortunately, cost-cutting pressures in government mean such principles can easily be forgotten. As so often with technological change, it will then be the poor and disadvantaged who find they have gained last and gained least from the new technology.

Privacy Policies for Data Protection

In some countries, data privacy legislation has been introduced although, globally, only just over one-third of nations fall into this category (Zammit, 2000). Legislation does vary but a typical example is given in Box 6.6.

Box 6.6   UK Data Protection Act

In 1998, the UK Data Protection Act was harmonized with legislation across the European Union. It specifies that personal data (digital or paper-based) shall be (Eversheds, 2000):

- processed fairly and lawfully;
- obtained only for one or more specified and lawful purposes, and shall not be further processed in any manner incompatible with that purpose;
- adequate, relevant and not excessive for the specified purposes;
- accurate and, where necessary, kept up to date;
- not kept longer than necessary for the purpose for which it was processed;
- processed in accordance with the rights of data subjects;
- made available to data subjects on request and corrected or erased where appropriate;
- properly protected by appropriate technical measures to prevent unauthorized or unlawful processing or accidental loss or destruction; and
- not transferred outside Europe unless to a country that provides adequate data protection.

The legislation has raised three particular problems for public agencies in Europe, including the UK (Bocij et al., 2003):

- *Conflict with other legislation*: Data Protection legislation appears potentially weaker than the more fundamental Human Rights Act, passed in 1998. The ability of government agencies to access data for investigative purposes (beyond just national security) under the Regulation of Investigatory Powers Act (2000) may also infringe the more protective laws.
- *Problems with international data transfer*: Weak legislation in the US covering personal data held by the private sector is deemed by some to be 'inadequate', thus raising barriers to outsourcing of e-government work to US-based firms. These firms have had to develop internal 'safe harbors' for European data.
- *Lack of clear guidance*: A number of public agencies have faced problems because of a claimed lack of clarity in implementing data protection legislation; for example, where important police intelligence data was wiped from records on the misguided understanding that its retention violated data protection principles.

Data protection legislation chimes very much with information resource management principles, and it has been a significant driver behind centralized data management. It has pressurized public agencies to identify someone senior and central who will be responsible and accountable for the accessibility, confidentiality and accuracy of data held on e-government systems. This person may be a CIO, although increasingly it is the heads of agencies who are legally to be held responsible for policy adherence.

Such pressures are increasing in some countries, such as the US and Canada, with the introduction of privacy impact assessments – mandatory procedures that aim to help public organizations 'determine whether new technologies, IS and initiatives or proposed programs and policies meet basic privacy requirements.' (TBCS, 2002: 1). They have also pushed public web sites into incorporating privacy principles and privacy statements that detail how a site collects data; how that data is used; who the data is shared with; how users can access and correct data; and how users can deactivate from the site or withhold data from third parties (Chaffey, 2002). This has become an issue of higher profile with increasing use of 'cookies': small files transferred into a user's computer when they access a web site that can be used to identify individual users.

Reflecting the access–privacy tension noted above, legislation is also acting to restrict agency activity; particularly setting limits on some of the grander 'one-stop shop' ideas (Wittkemper and Kleindiek, 2003). These ideas can still be applied to data that government already holds in areas related to national security, or where citizens can be persuaded to waive rights to restrictions on data use. In most cases, though, integrated e-government services are only going to be possible with new data gathered at a time when that integration and pooling of data is made known to service users. Where such services are not yet operational, it means public CIOs have to plan well ahead to think how data may be used in future, and to communicate that use clearly to data providers such as citizens or businesses.[6]

Security Policies for Protection of Data

From Figure 6.4, we can see security may be in tension with goals of access and/or income. Many ongoing security issues have been highlighted in earlier sections of this chapter. However, the growing use of web sites within e-government systems followed by the rise in global terrorism plus high-profile computer crime cases has thrown

the issue right to the top of the management agenda. There are concerns that the ease of 'web-izing' government data and the pro-access 'Information shall be free' mantra of the Internet has pushed things too far down the access path.

In 1999, for example, the US Pentagon closed down many of its .mil web sites having discovered those sites had made electronically available:

> a treasure trove of information, including the maintenance status of fighter aircraft engines, air refueling schedules, an Air Force 'how-to' manual for determining targets to attack, and army manuals on small unit tactics and the use of many weapons. ... The director of the Defense Intelligence Agency claimed threats to security no longer come from spies and moles but from simply releasing too much information. (Campbell, 1999: 3)

Despite this type of initial attempt to re-balance the access/security tension, in 2002 a number of governments felt the need to order further reviews. An example of such a review checklist is given in Box 6.7. This was in recognition of the belief that, alongside a mass of legitimate users plus opportunists such as 'mainstream' hackers, were potential groups determined and sustained in their efforts to uncover information that would help them cause harm to specific infrastructural or governmental targets.

The point about 'belief' does need to be noted. While no-one should underestimate the threat of terrorism, it does need to be kept in perspective. A 2002 study of incidents leading organizations to call on contingency backup services found 44 percent to be caused by hardware failure, 20 percent by software failure, 10 percent by power failure, 10 percent by disk failure, and 6 percent by fire, theft or air-conditioning failure (Mathieson, 2002). Less than 2 percent were the result of terrorism/cyber-terrorism.

Box 6.7   Reviewing Sensitive Public Information

The following questions will assist security professionals in reviewing sensitive infor-mation that has been, or could be, made publicly accessible.

- Has the information been cleared and authorized for public release?
- What impact could the information have if it was inadvertently transferred to an unintended audience?
- Does the information provide details concerning enterprise security?
- Does the information contain personnel information such as biographical data, addresses, etc.?
- How could someone intent on causing harm misuse the information?
- What instructions should be given to legitimate custodians of sensitive information with regard to disseminating the information to other parties such as contractors?
- Could this information be dangerous if it were used in conjunction with other publicly available information?
- Could someone use the information to target personnel, facilities or operations?
- Could the same or similar information be found elsewhere?
- Does the information increase the attractiveness of a target? (OCIPEP, 2002)

These beliefs are part of a perception that points to the public data tide washing back from an earlier high water mark of public access, as security outweighs access as a political issue. Partly in the wake of 9/11 and subsequent terrorist activity but more generally in response to rising cyber-crime, governments worldwide have been devel-oping and promoting data security policies, such those that underpin the US 2002 Federal Information Security Management Act. At their heart, such policies are typi-cally based around a risk assessment and mitigation approach: the type of hybrid general controls for data discussed in Chapter 4. However, there are new elements that are emerging including (DHS, 2003; OMB, 2005b):

- *Incident reporting*: Reporting of data secu-rity incidents both within and outside the agency.
- *Review*: Of data security policies to ensure they are working as intended;

that review being itself reported on to some central body, including the report-ing of any data deficiencies (agencies clearly having to balance here the embarrassment of reporting deficiencies versus the risk of some deliberately unre-ported deficiency later coming to public attention).

- *Collaboration*: Working with the private sector on areas of critical data infrastruc-ture, and sharing of knowledge and warnings.
- *Continuity*: Additional emphasis on robust contingency planning to ensure fallbacks in case key e-government systems are attacked.
- *Intelligence*: Greater efforts to identify sources of data attacks.

Alongside, there has been greater emphasis on raising awareness, properly performing threat assessments, and truly implement-ing the best level of data controls possible. One other major change has been the introduction of institutional mechanisms – such as the government-wide IT Security Offices being introduced in some countries and states/provinces – to drive implementation of such policies.

More controversially, the security measures being enacted worldwide are highlighting a tension that surfaces occasionally: the tension between security and privacy (Riley, 2002). It is often felt that data privacy and data security go hand-in-hand: making government data more secure also makes it more private. However, a split between these two has arisen because of a difference of interests: the argued security interests of the nation (including data security) are being pitted against the privacy interests of the individual (including data privacy) (Seifert and Petersen, 2002).

Anti-terror security measures have encouraged data gathering and data matching exercises that, in an earlier context, would be seen to violate privacy rights. In Canada, proposed new data measures have conflicted with privacy laws; in the UK, actual measures have conflicted with data protection legislation. To be a hybrid, then, in relation to data security means more than just combining hard and soft. It means steering a line between different laws and the different interests they represent: the state versus the data subject over privacy. And it means steering a line between different organizational interests: balancing the risks of security breaches and the constraints of security procedures against the need of users for free and easy access to e-government data.

6.3 POLICIES ON OTHER ISSUES

There are many other policy issues of relevance to e-government. Here, we discuss three: disability/accessibility; ergonomics; and Internet usage.

Disability/Accessibility

New technology offers ways to overcome some of the barriers faced by people with disabilities; including barriers of access to government data and government services. To ensure that full advantage is taken of this opportunity to reduce discrimination, a number of countries have introduced anti-discriminatory legislation. For example, in the US, section 508 of the 1973 Rehabilitation Act has been applied to e-government mainly through 1998 amendments; likewise Disability Discrimination Acts in both the UK and Australia cover IT/web applications in government (Howell, 2001).

In order to comply with the legislation, e-government managers have been introducing in-house policies covering the development of IS. In the US, for example, managers have to attend to six main types of technology (Access Board, 2001):

- *Software*: 'Most of the specifications for software pertain to usability for people with vision impairments.'
- *Web sites*: Again provisions mainly relate to 'ensuring access for people with vision impairments who rely on various assistive products to access computer-based information'
- *Telephones*: '[D]esigned primarily to ensure access to people who are deaf or hard of hearing.'
- *Multimedia*: For example captioning of video.
- *Self-contained, closed products*: Such as e-government kiosks, which must allow for private listening and touchscreen control.
- *Computers*: Again must allow non-keyboard forms of data entry, and alternative mechanisms for data output.

The policy requirements that relate to accessibility fall into two main types. First, there are very specific guidelines, such as those provided for e-government web site design (e.g. 'avoid using images to display text', 'avoid using absolute sizes for fonts', 'specify the language of text', 'avoid using emoticons' (ITO, 2002)). Second, there is a set of higher-level issues (DOJ, 2000; 2001):

- *Structures*: A designated agency official responsible for accessibility policies, processes and structures; an external voluntary advisory committee on disability and accessibility.
- *Systems*: Processes and structures for feedback on accessibility including an email contact and a system for complaints and for dispute resolution.
- *Processes*: Training of staff to raise accessibility awareness and skills; ensuring procurement of compliant technology; testing of web pages and other IT before live use in e-government systems; reviewing kiosks for accessibility barriers.

There tends to be relatively little room for balance or hybridization of disability-related policies: the law sets a clear threshold that must be achieved. However, in practice, e-government managers often seem to be 'satisficing' the issue: doing just enough to cover their backs but still leaving a gap between policy and practice. A test of US federal government web sites long after the 2001 deadline for compliance with disability legislation found over half still had accessibility errors (Stowers, 2003). A similar test in the UK found only two out of 1000 sites had attained the required level of accessibility conformance (*E-Government Bulletin*, 2004).

Ergonomics

Ergonomics can be defined as using knowledge of humans' physical and psychological characteristics to design and implement

technology, the arrangement of the work environment, and the organization of the job. By applying ergonomics in the design of e-government systems, health problems can be reduced and efficiency can be increased.

But what are the health problems that have been associated with computing? The main physical symptom is generally seen as repetitive strain injury (RSI) (Laudon and Laudon, 2005). This is damage that occurs through the heavy repetitive use of particular muscles. The commonest form is *carpal tunnel syndrome*, in which a nerve in the wrist is damaged by the repetitive tapping of the fingers on the keyboard. The impact is numbness or 'tightness' or pain in the hand that is often only temporary, but occasionally permanent. RSI is the most serious computer-related health problem. It has led to millions of US dollars'-worth of damages claims from employees who have suffered as a result of long hours of computer-based work. Other possible problems include neck, back or shoulder strain; eyesight problems such as soreness or tiredness; headaches; and skin rashes.

The causes of these problems may relate to the nature of the physical environment in which computing equipment is being used. These include lighting; the physical workspace in terms of design and placing of computer system parts and related work items; and heat, cold and humidity. Levels of radiation have been cited from time to time as a cause for concern. However, current thinking tends towards the opinion that, with modern equipment, especially monitors, radiation levels are too low to affect users' health (Willis, 2003a).

In a number of countries, growing realization about IT-related health problems, especially RSI, has led to ergonomics legislation. In Europe, for example, this legislation has tended to be a mixture of elements based on European Union directives and International Organization for Standardization ergonomic standards (such as standard 9241). This covers issues such as (Stewart, 2000):

- *equipment*: adjustability and clarity of monitors; keyboard design and adjustability; adjustability of work surfaces, chairs and footrests;
- *work environment*: space, light, reflection, noise, heat and radiation; and
- *software interface*: ease of use, adaptability, feedback on performance, nature of human–computer interaction.

The presence of this legislation has meant e-government managers must take actions within their agencies.[7] In general, though, typical policies will include not just actions but also a 'top and tail' of assessment of ergonomic risks, education and training to raise awareness, and ongoing evaluation (DAFS, 2000). Ergonomics issues impinge in two main areas of e-government systems development: design of new systems, and procurement of equipment. In both cases, legislative measures increasingly pressurize managers to incorporate ergonomic considerations into the e-government systems lifecycle.

In doing this, public managers face a difficult balancing act between the requirements of central legislation and the localized needs of the public agency. These may conflict where, for example, the agency has to make the best of an outdated physical environment, or where lack of money means what is ergonomically-best cannot be afforded. This balancing act can appear in the gap between policy on paper and policy in practice. eGovernment managers may develop an internal policy document that fully meets all legislative requirements, but may then not fully implement the document.

The Wider Context of Ergonomics

The types of policies and actions described above focus only on parts of the earlier definition of ergonomics: those related to physical well-being, to technology, and to the physical work environment. Ergonomics goes beyond these and so, too, do the health problems and causes that are associated with the use of IT in e-government.

Perhaps equal with RSI as a health problem is stress; a growing problem in the public sector (Doherty and Horne, 2002). This may be perceived directly by staff as a psychological condition, or may manifest itself in physical conditions such as headache or back ache. It is also likely to manifest itself in poorer work performance and complaints about other aspects of the work environment.

Stress can arise from problems with the physical environment but tends to arise more from the general arrangement and organization of work associated with IT. For internal users of e-government, we can therefore identify a number of potential stressors, including (Alter, 2002, Buchanan and Huczynski, 2004):

- *problematic job design*: such as the rewards, complexity, skills used, degree of personal autonomy, or rate and type of work required, or changes to job contents;
- *problematic management style*: such as autocratic styles or ones that place excessive deadlines and other time pressures;
- *difficult relationships*: with staff or clients, or limitations on communication and participation;
- *uncertainties*: about the future or about technology (e.g. fears about damage from radiation or dangers to pregnant women, even if this fear is unfounded); and
- *divided loyalties*: between groups or between home and work.

Stress may also arise from home- or leisure time-related events.

Dealing with IT-specific stressors, there is no evidence of any link between computer usage and either radiation dangers or an increased risk of miscarriage. However, an unfounded worry or concern can cause increased health risks. Given this, a number of public organizations have accepted that it may be beneficial to temporarily transfer a pregnant worker who is worried about computer work.

The other stressors are not covered here but they are often combated by approaches discussed in Part 2, such as full worker participation and consultation in any process of technology introduction; avoidance of computer monitoring of work; and structuring jobs so that they provide variety, feedback, and control (Baker, 1998; Armstrong, 2003). Unfortunately, there can be a Catch-22 here. Those workers most likely to suffer stress at work are those who are not in control of their work. They are also least likely to be able to bring about the changes in work that would reduce their stress.

As seen above, e-government managers have to take a hybrid approach to ergonomics that balances central and local needs. We see here that they can also benefit from two other hybrid components. First, from mixing hard and soft: attending not just to the technical issues such as lighting and positioning, but also to people-related issues such as consultation and job design. Second, by balancing the interests of different stakeholders: not just focusing on the interests of external stakeholders (likely to demand a minimization of expenditure) but recognizing the importance of agency staff, for whom spending more money and time on good ergonomics may ultimately reap greater rewards. This also reflects the value of taking a longer-term perspective: short-term expenditure on ergonomics may produce longer-term returns in higher staff productivity and also in lower costs of time off sick or, worse, litigation.

This room for maneuver and hybridization comes, in part, because legislation typically does not cover all aspects of ergonomics and/or does not specify what must be done in precise detail.

Internet Usage

As public servants spend increasing amounts of their working lives online, public agencies have been pushed to develop policies guiding online activity. As with many e-government-related policies, the driver for Internet use policy often seems to come from outside public agencies. It may be partly the drive of fear of litigation; it may be partly the drive of guidance from central agencies (see, for example, GSA, 1999); and it may be partly mimetic effects that spread from one agency to another. The overriding issue in all cases, though, seems to be concerns about the 'cyber-liability' of public agencies (Eversheds, 2000). Liabilities may cover civil issues (such as defamation by a public servant via an email or web site, or email harassment) or criminal issues (such as obscenity, spreading of computer viruses, or breach of copyright, data protection or other relevant legislation).

An example of such a policy is summarized in Box 6.8. This 'Internet Acceptable Use Policy' has to be signed by all employees. It represents one way in which public agencies are attempting to make usage of network-based systems more formal, consistent and organizationally rational.

Box 6.8   Internet Acceptable Use Policy, Kern County, CA

Policy components include (Pell, 1999):

- *Acceptable Use*: Internet use is intended to support organizational goals, within organizational guidelines.
- *Privileges*: Internet use is a privilege, not a right, which can be withdrawn.
- *Privacy*: Internet use can be monitored and employees can have no expectation of privacy.
- *Email Guidelines*: On good practice in email use over the Internet.[8]
- *Unacceptable Use*: The Internet is not to be used for purposes conflicting with departmental goals or for illegal or unethical purposes. This includes personal usage (though, see discussion in main text) and transmission of material that is likely to be pornographic, racist or sexist; that contains language inappropriate for an office environment; or that contains a virus. It also includes sharing accounts or sending messages in someone else's name.
- *Penalties*: Inappropriate use will result in account cancellation. Misuse can result in disciplinary action, potentially leading to job termination, or prosecution for illegal actions.
- *Services*: No warranties are provided, nor is there any responsibility for the accuracy of information obtained; there is no responsibility for damages suffered while using the Internet.
- *Security*: Security guidelines must be followed.

As in the example in Box 6.8, some public agencies are drawing up policies that bar personal usage of computing equipment and which provide for monitoring of that usage. Others adopt a 'missing middle' approach: they state that IT is to be used for work purposes (but avoid the word 'only'); they state that ICTs should not used for illegal, obscene, political, etc purposes; but they leave unstated the issue of more mainstream personal usage (e.g. City of Dayton, 2001).

The third approach is that some agencies do explicitly allow some personal usage, so long as it is not excessive, and so long as it does not fall foul of various unacceptable use prohibitions (e.g. City of Richmond, 2001). Monitoring in this case might not be random, but only carried out if there was some legitimate reason, with results kept confidential. Any productivity losses from this rather looser regime may be more than counterbalanced by greater employee morale, and greater freedom for a free flow of ideas and discussion on work-related topics.

Here, then, we again see a hybrid response that balances central and local, and the needs of different stakeholders. The capacity for hybridization has typically been greater for Internet usage than for the other policy areas discussed here because the legislative framework covers fewer elements and/or is looser in its guidance. However, this flexibility is changing over time as case law and concerns grow about cyber-liability.[9]

ACTIVITIES

Shorter In-Class Activities[10]

Section 6.1

a. Reflect on your own work and educational experience to discuss whether you feel it is better for e-government managers to manage performance of individuals or of groups.

b. Develop two points in favor and two points against the following statement: 'Performance management in the public sector is the same as performance management in the private sector.'

c. If you were managing the IS/IT function in a public agency, which one of the three financial control mechanisms listed in Box 6.3 would you prefer to be subjected to, and why?

d. Some of the performance criteria for progress towards e-government by US agencies cited in Box 6.4 can be given in more detail:

Integration of citizen one-stop services delivery through FirstGov.gov, cross agency call centers, and offices or service centers;
   Minimization of burden on business by re-using data previously collected or using XML or other open standards to receive transmissions;
   Intergovernmental deployment of E-Grants or Geospatial One-Stop; and
   Obtainment of productivity improvements by implementing customer relationship management, supply chain management, enterprise resource management, or knowledge management best practices. (OMB, 2003: 8)

Discuss how easy or difficult it would be to turn these criteria into measurable performance indicators.

Section 6.2

a. Discuss the following question: 'Does it matter if our children cannot access the electronic data that is being created today within government?' Come up with at least two arguments in favor of the answer 'Yes', and at least two arguments in favor of the answer 'No'.

b. Think of all the people in your local city/town. How is the spread of the Internet going to affect their ability to access personal and other data held by the public sector: will access be likely to be improved, worsened, or unchanged? You will need to differentiate between different groups within society.

c. Discuss which is more important: providing access to government data or protecting privacy of individuals on whom government keeps data.

Sections 6.2–6.3

a. 'eGovernment managers develop policies in order to reduce risks, not in order to deliver organizational benefits.' Discuss in pairs then plenary.

Section 6.3

a. The policy components listed in Box 6.8 are a few years' old. Do changes in technology, policy or political priorities mean they are now outdated?

Assignment Questions

Section 6.1

a. Based on a review of current ideas on motivation in the public sector workplace, develop a set of good practice recommendations for performance management of e-government-related staff.

Section 6.2

a. How has freedom of information (access) and data protection (privacy) legislation changed in your country of study over the past ten years? What impact has this had on data policies within public agencies?

Sections 6.2–6.3

a. Select a country with which you familiar. Identify the main e-government-related policies that a typical public agency in that country would need to develop. In what ways could these policies by hybridized?

Practitioner Exercises

Section 6.1

a. How is the performance of IS/IT staff currently managed in your organization? What improvements could be made to performance management? How could these improvements be implemented?

b. How is the performance of the IS/IT function currently managed in your organization? In your answer, be specific about indicators, measurement and control. What improvements could be made to performance management? How could these improvements be implemented?

c. How is the performance of e-government currently managed in your organization? What improvements could be made to

performance management? How could these improvements be implemented?

Section 6.2

a. What archiving procedures are in place in your organization? Are they set up to cope with electronic records? What improvements, if any, are needed to encompass electronic record-keeping?

b. How is the growth of the Internet likely to affect access to data and services for your organization's major client groups – will access be worsened, improved or unchanged? What actions should be taken?

c. Make some notes on the following questions:

- What data does your organization store on individuals – both employees and citizens?
- Who is allowed access to that data: (a) within your organization; (b) from other public sector organizations; (c) from private sector firms and individuals?
- Does this access conflict with privacy concerns?
- What is the relationship between income generation, access and privacy?
- What other issues of accessibility, confidentiality and accuracy does this storage raise?
- Are there any changes that could be made which would help to address these issues?

Note down any implications for e-government systems in your organization.

Sections 6.2–6.3

a. What e-government-related policies does your organization currently have? Consider all of the management issues and areas identified in Part 1: can you identify any policy gaps in your organization on this basis? Are policies honored more in the breach than in the observance: if so, does this matter?

NOTES

1. Two further 'Ps' – Principles and Place – are discussed in the Online Appendix for this chapter.

2. International evaluation studies are discussed further in the Online Appendix for this chapter.

3. See the Online Appendix for this chapter for more details on national e-government targets.

4. Further policy issues, relating to data quality and to other aspects of data access and privacy are discussed in the Online Appendix for this chapter.

5. This issue – the fact that there are many other divides besides just a digital divide in relation to government and disadvantaged citizens – is taken up in more detail in the Online Appendix for this chapter.

6. Some other issues around data privacy are noted in the Online Appendix for this chapter.

7. Details are provided in this chapter's Online Appendix of specific actions that managers can take.

8. A generic example of email guidelines is given in the Online Appendix for this chapter.

9. Specific issues of cyber-liability related to public sector email and web systems are discussed in the Online Appendix for Chapter 11.

10. Details of longer group activities are provided in the Online Appendix to this chapter.

Part Two
Implementing eGovernment

7

eGovernment System Lifecycle and Project Assessment

Key Points

- eGovernment projects typically involve a cycle of five stages: project assessment, analysis of current reality, design of the new system, system construction, implementation and beyond.
- eGovernment applications can be developed by many different methodologies over which participants may or may not have choice.
- Success in e-government comes from intelligent selection of individual techniques, from 'hybrid thinking', and from action on design–reality gaps rather than from slavish adherence to one particular methodology.
- Background understanding of a proposed e-government project comes from asking five questions: Who is involved? What is the problem? Why is the project happening? What constraints exist? What will change in the near future?
- eGovernment projects can be assessed in relation to their feasibility, priority, opportunity costs, and impact.
- Rational e-government project management deals with issues of how the project will be approached, who will do the work, what resources are required, and when elements will be delivered.

7.1 THE SYSTEM LIFECYCLE

Part 2 overall looks at the way in which new e-government systems are developed. Innumerable methods for systems development have been created, with a variance here or there, but all of them correspond more or less to four core stages:

- *analysis* of what is currently happening, and of whether and why a new e-government system is needed;
- *design* of the new e-government system's components;

- *construction* of the new e-government system;
- *implementation* of the new e-government system.

The method suggested in this part follows these stages, but also applies the logic of design–reality gaps discussed in Chapter 1. Any e-government systems project seeks to create a new situation that is different from the current one. The greater the difference between the new and current situations, the greater the degree of change that is required, and the greater the likelihood of system failure. Successfully planned e-government systems will therefore be those that require a manageable degree of change.

In order to assess this 'degree of change', the core of the systems development method described here will therefore consist of three activities:

- mapping out the realities of the current situation;
- designing a proposal for the new situation; and
- assessing the difference between the two, and reacting to that difference.

The design–reality differences could be assessed on each and every one of the elements listed in the onion-ring model of systems and their environment in Chapter 1. Here, though, the focus will be just on the seven ITPOSMO checklist dimensions also presented in Chapter 1, since these were identified as being necessary and sufficient to provide an understanding of design–reality gaps. As a reminder, these dimensions are:

- Information
- Technology
- Processes
- Objectives and values
- Staffing and skills
- Management systems and structures
- Other resources: money and time

Integrating these ideas into the four core stages listed above, and then topping and tailing them with assessment and post-implementation activities, the outline of the method presented in Part 2 can be described as a set of five stages:

1 *Project assessment*: Identifying possible e-government projects; outlining basic project parameters; and assessing whether or not to proceed with the project.

2 *Analysis of current reality*: Description and analysis of the seven ITPOSMO dimensions as they exist within the current situation of the organization.

3 *Design of the proposed new situation*: Setting objectives for the proposed new e-government system, and then describing in general terms how the seven ITPOSMO dimensions should be different for the new system to meet these objectives. Different options for the new system may be evaluated at this point.

4 *System construction*: Acquiring any new technology; undertaking detailed design of the new system; then building it, testing it and documenting it.

5 *Implementation and beyond*: Training users to use the new system; converting data to new formats; introducing the new system; monitoring and evaluating its performance and context; then undertaking any necessary system maintenance.

Assessing and mitigating risks (the degree of change between current reality and new proposal design) is identified as a separate activity. It could take place after general design. However, in practice, risk-related techniques are normally undertaken as an integral part of stages 1 to 3: a point discussed further in Chapter 10.

Overall, the stages can be called a 'systems development lifecycle' because the post-implementation stages may lead to the identification of a new e-government project, thus restarting the whole process again. The lifecycle is shown in Figure 7.1.

In practice, no method is as neat as this diagram might suggest because of two things. First, *parallelism*: activities running simultaneously. For example, analysis of current reality and general proposal design tend to overlap, with continuous analysis of the gap between the two. Second, *iteration*: looping back from a later step to an earlier

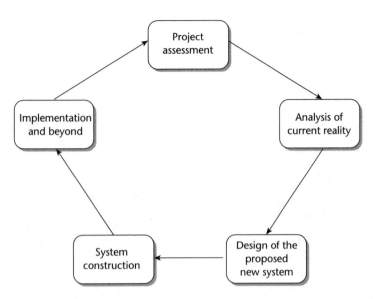

Figure 7.1   The e-government systems development lifecycle

one. For example, an issue thrown up during analysis of current reality may alter the basic project parameters and require re-assessment of the project. Alternatively, a problem during system implementation may lead to a realization that current reality needs to be re-analyzed and the e-government proposal redesigned.

Getting 'Behind the Method'

The approach described here is selected because of its perceived value, but there are many other methods that could be of relevance. One method used in a number of public sectors is SSADM: Structured Systems Analysis and Design Methodology, summarized in Figure 7.2 (Weaver et al., 1998: 5).

SSADM differs from the method presented in this book in two ways. First, as illustrated, it focuses mainly on the feasibility, analysis and design stages of the lifecycle, with relatively little to say about later stages. Second, it is a relatively 'hard' method that focuses in detail on data, processes and technology. Other methods – such as those based on 'soft systems' ideas – are more holistic and systemic in approach, and are more interested in human and organizational aspects of a situation.

The method presented in this book has both hard and soft components. We therefore would call it a hybrid method because it integrates these two different perspectives. It could also take the 'socio-technical' label introduced in Chapter 1 since it combines consideration of both the social (i.e. people and organizations) and the technical (i.e. data, processes and technology) (Avison and Fitzgerald, 2003).

No method is perfect but there are dangers for the public sector in adopting some of the harder methods. The public sector has had a tendency to choose such methods which then prove too old, inflexible, top-down, detailed, jargonized and

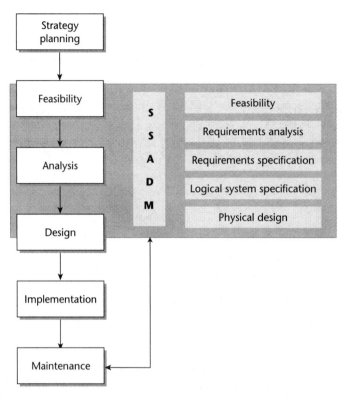

Figure 7.2   Overview of SSADM

time-consuming (Korac-Boisvert and Kouzmin, 1995). While these might have been appropriate to the routine clerical automations of the 1960s, they work poorly in politicized situations of change and uncertainty. Their selection has therefore been identified as a causal factor in e-government failures. In one UK e-government system failure, 'The tools employed using SSADM techniques were clearly inadequate in addressing the rich organizational realities involved.' (Dhillon, 1998: 9).

Beyond arguments about which method is best, it must be recognized that there is no room for maneuver in some situations. Some public sector organizations mandate that one method alone be used for systems development. In other situations,

choice of method will depend on factors such as:

- *The system developer(s)*: Methods that a developer has experience of will be preferred to those that are new. Developers also have innate preferences that are relevant. Some, for instance, will prefer hard methods; others will prefer soft methods.
- *The size of system*: Small e-government systems cannot justify such a comprehensive approach as that listed here. Instead, one or two of the most relevant aspects only need be used. The larger the system, the more one can justify a greater systems development effort.
- *The nature of the organization*: More participative, human- or user-centered

methods are difficult to apply in some public sector organizational cultures. In these cases, more top-down, centralized methods are likely to be employed.

It must also be recognized that – while the method presented here attempts to understand and work with differences between organizational rationality and personal politics (see Chapter 1) – it makes some assumptions that are organizationally rational. Among other things, these are assumptions about the logical structuring of activities, the purpose of management behavior, cause–effect relationships, and freedom to choose.

These assumptions will not hold in all situations. For example, systems development assumes that a large number of decisions will be taken about every aspect of the new system. In a risk-averse organizational culture, where decision making is avoided if at all possible, this may be difficult to achieve.

Public sector managers are frequently admonished for their failure to follow basic systems development techniques: assessing feasibility, setting objectives, analyzing requirements, and so on. In some cases, their failure to do so may be put down to impatience or to ignorance and lack of training.

In other cases, though, managers are well aware of what they are supposed to do. Their failure arises not from ignorance but from the gap between the assumed rationality of the development methods and the practical realities in which managers find themselves working. Thus e-government systems continue to fail in the public sector in spite of the plethora of available methods and the spread of information systems training. All this should act as a warning that any individual method may be of some assistance, but it may not all be applicable and cannot guarantee perfect results.

More important than slavishly following any one method, indeed, are two things:

- *Intelligent selection of relevant individual techniques*: System development methods for e-government should be seen as toolkits from which to pick and choose, rather than as one homogeneous block. As presented here or in other books, system development methods can seem long, complex and overwhelming. However, their only intention is to help you think, plan and apply lessons of best practice. With this in mind, applying just a few techniques is likely to be better than not planning at all.
- *Hybrid thinking*: This involves (adapted from Laudon and Laudon, 1995: 316):

  o Understanding problems before solutions. Suspending judgment so that, for example, e-government solutions are not prescribed until problems have been properly understood.
  o Understanding situations from multiple perspectives. First, from the perspectives of the different ITPOSMO dimensions: as an arrangement of information, as a collection of technology, as a set of processes, and so on. Second, from the perspectives of the different individuals and groups involved: computer operators, managerial users of information, politicians, IT staff, vendors, organizational clients, citizens, and so on.
  o Being open to a consideration of alternatives. For example, deliberating the possibility of not introducing new IT, but altering other aspects of the information system instead.
  o Being aware of the personal and organizational constraints that limit room for maneuver.

Overall, the presence of creative individuals who possess these skills, and an ability to close design–reality gaps matter more than any particular system development method.

7.2 PROJECT ASSESSMENT

Identifying a Project

New e-government projects typically arise in one of two ways. First, identification of a problem that needs to be solved ('If it ain't broke, don't fix it; if it is broke, do fix it.'). Second, identification of an opportunity which could be seized ('Even if it ain't broke, keep trying to improve it.').

Such problems and opportunities arise from many possible sources. These sources can be any of the factors identified in the onion-ring model illustrated in Figure 1.2. They can arise from the external environment or from internal sources. They can be rational or political or personal. They can form part of a broader strategy or program/portfolio or stand alone.

External examples include:

- complaints from citizens, politicians or the media;
- new legislation or directives or other pressures from external institutions, including those framed within the context of public sector reform;
- external economic, political or social crisis;
- technological innovation;
- observation of sister organizations; or
- the political need to project a more modern image for the organization.

Internal examples include:

- a previously conducted strategic planning exercise or consultancy report;
- a survey of staff problems or suggestions;
- shortfalls in work performance measures;
- financial resources being available that need to be spent on something before financial year end;
- an individual's desire to give their career a boost; or
- an individual's desire to earn kickbacks from IT suppliers.

In practice, e-government projects often seem to arise more from the garbage-can model of decision making than from any rational model; in other words, they are solutions (perhaps opportunities) looking for problems (Yildiz, 2003). If some rationality is to be introduced into the process then, once an idea for an e-government project has arisen from whatever source, four factors can be assessed:

- *Feasibility*: In practical terms, can this project be implemented successfully or not?
- *Priority*: If there are competing projects, which one should be given priority?
- *Opportunity*: Even if there are no competing projects, how else could the resources for this project be better invested?
- *Impact*: If the project is implemented, what impacts might it have?

Gathering Information on the Project

This sub-section describes the way in which information is gathered on a proposed e-government project in order to assess whether or not to proceed with it, using a basic – who, what, why – approach. If required, these can all be compiled together into an initial project proposal.

1 Stakeholder Analysis: Who is Involved?

Stakeholders are those individuals or groups who have a stake in the success of the new project. It is they who are the main determinant of whether the project proceeds or is scrapped, and of whether a project succeeds or fails. If in doubt about stakeholder identity, ask 'Who has the power/ability to make the project and system fail in some way?' Their views and objectives need to be understood, and there is increasing use of hybrid approaches to e-government that balance the

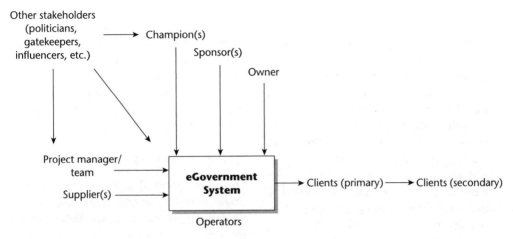

Figure 7.3   Stakeholder map for an e-government project

needs and interests of different stakeholders (Jupp, 2003).

Past discussion – for example in Chapter 5 – has identified a number of possible key stakeholders, summarized in Figure 7.3.

The stakeholders are:

- *Project manager/team*: Those who will analyze, design and build the e-government system.
- *Supplier(s)*: Those who will supply the technology and other resources required by the e-government system.
- *Operators*: Those who will be carrying out the activities/processes that make the e-government system work.
- *Clients*: Primary clients are on the immediate receiving end of what the e-government system does or outputs. Sometimes these will be outside government (e.g. citizens or businesses). Sometimes, though, these will be inside government (i.e. public servants): in this case, there may also be secondary clients who will be affected indirectly by the system since they are served by the primary clients (e.g. citizens served by those public servants).

- *Champion(s)*: The person (or group) who drives the project on and seeks to justify its implementation.
- *Sponsor(s)*: The person (or group) who pays for the expense and effort required to develop the new e-government system.
- *Owner*: The manager of the organization or department that will own and use the system, who is ultimately responsible for the system.
- *Other stakeholders*: Who have a significant influence on the project or on whom the project will have a significant influence.

One point to note is that two stakeholding groups can be identified: those involved with development of the e-government system; and those involved with operation of the e-government system. These groups overlap, but not completely.

In analyzing the stakeholders it is useful to ask:

- To what extent are the roles present? If there is no project champion, for instance, it is unlikely to succeed.

- To what extent is there overlap between the roles? If, for example, the sponsor, owner and champion are all the same person, this bodes well for the project.
- If roles are separated, to what extent is there conflict or cooperation between the different stakeholders? When there is conflict, the project may not succeed.
- From among all the stakeholders, who are the *opinion leaders*: those whom others will watch to see if they accept the new e-government system and the changes it may entail? Within the opinion leaders particularly, but within all stakeholder groups generally, what is the balance between:

  o *resistors*: those with a vested interest in the existing system, or those who have a general dislike of change; and
  o *adopters*: those with a vested interest in the new system, or those with are quick to pick up new methods and techniques?

2 Problem Statement: What is the Problem?

It is likely that most e-government systems are currently driven by a perceived problem rather than a perceived opportunity (though the management of public relations may demand that problems are presented as opportunities!). It may therefore be useful to create a *problem statement*: a single sentence that tries to encapsulate who or what the problem relates to, and what exactly is wrong, without trying to define a solution. This statement may well be defined by the most powerful stakeholders.

Understanding the true nature of the problem is not easy, and a significant part of the analysis stage – which comes next (see Chapter 8) – is likely to involve delving deeper into the problem. Thus, at this stage – if political factors make it possible – any statement should not be cast in stone, but

should be altered if further analysis makes it clear that the fundamental problem that needs to be addressed lies elsewhere. It may be appropriate to analyze the problem in some depth even now.

Where the project is truly opportunity- rather than problem-driven, an *opportunity statement* can be drawn up instead.

3 Project Rationale: Why?

This is a simple definition, possibly in a single sentence, of the main objective for the new e-government system sought by the most powerful stakeholders. In most situations it would relate to alleviating the previously identified problem (or making use of the identified opportunity). For some projects, this will fit within a strategic framework, discussed in Chapter 3. For some projects, a rather more detailed cost/benefit analysis would be required; a topic returned to in Chapter 9.

It is important to differentiate between formally stated objectives and the true drivers of an e-government project. These two things could be the same but in most e-government projects, they are not. Let us take the example of a new e-procurement system. The organizationally rational and formally stated objective for this might be 'to improve the efficiency of the department's procurement process'. But the true drivers could be things such as:

- a politician's desire to court the small business vote by spreading procurement more widely;
- an official's desire to demonstrate tangible signs of change in the department to political masters;
- a need to demonstrate greater transparency to overseas investors;
- a need to meet legislative targets for e-government.

Even if not spoken of publicly, these true drivers have to be recognized. Without them, you have no real answer to the question 'Why are we doing this?'.

4 Constraint Analysis: What Constraints?

Driver analysis – particularly of political and personal drivers – helps you understand what pushes an e-government project forwards. Constraint analysis helps you understand the roadblocks that hold an e-government project back.

Constraints will vary from situation to situation. You can use the ITPOSMO checklist to identify these. For example:

- *Technology*: What technical infrastructure (telecommunications, computer systems, etc.) is/is not available that the project may require?
- *Objectives and values*: Based on the stakeholder analysis and the subsequent set of questions, what support/opposition is this project likely to attract?
- *Staffing and skills*: How many/how few people could work on this project? What skills are available/not available that are likely to be relevant to this project? To what extent are these in-house, and to what extent held by external consultants, suppliers, and so on? Are the necessary client skills for system operation available?
- *Other resources*: How much/how little money is available for this project? How much/how little time is available for this project? Is there a deadline?
- *Other dimensions*: What other constraints exist that will affect this project (government policies or guidelines; quality of existing data; (in)flexibility of current procedures; quality of local IT suppliers; and so on)?

Any individuals involved in the process of e-government system development, can valuably identify their own constraints and 'room for maneuver'. This may include asking questions such as:

- *Personal objectives*: 'What do I personally want from this new e-government project?'
- *Personal qualities*: 'To what extent do I have the skills, knowledge and confidence to intervene in the process of system development?'
- *Direct control*: 'What money, time, human and other power resources (see Chapter 5) do I have direct control over that I could bring to bear on the e-government project?'
- *Indirect control*: 'To what extent do I have influence (see also Chapter 5) over other stakeholders? Could I influence them to change their objectives, to provide more resources, to choose a different consultant or supplier, and so on?'

Identifying room for maneuver is critical in understanding the extent to which an individual can and will make a difference to e-government system development. In many cases it will be limited because of politics: 'IT officials nationwide complain about their inability to stop elected officials from trying to please their constituencies by spending money on systems, some of which are doomed to disappoint before they're even plugged in.' (Barrett and Greene, 2001: 108).

5 Environmental Prediction: What Next?

A classic systems failure is to create a new e-government system suitable for today, but not for tomorrow. To guard against this, some type of 'crystal ball gazing' is required to anticipate future conditions within which the e-government application will have to operate. Typical points to be answered include:

- How long is the new system likely to last? Given the rapidity of change, not least technical change, many system projects only aim initially for a lifespan of a few years.
- How is the operation of the e-government system likely to change over its lifetime? Is it, for instance, likely to expand its coverage if successful?
- What kind of changes are likely to occur within the system's environment during this timeframe? Such changes may relate to the organization, to the main client or political stakeholders, to finances and other resources, to new technologies, to the economic and legislative and political environment of the public sector, and so on.
- Given all the changes, is the e-government system likely to be sustainable? Sustainable e-government systems require sustainable ITPOSMO dimensions. Above all, in the public sector, this relates to politics (objectives and values), money (other resources), and competencies (staffing and skills):
  - *Politics*: There must be a continuing need and rationale for the e-government system if it is to continue operating. There must also be continuing political support. A system is unlikely to be sustainable if it is dependent on a section head who will be rotated to another job in 18 months' time, or on an external consultant/champion who is soon to depart. There also needs to be an absence of support for a different system; yet pressure of prestige, career advancement, and from technology suppliers may encourage the premature abandonment of e-government systems.

  - *Money*: There must be sufficient money in future to cover the system's recurrent costs which, as described in Chapter 9, may be considerable.
  - *Competencies*: A system is unlikely to be sustainable if all the staff with operational or maintenance skills leave and cannot be replaced, or if those staff are re-assigned to a different project. There must also be some way to retain knowledge within the organization about the construction and operation of the system. System documentation, described in Chapter 11, can help achieve this to some extent, but not completely.

Project Summary Statement: The CATWOE Checklist

In thinking about and discussing a potential e-government project, it can be useful to have a single statement that summarizes the project. Such statements need to be concise enough to make them usable, but comprehensive enough to include the important aspects of the project. To help with this process, the CATWOE checklist can be used as a reminder of key system components (Bell and Wood-Harper, 2003).

The checklist, summarized in Figure 7.4, consists of:

- *Clients*: As identified under stakeholder analysis.
- *Actors*: The operators identified under stakeholder analysis.
- *Transformation*: What the e-government application is actually intended to do or achieve on a day-to-day basis: the way it changes inputs into outputs; this could be expressed in terms of transactions supported, or conversion of data into information.
- *Worldview*: The view or assumption that makes the e-government application

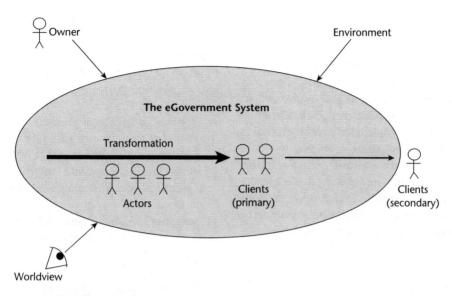

Figure 7.4 CATWOE summary

relevant or important; can be taken here to represent the main rationale behind introducing the new system.

- *Owner:* The person who has enough power to cause the e-government application to cease to exist; could be the sponsor or owner identified under stakeholder analysis.
- *Environment:* The important parts of the wider world that will impose conditions or constraints on the e-government application; can include future environmental changes.

The summary statement can either be written out as this CATWOE list, or as a single sentence that incorporates some or all of the elements. An example checklist for a new e-procurement system in a Department of Agriculture could be:

- *Clients:* The organization's suppliers.
- *Actors:* Purchasing section staff.
- *Transformation:* To support the process of tenders, bids and contracting.

- *Worldview:* To increase the average speed of the total procurement process from two weeks to two days.
- *Owner:* The Department Secretary.
- *Environment:* Limited financial resources; staff fears of job losses; Treasury pressures for efficiency gains.

A brief project summary statement incorporating some of these elements could be:

An e-procurement system owned at the highest level and run by the purchasing section that will support the process of tenders, bids and contracting, allowing a two-day average total-procurement time.

Assessing the Project: The 'Business Case'

As previously stated, e-government projects can be assessed in four principal ways – each of which is described here – to create (or refute) a 'business case' for the project.

1 Project Feasibility

This is the first quick and dirty attempt to check the gap that exists between current reality and the new design required in order to implement the proposed e-government system. The intention is to look at risks in order to assess whether or not it makes sense to proceed with the project.

At this stage, the assessment of some factors will be little more than guesswork since reality analysis has not been undertaken, let alone design. Therefore feasibility assessment can be returned to at regular intervals during the life-cycle as more information becomes known.

There are many factors that can be assessed in order to judge whether or not it is feasible to proceed with a proposed e-government project. We could group these under the ITPOSMO headings. However, to break the monotony of ITPOSMO for once and as a reminder that it is just one among a number of possible systems checklists, we will use a different list. Focusing just on some key points in the public sector, feasibility can be corralled under the PoTHOleS acronym: Politics, Technology, Hard cash (i.e. finance), Other lesser resources, and Sustainability. Each of these can be regarded as a pre-condition for successful development and operation of an e-government system:

- *Political feasibility*: Four things can be assessed here:

  o To what extent does the project have strong political/legal drivers?
  o To what extent is the new system supported by the key stakeholders, including clients?
  o To what extent will the interests of different stakeholders conflict over the new system?
  o To what extent will the new system be resisted by key stakeholders, including the actors who will actually use the system?

Putting these four elements together – drivers, support, conflict and resistance – provides your best overall guide to e-government feasibility. The other issues here are important, but not as important.

- *Technical feasibility*: Is it likely that the proposed system can run on existing or purchasable technology that will operate in the organization's environment? A technical specialist may need to advise on this.
- *Hard cash – financial feasibility*: Does the organization have access to sufficient finance to fund the development and operation of this e-government system?
- *Other lesser resource feasibility*: Does the organization have access to the time, people, skills and management capacity necessary to develop and operate the e-government system? This would include consideration of outsourcing options.
- *Sustainability*: Will the political and other resource inputs necessary to continue operating the e-government system remain available throughout its lifetime?

These pre-conditions can be reversed to identify circumstances in which proceeding with the e-government project as currently planned may not be advisable:

- if it lacks support, especially among key stakeholders such as senior managers, politicians and external clients;
- if it will create conflict between stakeholder groups;
- if it will be resisted by key stakeholders;
- if it requires complex or leading-edge technology;
- if there are insufficient funds to develop and operate the system;
- if there are insufficient other resources to develop and operate the system; or
- if necessary inputs will not be available for the intended lifetime of the system.

As well as drawing these up as a list, you can also represent them via a modified force-field diagram that sets drivers against constraints (see Chapter 9 for a slightly different example).

2 Project Priorities

One way to choose between projects is to look at their assessed feasibility, and prioritize those projects that look most feasible. More formal/rational ways of prioritizing according to the balance of costs and benefits are described in Chapter 9. A simple variant on this is the question: 'What level of resources is it worth investing in this project?' Yet other criteria were outlined in Chapter 3, relating to impact and implementation factors, that may set the project within a more strategic or portfolio perspective.

Ultimately, though, priorities may well be determined by the personal objectives of the most powerful stakeholders. If feasible, one could get them to rate the perceived importance of projects. Some such rating methods are described in Chapter 9.

3 Project Opportunity Costs

Only rarely is the question asked: 'What else could we invest these resources in if we did not invest them in this e-government project?' If the question *is* asked it can produce surprising results. Stakeholders may suddenly become aware that a large amount of money and time is about to be spent on something that no-one particularly wants.

4 Project Impacts

eGovernment systems are increasingly interwoven into the fabric of the public sector and, as a result, they have a growing impact on the work of the public sector. At this point in the lifecycle, then, impact assessment exercises may be conducted, such as the privacy impact assessments described in Chapter 6.

Project Planning and Management: How, Who, What and When?

Once a decision has been made to proceed further with an e-government project, plans are normally made for that project. This will typically involve decisions about:

- *How*: The approach to systems development to be used; the main stages and tasks that will have to be undertaken in order to develop any new system; and the deliverables that form their output (reports, diagrams, decisions, acquired or developed IT, etc.).
- *Who*: The staff involved in systems development from both inside and outside the organization.
- *What*: The financial, technological and other resources that will be required for development.
- *When*: The timetable that will be worked to. Project milestones can be inserted as points for project review based on time (e.g. every week), money (e.g. after a certain amount has been spent), or on the deliverables (e.g. after the project assessment, after the analysis of current reality, etc.).

Formal project management techniques are sometimes used here, for large or well-structured projects. Some of these techniques were described in Chapter 5. For example, Gantt charts can be used to plan when particular activities will be undertaken and when particular resources will be required. Formal planning may also include separate consideration of how system quality will be assured.

As noted in Chapter 5, though, a wholly rational approach to projects may not be best. For many projects, a more hybrid approach will be suitable. This recognizes systems development as a flexible process of discovery, gradual understanding and iteration, more than the step-by-step implementation of pre-arranged activities. If e-government projects are planned around the step-by-step ideal they will, at the least, probably over-run their schedules and/or budgets. At worst, they will not see the wood for the trees; focusing so much on quantitative factors that the system produced fails to meet user needs, political requirements and the like. Instead, such projects need flexible contingency plans. They also need to be managed using the techniques discussed in Chapter 10 on closing the design–reality gap, which can be seen as part of separate risk assessment and mitigation.

In terms of staffing, a project team will need to be put together representing key stakeholder groups bringing together political, management, user and technical inputs. A key success factor will be ensuring that the team is also hybrid in its competencies (for more detail, see Chapter 12).

In terms of technological resources, the planning, management and development of e-government systems can be supported by IT in various ways (Yeates and Cadle, 2002):

- *Primary office automation*: Word processing to record text details of systems and to create proposals and reports; databases to record details of different e-government projects or of staff attached to such projects; and spreadsheets to record financial details of projects.
- *Secondary office automation*: Graphics packages to create the various different diagrams used in e-government systems development; and project management packages to manage the human, financial and other resources of each e-government project.
- *Programming languages*: These are used to create the e-government system software.
- *Computer-aided software engineering tools and systems*: These provide support for all or part of the development process; they might help, for example, to record and revise e-government systems and other processes; they may include data dictionaries.
- *Groupware*: This typically provides a set of software tools that can be used to facilitate group communication, decision making, and documentation.

ACTIVITIES

Shorter In-Class Activities[1]

Section 7.1

a. 'You don't need to plan e-government systems. You just get on and build them.' Discuss in pairs then plenary.

b. What steps would you follow in developing a new e-government system? Discuss in pairs then plenary.

c. What kind of e-government systems developer would you be? Identify yourself on a continuum from hard to soft development methods.

Section 7.2

a. Discuss which of the PoTHOleS factors you believe is the most important in determining the feasibility of an e-government project.

b. On assessment, you find that your e-government project does not appear feasible. Identify two actions you would take in this situation.

c. Discuss what e-government projects need: more or less formality in their planning.

Assignment Questions

Section 7.1

a. Compare and contrast the hard and the hybrid/socio-technical approaches for developing e-government systems. What are the implications of these approaches (a) on the process (assess, analyze, design, construct and implement) of introducing e-government systems, and (b) on the skill requirements of systems developers? If you had to choose between these approaches for the public sector, which one would you follow, and why?

b. Compare and contrast development of information systems in the public and private sectors.

Practitioner Exercises

Section 7.2

a. What is the relevance and applicability to your public sector organization of all the techniques described in the project assessment section? Note down any implications of your answer for e-government systems development in the organization.

eGovernment Project Development Exercises

This is a set of exercises intended either to put the techniques of Part 2 into practice, or to practice the techniques of Part 2. If you are working on a live project, you can do the former;

if working on a practice project, you can do the latter. Practice projects could be identified from any local public sector organization – local arms of central/federal government agencies; state/city/local government departments; local public libraries; local public schools; local public health facilities; and so on.

1   Select the possible e-government project, and undertake stakeholder analysis.
2   Write a brief problem/opportunity statement for the project.
3   Write a sentence of project rationale. Make sure you identify true political drivers.
4a Write a list of project constraints. Which is the most critical constraint?
4b Write down your own room for maneuver. How will this affect what you can do on the project?
5   Answer the 'crystal ball' questions listed in the main text and assess for how long the project is likely to be sustainable.
6   Create a CATWOE list for the project.
7   Assess the project's feasibility, priority, opportunity costs, and impact.
8a Select the type of approach to project planning and management that will be used: rational, behavioral or hybrid (see Chapter 5 for further details).
8b Set out plans for the how, who, what and when of the e-government project. Include details of those risk mitigation techniques listed in Chapter 10 that you may wish to employ.
8c Identify the IT to be used in supporting management and development of the e-government system.

NOTE

1. Details of longer group activities are provided in the Online Appendix to this chapter.

8

Analysis of Current Reality

Key Points

- Before introduction of an e-government system, information needs to be gathered about the reality of the current situation.
- To build an accurate picture of current public agency reality, use the ITPOSMO checklist to cover both hard and soft aspects; use triangulation of different sources and methods; and gain the trust of those sources.
- A mixture of hard and soft techniques – IS audit, IS analysis, people analysis, problem analysis, context analysis – are needed to build an overall picture of current reality.
- A key skill in mapping current reality is the ability to distinguish what *ought to be* happening from what *is actually* happening.
- Use of diagrams can be valuable in eliciting information from stakeholders, as they help people to understand the situation and encourage further contribution.
- The 'rich picture' is a valuable technique for recording a holistic summary of current reality, while diagramming techniques such as process maps, data flow diagrams, and entity-relationship diagrams can be used either to represent current reality *or* to summarize the new e-government system design.

This chapter comprises two main components. First, the main approaches to use in gathering information about the reality of the current situation into which an e-government system may be introduced. Second, a set of more specific techniques that can be used to elicit and record this type of information. These techniques are mainly diagram based.

8.1 METHODS OF ANALYSIS

Overview of Data-Gathering Methods

As just noted, information now needs to be obtained about the current reality of the situation into which an e-government system may be introduced. To facilitate comparison with system design (see Chapter 9), current reality will be analyzed in relation to all the ITPOSMO dimensions (see Chapter 1): information; technology; processes; objectives and values of stakeholders; staffing and skills; and management systems and structures. It is assumed that the time and money issues are already understood from the feasibility assessment. It many cases, it may be appropriate to also gather data on the additional O: the outside world of environmental factors and context.

In brief, there are four main data-gathering techniques that can be used to understand current reality:[1]

- *Interview/discussion*: Talking to individuals or groups about the current situation.
- *Questionnaire*: Gathering background information using a survey of stakeholders.
- *Document analysis*: Reviewing current manuals, regulations, policies, contracts, memos, reports, and so on.
- *Observation*: Looking at what currently goes on, including the use of any current information systems.

It can be quite a challenge to uncover the reality of a public sector organization – the reality that lies beneath the surface impressions.

For example, when gathering information about current reality, there is a tendency to present a picture of what, according to organizational rationality, *ought* to be going on, rather than what actually *is* going on. Overcoming this is not easy. The pressures maintaining the mirage of organizational rationality are strong in textbooks, in the actions of consultants and vendors and their sales pitches, in the conceptualization of much IT, and in the language and assumptions of organizational meetings and documents.

Analysts themselves can also be part of the problem. They may impose their own worldview on the data gathering. For example, they may see a public agency through a private sector lens, failing to pick up the real ways in which government is different. Or, they may see current reality through a technical lens, failing to identify the 'soft stuff' of people and politics that strongly determines e-government trajectories.

Yet the key to good data gathering is the ability to get beyond the façades and the lenses and to uncover, for instance, the informal systems that are used and the formal systems that are unused. Part of this depends on ensuring all the ITPOSMO dimensions – both hard and soft – are covered. Part also depends on the analyst. Someone familiar with the organization will have an inherent advantage through their own knowledge and through their ability to win the trust of internal stakeholders. Equally, someone familiar with the client and other stakeholder communities may be better able to win the trust of external stakeholders.

Being trusted – persuading stakeholders that you are 'on their side', that what they say matters, and that you will maintain any necessary confidentiality – is a vital part of data gathering. So too is *triangulation*: building a picture of reality from several different sources and methods. This can mean talking to several different people and/or using more than one of the four main techniques described above. In summary:

Trust + Triangulation = Truth

There is, however, a limit to triangulation; indeed, to the whole idea of mapping 'current reality'. This limit arises from the fact that each person's reality differs: what a senior official perceives as the reality of the public agency is not the same as that perceived by, say, a junior clerk or by a citizen-client of the agency. It may therefore be more accurate to talk of mapping 'current realities'.

It is the overall intention of the initial systems development stages to compare reality with a new proposed design. If there is one complete reality per stakeholder of everything from information to management systems and structures, this will obviously be a very lengthy process.

In practice, for most of the ITPOSMO dimensions of comparison, the stakeholders will define a common reality, or one can be agreed. For example, this is likely to be the case with descriptions of:

- current technologies;
- the information and processes currently in use;

- staffing and skills; and
- management systems and structures.

Differences in these descriptions often arise because some stakeholders are not aware of the true situation, and their view is therefore mistaken. Differences *do* arise in the more personal elements of the ITPOSMO checklist, particularly objectives and values. Here, each stakeholder's reality *will* need to be treated as separate, and compared separately with the new design proposal.

The analyst needs to be aware that all realities are not equal. During data gathering, analysts will find some realities dominate the discussion. These will typically be the realities of the powerful stakeholders: 'power is to have your definition of reality prevail over other people's definition of reality' (Chambers, 1994: 19). These stakeholders may not be the same as those who matter most to development and operation of the new e-government system. If there are differences, the analyst must try to ensure that the realities of other stakeholders are heard and taken into account.

Specific techniques for gathering and then recording information about the current reality of public systems will now be described in more detail.

Information Systems Audit: Technology, Staffing and Skills, Management Systems and Structures Dimensions

An information systems audit, like that described in Chapter 3, can be undertaken to identify many of the elements of current reality, including at least three of the ITPOSMO dimensions:

- any technology currently in use (or available but unused);
- pertinent staffing arrangements and skills being used or available; and

- the management systems and structures of relevance to the current information system (which may or may not be computerized).

Information Systems Analysis: Information and Process Dimensions

This deals directly with the seven CIPSODA tasks of an information system, as described in Chapter 1: capture, input, processing, storage and output of data plus decision making and action. It can be systematically analyzed to record the data and tasks for each of these seven activities plus the communication of data between tasks. For these eight tasks (CIPSODA plus communication), analysis tends to focus at least on: what is being done, and who is doing it. It may also focus on the *way* in which things are being done.

Since output forms the most critical part of the system, this part can be examined in more detail by asking:

- *Who* is getting *what* information?
- *When* and *where* do they get it?
- *How* do they use it for decisions and (trans)actions and *why*?

There is also likely to be an examination of the quality and value of the information being output: Are information outputs meeting user needs? How CARTA (complete, accurate, relevant, timely and appropriately presented: see Chapter 4) are information outputs? This can include identification of potential cost/benefit failures in current information systems.

In addition, there can be analysis of *administration*: the tasks involved in operating and maintaining the current information system, and of *management*: the tasks involved in supervising other tasks, including management and control of data.

It is critical to remember that this exercise does not aim to map what *ought* to be happening with e-government, but what *is actually* happening. Some of the tasks described may well be informal; that is, based on the dictates of personal politics rather than adhering to some ideal-type, organizationally rational model. It is also quite possible that some of the system components are absent from the existing system. They should not be inserted, but should be noted as a reflection of possible problems with the system or of non-organizationally rational functioning.

One way to keep analysis centered on reality is to focus on key real-life events that trigger processes and the movement of data. Stakeholders can then be asked to answer questions such as, 'What happens then?' or 'What do you actually receive or send out at that point?' In many cases, this will identify chains of public information systems, where the output from one system forms the input to the next.

The data components can, in some cases, be recorded using an entity-relationship diagram. The process components can be recorded using a process map. Data and process components can be recorded together using a data flow diagram. All of these are described below.

People Analysis: Objectives and Values Dimension

The techniques already described are relatively hard in their approach. The key to a balanced and hybrid approach to reality analysis will be the inclusion of softer techniques that address the human aspects of public information systems.

There are techniques, derived from psychological theory – such as personal construct theory – that can be used to expose human objectives, motivations and other values. However, these are difficult to use in the context of most e-government projects because of their time and skill requirements, and because those questioned do not see the relevance of the techniques.

It is therefore more practical to approach these issues in other ways. A couple of techniques are described below that can be applied with the key internal and external stakeholders. In each case, the information elicited is likely to be richer if informal, one-to-one discussions are used rather than questionnaires or group work.

SWOT Analysis

This involves getting key stakeholders (including clients) to identify the internal strengths and weaknesses, and the external opportunities and threats relating to an organizational system. In some cases, this may be the whole organization (in which case this may be part of a broader strategic approach, as described in Chapter 3). In other cases, it could be the current system that may need to be amended. SWOT provides both direct information that can be used in planning the new e-government system, and indirect information about the current reality of stakeholder objectives and values.

Personal Objective Setting

Key stakeholders can be asked directly about their personal objectives vis-à-vis the proposed e-government system: what do they want or expect from the new system? Such objectives may also emerge from the other techniques described in this chapter. Client examples might include cheaper or better service. Employee examples might include better job satisfaction or improved career prospects. Politician examples might include fewer complaints from clients, or more business/employment opportunities.

These may be relatively easy to uncover if they are wholly or partially congruent with rational objectives. More difficult to tease out unless the analyst is well trusted might be non-congruent objectives such as removing power or resources from political rivals: one technique is to keep asking 'Why': Why are users seeking certain benefits from a new system? Why are they disaffected with the current system? It can also be useful to expose current values by asking what stakeholders do *not* want the new system to deliver or to change.

By whatever means, the analyst does need to keep pushing on these – they will expose the drivers to e-government that are critical to both comprehending and succeeding.

Problem Analysis: Multi-Dimensional

Despite the headings above, most of the foregoing activities are description rather than analysis. They answer the 'where are we now?' question for the ITPOSMO dimensions, but they may not do much more. Analysis, however, requires more and requires an answer to a further question: 'What's the problem/opportunity?'

Here we focus on problems. Change – such as a new e-government system – can only be effective if it addresses the right problem and addresses it correctly. The problem must therefore be analyzed and understood. This may well require a more holistic focus on the problem than the rather reductionist dimensions of ITPOSMO can provide.

The intention of problem analysis is two-fold. Most straightforwardly, it aims to avoid a common cause of e-government systems failure, when inadequate analysis and understanding leads to a focus on the wrong problem: see Box 8.1. Problem analysis will also help to generate ideas about personal objectives, values and priorities that can be used to help build the map of current organizational reality.

Box 8.1   Identifying the Wrong Problem

A government was experiencing poor participation rates in elections. A naïve analysis indicated that a key problem was the transaction costs of voting: citizens found it a burden to seek out the polling station and cast their vote. Therefore a costly project was initiated to enable much easier voting – by cell phone or via the web. Heavy investments were made in the security systems necessary for such e-voting.

A follow-up study showed that participation rates had hardly shifted, with limited take-up for the e-voting channels. Further analysis revealed that the wrong problem had been identified for action. The true underlying problem was not the small burden of time and effort to vote, but the alienation of citizens from politicians and the political process. It was this human problem that needed to be addressed, not the largely technical issue of how votes are actually cast. The e-voting initiative was an expensive waste of time and money because it was trying to solve the wrong problem.

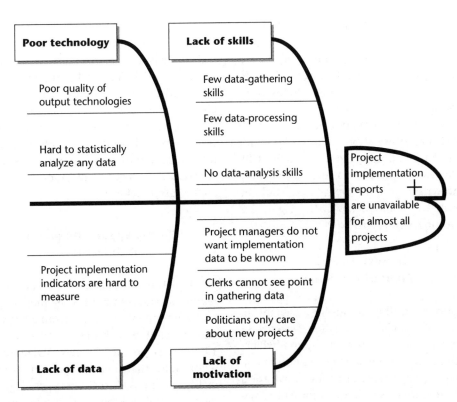

Figure 8.1   Fishbone diagram

One starting point for problem analysis would be the project summary statement described in Chapter 7. This simple statement can be investigated further in various ways. Typically, a 'problem chain' can be created. This takes the initially stated problem and asks 'Why is this a problem?' in two ways: first, working 'upstream' to understand the causes of the stated problem; second, working 'downstream' to understand the symptoms of the stated problem, which provide the rationale for addressing the problem. Stakeholder questions can also be asked about who is having the problem, who wants the problem solved, and why.[2]

It is important at this stage not to jump to solutions. Statements such as 'It's a problem that we don't have a portal,' focus on solutions, not problems. They need to be investigated further to uncover both causes and symptoms in the problem chain.

A complementary technique is the fishbone or cause/effect diagram. This is a means for recording data on problems from, for example, a group brainstorming exercise. It begins by setting the problem statement as the head of the 'fish'. Other causes can be added at the start or as brainstormed: the main causal factors or domains as the main bones of the fish skeleton; and minor causal elements within those main factors as minor bones projecting from the major bones. An example is shown in Figure 8.1 related to management information systems for a set of community development projects.

As with the other diagramming techniques discussed below, there is nothing magical about the fishbone diagram. It is just a simple technique that encourages people to contribute ideas and, in turn, helps communicate those ideas back.

Where the problem does, or may, relate to an existing information system, one major bone can be allocated to each of the CIP-SODA tasks or each of the CARTA data quality characteristics. Alternatively, bones could be allocated to components of the Figure 1.2 onion-ring, or to ITPOSMO.

Context Analysis:
Multi-Dimensional

As shown in the onion-ring diagram in Figure 1.2, public information systems sit within a wider organizational system which, in turn, sits within a wider environment. Factors within this broader context will affect both the current and future information systems. These broader factors – such as drivers to e-government, which often come from political pressures outside the agency – may have been thrown up by one of the other techniques described above. They may also have been identified by the kind of strategic exercise described in Chapter 3. However, as part of a hybrid approach – ensuring both social and technical factors are considered – it may also make sense to revisit contextual influences on current public information systems in case they are important. Key aspects of this review could be recorded using the rich picture described below.

8.2 RECORDING TECHNIQUES

The elements described above can be recorded as text. However, using diagrams offers some significant benefits, because diagrams help to simplify, formalize and communicate representations of public sector reality.

Thanks to these strengths, diagrams are also a useful way to elicit information from stakeholders. Indeed, diagrams may be used primarily for eliciting rather than recording information. First, because diagrams help clients, staff and other stakeholders to understand a situation more easily than other means. Second, because diagrams are interesting and therefore stimulate people to contribute further. Key diagram techniques are discussed below.[3]

Reality-Specific Diagrams:
Rich Pictures

A rich picture is a diagram rich in detail that represents and summarizes the most important components of a government system and its context (Checkland and Scholes, 1999). It is one of the few diagramming techniques that helps represent current reality, as opposed to some theoretical and rational ideal. It is also one of the few diagramming techniques that is hybrid; mapping both hard and soft elements in and around a government system. It is therefore of great value to analysts, particularly given the key role that personal interests, politics and culture play in the public sector generally and in e-government specifically.

There are no hard and fast rules about rich pictures, but typically a rich picture would contain:

- *Structures*: Details of both formal and informal structures. For example, an organizational map (*organigram*) for all relevant parts of the organization and related organizations, but also an indication of informal relationships.
- *Processes*: Details of both formal and informal processes. For example, the organizational activities that do take place, but also an indication of those that are not working.

- *People*: The key stakeholders and relationships (good or bad) between them. For example, the rich picture could indicate political rivalry or poor communication between two key individuals.
- *Values*: Relevant feelings and beliefs of stakeholders. For example, the dissatisfaction of current clients, or their personal objectives.
- *Environmental factors*: Key constraints, key external individuals and organizations, and a boundary line between the system and the 'outside world'. For example, the presence of new legislation that both drives and constrains what can be done.
- *Symbols*: Diagrammatic summaries. For example, a line with a cross on it to represent poor communication or a poor relationship; or an eye to represent a monitoring function. A key that explains these will need to be appended unless all those using the picture are familiar with its conventions.
- *Supporting statement*: A written or verbal explanation that helps the rich picture be understood and provides more detail about particular aspects.

There is no set method for creating a rich picture, but one way to start is with the formal structures, then adding the elements one-by-one as listed above. As with *all* the recording techniques listed here, a key stage in recording is to show the diagram to others working within and served by the public agency to check it for suggested changes. An example of a rich picture for a procurement system is shown in Figure 8.2.

Example Supporting Statement

The rich picture shown in Figure 8.2 describes the current situation in the Department of Agriculture's procurement system. Orders for new items are sent regularly to the Purchasing Section within the Finance Department. Because of process problems and poor purchasing staff motivation, the procurement process is lengthy and can be erratic. The Purchasing Section manager is interested in improving this situation. He sees a web/Internet-based e-government application as a solution and, through an informal contact, can obtain the technical assistance that will otherwise be hard to get from an IT Department that jealously guards prioritization and ownership of any IT-related projects. However, there are financial constraints within the Finance Department. In addition, the Finance Department's Director, while aware of pressures, is not keen on e-government solutions because of his own lack of relevant knowledge and experience. Clerical staff are also fearful of greater use of IT in their work. Countervailing this, the Chief Secretary of Agriculture recognizes that she must respond to external pressures from both the Treasury and certain politicians. Considerable work to address underlying problems and achieve greater consensus between major stakeholders will be required before the introduction of a new e-procurement system could be considered.

The strengths of the rich picture as a recording technique are that it provides:

- A holistic, overall view of the situation.
- A means of recording some of the key soft features of a situation, such as politics, subjective viewpoints, disagreements, and other constraints.
- An enjoyable and stimulating means by which to elicit information from clients, staff and other stakeholders in order to communicate information to them. It can be especially helpful in getting stakeholders to talk about informal realities, and in steering them away from organizationally rational but false statements about the current situation.

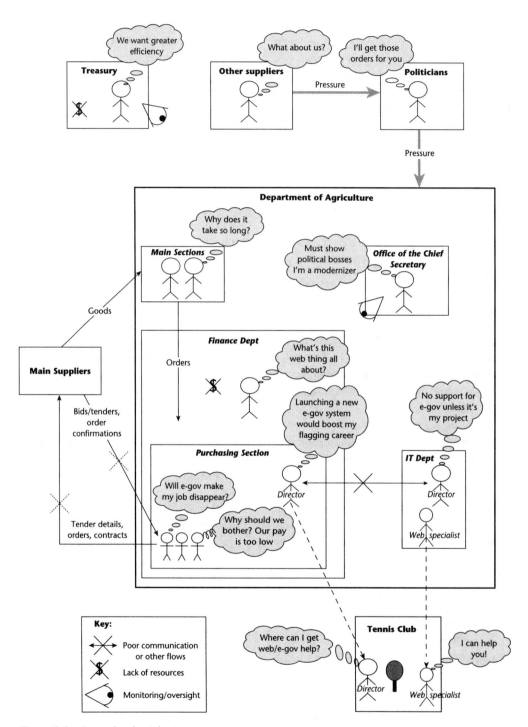

Figure 8.2   Example of a rich picture

The rich picture does have weaknesses:

- It may not be appropriate to certain organizational or national cultures; for instance, some cultures might regard the picture as childish.
- It may not be suitable for circulation because the content may be too sensitive; such content might include rivalries between key individuals, or the negative attitudes of certain groups.
- It may become complex, and thus harder to understand, if it tries to represent all the elements of context.

In the first two situations, analysts may find the rich picture is just for their own personal use.

Analysis of the rich picture often indicates the constraints within which any new e-government system must operate, particularly political constraints. These can be checked against, or incorporated into, constraint analysis. The rich picture may also record some of the key problems of current reality, which can be used as a starting point for more in-depth problem analysis.

Design/Reality Diagrams

The rich picture is particularly suited to representing current reality. Other diagramming techniques – such as those presented below – can be used either to represent current reality *or* to summarize the new e-government system design. Although these diagrams are simpler than rich pictures, this dual purpose creates a confusion that can interfere with their utility.

When recording reality, it is all too easy to slip into drawing what should be happening in the organization rather than what is actually happening (i.e. to confuse rationality/design with reality). The reverse can also happen when recording designs, but it tends to be less of a problem. Because of this, these techniques are used far more in practice for design (i.e. alongside the activities described in Chapter 9) than for reality analysis. Nevertheless, if used carefully they can be valuable for the latter too, as described below.

Process Map

The rich picture mainly provides a view of context. Any processes listed are described only in very simple and general terms. It may therefore be useful to have a more detailed record of the formal or informal processes involved in the operation of a particular organizational system. One technique that can be used for this is a process map.

A process map is a diagram indicating a sequence of tasks that make up one or more organizational processes. In the diagram, tasks are typically represented as numbered circles or ellipses, with the flow of activity from one task to the next indicated by arrowed lines. For example, the tasks of a procurement process could be represented by the process map shown in Figure 8.3. This shows a procurement system that is currently working properly.

Process maps can be quite easy to create, particularly if they represent simple, formal public sector processes such as the one above, since these relate directly to the tasks that are apparent from process analysis. However, the following steps can be used to create a process map:

1 Most processes have a starting point, so identify this and write down a short summary description of this initial task. Every task description should contain a verb (i.e. a 'doing word').

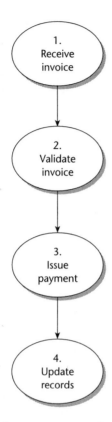

Figure 8.3   Process map example

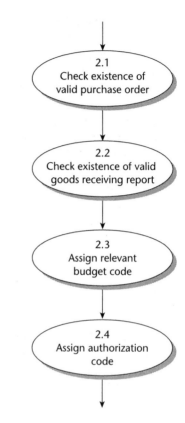

Figure 8.4   Exploded process map

2 Thinking through how the process works in practice from the process analysis, write down a similar description of the next stage (i.e. task), and the next stage, and so on until an obvious end point is reached.

3 Draw a diagram of the tasks, with arrows to indicate the flow of process from one stage to the next.

4 Draw boundary lines, if necessary, to indicate those tasks that naturally group together in processes or sub-processes.

Process maps can be drawn at various levels of detail. Greater detail could be added, for example, by 'exploding' some of the tasks into a series of smaller sub-tasks, each showing more precisely the steps that are involved. This activity is sometimes called *functional decomposition* or *leveling* and could be used if the system is a particularly complex one.

For example, the 'Validate Invoice' task could be exploded into the process map shown in Figure 8.4.

Process maps can record informal activities just as well as formal ones. For example, a typical informal stage in the recruitment process could be recorded as in Figure 8.5. The strength of the process map as a recording technique is that it provides an easy way to understand and discuss what is

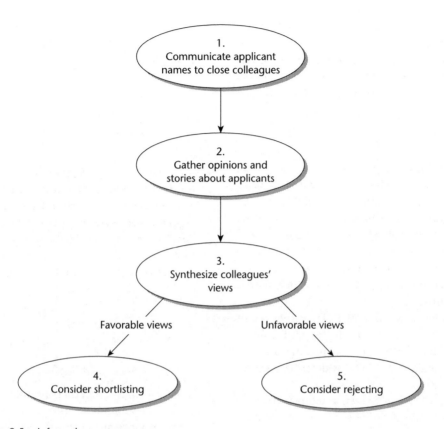

Figure 8.5   Informal processes map

being done in an organizational system. One weakness is that it only provides details of processes, not of other critical system components, as a rich picture does. Put another way, this is more a hard than a hybrid technique, so it would need to be supplemented by mapping of softer elements. In practical terms, as well as ease of rationality/reality confusion, it can also be difficult to know what level of detail to go into.

Analysis of the process map can highlight potential problems with current government systems, such as:

- tasks or sub-processes that are supposed to be undertaken, but are not;

- tasks or sub-processes with no clear purpose and no clear value-added for the organization;
- the same tasks being repeated in different parts of the system;
- apparently simple systems that involve a large number of tasks or staff or a large amount of time;
- process bottlenecks that slow down a whole system;
- tasks that could be undertaken in parallel, but that are not; and
- systems that involve a lot of iteration, or a heavy load of administration and management tasks, or a lot of exceptional tasks to cope with anomalies, or a lot of corrections, reworking or re-entering of data.

It may also necessary to step back from the detail and ask more holistic questions such as, 'Why does the organization undertake this process?' or even, 'Why does the public sector – as opposed to the private or non-profit sector – undertake this process?'

Data Flow Diagram

A data flow diagram (DFD) is a structured diagram that shows not only the tasks/processes involved in a public sector system, but also how data moves between those tasks, and where that data is stored. It therefore represents some of the main components of an e-government system within a single diagram, and is quite widely used as a technique.

Individuals can draw DFDs as they see fit. However, a number of standard conventions have arisen in drawing the principal components of a DFD, as described below.

- *A flow of data*: Shown as a line with arrow. Data will flow between any of the other elements of the diagram: tasks, stores and entities. As with all the components of a data flow diagram, the data flow is described wherever possible. For example:

Employee details

- *A task that transforms data*: Shown as a rectangle with curved corners (or a circle or ellipse). Data flowing in is different from that flowing out. As with the other elements, tasks may be numbered to aid clarity. For example:

1.2
Prepare
budget

- *A store of data*: Shown as an open-ended rectangle (or two parallel lines). For example:

Account file

- *An external entity*: Shown as a square (or double square). External entities usually lie outside the boundaries of the e-government system. They can be either *data sources*, that send data, or *data sinks*, that receive data. External entities are often a person or group. For example:

Accountant
General

Putting all these together produces the DFD. We can build on the process map above to produce an accounts payable DFD, shown in Figure 8.6.

This diagram shows invoices being received from suppliers and then validated against existing purchase orders and records of goods received. The payment is then issued to the supplier and relevant records are updated. Several points are worth noting:

- The boundaries set here are fairly arbitrary: if relevant, details of the order and purchasing system could have been added before process 1, and details of management reporting added after process 4.
- Just like process maps, DFDs can be drawn at various levels of detail, and a much more detailed DFD could be created. A DFD that provides the least detail and the broadest perspective on a system is known as a *context diagram*; below that is a *level 0 data flow diagram*.

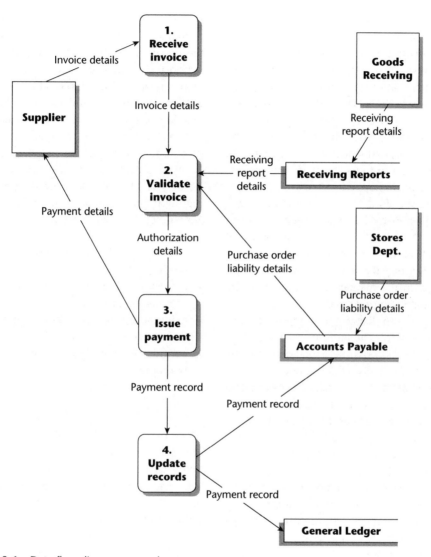

Figure 8.6   Data flow diagram example

- The entities – supplier, goods receiving, and stores department – are all external to the procurement system, but provide data to it.
- Alongside these data flows there are flows of documents, which frequently hold that data; there are also flows of resources, such as the ordered goods and services.

DFDs can be created in the following manner:

1   If a process map has already been created, it is checked to ensure that it contains a complete set of the tasks that take place in the system. If there is no process map, then one needs to be created, starting with the first source of data and the first task.

2   Starting with the first task, identify the people or things from which data comes (sources) and those to which data goes (sinks). Then identify the stores in which data about similar items is or should be held. Then identify what data flows move to the next task.

3   Then think what the next task in the process is, and repeat step 2 for that task. Continue until all tasks in the process have been mapped.

4   Data should flow between the identified tasks and data stores. Check that each task has data flowing in and out, and that each store has data flowing in and/or out. If it does not this is either an error in the diagram or a fault with the system being mapped.

5   Review the diagram and amend as necessary with the aim of making it as simple as possible, for example by removing tasks which merely involve transmitting rather than processing data (tasks 1 and 4 in Figure 8.6 could be candidates); and as comprehensive as possible, for example by adding tasks or flows that have emerged as important.

6   Discuss the diagram with the clients, staff and others involved to see if the system has been correctly summarized, and that it copes with the various events that trigger system activity.

7   If the diagram is to be a complex one, it can more easily be drawn in sections relating to discrete activities, which are subsequently assembled into a final diagram.

8   If required, do a new diagram that explodes particular tasks to show more detail and exceptions to general flows.

The strength of the DFD as a recording technique is that it is richer than the process map. Since it includes data, it encapsulates some of the key elements of an e-government system. Its weaknesses compared to the rich picture are its failure to include critical system components such as values and politics; like the process map, this is a hard rather than hybrid technique. Compared to the process map, it is more difficult to produce and more difficult for others to understand and use. In practical terms, flows of data and flows of resources can become confused. As with a process map, it can be hard to get the level of detail consistent throughout the diagram.

Analysis of the data flow diagram can highlight potential problems with current government systems, such as:

• tasks that receive no input or produce no output;
• data stores that are maintained but not accessed by any task;
• external entities that do not provide or do not receive necessary data; or
• confidential data being accessed for the wrong tasks.

Entity-Relationship Diagram

All of the 'things' about which data is kept are called entities. The data identified as being used within an existing or planned information system can therefore be grouped as entities. Entities are a category of things rather than the individual things themselves, for example, 'Welfare claimant' rather than 'Mr Jones'; 'Voter' rather than 'Sarah Antonelli'.

Often the best way to test if something is an entity is to ask yourself, 'Is there more than one of them in this particular context?' For example, in the case of an e-government system for an individual construction project, the entities might be 'Employee' or 'Equipment item'. They would not include 'Project'. In the case of a higher-level e-government system for the Department of Public Infrastructure, though, 'Project' might be an entity.

Typical entities found in internal-facing e-government systems include: Employee, Job, Department, Training event, Budget head, and Equipment item. Entities found in external-facing e-government systems could include things like: Client, Complainant, Claimant, Service user, Taxpayer, Supplier, Voter, Bid, Contract, Order, Invoice, Payment, Project, License, Application. Note that entities can be both physical items or transactions. Once identified from the information analysis and/or via a DFD, these can be recorded on an entity-relationship (E-R) diagram, which shows all the entities in an e-government system and their relationships to each other.

There are four different possible relationships that can exist between any pair of entities, forming four different components of an E-R diagram. Where applicable, the relationship is given some description on the diagram.

- *No relationship*: The entities are not linked in any way. For example, Vehicle and Library book.

- *One-to-one relationship*: The first entity is related to one and only one instance of the second entity, and vice versa. For example, Licensee and Fishing license: each licensee holds only one fishing license, and each fishing license relates to only one licensee.

- *One-to-many relationship*: The first entity can be related to more than one instance of the second entity, but the second entity is related to one and only

one instance of the first entity. For example, Department and Employee: each department can employ several employees, but each employee is employed by only one department. If the order in which the entities are written is reversed, this is called a many-to-one relationship.

One-to-many:

Many-to-one:

- *Many-to-many relationship*: The first entity can be related to more than one instance of the second entity, and vice versa. For example, Project and City District: each project can cover more than one city district, and each city district can be involved in more than one project.

These can all be put together if several entities are found in the information system. For example, a functioning accounts payable system might be found to include the following entities: Supplier, Stock item, Purchase order, Invoice, and Budget code. An E-R diagram for this system is shown in Figure 8.7. The diagram has been simplified since it should also contain relationships between Purchase order and Stock item, and Supplier and Invoice.

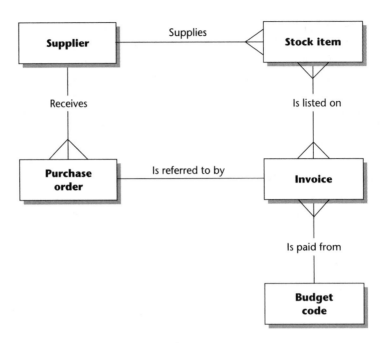

Figure 8.7   Entity-relationship diagram example

Entity-relationship diagrams can also be used to record each entity's attributes; that is, the data elements that store information on the characteristics of each entity. Once every data element has been associated with the relevant entity, the *key attribute* may appear underlined. It provides a unique identifier for each instance of any entity. An example is illustrated in Figure 8.8.

The strengths of the E-R diagram are that it provides a relatively simple record of information being used. When used for design purposes, it provides a direct link to database design. The weaknesses are that it may be of little relevance to any except formal, properly functioning, well-structured, database-oriented government systems. The diagrams can also be hard to produce: it can be hard to distinguish one-to-many and many-to-many relationships, to work out whether something is an entity in its own right or an attribute of

another entity, and to understand whether you need to model relations longitudinally (i.e. all the hunting licenses a citizen has ever had) or cross-sectionally (i.e. just the hunting license that the citizen holds now).

Analysis of the E-R diagram can highlight potential problems with current systems, such as:

- a lack of information systems links between data entities that should be related;
- a duplication of data in different entities that could be rationalized;
- failure to identify a primary key attribute for the entities, so that data records have no way of being uniquely identified;
- an absence of necessary attributes or a presence of unnecessary attributes; or
- the content of certain attributes being unclear or misleading.

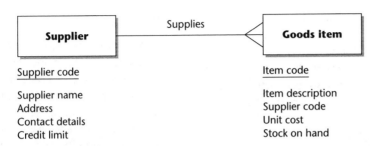

Figure 8.8   Entity-relationship diagram with attributes

Other

There are other recording techniques. *Flow-charts*, for example, are essentially process maps that cover very structured public sector processes, such as tax calculations or welfare decisions. They have a set of standard symbols covering tasks such as input and output, and yes/no decision points. *Organigrams* chart the formal organizational structure within a public agency. This is typically shown as a hierarchy of boxes with job titles from most senior to most junior staff member in all or part of the agency. As noted above, a simplified organigram can be used as the starting point for a rich picture.

ACTIVITIES

Shorter In-Class Activities[4]

Section 8.1

a. Discuss which will be most effective in analyzing situations for potential new e-government systems: individual interviews, group discussions, questionnaires, document analysis, or observation. Be prepared to defend your choice.

b. You have been asked to act as a consultant for a new web-based system to help the Department of Small Business Development support local small companies. How exactly will you win the trust of the key stakeholders? How exactly will you triangulate your sources of data?

c. 'All this stuff about analysis is just a waste of time. Design is all that matters for a good e-government system.' Discuss in pairs and/or plenary.

d. 'This soft stuff about people and politics is bunk. All that matters in analyzing a system for an e-government project is understanding current processes and data.' Discuss in pairs and/or plenary.

e. Look at the following problem statements, and decide which might be technology-related and which might not:

- 'I can't create proper service reports because the service data sets provided are never complete.'
- 'I can't work out what the correlation is between size of funding and number of jobs created on these federal employment schemes.'

- 'There are just too many clients to continue recording details on the paper-based pro-forma.'
- 'The staff in district offices are being very unhelpful about supplying the data we need for this equal opportunities survey.'

How would you go about investigating these problem statements further?

f. Review the case in Box 8.1. Discuss why you think the wrong problem was identified. What good practice lessons are there here for other e-government projects?

Section 8.2

a. Using an example of a rich picture that relates to the public sector, discuss whether or not you think this would really be useful as part of an e-government project.

b. Practice drawing a quick process map (maximum of four tasks) for a very simple, common process, like making a cup of tea.

c. Draw the appropriate E-R diagram for the entity pairs shown in the table below. Note that your answer may depend on your interpretation of the relevant e-government system; for example, whether or not it is to keep a historical record of transactions.

Assignment Questions

Section 8.1

a. 'Analysis is just a waste of time. Design is all that matters for a good e-government system.' Discuss.

Section 8.2

a. The following recording techniques – rich pictures, process maps, DFDs, and E-R diagrams – can all support the analysis and design of new information systems. Would the development and use of these diagrams be different or the same in the public sector as compared to the private sector?

b. Select any public service situation with which you are familiar. Draw up a rich picture for that situation. Analyze what e-government-related issues emerge from the rich picture.

Practitioner Exercises

Sections 8.1–8.2

a. What is the relevance and applicability to your public sector organization of all the reality analysis techniques described in this chapter? Note down any implications of your answer for e-government systems development in the organization.

eGovernment Project Development Exercises

1 Conduct an information systems audit covering those parts of the organization that the new e-government project is likely to affect.
2 Conduct an information systems analysis for the current reality related to the e-government project.
3 Work with key stakeholders (including yourself where relevant) to identify their objectives and values; for example by

Mother	Child	Voter	Political party	Job	Employee
Tax code	Taxpayer	Borrower	Library book	Car	Star sign
Project	Funding source	License	License holder	Disease	Patient

conducting a SWOT analysis or by directly collecting personal objectives.

4   Draw up a fishbone diagram for any main problem that exists within the current reality related to the project. Use this and other questions to build a picture of problem causes and symptoms.

5   Use the earlier analyses plus context analysis to create a rich picture for the current reality related to the project. Try to include all of the elements listed in the text as part of a rich picture, from structures to a supporting statement. Do not worry about your drawing abilities: you do not have to be a great artist in order to create a rich picture. Once you have done this, note down answers to the following questions:

- Will it be possible to use the diagram you have just created in your organization?

- If not, why not? If so, for what purposes can it be used: personal use; presentation to other individuals; presentation to, and discussion with, a group; etc?
- What problems does the picture highlight?

6   Draw a basic process map (i.e. with something like four to six processes) for the current reality related to the project. Check its accuracy with colleagues, and then analyze it for potential problems.

7   Draw a basic DFD for the current reality related to the project. Check its accuracy with colleagues, and then analyze it for potential problems.

8   If more than one entity is involved, draw an E-R diagram for the current reality related to the project. Check its accuracy with colleagues, and then analyze it for potential problems.

NOTES

1. A more detailed, rational approach to data gathering is discussed in the Online Appendix for Chapter 4.

2. Some further detail on questions for problem analysis is provided in the Online Appendix for this chapter.

3. Further examples of these diagrams are provided in the Online Appendix for this chapter.

4. Details of longer group activities are provided in the Online Appendix to this chapter.

9

Design of the New eGovernment System

Key Points

- Hard approaches to e-government design often fail; a successful approach must be hybrid, encompassing both hard and soft elements and all ITPOSMO dimensions.
- Hybrid design of e-government objectives steers between organizational and personal interests.
- Design of e-government information is based on questions that follow the CIPSODA model.
- Design of e-government technology typically deals first with software and then the hardware, though choices may be constrained by technical, financial or political factors.
- Hybrid design of e-government processes attempts to optimize or improve or redesign public processes rather than to radically reshape them or to leave them untouched.
- Design of human systems for e-government covers staffing, skills and management, including the key issue of incentivizing change.
- Traditional approaches to cost/benefit analysis of e-government proposals have far greater symbolic or political than objective or rational value; they are best replaced with hybrid approaches.

Too many e-government systems are designed from a hard perspective – focusing design on the technology, the data it handles, and related public sector processes only (Parrado, 2002; Riley, 2002). Hard approaches are attractive because they are relatively simple and easy, because they reflect the 'e' in e-government, and because they reflect the technical background of many designers. However, hard approaches often end in failure because they ignore the soft human, political factors that have such a critical impact on e-government projects.

A successful approach to e-government design must therefore be a hybrid approach: one that encompasses both hard and soft elements; in other words, all of the ITPOSMO dimensions outlined in Chapter 1. In theory, all of these eight dimensions within a current public system and its components – from the information out to even environmental factors – could be redesigned. In practice, design tends not to focus on environmental issues. In this chapter, therefore, we will cover six main dimensions of change within five overall design headings:

- *objectives*;
- *information*;
- *technology*;
- *processes*; and
- *human systems* (staffing, skills and management).

Estimations of required time and money (the 'other resources' dimension) will already have been made during the project assessment stage. Further details on cost estimation are provided at the end of this chapter.

Despite the criticism of hard approaches to e-government, you will find that, in considering the design of e-government components, a relatively hard, rational approach will be taken; particularly in covering information, technology and process design. Discussion of objectives and human systems refers a little more to soft, political issues. However, it is one of the disappointments of systems design that so few guidelines are offered from anything other than a hard, rational perspective. Rational design techniques can be located within contextual constraints, but there are few robust ideas that put behavioral or even hybrid notions at the heart of, say, information or technology design for e-government.

Each of the five components of design will be discussed separately and in turn but, in practice, e-government design is not a neatly separated step-by-step process. Each component is affected by all of the others, and the choices made about each component need to be compatible. Therefore there is likely to be some iteration in the process of choice in order to get everything to fit together. This iteration may go a little way to hybridize the design process. In addition, as discussed in Chapter 10, there can be iteration due to design–reality gap reduction, which helps further to knock some of the overly rational edges off e-government design.

As noted in Chapter 8, the design for the new e-government system can be recorded using diagrams. In mapping out current reality, diagrams are used to represent what is really happening. In recording the design of the new system, diagrams are representing a theoretical situation that is intended to come about, but that may not bear any relation to current reality. Thus, again, these diagrams are hard, rational tools, with nothing soft or hybrid on offer to support design such as the rich pictures that can support analysis.

As noted above, the rational techniques described in this chapter can be located within their context. To do this, many of the outputs from the feasibility and analysis processes – such as constraints, problems and influencing factors – can be carried forward as key inputs to design. It will also be useful to refer back to the earlier 'What Next?' analysis described in Chapter 7. This will help ensure that choices – principally those about information and technology – are future-proofed and sustainable, and do not just focus on current needs. Finally, data from analysis of objectives can also be carried forward, since these help to form an initial and overall framework for the new design.

9.1 SETTING OBJECTIVES

The design and development of a new e-government system requires some guiding framework. A project summary statement may provide this to some extent, but most projects will require a set of objectives to work to. Taking account of the framework of constraints and future changes, these can be based on the previous problem statement, project rationale statement, problem analysis and/or personal objective setting.

Objectives are often stated in terms of the benefits sought from the proposed new e-government system, and may be a mirror image of any identified problems. Objectives for an e-procurement system, for example, could include:

- to reduce the time taken to procure goods and services;
- to increase the accuracy of ordering and payment; and/or
- to increase the motivation of purchasing section staff.

If there are a number of objectives, these can now be prioritized in order to provide a principal focus for subsequent system development.

Organizationally rational approaches to systems development may recommend that these objectives are derived from wider organizational objectives. However, as analyzed in Chapter 3, the concept of 'organizational objectives' is flawed. eGovernment objectives based on organizational objectives may differ considerably from the personal objectives of key internal stakeholders.

A hybrid approach is therefore needed that steers carefully between the formal design conceptions (typically phrased in organizationally rational terms, and hopefully relevant to reform or client needs rather than technical agendas), and public sector realities (that deal with personal, political agendas). This hybrid approach requires that the gap between these two – between design and reality – is closed. Closure could involve making the objectives stated here more closely resemble some of those derived under the 'personal objective setting' described in Chapter 8. Alternatively, it could involve changing personal objectives through the kind of motivational and participative techniques described in Chapter 10.

Rational approaches may also recommend that e-government objectives are made

SMART: Specific, Measurable, Agreed, Realistic and Time-bound (RIU, 2003). This can be valuable. Without specificity, measurement and timing, it is difficult to know whether or not any new system has achieved the objectives that were set for it. However, in some public organizational cultures, managers may try to keep objectives vague to reduce the danger that they will be held to account for failing to meet those objectives. Keeping objectives simple and flexible may also increase the chances that those objectives are met.

9.2 INFORMATION DESIGN

It should not be assumed that the information provided by any existing information system meets current needs. Data may be disseminated to clients because 'we have always done it that way', even if that data is of no value to either the client or the public agency. Similarly, there may be information that stakeholders would like to access, but which is not being gathered or created. Some analysis of information requirements is therefore often appropriate.

The information required within the new e-government system can be planned using a set of questions about the key information functions. Roughly, this runs the CIPSODA model (introduced in Chapter 1) backwards, starting with the most important information element: output.

Output Requirements

How will information outputs meet system objectives:

- Who will expect output from the new system? These are the 'clients' of stakeholder analysis. If not already known, then primary (direct) and secondary (indirect) users of output can be identified both inside and outside the organization.

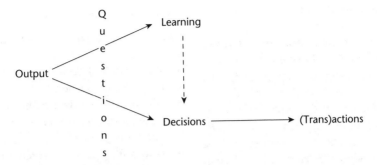

Figure 9.1   Determining information needs

- What information will they require to be output from the system? This is the second most critical question to be answered in the whole of the design process. (For the most critical, see the discussion below on individual motivation.)

  It can be divided into parts. First, one might ask: 'What questions should the new system be expected to answer for them?' As indicated in Figure 9.1, this can be applied to both learning and decisions/actions. Alternatively, one might ask: 'What information is required to support the transactions (decisions and actions) that users want to undertake?'

  More formal techniques for analyzing information needs – such as information engineering and critical success factors – were mentioned in Chapter 3. In some ways, these can be seen to more strictly run CIPSODA backwards:

  - o A: Start by investigating which actions/transactions of users are most important in the project context.
  - o D: Investigate what decisions users need to take to support those actions.
  - o O: Investigate what information users need from e-government systems to support those decisions.
  - o Other elements follow as described below.

These and other techniques attempt to understand the new e-government system in its overall context rather than simply asking users directly, 'What information will you need?' Such a question is not easy to answer: stakeholders find it hard to know what they want – especially in informational terms – unless given some guidance. Ideas on guided approaches could include the following type of tools (Afferson et al., 1995):

- o An information log book run over several weeks: In the log book, users record details of the questions they need answering, the context, whether or not they got answers, from which source, and the value of those answers. For other types of client, one can use a service log book that focuses more on the actions that clients need to undertake via a system.
- o Structured interviews: Questioning users on critical success factors for a particular government system, on overall information priorities and needs, on main issues of concern and problems, and getting users to review existing outputs from a data quality (CARTA: completeness, accuracy, relevance, timeliness, appropriateness of presentation) point of view.
- o Prototyping to see what information content users want.

Information needs can also be teased out through observation and through group interviews or brainstorming. Group-based techniques will often try to come at the issue of information needs from a variety of angles: starting with critical success factors and working back to decisions and information; starting with current organizational problems and working back to decisions and informa-tion; starting with measuring public service quality and working back to deci-sions and information.

- Why do stakeholders require this infor-mation? How does information output meet system objectives? This helps to understand, justify and refine informa-tion needs.
- How often and when and where will the e-government system be expected to produce information output?
- In what format will the system be expected to produce information output? This and the previous question might include a consideration of personal prefer-ences. For example, preferences for the channeling, format and content of infor-mation can differ from person to person. There might also be a consideration of user abilities, to ensure that the output will be understood. Where several users are involved, this may merely create a general need for a flexible output interface.
- What characteristics should the informa-tion output possess:

  o How complete, accurate, relevant, timely and appropriately presented does the output information have to be?
  o What other qualities are required of out-put information: such as confidentiality, integrity, scarcity, sense-making power, symbolism, and so on?

Capture and Input Requirements

How will input data meet output needs:

- What data will have to be input to produce the required outputs?
- Where will the data come from, and in what form, in order to produce the required outputs?
- How will data be captured and input to the e-government system?

Process Requirements

How will processing turn input data into output information? In particular, what processing functions are required to convert the input data into the required outputs? Some basic functions include: classification, sorting or rearranging, selection, aggrega-tion, calculation and comparison.

Storage/Retrieval Requirements

How will storage hold data needed for processing and output:

- What data will be stored and retrieved in order to produce the required output?
- In what way does the data need to be stored?

Communication Requirements

How will data be transmitted to support other tasks:

- What data will be transmitted as part of the tasks of capture, input, processing, storage/retrieval and output?
- Where, or to whom, will the data be transmitted?
- How will it need to be transmitted?

These questions are also a reminder that, as noted in Chapter 8, public sector informa-tion systems can exist in linked chains. If this is the case, determination of information requirements will have to be undertaken for each individual information system link in the overall e-government system.

If appropriate, an E-R diagram (see Chapter 8) can be used to represent the information that will be required by the new e-government system. This can be used to highlight:

- the entities about which data must be stored on the new system;
- the entities' relationship to each other;
- the attributes of each entity about which data must be stored; and

- the primary key attribute that will be used to uniquely identify each instance of each entity.

This can be a moment to review and rationalize the structure of the e-government system's data. Techniques such as 'normalization' can be used to reduce the data structure to its most efficient form by removing all data redundancy. A revised E-R diagram can then be drawn.

Putting all this together can produce quite a substantial document listing information requirements, as can be seen from the sample given in Box 9.1.

Box 9.1   Information Design Requirements for Human Resource Information System, Hillsborough County, FL

The information design requirements run to nearly 30 pages (HCPD, 2000). Some illustrative sample requirements are given here.

Capture/Input:

- Allow data to be captured from the following: keyboard, telephone, touch screen, mouse, scanner, pen, voice, fax, bar code, remote data entry.
- Support file import from: spreadsheets, word processing, database management system, payroll systems, scanners, cameras, electronic time clocks, and so on.

Processing:

- Allow transfer of employee from one organization to another without data re-entry and with history of changes.
- Support: calculation of salary range (min, mid, max); calculation of bonus payments; maintenance of salary history; flagging of high-performance employees; tracking and charting of progress of minorities; year-end carry-over calculations for benefits; calculation of estimated and actual employee benefits.

Storage:

- Allow organizational classifications broken down by: division, region, district, department, section, project, task, client, and so on.
- Support employee classification by: salary grade, job evaluation, bargaining unit, full-time/part-time, cost center, and so on.

(Continued)

Box 9.1   Continued

- Support: hyphenated last name of varying length; Asian, French, Hispanic and other character sets; married and maiden names; common name or nickname that employee is addressed by.
- Support: multiple employee addresses; unlisted flag for telephone numbers; emergency contact information; employee language preference.

Output:

- Support output of: organization charts, line graphs, bar charts, pie charts, and so on.
- Export files to: spreadsheets, word processing, DBMS, payroll systems, email systems, and so on.
- Provide reports: notification of employee when benefit eligibility dates are reached; succession planning reports; summary benefit statements; affirmative action; quarterly wage summaries; pension to payroll reconciliation.

9.3 TECHNOLOGY DESIGN

This involves thinking through alternative ways in which technology can meet stated objectives and information requirements, and selecting one of the alternatives. The information systems audit should have provided information on current trends, standards and technologies available to clients and sister organizations, from which choices about designs can be drawn. Potential suppliers may be circulated with general details of requirements in order to produce initial expressions of interest and an outline of ideas about possible technology designs.

All this assumes that alternatives are possible: earlier constraint analysis may have identified that they are not, for example where one stakeholder imposes a particular solution. This can sometimes be the case where a senior official becomes convinced, through ignorance and/or the persuasion of external advisors and/or the desire to impress others, that the organization requires state-of-the-art technology. In such cases, there may be little room for maneuver on technology design and the likelihood of technical failure is high. There may also be financial constraints that limit the available choices.

Where there *is* room for maneuver, one option that can always be considered is the 'no new IT' option.

Software Design

In designing the IT component of an e-government system, software is typically the first focus because it is software that actually does the work. If hardware is designed first, there is a danger that it will not be able to run the necessary software. Three design choices must be made, as described below.

Type of Application

Based on the identified information requirements – primarily those concerned with output and processing – a choice can be made of the type of application needed to fulfill these requirements. Applications can be categorized in many different ways, but one can see them as relating to three main areas:

- *Improved data handling*: Such as an ERP (enterprise resource planning) system to handle the agency's data infrastructure, or an office automation system to handle its documents.
- *Improved decision making*: Such as an information system of local economic and social indicators to support strategic decisions about community regeneration.

- *Improved interaction*: Such as an intranet to support internal communication, or a web portal to support external transactions.

Checking the capabilities of particular applications against requirements should indicate which is most suitable. Two examples of software capability requirements are given in Box 9.2, indicating quite different types of application needs. This can also be the opportunity to decide which of the listed capabilities is most important.

Box 9.2   Software Capability Requirements for eGovernment Systems

Computer Aided Dispatch

The County of San Bernardino in California (CSB, 2001) needed to improve its emergency dispatching system. Its software capability requirements included the following, showing a strong focus on data handling and decision making:

- Respond within two seconds for 90% of transactions.
- Accept set incident data on a pre-formatted screen and validate input codes.
- Interface with the existing 911 systems and support a geographic information system interface.
- Support transfer between dispatchers and priority interrupts for more urgent calls.
- Detect and handle duplicate reports of the same incident.
- Identify location-specific threats, hazards and prior incidents.
- Provide dispatchers with a display of pending incidents.
- Automatically route calls to dispatchers but allow dispatcher control over call selection.
- Provide dynamic support for selection of units to respond to an incident, and support multiple service dispatch including public works and animal control.
- Keep time-stamped records of all incidents handled.

Web Content Management

Columbia County in Georgia (CCBC, 2003) included the following software capability requirements for its new web content management system, indicating a mixed focus on data handling and interaction:

(Continued)

Box 9.2   Continued

- Enable creation and management of web pages.
- Allow three levels of content approval.
- Allow images and files to be readily uploaded.
- Enable content to be marked as time sensitive.
- Allow site visitors to search content, and support search engine indexing.
- Support online polls, discussions, forms and newsletters.

These capability requirements were divided into 'core' and 'additional'.

Method of Software Development

There are four basic ways in which to develop the software application that lies at the heart of the e-government system, one of which needs to be selected:

Off-the-shelf package This either works immediately on purchase or merely requires organization-specific data to be entered. An example might be one of the many standard accounting packages. Compared to other choices, its main potential advantages are lower cost, relative speed and ease of implementation, limited program errors (*bugs*), greater subsequent portability of data, and some reduced in-house skill requirements. Much of this, however, depends on the package developer and their volume of sales.

The package's main disadvantage is that it may not quite fit organization or user requirements. This may especially be the case for public sector organizations which buy packages aimed at the private sector market, and for non-US organizations buying packages aimed (as the majority of packages are) at the American market. The second disadvantage is the mistaken presumption that, when buying a package, other stages in the e-government systems development lifecycle can be ignored or skimped.

Customized package This is an off-the-shelf package that is altered to fit organization/ user needs. An example might be a spreadsheet filled in with organization-specific data, calculations and models. Another example would be a standard ERP package modified to fit a particular public sector organization's procedures. Customized packages can be a good compromise between packages and custom-built software. Many public agencies therefore choose packages that could be customized even if there is no immediate requirement. However, the outcome depends heavily on the qualities of the people doing the customization, and the extent of customization required.

Custom-built application This is software built from scratch to meet organization/user needs. For example, the organization's revenue collection procedures might be so particular that a system is specially written, either by an in-house team or by a local software house. If done well, the custom-built application can provide the best fit to needs. However, it is likely to be the most expensive method. It is also liable to design, implementation and possibly maintenance problems. With the increasing popularity of the first two options, very careful consideration has to be given before choosing this route.

System re-engineering This is the redesign and rewriting of an existing software application. For example, changes in electoral regulations might mean that an existing e-voting system no longer meets requirements. However, if many of the basic procedures remain the same it could make sense to modify the existing application. Given the existing base of software that has already been paid for, this can be cheaper than getting a new application. Much depends, though, on how well the existing application has been written and documented. If it is poorly structured and documented and if the original developers are no longer available, then it may well be better to start with a new application.

Operating System

The operating system that is to run 'underneath' the application needs to be selected. Choice may be constrained. For example, the application selected may only run with one operating system. Considerations of cost and inertia in the public sector may restrict the choice to the operating system already in use within the organization. Choice may also be restricted by what is available in client organizations. This may feed back into revised consideration about the method of software development since operating system choice may open or close certain method options.

Hardware Design

Three main design choices need to be made, as described below. Hardware choices are often heavily constrained by factors such as available finance, the existing hardware base within the organization, pre-existing contracts, and local supplier characteristics. They are also constrained by – and may

in turn constrain – software design choices. There may therefore need to be some iteration in the process of technology design to produce viable combinations of software application, operating system and hardware.

Hardware choices are framed in terms of information requirements. Some of these can be used to partly specify the performance requirements for new hardware, such as those about frequency of output, but further questions may need to be asked. For example:

- For each of capture/input, storage/retrieval, processing, output, transaction and communication: How much data will be involved on average and at maximum?
- How many users, at most, will wish to use the system at any one time?
- Where will those users be?
- How quickly will users need a response from the system?
- How often will old data items need to be deleted and new ones added?
- How reliable and secure will the system need to be?
- What backup and recovery services need to be provided?

A basic example of hardware design requirements is given in Box 9.3.

Computer Size

Depending on the earlier information requirements, especially for the volume and security of information processing, the broad type and performance of computer required is sketched out. Issues of necessary computer portability can also be considered here.

Specialist Hardware

There may be a requirement for specialist hardware, such as particular input or output devices like scanners, radio-frequency ID tag readers, and so on.

**Box 9.3   Technical Architecture Requirements for a Human
Resources Information System, Hillsborough County, FL**

Hardware requirements for the HRIS included the following (HCPD, 2000):

- Client/server computing architecture.
- Support for high-end databases: Informix, Oracle, SQL Server, Sybase.
- Support for database server platforms: AIX, HP Unix, Novell, Windows 95, Windows NT.
- Provision of distributed database capability.
- Support for TCP/IP network protocol.

Information Systems Architecture

Choices are made about computer architecture and connectivity, and data management architecture. Choices can relate to issues such as the relative balance of power and distribution of data between desktop and central server computers. Choices are determined in part by the computer size choice already made, requirements for shared output or communication of data, other information requirements, and contextual constraints such as the likely IT base to be found among citizen- or business-users of the e-government system. In most situations, a network will form part of the information systems architecture.[1]

9.4 PROCESS DESIGN

This involves thinking through alternative ways in which organizational processes can meet stated objectives, and selecting one set of alternatives.

The question of process change needs to be handled carefully. Not changing processes at all, while low-risk, can mean that efficiency gains are not achieved, and many e-government projects are criticized for thinking too much about technology front-ends and failing to change underlying processes (Jupp, 2003). At the other extreme, though, radical redesign of government

processes – as advocated by business process re-engineering (BPR) – is high risk. It runs counter to the principle of design–reality thinking, which helps to explain the very high failure rate of public sector BPR projects (Hanrahan, 2003).

A hybrid approach to the extent of design change is probably best. This would take a less radical, more incremental approach that attempts to optimize or improve or redesign public processes rather than to radically reshape them or to leave them untouched.

There are two groups of tasks that form key e-government processes, and about which decisions have to be made in an e-government project:

- *Core information system tasks*: At least some of the tasks required will differ from those of 'current reality' because there is a move from an old to a new information system in e-government development.
- *Wider system tasks*: These tasks will be placed somewhere on the untouched – optimized – redesigned – re-engineered continuum.

Each of these is discussed a little further below. In all cases, the individual tasks or overall processes can be designed and mapped according to the checklists shown in Box 9.4.

Box 9.4   Process/Task Design Descriptions

For each of the identified tasks or processes, one can simply ask two questions:

- What is to be done?
- Who will do it?

A more comprehensive approach would also add:

- When will it be done?
- Where will it be done?
- How will it be done?
- Why will it be done?

Alternatively, the CATWOE checklist described in Chapter 7 can be used for each of the tasks/processes which, in this case, can be summarized as meaning:

- *Client*: who receives the output of the process.
- *Actor*: who is responsible for undertaking the process.
- *Transformation*: what the process involves.
- *Worldview*: the purpose of the process.
- *Owner*: the manager of the process.
- *Environment*: any external factors that impinge on the process.

The theoretical design for the new tasks/processes can be summarized using a process map, or can be combined with new information design to produce a DFD that represents the proposed ideal of the required e-government system. Chapter 8 provides further details on both diagram types.

Core Information System Tasks

The information systems model introduced in Chapter 1 can be used to provide a framework for design, in a similar way to that already described for analysis of current reality. Each set of tasks designed should be the theoretical ideal set (at least within existing constraints) required for each activity:

- *Capture/input*: The tasks required to get data into the proposed e-government system, including application controls such as those described in Chapter 4.
- *Processing*: The tasks required to change input data into output information.
- *Storage*: The tasks required to store and retrieve data.

- *Output*: The tasks required to extract information from the system.
- *Communication*: The tasks required to communicate data between the other tasks defined here.

The issue of data quality and stakeholder motivation was described in Chapter 4. Bearing this in mind, one set of tasks that could be designed in is that which feeds back information from the system to those responsible for gathering and inputting.

In addition, decisions have to be made about *administration* (the tasks required to operate and maintain the new e-government system) and *management* (the tasks by which all other processes will be supervised). These tasks will include those connected with data

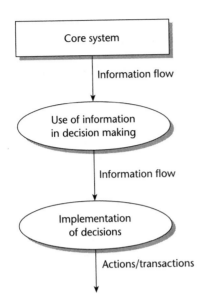

Figure 9.2   Key wider system tasks

management as described in Chapter 4, and those connected with external policies, such as those described in Chapter 6.

Wider System Tasks

One set of tasks that should come under particular scrutiny are those involved in making use of the information that is produced by the e-government system, for internal decisions, for external transactions, and so forth. These are illustrated in Figure 9.2. Unless these are effective, the whole e-government system may be of little value. Where they involve external clients, though, it may not be easy to effect change. Other individual tasks or whole processes may need to be redesigned if the earlier analysis of existing processes drew attention to problems, or if information system changes will create wider system changes.

9.5 HUMAN SYSTEMS DESIGN

This involves thinking through alternative ways of organizing work and work structures in the new e-government system in order to meet stated objectives, and selecting one set of alternatives. Whereas the process design phase focused on *what* is to be done, this phase focuses on *how* it is to be done, and *by whom* (Pearlson, 2001).

The design and organization of work and structures varies greatly from situation to situation but some generic guidelines are provided below.

Key Human Systems Design Questions

Design begins by revisiting what is to be done, and converting it into how it is to be done. The starting point will be task specifications: a consideration of the overall responsibilities that are required in order to successfully operate and use the new e-government system, based on the technology and process design. This can then be developed into a set of skill, knowledge and attitude specifications that are required in order to successfully complete the required tasks.

Some of these tasks may involve external clients, and questions can then be asked about the match of competency requirements to those actually existing within the client population. Where tasks involve internal staff, issues of job design and specification will next be covered. The generic task and competency requirements just described form an input to this, but two other issues must be determined before job specifications can be finalized.

First, there is the question of who will do the internal tasks. Can existing staff be provided with the new skills and responsibilities, or do new staff have to be brought in?

Which staff will use which skills? For example, is it more efficient for managers to enter and extract data themselves, or to work through more junior staff? Job design may go as far as asking which tasks will be allocated to which staff.[2]

Second – having outlined the tasks, competencies, jobs and staffing required – management structures can be questioned: will the existing organizational structures be appropriate for the new e-government system, or is structural redesign seen as a requirement? Although a higher-level issue, this may have an impact on job design.

Having done all this, you can then finalize job specifications/descriptions (the requirements of particular jobs involved with the new e-government system), and of person specifications/descriptions (the competencies required of those who will fill these jobs) (Berman et al., 2001; see also PTI, 2004).

Overarching Human Systems Design Issues

As described so far, the human systems design activity for e-government may sound relatively simple and straightforward. However, there are other factors that will influence the answers to the key design questions. Some of these are discussed below.

Individual Motivation

From the initial stakeholder analysis, it should be clear who is likely to be affected and unaffected by any new e-government system. For those stakeholders who are internal to the public sector, design could be framed in terms of the contributory factors to job satisfaction: as Herzberg (1987) puts it: 'If you want people motivated to do a good job, give them a good job to do.' An example is given in Box 9.5.

Box 9.5   Designing Satisfaction into eGovernment Jobs

Job satisfaction can be seen as the converse of the stressors discussed in relation to ergonomics in Chapter 6. For example, job satisfaction is likely to be higher when a job (Doherty and Horne, 2002, Mullins, 2002):

- requires use of higher-level rather than lower-level skills;
- is controlled by the employee rather than by a supervisor;
- forms a meaningful whole rather than being just one small part of an overall operation;
- makes a significant and visible contribution to the public agency;
- provides feedback on performance that is rewarded in some way;
- involves a variety of different tasks rather than repetition of the same task;
- involves social contact with others; and
- is undertaken in a pleasant working environment.

Such factors were built into the design of jobs for staff in a new computerized call center for Newham local government in London (Holmes, 2001). Their jobs were upskilled and made varied and holistic by allowing staff to field the whole gamut of possible call topics, and by getting them to 'close' every call: taking responsibility for following up each query until it is satisfactorily resolved. In combination with a new call center office, and the contact and positive feedback of sorting out callers' problems, this has provided a high level of motivation and job satisfaction.

Given the growing recognition of the importance of the individual public servant, design must also encompass the specific issue of reward and punishment. Put at its most blunt, all stakeholders involved – both internal and external – will ask of the new e-government system the critical question: 'Why should I: what's in it for me?' A satisfactory answer for the public servants involved may require the design of new rewards and incentives. This is discussed in more detail in Chapter 10.

Contextual Factors

Human systems design for e-government can also be framed by contextual factors such as the following.

Philosophy/culture Particular public agencies may have particular over-arching management philosophies. For example, an agency which adheres more to McGregor's widely used management perspective, *Theory X*, will tend to believe that staff are inherently lazy, lack ambition, dislike responsibility, and need to be closely controlled (Armstrong, 2003). In such agencies, the human systems are unlikely to be designed to allow autonomy and flexibility. On the other hand, in an agency adhering more to *Theory Y*, managers will tend to believe that staff find work to be a natural activity, have inherent motivation and potential for development, and will accept and even seek out delegated responsibility. Such managers are likely to support job design that allows autonomy and flexibility.

Agreements and legislation The design of the human systems for e-government is both enabled and constrained by a continuum of guidelines from word-of-mouth understandings up to legislative regulation. Where e-government can bring efficiency gains, such guidelines can mean that, instead of the efficiency gains being designed to deliver staff retrenchment, they must be designed to deliver staff redeployment only. There is a danger with e-government of polarization: of elite groups gaining more from change, and of marginalized groups being further marginalized. Regulations, for example on equal opportunities, may pressurize designers to specifically avoid such polarization – and to specifically consider the impacts on marginalized user groups – in designing the human systems for e-government.

Human systems design will also be guided by the job classification schemes in use in the public agencies involved. These will typically require the positions involved to be fitted into existing categories, which can be awkward given the evolving nature of e-government.

Stakeholder tensions Being a hybrid can mean steering a difficult line between competing interests. In e-government system design, this may arise as a need to balance the interests of staff against the interests of clients. Transforming public services through IT might deliver a very efficient, client-centered service. But what if this came at the cost of job cuts and shift patterns that take public servants away from their families? All stakeholders in an e-government system have rights that must at least be recognized in the process of design.

9.6 EVALUATING PROPOSALS AND ALTERNATIVE DESIGNS

There are three main possible outcomes from the design process:

- Pre-existing constraints or the nature of requirements determine that it is possible to proceed with only one set of e-government designs, and system development moves directly on to the next stage.

- For whatever reason, the design process produces only one set of e-government designs, but a 'go/no go' decision is still required to determine whether or not system development should proceed.
- The design process produces more than one set of e-government designs, from which choices must be made about which design is 'best'.

In either of the last two situations, some process of evaluation is required. Evaluation can mean identifying the extent of change required between current reality and the proposed design(s). A quick and dirty version of this was described under the PoTHOleS list of factors in Chapter 7. A more detailed examination will be provided in Chapter 10.

However, evaluation can also be thought of in terms of value. This can be considered by looking at one side of the coin: costs, or by looking at both sides of the coin: costs and benefits.

Cost Analysis

Cost has already been discussed in Chapter 7, but here we look in more detail at estimation of the expenditure that will be required by the new system or design. There is a tendency to grossly underestimate the costs of e-government systems for two reasons. First, because cost estimation tends to focus on the initial investment – capital – costs rather than the ongoing operational – recurrent – costs. Second, because many of the costs (e.g. of staff time) are hidden under other budget heads (e.g. staff salaries).

For many e-government projects, recurrent costs are greater than capital costs, and hidden costs are greater than overt costs. Only thorough analysis will provide realistic

estimates. This has been attempted through 'total cost of ownership' (TCO) approaches that indicate a cost 'iceberg' in which something like four-fifths to nine-tenths of costs fall into the recurrent/hidden categories (Rabone, 1999, Boddy et al., 2005). Yet only a minority of government departments even consider TCO, let alone try to calculate it (Kennedy, 2003).

Table 9.1 provides an example of the type of total costs that an e-government system could involve. For each cost, the table indicates whether it is typically:

- a one-off capital investment cost or a continuing recurrent cost or both (in which case the main component is listed first); and
- an overt cost or a hidden cost or both (in which case the main component is listed first).

In addition there are costs that are even more deeply hidden: potential negative impacts that can arise with the growth of e-government (e.g. Heeks, 2000d; Korac-Kakabadse and Korac-Kakabadse, 2001; Svensson, 2002):

- loss of informal information channels;
- loss of flexibility and adaptability;
- loss of human input to decisions;
- increased dependency and vulnerability;
- content-impoverished communications;
- data overload; and
- increased inequalities.

These are very hard to quantify, and we will return to this point later in the chapter. There is also an assumption, in exposing these sources of cost, that there is a desire by those involved to understand the true costs of the new e-government system. In some situations, this will be the case. In others, though, stakeholders may wish

Table 9.1   Costs of an eGovernment System

Cost	Capital (C) or Recurrent (R)	Overt (O) or Hidden (H)
Initial hardware and software	C	O
Initial telecommunications	C	O
Travel and communication costs of system development	C	O/H
Site preparation (electrical and network wiring, refurbishment of rooms, air-conditioning, etc.)	C	O/H
Transition/conversion costs (e.g. retaining old system or changing data formats)	C	H
Installation and delivery	C	O/H
External consultants and contractors	C	O
Documentation	C	H
User training courses and system publicity	C/R	O/H
Accessories, consumables, ancillary equipment (e.g. furniture, uninterruptible power supply)	C/R	O/H
Backup systems in case of failure	C/R	O/H
Training, salary and overhead costs of information systems (IS) staff for system development, operation, maintenance and support	R/C	O/H
Recruitment, training, salary and overhead costs of any new internal user or IS staff	R/C	O/H
Non-IS staff salary and overheads from time spent on system development, on sorting out implementation and ongoing operational problems (system crash, viruses, etc.), on being trained, on learning the system, and on providing support to other users	R/C	H
Opportunity costs of work displaced by staff time spent on system development and on operational problems and support	R/C	H
Incentive or redundancy payments for internal users and IS staff	R/C	H/O
Fraud, kickbacks, theft, use of system for personal gain, playing games, and other non-productive behavior	R/C	H
Insurance	R	O
Upgrades	R	O/H
Ongoing operational costs (e.g. electricity, health and safety inspections, spares, maintenance contracts)	R	O/H

either to deliberately exaggerate or to deliberately underestimate true costs.

Formal Cost/Benefit Analysis

Cost/benefit analysis (CBA) is a formal technique intended to assess the costs and benefits of any course of action. It extends cost analysis by adding in the financial value of benefits that the proposed e-government system or particular design(s) is expected to

bring. Organizationally rational management sources cite CBA as a central evaluation technique and provide a number of variants (Doherty and Horne, 2002, Gupta et al., 2004). These variants include:

• *Simple analysis*: This adds up costs and adds up benefits for the proposal over a set time period and then compares the totals for the two. A feasibility evaluation would look for benefits to exceed costs. A priority or other comparative evaluation would

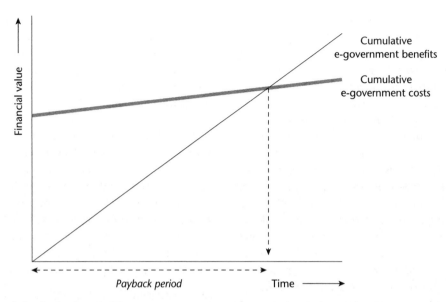

Figure 9.3   Payback period for an e-government system

select the option with the greatest excess of benefits over costs. The *cost–benefit ratio* (of total costs to total benefits) is sometimes used as a single indicator of this.

- *Discounted cashflow analysis*: This 'discounts' future costs and benefits by progressively reducing the size of these costs and benefits for each year of the time period. The further into the future costs and benefits lie, the more they are discounted (i.e. reduced). This incorporates a chronological view of value which recognizes that, for example, $10-worth of benefit delivered in five years' time is worth less than $10-worth of benefit provided now.
- *Payback analysis*: This calculates how long it will take for the cumulative costs of the proposed e-government system to be exactly balanced by the cumulative benefits, as illustrated in Figure 9.3.

Implementation Problems

These organizationally rational techniques face serious practical limitations for

several reasons (Rocheleau, 2000; UNDESA, 2003a):

Most benefits and some costs are unquantifiable Objective CBA requires a financial value to be put on all costs and benefits. As stated above, this can be difficult for costs, some of which are hidden. It is even more difficult for benefits, as a sampling of potential e-government system benefits shows:

- anywhere/anytime delivery of services to citizen/business clients;
- faster or better decision making by public officials or by clients;
- increased ability of public agencies to cope with complexity and uncertainty;
- new intra- and extra-organizational patterns of working.

How can we place a financial value on these benefits? How much is it worth for a citizen to submit their tax return at midnight rather than 4pm thanks to an e-government site? How much is it worth for a politician to make a slightly better policy decision thanks to IT-enabled inputs from citizens? How much is it worth for a cross-agency team to work together a bit more easily thanks to an intranet?

In most cases, the answer is 'no-one knows'. Valuation is particularly a problem for the public sector because a key quantifiable benefit that can sometimes be linked to new IT systems – new income earned – is frequently absent: some licensing systems can charge user fees but most public agencies and most e-government systems are not income-generating. So, in most cases, objective CBA is a technique that fails to reflect true costs and benefits of e-government.

If CBA is allowed to guide decision making, these shortcomings can mean two things. First that there is an overemphasis on one quantifiable benefit that can exist for the public sector: saving labor costs. Proposed systems that could improve organizational effectiveness (rather than just deliver labor-saving efficiency) may be rejected because their benefits are not financially quantifiable. This has constrained the spread of e-government in some public sector organizations, such as short-sighted US states which insist on a 'loan and payback' arrangement for IT-based systems.

Second, that proposals may seek to cut costs in order to match the few benefits that can be quantified. This can lead to sub-optimal design choices that have to be – very expensively – amended soon after project implementation.

These problems have particularly plagued the public sector. Lack of understanding about e-government systems is commonplace among senior managers and politicians. They are therefore keen to focus on the apparent certainties of CBA, cost savings and efficiency gains. Yet the consistent message of study after study is that e-government is not producing net cost

savings (UNDESA, 2003a). Research in the UK, for example, indicates e-government saves central and local government roughly US$500 million per year (Kable, 2003). Great; except that saving is only achieved by spending at least US$2 billion per year.

Systems development is an uncertain process eGovernment systems development frequently ends in whole or partial failure, in cost overruns, and in changes of direction due to political change. This uncertainty means that, even for those costs and benefits that can be given a financial value, that value is a guess liable to differ significantly from any true value realized upon implementation.

Other problems These include the lack of baseline internal and external financial information in some public sector organizations, and the confusion in attributing impacts (including benefits) to either new IT or to simultaneous organizational change.

The True Role of 'Objective' CBA

The implementation problems just noted are a serious enough challenge to CBA. However, the type of CBA outlined above is equally undermined by the domination of behavioral models in decision making about information systems (Walsham, 1989; Grindley, 1991). Many decisions about information systems – including e-government – are ultimately made on grounds of self-interest or subjective feelings. For example, a study of successful e-government projects in UK local government indicated that decisions to proceed with them had been a 'leap of faith' shaped by political agendas rather than rooted in rationality (Greenwood, 1999). CBA's only role in these circumstances is to support a decision that has already been made. Figures are often manipulated in the CBA in order to ensure this result.

Because of this and its implementation problems, formal and detailed CBA is frequently of little formal value, and surveys find little evidence of its use in US and other industrialized country e-government projects (Cohen and Eimicke, 2001; e-Envoy, 2001). Where such CBA is used, to bolster an already-decided case or at the insistence of senior managers, politicians or outside agencies, the analysis is rarely worth the paper it is written on. As one survey found:

83% of IT directors admit that the cost/benefit analyses supporting proposals to invest in IT are a fiction. (Grindley, 1991)

The Tax Systems Modernization project in the US Internal Revenue Service is one example (Margetts, 1999). It was subject to strong external pressures from Congress and from the Office for Management and Budget to show a quantitative return on investment. For the reasons given above, this could not be done using real figures. Figures still had to be presented but they had 'very little to do with reality', transforming the process from 'a scientific analytical exercise [*into*] ... a political exercise' (ibid.: 97).

Formal CBA with pages of calculations should thus be treated with great caution. It is required for many e-government projects, but the numbers are likely to be flawed and the analysis is likely to have far greater symbolic or political than objective or rational value.

Hybrid Cost/Benefit Analysis

This is not to argue that costs and benefits are unimportant. The costs of any proposal still need to be understood, as do the benefits. If financial values for major benefits are known or can be estimated, they can be compared with costs using simple back-of-an-envelope calculations. Politics permitting, this can help to eliminate patently wasteful and impractical e-government proposals. It

can also bolster the case for projects that may produce significant cost savings. Thus objective analysis needs to steer the hybrid course between the errors of completely ignoring the figures, and of undertaking financial analysis in unjustifiable detail.

A further reaction to the problems noted above is to focus more on change/risk assessment (see Chapter 10) than on CBA, since the former is a more important issue for e-government.

Yet another reaction – recognizing the central role of personal politics and intuition in e-government decision making – is to adopt more subjective methods of CBA. These involve asking the key stakeholders to give a personal rating of costs and benefits, typically on a scale of 1 to 10. For example, costs might be divided into the tangible (financial expenditure) and the intangible (such as loss of motivation, or fears about data security). Similarly, benefits might be divided into the tangible (such as efficiency gains) and the intangible (such as effectiveness gains). A sample scoring table for evaluating three different e-government design options is shown as Table 9.2.

This type of approach can also be represented using a modified force-field diagram. Perceptions of benefit for a particular e-government proposal can be listed on the left-hand side of the diagram, with the length of arrow matching the relative strength of feeling about the benefit. Perceived costs and risks are listed on the right. For example, a tax accountant who, overall, did not support a proposed e-government system for online tax filing might record the analysis shown in Figure 9.4.

If different e-government projects or options have to be prioritized using this method, then those rated high benefit with low cost and risk would tend to take first priority. Those rated low benefit with high cost and risk would probably be abandoned.

Table 9.2   *eGovernment Cost/Benefit Scoring Table*

eGovernmment design options	Tangible costs	Intangible costs	Tangible benefits	Intangible benefits	Total
Option 1	−5	−4	+3	+3	−3
Option 2	−4	−5	+6	+5	+2
Option 3	−6	−6	+5	+7	0

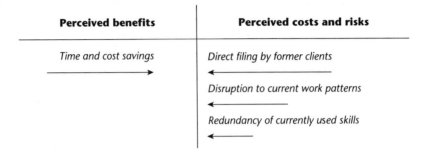

Perceived benefits	**Perceived costs and risks**
Time and cost savings	*Direct filing by former clients*
	Disruption to current work patterns
	Redundancy of currently used skills

Figure 9.4   Force-field diagram

ACTIVITIES

Shorter In-Class Activities[3]

Chapter Introduction

a. Why are so few e-government design techniques drawn from soft/behavioral or hybrid perspectives?

Section 9.1

a. Objectives listed for a US local government document management system (Keen, 2000) were that the system:

- will route documents electronically;
- will store documents electronically that will allow immediate retrieval;
- will meet current and future needs of document storage and electronic document routing (workflow) between the Register of Deeds, Appraiser, Clerk and Treasurer; the system should also allow images to be shared and accessed by each department;

- will meet legal requirements of storing archival documents on microfilm;
- will have the capability to be accessed by external clients from the Internet;
- will have the capability of converting archived, microfilmed copies of documents to digital images.

Compare these objectives with the discussion in Section 9.1, and comment upon them.

b. Discuss which matter more for a planned e-government system: organizationally rational or personal/political objectives.

Section 9.2

a. 'eGovernment systems increasingly deliver services, not information – so information design is redundant for modern systems.' Discuss.

b. Look at the information design requirements list in Box 9.1. Does it support the
idea that output requirements are the most
important?

Section 9.3

a. 'The needs of public agencies are so unique
that they are always best advised to go for
a custom-built e-government application.'
Discuss – you can incorporate the examples
in Box 9.2 into your discussions if you wish.

b. Why do think there are multiple databases
and server platforms listed in the Box 9.3
requirements list?

c. Identify two items of specialist hardware that
can be of value to e-government systems.

Section 9.4

a. Pick any process with which the class is
familiar (ideally government-, otherwise
education-related). Answer all the process
questions from Box 9.4 for that process.

b. Discuss briefly whether it is better to be
radical or incremental when redesigning processes for a planned e-government system.

Section 9.5

a. Discuss whether or not you would find a job
more satisfying if it was designed according
to the criteria outlined in Box 9.5.

b. In pairs, take opposing management
philosophy positions – one for Theory X,
one for Theory Y. How will your different
positions create differences in your design
priorities for the human components of
new e-government systems?

Section 9.6

a. Costs listed for a US local government
document management system (Keen,
2000) were:

- Main servers: US$70,700
- Standby server: US$3,600
- Archive writers: US$120,000
- Microfilm scanner: US$20,000
- DVD tower with DVD writer: US$18,900
- Workstations: US$11,500
- Software licensing: US$109,000
- Adapter cards: US$8,000
- Installation: US$10,000
- Training: US$6,000
- Ongoing maintenance: US$57,000 (15 per-
  cent of hardware and software purchase)
- Miscellaneous and contingency items:
  US$46,000 (10 percent of total system costs)

Discuss this list of costs in the light of the
section on cost analysis.

b. In pairs, imagine you are the project owners for a new e-government system.
Would you want a CBA for the system
before proceeding? If not, why not? If so,
what type of analysis?

c. You work for the local development
authority, which issues permits for new
construction projects. There is a plan to
create an e-government system that will
issue these permits online. In pairs, draw
up a force-field diagram of perceived benefits versus perceived costs and risks.

Assignment Questions

Sections 9.1–9.5

a. What would be meant by a hybrid
approach to e-government system design?
How would this differ from other design
approaches?

b. In what way would design for public
sector e-government systems differ
from design for private sector e-business
systems?

Section 9.6

a. Discuss the role of CBA in e-government projects.

Practitioner Exercises

Sections 9.1–9.6

a. What is the relevance and applicability to your public sector organization of all the design techniques described in this chapter? Note down any implications of your answer for e-government systems development in the organization.

eGovernment Project Development Exercises

1   Set objectives for the new e-government system.

2   Analyze the data/information requirements for the new system: output, capture/input, processing, storage/retrieval and communication.

3   Make choices about software and hardware design for the new e-government system. For software design, this will cover: type of application, method of software development, and operating system. For hardware design, this will cover: computer size, specialist hardware, information systems architecture, and network design.

4   Make choices about process design for the new e-government information system and for wider system processes, representing these choices using a process map.

5   Make choices about the human systems design for the new e-government system covering task, job and structural design and specification. Bear in mind issues of individual motivation and context.

6   Using the table below, estimate the total costs for the proposed e-government system over its expected lifetime (e.g. a five-year period). By differentiating capital and recurrent costs, try to estimate the expenditure in each year of the period. How does this compare to the likely financial resources available for the system? If there are specific design options, make a cost estimate for each of these.

7a.   Starting with the cost figures produced – and only if it makes sense to do so – undertake

Item	Cost
Initial hardware and software	
Initial telecommunications	
Travel and communication costs of system development	
Site preparation (electrical and network wiring, refurbishment of rooms, air-conditioning, etc.)	
Transition/conversion costs (e.g. retaining old system or changing data formats)	
Installation and delivery	
External consultants and contractors	

Item	Cost
Documentation	
User training courses and system publicity	
Accessories, consumables, ancillary equipment (e.g. furniture, uninterruptible power supply)	
Backup systems in case of failure	
Training, salary and overhead costs of IS staff for system development, operation, maintenance and support	
Recruitment, training, salary and overhead costs of any new internal user or IS staff	
Non-IS staff salary and overheads from time spent on system development, on sorting out implementation and ongoing operational problems (system crash, viruses, etc.), on being trained, on learning the system, and on providing support to other users	
Opportunity costs of work displaced by staff time spent on systems development and on operational problems and support	
Incentive or redundancy payments for internal users and IS staff	
Fraud, kickbacks, theft, use of system for personal gain, playing games, and other non-productive behavior	
Insurance	
Upgrades	
Ongoing operational costs (e.g. electricity, health and safety inspections, spares, maintenance contracts)	

a quick and dirty quantitative CBA of the new e-government system.

7b. Rate the costs and benefits of the new e-government system according to the subjective method described. If there are specific design options, use this approach to help choose between them.

NOTES

1. Some detail on network design is provided in the Online Appendix for Chapter 3.

2. The issue of task allocation is discussed in further detail in the Online Appendix for this chapter.

3. Details of longer group activities are provided in the Online Appendix to this chapter.

10

eGovernment Risk Assessment and Mitigation

Key Points

- Because most e-government projects fail, risk assessment and mitigation are essential.
- Risk assessment can be carried out by analyzing the gap between current reality and the design assumptions of an e-government project.
- When large design–reality gaps are present, risk mitigation options are summarized by the ZABC checklist.
- Risk mitigation through change occurs by gap reduction: changing the design of the e-government project to make it more like reality and/or by changing current reality to make it more like the assumptions/requirements within project design.
- Generic gap reduction techniques include legitimizing current reality, customization, client–vendor relationship management, incrementalism, and scope limitation.
- Specific gap reduction techniques to deal with stakeholder objectives and values run along a continuum of involvement, from the relatively arms'-length approach of reward and punishment, through the median approach of passive participation, to the intense involvement of end-user development.
- Any e-government risk mitigation technique can be analyzed in advance to see if it is appropriate to public sector realities.

Preceding chapters have presented a comforting set of steps and techniques intended to help build a sound e-government system. The discomforting fact is, though, that most e-government projects fail in some way, as noted in Chapter 1. It therefore makes sense to perform some kind of risk assessment – and mitigation where necessary – within the e-government system lifecycle.

In general terms, we can pose the following questions about risk assessment and mitigation:

- *Why*? The aim of risk management is to stop e-government projects failing.
- *When*? Assuming a typical project lifecycle of assessment–analysis–design–construction–implementation, then typically you would do a quick and dirty risk assessment during the assessment stage, and a more detailed assessment during the analysis stage. Risk mitigation activities could take place at any point, though might be particularly focused on analysis and on design. This is

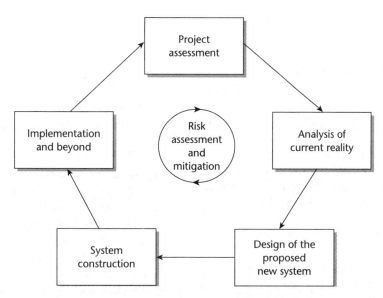

Figure 10.1   The place of risk assessment and mitigation in the e-government system lifecycle

summarized in Figure 10.1, showing that this chapter breaks the stage-by-stage pattern of Chapters 7–9. In general, the earlier you assess risk, the harder it is to know the risks accurately. But the later you assess risk, the harder it is to do anything about the risks identified.

- *Who?* A small team consisting of a mix of different stakeholders is the best unit to assess risk. The fewer people involved, the greater the chance that you miss an important risk. The more people involved, the higher the time and financial and other costs of the exercise.
- *How?* The remainder of this chapter is taken up with answering this question, focusing on the notion of design–reality gaps.[1]

10.1 RISK ASSESSMENT THROUGH GAP ANALYSIS

It is not easy to analyze the gap between current reality and the design assumptions and requirements of a proposed new e-government system. There are no hard and fast rules that say 'this gap is OK' or 'this gap is too large'. Any assessment of gaps – and, hence, of project risk – must therefore be subjective, and based on opinion and experience. If one accepts this subjectivity, then rating scales can be used, as described below:[2]

1   Using each of the seven ITPOSMO dimensions in turn, analyze two things. First, the organizational reality relating to that dimension that exists right now at the time of analysis. Second, the conceptions/requirements within the design of the e-government application.

2   For each one of the dimensions, give a numerical rating to indicate the size of the design–reality gap on that dimension. The rating for each dimension's gap can be anywhere on a scale from zero to ten. As a guide, illustrations are just given here for gaps corresponding to ratings of zero, five and ten, but all

numbers in the range are possible. Illustrative ratings:

- o 0 rating would indicate *no change* between the design proposal and current reality;
- o 5 rating would indicate *some degree of change* between the design proposal and current reality;
- o 10 rating would indicate *complete and radical change* between the design proposal and current reality.

3 Thus, for example, taking the first dimension – information – 0 would indicate that the information used in the e-government application was exactly the same as the information currently really being used. A rating of 5 would indicate that the information used in the e-government application was somewhat different from the information currently really being used. A rating of 10 would indicate that the information used in the e-government application was completely and radically different from the information currently really being used. This rating would be done by comparing information analysis of reality (see Chapter 8) with the new information design (see Chapter 9).

The other six dimensions to be rated from 0 to 10 are:

- o the technology used by agency and clients (comparing the requirements contained within the design of the e-government application versus the real situation now identified by an information systems (IS) audit);
- o the work processes undertaken in the agency–client system (comparing the processes needed for successful implementation of the e-government application versus the real situation now);

- o the objectives and values that key stakeholders need for successful implementation of the e-government application versus their current real objectives and values (this data would be produced by comparing the new system objectives and the rewards/values of the new human systems design with the objectives and values emerging from earlier people analysis);
- o the staffing numbers and skill levels/types required by the agency and clients (comparing the requirements for successful implementation of the e-government application identified by the new human systems design versus the real situation now identified in an IS audit);
- o the management systems and structures required in the agency (comparing the requirements for successful implementation of the e-government application identified by the new human systems design versus the real situation now identified in an IS audit);
- o the time and money required to successfully implement and operate the new application compared with the time and money really available now.

Where diagrams have been used – for example, a process map of the current process and one for the new process – they can support this comparison.

4 The simplest and crudest thing to do now is to add up the rating numbers for all seven ITPOSMO dimensions and interpret them according to Table 10.1.

A slightly more detailed approach is to present the scores for each individual dimension using a table or a diagram arranged to show the gaps in size order from largest to smallest. The dimensions with the largest gaps are those that

Table 10.1   *Risk Ratings and Outcomes for eGovernment Projects*

Overall rating	Likely outcome
57–70	The e-government project will almost certainly fail unless action is taken to close design–reality gaps.
43–56	The e-government project may well fail unless action is taken to close design–reality gaps
29–42	The e-government might fail totally, or might well be a partial failure unless action is taken to close design–reality gaps
15–28	The e-government project might be a partial failure unless action is taken to close design–reality gaps
0–14	The e-government project may well succeed

should be prioritized for action if risks of failure need to be addressed. Ideas about actions to take are discussed below.

These seven rating scales can be used by a single individual, such as a project consultant or project manager, to help them with their own understanding and recommendations. Alternatively, a more participative approach can be used. The seven scales can be presented to a group of key project stakeholders (both internal and external) in a facilitated workshop. The stakeholders discuss and rate each dimension. The main problematic design–reality gaps are identified. The workshop then moves on to work out how best to close those gaps. This mirrors the approach of 'soft systems' methods (Bell and Wood-Harper, 2003). These often advocate recognition of gaps as potential changes, which can then be discussed in participative fora to identify those that are desirable and feasible.

Design–reality gaps can be thought of as constraints or risks to implementation of an e-government project: they give a sense of what may make the project fail. They may not give a good sense of what may make the project succeed: the drivers. The drivers can be analyzed as well, and illustrated along-

side the gaps/constraints/risks using a force-field diagram with drivers on one side and constraints on the other. Strong drivers can push a project forward even where the risks/constraints (i.e. design–reality gaps) are large. But a project with weak drivers may be derailed by even quite small design–reality gaps.

Overall, this technique is relatively simple and quick to understand and put into practice. One key advantage is that it matches the unique situation of each individual e-government project, rather than imposing a 'one size fits all' concept.

On the downside, this gap analysis technique tries to cram a lot of issues into each single dimension (particularly into 'objectives and values' and 'staffing and skills'), and it will not work well if there are competing designs or competing ideas about what counts as 'reality' (e.g. between internal staff and external clients). Nor does it make value judgments about current reality: that reality might be highly dysfunctional, perhaps even corrupt, so you might want an e-government design that was very different from the current reality. But design–reality gap analysis tells you only about the risks of change, not the benefits (see also the point below about high-risk, high-gain projects).

Figure 10.2   Risk mitigation alternatives

10.2 RISK MITIGATION THROUGH GAP PREVENTION OR REDUCTION

Risk assessment through analysis of gaps is only one element. You also need to take action if there are large gaps and a high risk of failure. Options for action are summarized through ZABC:

- *Zap the project*: Abandon the e-government initiative.
- *Alter the project*: Change some of the initiative parameters to try to make it more feasible. It is this option for action that is the main focus of this chapter.
- *Be selfish*: If the change initiative seems likely to fail but it cannot be zapped or altered, then focus on personal goals and personal gains that can be extracted from the initiative such as training, expertise and experience, money, or equipment.
- *Change your job*: More radically if the e-government initiative seems likely to fail, change job either within the public agency to get away from the project, or to another organization.

The specific ZABC outcome will partly be dependent on the drivers which (see Chapter 7) may have been identified via force-field analysis during feasibility assessment. If drivers are strong, then it is likely that the project will continue, possibly with some alterations. Only if they are weak, will there be a realistic chance of zapping the project.

As just stated, this chapter will focus on altering the project through risk mitigation techniques that either (a) prevent large gaps

arising in the first place, or (b) reduce those gaps once they have been identified. In the latter case (summarized in Figure 10.2), taking action means either:

- changing the design of the e-government project to make it more like reality; and/or
- changing current reality to make it more like the assumptions/requirements within project design.

Selected techniques will, of course, depend on the dimension(s) in which the gap occurs. Take the example of a financial gap along the 'other resources' dimension. This gap could be reduced by scaling-down the project remit and thereby reducing cost (design change). Or it could be reduced through public–public or public–private collaboration that increases the supply of available finance (reality change).

A sample of risk mitigation techniques to accomplish gap prevention or gap reduction is presented in more detail below. This is not a comprehensive review of all dimensions, but an indication of some ways in which public agencies try to improve the success rate of e-government initiatives. Some techniques are *generic*: they relate to one or more ITPOSMO dimensions. Other techniques are *specific*: they relate to one specific dimension.[3]

Two final points should be made. First, e-government systems that require a greater design–reality gap – that is, a greater degree of change – may bring greater organizational benefits (though there is no necessary link between size of change and size of benefits).

In some cases, therefore, a trade-off is being made: reducing the size of the design–reality gap may increase the chance of system success but also reduce the organizational benefits of that system. Certain public officials might baulk at this and be inclined to adopt a 'high-risk, high-gain' strategy instead.

Second, in selecting a technique for a particular e-government project, one should ensure that the technique is not only desirable but also feasible. There is no point considering techniques that could reduce risks in theory, but not be implemented in practice. This issue will be revisited at the end of the chapter.

Generic Gap Reduction Techniques to Reduce the Risk of eGovernment Failure

Legitimizing and Mapping Current Reality

To succeed in e-government – and to properly identify design–reality gaps – you have to understand current reality. Yet this may be difficult to achieve. eGovernment leaders can help by 'legitimizing reality': by encouraging stakeholders to express the difference between prescriptive models of what they *should be* doing, and real depictions of what they *are actually* doing.

Techniques for exposing and mapping organizational and client realities such as those described in Chapter 8 play a role here. Self- and third party observation helps expose realities. Use of soft systems tools such as rich pictures helps map realities. Prototyping – described further below – helps both, particularly helping users to understand their real information needs.

Customization to Match Public Sector Realities

The approach to e-government during the 1970s and 1980s has been criticized for reinventing the wheel by custom-building each IT solution from scratch (Willcocks, 1994). In the 2000s, there is a danger that the pendulum is swinging too far the other way. Government agencies too readily try to install ready-made digital solutions that have been designed for private sector firms.

The problem is that private sector and public sector remain fundamentally different. Solutions designed for the former do not necessarily match the realities of the latter, and can create a classic situation of square pegs and round holes; and of large design–reality gaps.

To combat such problems, managers of e-government projects must be competent enough and confident enough to demand designs that match government's unique reality. The keywords for such projects must be 'customized' not 'off-the-shelf'; 'adapt' not just 'adopt'.

In many cases, this will require national and/or sectoral and/or in-house e-government development capacities to be strengthened. This will also affect selection of software vendors and developers. One key criterion will be their demonstrable willingness and ability to understand client contextual realities and to customize e-government systems accordingly.

Client–Vendor Relationship Management

As discussed in Chapter 5, the squeeze on public sector skills and cash means that e-government projects are increasingly outsourced to the private sector. This can exacerbate the traditional gulf between developers and clients, by stirring in an additional clash of culture and values seen, for example, in the collapse of the State of Connecticut's major outsourcing deal, caught between 'political acceptability and profitability' (Kieley et al., 2002: 344). Gaps between vendor design and client reality readily emerge in outsourced projects.

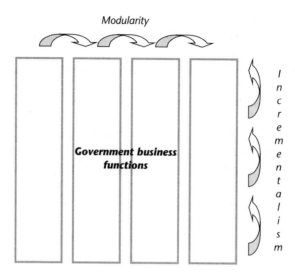

Figure 10.3   Modularity and incrementalism on e-government projects

To reduce these design–reality gaps, much more attention needs to be paid to active management of the client–vendor relationship, as also discussed in Chapter 5. Successful e-government projects are adopting innovative approaches to build mutual understanding and shared objectives. Gap reduction techniques include vendor shadowing of key client staff, joint team-building events, joint profit sharing and open book accounting.

For government, this heightened focus on supplier relationship management means the development of new skills and roles, including relationship building, contract facilitation, contract monitoring and vendor development. It also means a renewed emphasis on other roles that must remain in-house such as strategic management, business analysis and change management.

Step-by-step: Modularity and Incrementalism

The bigger and bolder the e-government project, the greater the risk of failure. Developers must reconfigure such projects to limit the extent of change (i.e. of design–reality gap) at any given time.

Stretching project time horizons is one technique. There is also a growing consensus behind modularity (supporting one business function at a time) and incrementalism (providing stepped levels of support for business functions) within e-government projects (see Figure 10.3).

This was put into practice in the US, 1996 Clinger-Cohen IT Management Reform Act, which 'required agencies to procure their largest systems in increments, or modules, rather than single 'grand design' acquisitions.' (Wolfe, 2001: 238). It was also used in Singapore's eCitizen project. This was first launched as a pilot system for proof of concept. Then a single package of services, related to education, was put onto the system. Once this was found to work satisfactorily, other services (births then employment then college registrations, etc.) were added one by one, with each one being fully checked and evaluated before the next was

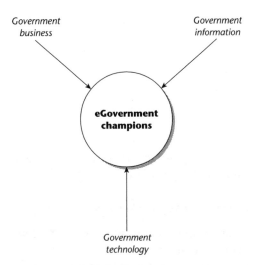

Figure 10.4   The capacities of hybrids for e-government projects

added. The full system was only launched two years after initial piloting (UNDESA, 2003a).

Hybrids and 'Tribrids'

Design–reality gaps often arise in e-government because of a 'two tribes' mentality that afflicts most governments: a variant on the issue of divisions already identified in Chapter 2. IT designers understand technology but not the realities of government. Public officials and politicians understand the realities of government but not the technology. To close these gaps, projects need to develop and use the hybrid professionals who understand both perspectives. We might even call them 'tribrids' (see Figure 10.4) if they can combine three aspects: understanding the technology *and* the business of government *and* the role of information in government. The development of hybrids is discussed in further detail in Chapter 12.

Scope Limitation: KISS and Automation

eGovernment projects sometimes fail because they try to change too many things at once. One way to address such over-large design–reality gaps is to cut down the scope and ambition of the project design; sticking with the valuable design motto *KISS*: *Keep it Simple, Stupid*. One way to incorporate KISS is by trying to freeze all except the technology dimension. How? In some cases by simple automation of existing activities. The intention is to retain the same information, same processes, same management systems and structures, and so on, but merely change them from manual to computerized operations. In other words, you attempt to create no design–reality gap (no change) on most ITPOSMO dimensions. Although criticized in hindsight as being insufficiently bold or for computerizing inefficiency (see the Vermont case discussed next), simple automation can be a very good – and successful – way to institutionalize new technology in a particular aspect of public sector operations.

Scope Limitation: Processes before Technology

Another variation on the idea of freezing some dimensions is to postpone introduction of new technology, and focus first on improving processes. IT is no cure for poor management or poor governance, and broad/deep problems with current public sector processes need to be addressed first before new technology can be of wider value to a program of change. The State of Vermont ran into this problem in the mid-1990s, automating a set of personnel procedures that were inefficient and ineffective, and thus ending with an inefficient, ineffective e-government system (Cats-Baril

Figure 10.5　Typology of e-government applications

and Thompson, 1995). The Office of Defense Trade Controls in the US stumbled similarly when automating its licensing procedures for munitions exports before first reforming those procedures (OIG, 2002).

Reality-Supporting not Rationality-Imposing Applications

There is a continuum of e-government applications, as shown in Figure 10.5 (Heeks, 2005).[4] At one extreme, there are 'rationality-imposing applications', such as decision-support systems. These include in their design a whole series of assumptions about the presence of rational information, processes, objectives and values, management structures, and so on. These rationalities must either be present in the organization as a pre-condition for successful implementation of this application, or they must be imposed. In many government organizations, the introduction of such applications will not succeed because of the large gap between the application's required rationalities and current organizational realities.

At the other extreme, there are 'reality-supporting applications' such as word processing or email. By comparison with rationality-imposing applications, reality-supporting applications require fewer rational pre-conditions or impositions. They can therefore work successfully in a wider variety of government organizational situations. eGovernment projects will therefore be more likely to succeed if they focus on

'reality-supporting' rather than 'rationality-imposing' applications.

Supporting Informal Information Systems

Informal information systems can be damaging to a public agency and its clients, and there are arguments for stamping out such systems. On the other hand, such systems play an essential role in the public sector, and one that may become increasingly valued with growing recognition of tacit knowledge as an organizational resource. Supporting informal information systems can mean that several potential dimensions of change – such as objectives and values, staffing, management and structures – are frozen and do *not* change. Risks may therefore be reduced. Ways to support such systems include using the reality-supporting e-government applications identified above, and finding ways to build up informal relationships through social networking. When Scottish Enterprise, a government agency based in Glasgow, wanted to create a 'workplace of the future' for its staff, it made a deliberate attempt to harness the organization's human knowledge resources by supporting informal information systems (Bell, 2000). Initiatives included cross-functional work teams, an open office layout to encourage communication, informal wire-free workspaces to encourage face-to-face discussions, an onsite staff café, and the introduction of a comprehensive internal email service. The result of supporting informal systems has been claims of up to 50 percent higher productivity (WF, 2002).

Dimension-Specific Gap Reduction Techniques to Reduce the Risk of eGovernment Failure

A number of dimension-specific risk mitigation techniques are discussed in Chapter 5.[5] These include innovative ways to increase income to close finance gaps, and the use of outsourcing and consultants to close staffing and skills gaps. A summary of techniques for all dimensions is presented in Box 10.1 below. The remainder of this chapter will focus on more detailed discussion of risk mitigation (i.e. gap closure) for the most important dimension: that of objectives and values.

10.3 CHANGE MANAGEMENT: ADDRESSING THE GAP OF STAKEHOLDER OBJECTIVES AND VALUES

Key stakeholders – funders, managers, operators, users, clients, and so on – must support (passively or, ideally, actively) a proposed e-government project if it is to succeed. For any human to support a project, that project must align with at least some of their personal objectives and values. Put more simply, the e-government project must provide each stakeholder with at least some positive answer to the key change management question we all ask of any project: 'Why should I: what's in it for me?'.

This is the most critical question that must be answered during analysis and design of an e-government system because it grapples with the politics and self-interest that are the strongest determinants of e-government success or failure. As ever from a design–reality perspective, getting a positive answer will either involve altering the reality of current stakeholder objectives and values and/or altering the project design.

These risk-mitigating alterations can be undertaken in a variety of ways as part of the change management process. In this section, the techniques described can be seen as representing a continuum of involvement, from the relatively arms'-length approach of reward and punishment, through the median approach of passive participation, to the intense involvement of end-user development.

Changing Stakeholder Self-Interest: Reward and Punishment

Self-interest may come from some immutable drive for survival within the human psyche, but the way it manifests itself changes all the time. Stakeholder self-interest can therefore be manipulated by external factors, to align it more with other stakeholders' interests or with those of the organization. Put another way, stakeholder motivations can be altered to make them support, or at least not resist, the introduction of a particular reform-enabling e-government system. Any gap of objectives, values and motivations can therefore be reduced.

One way in which this manipulation takes place is through the use of financial rewards for primary users. For employee stakeholders, this could be in the guise of an 'e-government skills payment': a one-off award or a regrading in recognition of the additional skills or responsibilities that go with use of new technology. In some cases, this

Box 10.1   Dimension-Specific Risk Mitigation Ideas

Information Dimension

- Undertake a professional requirements analysis in order to draw out true information needs of stakeholders.
- Use prototyping – getting users to use a test version of the e-government application – in order to help them explain what information they really need.

Technology Dimension

- Investigate ways in which government reforms could be delivered without IT.
- Investigate ways in which government reforms could be delivered using the existing IT infrastructure.
- Avoid leading-edge technologies in e-government design.
- Investigate opportunities for use of donated or recycled equipment.

Process Dimension

- Keep doing things the same way, only with the addition of some new technology (see generic point above about automation).
- Avoid business process reengineering; instead, at most, look at optimization or minor modification of existing processes within the e-government application design.
- Consider a two-stage approach: in the first stage, processes are optimized without any change to IT; in the second and later stage, new IT is brought in.

Objectives and Values Dimension

- Use rewards to alter stakeholder objectives and values (e.g. incentives for e-government take-up for clients; or messages of management support, better pay, better working conditions, career advancement, etc. for internal staff).
- Use punishments to alter stakeholder objectives and values (e.g. higher costs for use of non-e-government channels for clients; or threats, reprimands, transfers, worsened pay and conditions, etc. for internal staff).
- Communicate with stakeholders about the system: sell the true benefits and address the true negative aspects.
- Get key stakeholders (those regarded as key opinion formers or those vociferous in their resistance to the e-government application) to participate in the analysis and/or design of the e-government application.
- Base e-government application design on a consensus view of all main stakeholders.
- Use prototyping: this helps incorporate stakeholder objectives in the design, and also helps to make actual stakeholder objectives more realistic.
- If feasible in skill, time and motivational terms, get users to help develop and build the e-government application.

Staffing and Skills Dimension

- Outsource contracts in order to improve the current reality of available competencies (though this may increase other gaps).
- Train staff and/or clients to improve the current reality of competencies.
- Simplify system interfaces to make usage easier.
- Improve recruitment and retention techniques to reduce competency (staff) turnover.
- Make use of external consultants (though this may increase other gaps).
- Hire new staff to expand the volume of current competencies.

Management Systems and Structures Dimension

- Make an explicit commitment within e-government application design to retain the existing management systems and structures.

Other Resources Dimension

- Prioritize e-government applications that maximize revenue generation for government (e.g. those dealing with tax, fees, fines, etc.).
- Seek additional financing from central government agencies.
- Take out loans from private sector institutions.
- Get private firms to develop, own and operate the e-government application.
- Charge business or wealthier users of the e-government system.
- Scale down ambitions of the e-government project.
- Extend timescales of the e-government project.
- Negotiate central/shared agency IT agreements to reduce hardware and software costs.
- Use 'one for all' contracts that are reusable.
- Use project management techniques to reduce waste and delays.
- Outsource contracts in order to reduce time (and possibly costs) gaps.
- Make use of open source software (though cost savings are often less than anticipated).

---

has been little more than a bribe to persuade users to stop complaining about a new system or to withdraw a threat of employee action.

There are often constraints on the innovative use of payment rewards in the public sector, so other examples of the 'carrot' approach for employees include:

- explicit messages of support for the system from senior managers or politicians, possibly suggesting that staff career progress will benefit from accepting the system;

- offering training courses for stakeholders, perhaps in a desirable location;
- improving the stakeholders' working environment;
- providing stakeholders with new job titles or other non-financial rewards; or
- involving stakeholders more in the process of systems development (see below).

In India's public sector railway system, a major program was introduced to reform travel reservations through computerization (Heeks, 2000c). There was potential for considerable resistance to this change from front-line clerical staff involved. However, the danger was averted, partly thanks to encouraging statements made by senior public servants and politicians. In large measure, though, the rewards provided were those of a changed working environment. Reservation offices were provided with good lighting and air conditioning. Clerks were encouraged to think of themselves as skilled computer operators, even to the extent of being issued with white coats of the type that laboratory technicians wear. All of this was a great improvement from the Dickensian setting of the pre-computer reservation offices. As a result, the reform was implemented with few problems.

Given evidence of relatively poor take-up of e-government systems (Accenture, 2003), carrots are also needed for external clients. This can take the form of quicker or cheaper service via the e-government route. Australia's SmartGate automated passport checking system, for instance, offers travelers the benefit of faster service as an incentive to support and use the system. Rewards can also be financial: Singapore's Inland Revenue Authority encourages use of its e-filing system by including filers in a cash prize draw; Canada's Corporations Directorate charges C$200 for online filing, C$50 less than for the paper-based route.

The 'stick' approach has also been used to modify perceived self-interest. Staff may be threatened with worse job content, with stagnating pay or careers, with transfer, or even with retrenchment if they continue to resist the new system. For example, public officials in Dubai who failed to make the transition to e-government-based working within 18 months were told by the country's Crown Prince that they would be fired (Holmes, 2001). For clients, the stick is the fact that service via non-e-government channels is quantitatively or qualitatively worse.

A variant used with employee stakeholders is the 'removal of stick' approach. In such cases, there may be some threat (real or invented) such as job losses or deskilling or loss of personal power that the new e-government application is felt to pose to stakeholders. If those managing the development process then remove this threat, it may cause stakeholders to feel their interests are being served by the new system.

In general, these examples relate to direct and individualized incentives. However, the drivers behind e-government projects – which are often contextual and political and/or legal – will also provide incentives. For example, many projects are driven by centrally set e-government targets associated with agency-level rewards and punishments (e.g. additional funds for success versus funding withdrawal for failure, or public acclaim versus 'naming and shaming') that are fairly readily converted into individual incentives.

Communication and Expectation Management

Communication during an e-government project can be a one-way process of telling those involved what will be happening. This helps to reduce stakeholder uncertainty and ensure there are not too many surprises. It also ensures that expectations about satisfaction of, or conflict with, self-interest do not become overblown. It provides stakeholders with a sense that they are involved and that their interests are not completely divorced from e-government objectives.

Assuming it moves beyond mere awareness-raising, then communication and expectation management will have two main elements. First, selling the benefits of the new system to stakeholders; in particular, communicating the personal benefits that will emerge. Second, discussing the negative aspects of the new system directly and denying them if untrue or admitting them if true. Honesty about negative outcomes is widely advocated as a technique, though many managers find it hard to accept and employ.

When New York State's Department of Agriculture and Markets embarked on automation of its dog licensing service, frequent communication with stakeholders throughout system development was seen as vital to success. A clear, concise newsletter was sent out to all stakeholders during development, supplemented by phone calls and meetings that kept key individuals further informed (Dawes et al., 1997). The result was a successfully implemented system that increased efficiency.

Participation

A gap can arise between reality and design if the design proposal represents the interests of only one stakeholder, or one stakeholder group. This can occur around the four-way division between senior managers, politicians, mainstream staff and IT staff described in Chapter 2. It can also occur around the division between internal government staff and external citizen/business clients. Generally, it will occur if some of the key stakeholders are not represented in the system development process.

The likelihood of such gaps arising can be reduced, then, if all the stakeholder groups participate in systems development. Participation is widely cited as a critical success factor in the e-government development process (e.g. Cook et al., 2002; Detlor and Finn, 2002). When the US State Department built WRAPS, its Worldwide Refugee Admissions Processing System, the system was intended to help volunteer organizations resettle refugees in the US. A key element in the system lifecycle was the participation of representatives from these organizations 'to ensure that the information and statistics that WRAPS produces would satisfy their requirements' (Fulton, 2003: 139).

When putting together the project team to oversee e-government development, a check can be made to see if all major stakeholder groups are represented. Looking to the internal stakeholders, at least four roles will normally be present if a participative approach is used, adapted from the 'IT square' illustrated in Chapter 2 (Figure 2.2):

- senior managers and politicians with the power to allocate resources and have decisions implemented (their particular case is discussed further below);
- IT staff who can provide the necessary technical input;
- mainstream managers within whose work sections the new system will be introduced, and who will use the system's output;
- primary users who will actually operate the new e-government system.

In addition, larger projects may involve other specialist staff such as finance and human resource specialists. There will also be a need for collaboratory participation across institutional boundaries for cross-government and intersectoral e-government systems. Finally, as discussed in more detail below, client groups might be involved.

Other roles that may be addressed are those of key opinion leaders, who can be involved early. In particular, those opinion leaders who might resist the changes may be targeted. Nothing kills off resistance better than getting those likely to resist to participate in and 'own' the systems development process.

As a way of encouraging participation, some governments have developed best practice guides or standard methodologies that incorporate participation. Thus the UK government's PRINCE 2 method – though painted in Chapter 5 as very rational – nonetheless includes procedures for involving management, users and other stakeholders in the development process.

The larger the project team, though, the greater the cost in staff time and the longer it takes to communicate and to make decisions. There are therefore pressures to keep the team small, and so exclude some stakeholders. In this case, then, a participative approach will at least involve two-way communication with non-team stakeholders and getting their feedback about current reality and about new design proposals.

Involving Senior Officials

The support of senior public officials is identified by studies as a critical success factor in e-government systems development perhaps more than any other factor (Pascual, 2003). For example, South Africa's ambitious Cape Gateway project to provide a full data/services portal was only possible because it was championed by a senior Minister (Levin and Dingley, 2003). Similarly, the development of agency intranets in US federal government has only progressed where there has been support at secretary or deputy secretary level (Mahler and Regan, 2003).

In cases where senior staff become positively involved, their support:

- brings access to organizational resources, including political clout;
- signals the importance of the project to other stakeholders; and
- may suppress some types of user resistance.

Where there is a lack of commitment, this arises from two particular gaps, as described below.

A gap of objectives   Where senior staff do not feel their interests are being served by the proposed e-government system, they will not support it.

This gap can be addressed by ensuring that senior staff participate in the system development process, and that their interests are considered in setting system objectives. Given that senior officials' support is such a key factor, it may sometimes be relevant to let system objectives be almost entirely determined by senior staff. Of course, the danger here is of ignoring other stakeholders and thereby running the risk of system failure.

Everyone complains that e-government projects suffer from political cycles – the four years between elections, or the two-year tenure of senior officials in particular posts, or the annual funding round. But these cycles are a fact of life that shape the objectives of senior figures in the public sector. The cycles must be recognized and built into the project design. They mean – whatever the ultimate ambitions of the project – that it must show some fairly quick deliverables; hence, the endlessly repeated e-government mantra of 'Think Big, Start Small, Scale Fast', which specifically matches the political realities of the public sector.

A gap of knowledge or skills or attitudes Where senior officials do not understand IT or the role of information systems and where they lack systems development or project management skills and confidence, they may try to suppress new e-government systems. They do this partly because they feel unable to control the systems development process, and because they fear that exposing their ignorance will undermine their authority. This is a particular problem for the public sector, where the lack of IT/IS-related competencies is higher than in the private sector (Say, 2002b).

This gap is mainly addressed through training and presentations, though special allowances may need to be made for senior staff. For example:

- they may be trained first, before all other staff, to give them a head start;
- they may be sent to some prestigious training institution commensurate with their perceived importance;
- they may be trained one-to-one, to avoid having to expose their ignorance to other staff members.

In the UK Home Office, for example, senior managers were among the first to be trained in updated IT skills as part of a broad e-government-enabled modernization program (*Government Computing*, 2003b). Their training was provided via one-to-one sessions in their offices, and has resulted in development of both competence and confidence in using laptop-based systems.

Attitudes can be addressed using the attitude training techniques described in Chapter 5. Producing an e-government system (or even just a demonstration) that meets some senior official's need – even a minor one – can also help to change attitudes. Use of prototyping (see below) can also help.

Even simpler can be a demonstration of systems already in use, of which senior managers and politicians are unaware. Many governments run these as a day or week event; for example, the Australian government ran an eGovernment Week (*SMH*, 2002). This was aimed at the public in part, but also at closing knowledge and attitude gaps amongst politicians, legislature staff and government managers.

Senior officials are also particularly susceptible to presentations that pander to their vanity and insecurity, of the 'Your peers in sister organizations have got wonderful new e-government systems, don't you think you should have one too' variety.

Unfortunately, the message of such presentations and of management training may be to wrongly over-emphasize the technology and under-emphasize information and contextual factors in reform. The result may be a job half-done that is worse than not being done at all. Senior managers may be converted into semi-literate IT idolizers who feel technology will solve all problems. They rush headlong into e-government, but using the wrong approach and in ever-changing directions blown by the winds of technology fads and fashions.

Involving External Clients

Increasing numbers of e-government systems involve external clients. Closing the gap between system design and client realities means involving those clients in some way. This is a cornerstone of e-government success, with a clear relationship seen between ratings of success in e-government service quality and level of client consultation (Accenture, 2003). Yet a review of major US e-government system proposals revealed only nine out of 23 even discussed how to identify client needs (GSA, 2003).

Where clients are involved, the trend with e-government is to involve them earlier and deeper in the lifecycle. Where previously clients would have been brought in at the point of testing, now they might be brought in to analyze current problems or to define key system objectives. Such consultation typically means talking with clients through interviews or focus groups. As an example, the Danish government used a panel of 400 business representatives to help provide input about the design of its enterprise portal. Similarly, the successful delivery of online services by Tameside Council in the UK has been underpinned by a citizens' panel and by broader polling that ensure client needs drive e-government objectives and direction (SOCITM and IDEA, 2002).

A more radical participative approach would include clients in the actual project team in some way. This may seem fairly obvious where those client groups are going to be the key users of the e-government system, yet such inclusion is rare. It is rarer still to include external client groups for an internal e-government system even though they are likely to be affected by such systems and, hence, should be identified as system stakeholders.

Active Participation and Consensus

Allowing stakeholder groups to be heard does not necessarily mean that they are listened to, and some approaches may just pay lip-service to participation. This 'passive participation' may still be of value. It can make stakeholders feel that they are involved, and therefore make them view the new system more positively. However, reducing design–reality gaps is more likely if the intention is that participation should be an active process.

One way of making participation active is to allocate particular tasks to particular stakeholders, as described in the section below on user involvement. However, this still allows gaps to emerge between one group's designs and other groups' realities. Closing these gaps may require the use of active participation techniques to build *consensus*.

In essence, this requires the different stakeholder groups to develop an agreed view of reality and/or problems and/or objectives and/or design choices. For example, all stakeholder personal objectives could be combined and compromised in order to create a single set of agreed reform objectives. Such consensus involves perceived

self-interest being made to converge with perceived group (or even organizational) interests.

One of the skills of being an e-government hybrid is in balancing the different interests of different stakeholder groups. It means deciding whether to demand a single consensus output that recognizes all groups, or whether to allow one or two stakeholder groups to dominate, in which case there will be no consensus.

Consensus can be created using relatively formal techniques, which are sometimes known as 'joint application development' (JAD) techniques when applied to information systems (including e-government) development. These bring different stakeholder groups together for a structured meeting with a facilitator. Meeting participants and outputs are agreed beforehand. Where plenary meetings are difficult, the facilitator may become more of a negotiator and mediator, going round to stakeholders one-by-one trying to narrow down differences.

For example, when New York State wanted to apply web-based technologies to payment claims for its Child Nutrition Program, it adopted a JAD-centered approach (Connell, 2001). Public servants from education, finance and IT were brought together with consulting staff to agree issues such as the business rules being applied to the program, and the data requirements. Although this required more time and effort than a more top-down/single-view approach, it led to savings because changes did not have to be made later in the e-government lifecycle.

Consensus can also be created indirectly. For example, a group of stakeholders can be set a task, such as creating a diagram of the e-government system, or producing a single, final version of some rating table for subjective cost/benefit analysis. The group is focused on the particular output required. In practice, though, the output may be much less important than the process of working together, of mutual learning through sharing knowledge and values and perspectives, and of reaching some kind of agreement.

In addition, training has a role to play. It can help in group-forming and in trying to reduce the 'distance' between stakeholder positions. Finally, consensus can be achieved by locating multiple stakeholder roles within the same individual, the ultimate expression of which is end-user development (see below).

Prototyping

Prototyping is a form of active participation. It is the use of a working model of the final e-government system, which users can see, comment on, and have revised before the final version is produced. The prototype can be presented to stakeholders by being either demonstrated to them or used by them. Their reactions can be recorded about system elements they would like kept, removed, altered, and added.

Reactions and suggestions can be probed further by individual and group discussion during prototyping or after. Prototyping – like other participative techniques – therefore demands developers who listen to, and empathize with, other stakeholders.

Next, revisions to the prototype are planned and implemented, and the process of presentation and stakeholder reaction can be re-run. Iterations around this cycle may continue several times until stakeholders are satisfied. The scope of this cycle may need to be widened if issues raised during prototyping indicate, say, that the initial focus of reform or the initial project feasibility assessment were misguided.

The main benefit of prototyping is that, being faced with an actual e-government system, stakeholders can express requirements or objectives that they would otherwise find hard to state. Such requirements may be quite general (e.g. about the overall objectives sought from a government reform process) or may be quite specific (e.g. a comment on the nature of the system interface). The presence of a system helps focus stakeholders' attention, imagine what they need from the system, and point out what they do not like. In turn, this means that:

- the final e-government system is more likely to match stakeholder objectives;
- stakeholders are more realistic in what they expect from the final system;
- the final system *may* be produced more quickly; and that
- major problems are spotted earlier, and can therefore be addressed at lower cost.

Design–reality gaps of objectives and values but also finance and possibly time may therefore be tackled.

Such benefits were found when prototyping was used in development of an integrated service delivery system for local government in the Netherlands (Leenes, 2002). This not only led to improvements in the system, but also to greater levels of interest and commitment from staff, managers and politicians in local government. Although receiving a rather cooler initial response, the prototype for the US Business Advisor service portal for small enterprise was similarly valuable (Fountain, 2001). It generated a large amount of feedback – channeled through user focus groups – that led to redesign of content, services, interface and tools. This also helped to align expectations within the business community more closely with what could be delivered online.

Like any technique, prototyping can have its drawbacks (Avison and Fitzgerald,

2003). Time pressures may force premature acceptance of the prototyped system as a final system before all requirements are fully analyzed, before non-technical components of the system are designed, or before the system is properly tested and documented. Prototyping may encourage corners to be cut, yet it does not substitute for techniques to analyze reality or to create consensus or for good communications between IT staff and users. It can also be difficult to engage users – particularly external clients – in the prototyping process without some direct incentives, such as payment.

Nevertheless, prototyping is increasingly used in development of e-government systems and is often cited as a critical success factor in the development process (Brown, 2001; HPG, 2001). Systems development methodologies that incorporate prototyping have been around for many years. For example, prototyping has been successfully incorporated into Dynamic Systems Development Method. This provides a standard, non-proprietary approach to systems development that combines both rapid and joint application development methods (Bocij et al., 2003). It has been adopted for certain projects by a number of government agencies worldwide.

Such combinations of prototyping and active participation can be particularly effective. The Royal Netherlands Air Force, for example, used both techniques through a management game involving the simulation of the entire organizational information system for a planned air base. Not only did this create a shared vision for change among participants, it also facilitated discussion of key issues, and created a sense of unity between those involved. As a result, this has been recommended as a standard approach to public sector change (Quanjel and Wenzler, 1998).

User Involvement and End-User Development

IT staff and senior managers can easily fall into the trap of idolizing new technology, and develop a belief that the formal objectivity of technology represents the best path for organizational change. Senior managers and external consultants can easily develop a belief that formal and objective models of the organization represent best practice that should be aimed for. All these groups may therefore attempt to impose technology-/rationality-driven designs on the change process.

Of all the stakeholders, the users are those who tend to be most rooted in current system realities, and who best understand when technology-/rationality-driven models will be inappropriate. Giving users a bigger say in systems development can therefore help guard against e-government failure. In the US State Department, for instance, a review of the successful e-government systems found:

> Practically all of the innovations were initiated and developed by individuals who were part of the user community that they were designed to serve. (Fulton, 2003: 167)

A number of techniques for involving users in the e-government development process have been described above. Another technique is a hybrid division of roles, as described in Chapter 2, that allocates certain systems development responsibilities to users. Typical examples can include:

• making one of the users responsible for managing the whole e-government project;
• getting a user or user group to undertake the analysis of current reality;
• getting a user group to recommend which of various e-government design options should be adopted;
• making users responsible for process design while IT staff work on technical design;

- getting a user to write the system documentation;
- having the training designed and delivered to users by users;
- requiring a formal user acceptance test of the new system.

In the development of a new intranet for the US Department of Transportation, for example, user-managers were involved throughout the development lifecycle (Mahler and Regan, 2003). Program and personnel managers who would be key users of the intranet were put in charge of design decisions for the intranet covering not just functions but also terminology and layout. They were responsible for pilot testing intranet prototypes. They also ensured that the language of the project remained rooted in user experiences rather than drifting off into 'web-speak'. As a result, there was a good fit between user needs and intranet outcomes.

The ultimate expression of this process of giving responsibilities to users is *end-user development*, which vests all – or almost all – systems development roles in a single person. This will close the design–reality gaps of information needs, and of objectives and values. It can significantly reduce the money and time resource requirement, and end users are most unlikely to create unmanageable levels of change for themselves on the other ITPOSMO dimensions. As such, end-user development should greatly increase the chance of producing a successful e-government system.

However, as described in Chapter 2, there can be drawbacks (Bocij et al., 2003). By focusing on users, one may lose focus on other stakeholders; for example, delivering a system that is user-friendly but politically unwelcome. Allowing insufficiently skilled users to develop systems can lead to poor quality analysis, design, construction and

implementation. To combat this, either user training or some type of hybrid responsibility-sharing compromise between users and the IT section is appropriate in order to provide the knowledge and skills support that users need. Such an approach was employed when Western Australia's Department of Conservation and Land Management needed a new computerized system to support environmental assessments (Hobbs and Pigott, 2001). Users laid out their information needs using spreadsheets; a technology with which they were familiar. IT staff then helped them translate those needs into an operational system based around database software.

Even where this type of support can be provided, it must be recognized that end-user development is only appropriate for certain types of e-government system but that, if adequately supported, it represents a significant improvement on other systems development methods by inherently managing the degree of change. While such ideas are slowly gaining acceptance in relation to internal staff users, they still represent a 'radical fringe' view when applied to external client users. Yet, with growth of, and increasing need for, client-focused approaches to e-government, such radical ideas must increasingly be contemplated.

10.4 CONCLUSION: THE APPLICABILITY OF THESE TECHNIQUES

The essence of design–reality gaps as an approach to e-government risk assessment and mitigation is that it is contingent: matching itself to the particular public agency and context. The focus, though, in this chapter has been on the contingency of the e-government system's content (the *what*) rather than on the contingency of the e-government development process (the *how*). In other words, we have focused on matching the final e-government system to its context, but have not thought about matching e-government risk techniques to their context.

We must now do the latter in order avoid presenting the risk mitigation techniques in a prescriptive, 'cookbook' manner. We must therefore not say 'participative approaches will always be part of successful e-government implementation'. Instead, we must say 'first analyze the situation to see if these particular conditions hold; if they do, then participation is more likely to be of value; if they do not, then participation is less likely to be of value.'

For example, user-participation techniques for e-government development are unlikely to work well where (adapted from Heeks, 1999c):

- internal/external users lack information about participative techniques and about the new e-government system (information dimension);
- the objectives of senior officials are not to share power and the values of the public agency are authoritarian and hierarchical (objectives and values dimension);
- users lack the skills and confidence necessary to engage in participative processes (staffing and skills dimension);
- the management style and organizational structures of the public agency are highly centralized (management systems and structures dimension); and/or
- the agency lacks the time and money to invest in participative approaches (other resources dimension).

From this example, it can be seen that we can apply the design–reality/ITPOSMO model to the process of e-government implementation. We can say that risk assessment and mitigation (and other implementation)

techniques are less likely to work where there is a large gap between the design assumptions/requirements inherent within those techniques and the realities of the public agency or context in which you try to apply them. We can therefore use the design–reality gap model to assess not just the feasibility of a particular e-government system design, but also the feasibility of particular e-government implementation techniques.

The risk mitigation techniques discussed in this chapter are therefore likely to help e-government, but they cannot always be applied. The techniques are fairly well known, but the continuing high failure rate of e-government initiatives is a reminder that there is no panacea. All will depend on the design–reality gaps for those techniques, and on the room for maneuver that stakeholders have. In addition to undertaking gap analysis, those interested in applying the techniques in this (or other) chapters are therefore advised to run through the room for maneuver checklist presented in Chapter 7, focusing on their capacity to introduce new techniques. Some ideas on extending one's room for maneuver in e-government are discussed in the section on politics in Chapter 5.

If the techniques described cannot be applied, or if they are being applied unsuccessfully, and the overall design–reality gap for an e-government project is still felt to be sizeable, then action A identified in Section 10.2 above is no longer an option. The courses that remain are those of Z, B and C discussed earlier.

If the e-government application does proceed and then fail, this should not be written off as a completely negative experience. Failure provides powerful opportunities for organizational learning (though whether these are recognized and taken up is another matter discussed further in Chapter 11). Failure may also leave a residue that is built upon. For example, fear or ignorance of particular new technologies may be reduced. The e-government infrastructure may later be used for other purposes. Thus, even if unsuccessful, the introduction of new IT and information systems is still a way of changing current reality in the public sector.

ACTIVITIES

Shorter In-Class Activities[6]

Introduction

a. 'Risk comes in the future, and is unknowable. Therefore we should not waste time worrying about it in e-government projects.' Discuss in pairs then plenary.

Section 10.1

a. The following passage describes both design and reality for an anonymous planned e-government system to assist with personnel management in several government departments. Read the passage, and then discuss your estimated rating (on a scale of 0–10) of the gap between design and reality:

  The e-government design incorporates a new set of security procedures, which bar clerical staff (those who do the data entry work) from amending personnel records of managers and senior officials. The current reality is that clerks are allowed to amend all records except those of senior officials that are explicitly identified as confidential. Related to security, the design assumes the acceptability of electronic signatures, which would allow forms and other formal documentation to be passed between departments. In reality, electronic signatures are not yet legally acceptable. The design also assumes a change in location of many processes, even though many of the basics of personnel record-keeping would remain as they are in current reality (except for their partial automation).

b. Which is it more important to understand for an e-government project: the drivers or the risks? Discuss in pairs then plenary.

Section 10.2

a. You are a junior analyst working on an e-government project. Following your risk analysis, you are convinced the project is going to fail. Considering you junior position, what would you be most likely to do next?

b. Discuss which is easier to change on e-government projects: design or reality.

c. In pairs, then plenary, discuss whether it is better for the public sector to go for low-risk, low-gain or high-risk, high-gain e-government projects. What are the implications of your conclusions for risk assessment and mitigation?

  (As a supplementary: does high-risk always mean high-gain, or can e-government projects be high-risk, low-gain?)

d. You have a simple task to complete: stand up and write your name down on a piece of paper. The only complication is that – at the same time as you try to write your name – you must pat your head, count backwards from 10 to 0, and dance. Reflect on your experience to understand what happens if you try to change several ITPOSMO dimensions at once on an e-government project.

e. To avoid creating too much change, it makes sense to separate the redesign of government processes from the automation of those processes. Discuss which way round it would be best to sequence these changes: process redesign then automation, or automation then process redesign.

f. Identify at least two further examples of each of a 'reality-supporting' application and a 'rationality-imposing' application used in the public sector.

g. Select three or four of the risk mitigation ideas in Box 10.1. Identify whether they are mainly concerned with changing e-government design, or mainly concerned with changing current reality.

Section 10.3

a. Better e-government projects can provide a good answer to the 'Why should I: what's in it for me?' question for all stakeholders. Imagine a new e-government system is planned to enable online tax payments. Provide a good answer to the 'Why should I: what's in it for me?' question for the following three stakeholders: a politician with an interest in improving tax; a clerical staff member of the country's main tax agency involved in processing tax payments; and a citizen tax-payer.

b. You are the project leader for a major e-government project. You sense that the objectives and values of some current staff are out of synch with the project's inherent goals and values. What would be your preferred method for creating greater alignment of objectives and values, and why: reward/ punishment, awareness- raising, communication, passive participation, active participation, prototyping, or end-user development?

c. Discuss in pairs, then plenary, whether the support of senior officials is really that crucial to the success of e-government projects.

Section 10.4

a. 'The public sector is not capable of learning from e-government failures.' Discuss in pairs then plenary.

Assignment Questions

Sections 10.1–10.2

a. Identify a detailed e-government case study. In selecting the case study, you should ensure that there is enough detail to answer *all* the following:

1 Who were the main stakeholders involved in the change?
2 Using each of the ITPOSMO dimensions in turn analyze two things. First, the organizational reality relating to that dimension that existed prior to/at the start of the change. Second, the assumptions/requirements within the initial design of the change initiative.
3 As you analyze the design and reality for each dimension, also estimate the gap between the two on a scale of 0–10.
4 Make an overall assessment of the extent of gap between design and initial reality.
5 On the basis of your design–reality gap analysis and any other relevant evidence, summarize the main constraints to introduction of the e-government system.
6 Make an overall assessment of whether the system was a success or some kind of failure. Relate your assessment to your findings about design–reality gaps.
7 If the system was some kind of failure, suggest both specific and generic ways in which design–reality gaps could have been closed in order to increase the likelihood of success. If it was a success, how were design–reality gaps kept small or closed during the implementation of the e-government system?

b. What would a hybrid approach to e-government risk assessment and mitigation look like?

Sections 10.1–10.4

a. How should approaches to information systems project risk assessment and mitigation be similar and different in the public sector compared to the private sector?

Practitioner Exercises

Sections 10.1–10.2

a. Either, for an e-government project that has already been completed, undertake the first assignment given above. Or, for a project that has not yet been completed, undertake the project development exercise given below.

Sections 10.1–10.4

a. What is the relevance and applicability to your public sector organization of the risk assessment and mitigation techniques described in this chapter? Note down any implications of your answer for e-government systems development in the organization.

eGovernment Project Development Exercises

1 Using each of the ITPOSMO dimensions in turn, analyze two things. First, the organizational reality relating to that dimension that currently exists (i.e. the reality as identified during the analysis phase). Second, the assumptions/requirements within the initial design of the new e-government system, as identified during the design phase.
2 As you analyze the design and reality for each dimension, also estimate the gap between the two. You can use the rating scale approach described as an individual or with a group.
3 Make an overall assessment of the extent of gap between initial design and current reality.
4 On the basis of the design–reality gap analysis and any other relevant evidence, summarize the main constraints to introduction of the new e-government system.
5 Suggest both specific and generic ways in which design–reality gaps could be closed or kept small during the implementation process in order to increase the likelihood of success. If necessary, revise the system design.

NOTES

1. A simpler factor-based variant on this approach is shown in the Online Appendix for this chapter. Links to other risk management approaches are also provided in the Online Appendix.

2. Further variations on the basic gap rating approach presented here are discussed in the Online Appendix for this chapter. The Online Appendix also provides a worked and a real-world example of risk assessment via gap analysis.

3. The Online Appendix for this chapter provides two real-world examples of using design–reality gap analysis to highlight both generic and specific techniques of risk mitigation.

4. A more strategic view on this continuum is given in the Online Appendix for Chapter 3.

5. There is also discussion in the Online Appendix for Chapter 5.

6. Details of longer group activities are provided in the Online Appendix to this chapter.

11

eGovernment System Construction, Implementation and Beyond

Key Points

- Once high-level design of the new e-government system is complete, specific purchasing, construction, and implementation follow.
- If existing systems cannot be re-engineered, then new hardware and software needs to be procured, typically by using a checklist-and-scoring method.
- Final construction of an e-government system involves installation, detailed design and production, testing and documentation.
- Training for e-government is planned using who, why, what, when and where questions.
- Incremental methods of e-government introduction may be less efficient but more effective and less risky than 'big bang' methods.
- eGovernment projects need to concentrate efforts on marketing and support, avoiding the dominant 'build it and they will come' mentality.
- There are significant barriers to post-implementation evaluation of e-government systems, even though this provides a valuable guide to systems improvement.

Once a design for the proposed new e-government system has been agreed, the development cycle can proceed to the remaining stages: that of actually constructing the new system and then implementing it. This chapter describes the steps in system construction:

- acquiring any necessary new technology;
- undertaking detailed system design;

- constructing the new e-government system, and
- testing and documenting the system.

It then discusses the planning of implementation processes, including:

- who will be trained and why; and
- how implementation will be timed, according to what method.

The chapter concludes with a description of post-implementation techniques to market, support, upgrade, monitor, evaluate and maintain the developed e-government system.

11.1 PROCUREMENT FOR ᴇGOVERNMENT SYSTEMS

The previous stage – design – laid out a series of general system objectives and specific system requirements that the new e-government system was intended to meet. Within these parameters, general decisions about IT were made. New technology now needs to be acquired. Of course, this is only appropriate if any existing IT system is not suitable and also, for software, if a new software package (rather than re-engineered system) is to form the basis of the e-government system. The timing of this stage may also vary: where outsourcing or consulting are used to develop the e-government system, the procurement will be of services rather than products, and it will likely precede some aspects of analysis and design.

The approach to acquisition needs to be decided at the start. Five options are common in the public sector (DPWS, 1998: 15). They are not mutually exclusive: it is possible that each one is found, sequentially, in the same acquisition process:

- *Expression of interest*: 'Based on an informal statement of the agency requirements. This may also be initiated to determine the nature, extent and cost of available solutions.' It is unlikely to go into the detail – especially not the technical detail – of full requirements.
- *Request for proposal*: 'Based on a more detailed statement of requirements than

the Expression of Interest. It may be initiated to explore the range of solutions that are available from the potential suppliers without binding either the agency or the supplier.'
- *Request for tender*: 'With the detailed requirements and conditions to elicit a comprehensive and comparable response from suppliers.' (In practice, many requests for proposal (RFPs) actually conform to this description.)
- *Price quotation*: A simple price request from suppliers for a specific item or items.
- *Period contract arrangement*: This sets a time period for a relationship between public agency and supplier typically relating to the provision of particular goods and services, such as a software package or delivery of IT training.

Setting Acceptance Criteria

The information and technology performance requirements decided earlier (see Chapter 9) provide guidance on the technology to be selected. In addition, more general requirements about the technology – such as those listed in the Appendix at the end of this chapter – may also be used. These requirements together can be laid out as a checklist against which alternative possibilities are scored. As with the techniques described in Chapter 10, all requirements can be treated equally or they can be prioritized in some way that will allow them to be weighted. For example, the requirements could be divided into mandatory (weighted 10), important (weighted 5), and desirable (weighted 2).

Scoring can either be subjective, by individual or group, or – if applicable – can be done on the basis of some more objective performance test. Such objective tests could provide an absolute threshold, such as rejecting any system that could not hold more than 50,000 data records. Alternatively, the test could be relative, scoring from 1 point for a system response time of more than 20 seconds to 10 points for a response time of less than 2 seconds.

Subjective scoring is valuable since it helps address a potential rationality–reality gap. Rationally, managers should prioritize the features that users *need* more than the features they *want*. In reality, though, a new e-government application must address wants if users are to support it. Where objective, external analysis and design tend to emphasize needs, subjective scoring helps shift the balance back towards wants.

Decisions need to be made about how checklist items are to be validated. Methods include:

- *Written response from vendors*: The least trustworthy method, which compares poorly with any form of demonstration.
- *Demonstration of technology*: Could involve visits to the sites of the supplier's other public sector customers.
- *Benchmarking of performance*: Needed for performance tests and requiring a demonstration under particular, agreed conditions.
- *Full acceptance testing*: Typically requires a demonstration under conditions that are as similar as possible to those that will apply to the real new e-government system. Demonstrating hardware, for example, requires loading chosen software and organizational data onto the computer system to see how it performs. System users – including representatives of external client groups when relevant – are invited to try out the system.

Technology acquisition is the moment during system development when most

money changes hands. It can therefore be a highly charged and politicized process with aggressive and even underhand lobbying by vendors and/or their internal contacts. In practical terms, this means that politicians or staff not otherwise involved may try to push themselves forward into the decision-making process. It can also mean that logically drawn-up checklists of criteria may be modified or ignored. Such activities represent the gap that can exist between the rationality of the systems development process and the reality of public agency functioning. It is relatively easy to note them informally as a constraint but much harder to do anything about them since room for maneuver can be limited.

The Appendix at the end of this chapter provides more detailed checklists for the selection of three key elements of a new e-government system: the software, the hardware, and the supplier (vendor).

The Procurement Process

A complete checklist can now be assembled from:

- earlier information design requirements;
- earlier technology design requirements; and
- the general requirements that emerge from the questions listed in the Appendix below.

This checklist can be used as the basis for an expression of interest or a request for proposal/tender that is issued publicly or sent round to pre-selected suppliers. The request may include:

- general background information about the system, including objectives;
- details of tender submission procedures and timetables;

- the supplier information that is needed;
- the requirements checklist and details of how requirements will be validated;
- any financial, timing or other systems development constraints; and
- any relevant contractual conditions.

Alternatively, suppliers may just be asked to provide a price quotation. This is often appropriate for simple e-government technologies. It may also be appropriate when the same producer's technology can be obtained through several different suppliers (in which case a separate technology decision-making process would be used).

In either case, tenders, proposals or quotes are requested and received. They are then reviewed and shortlisted, with a supplier briefing if necessary, and checklist items are validated against acceptance criteria. Finally, a decision is made. Decision making may involve the use of weighted criteria, as illustrated in Box 11.1.

Any contract and price negotiations are finalized to allow the choice of supplier to be finally approved, and then the contract or order is signed. The contract itself is likely to be a combination of general and specific conditions. An example of contract elements is presented in Box 11.2.

Box 11.1   Weighting Criteria for a Human Resources Information System RFP, Hillsborough County, FL

Responses to the request for proposal were shortlisted to three proposals based on those who scored best out of 200 points (HCPD, 2000). That 200 represented the sum of a preliminary and a post-preliminary score. Preliminary score items (total 100 points) were: methodology (15 points), project staff (10), human resources information system (HRIS) application experience of firm (10), government experience of firm (10), functionality (30), contract cost (25). Post-preliminary score items (total 100 points) were: oral presentation (45 points), site visit(s) (10), detailed contact information from investigation of past performance (45).

The final decision was made on the basis of a 200-point evaluation of best and final offers from the suppliers. Of those points, 100 were made up from the post-preliminary score items. The remaining 100 were: revised methodology (30 points), revised project staff (20), revised contract cost (50).

Box 11.2   Elements of eGovernment Contracts

The following elements are found in typical e-government contracts (Stevens, 1999; DFA, 2001; MCC, 2003):

- *term*: the contract period;
- *contracting*: identity, status and sub-contracting limitations for contractor;
- *scope of work*: outline of main contract scope – the goods (or services) to be provided and the schedule of delivery;

(Continued)

Box 11.2   Continued

- *requirements*: fuller details of particular goods or services to be provided, such as technical support or training, with any performance requirements;
- *acceptance*: standards and procedures for inspecting and accepting goods or services produced;
- *reporting*: mechanisms and schedule for reporting on contract progress;
- *payment*: invoicing, payment and taxation arrangements; plus any discounts available for bulk or early payment;
- *records and audit*: quality/nature of records to be kept by the contractor and made available for audit;
- *maintenance and warranties*: the contractor's responsibilities for maintaining the hardware/software supplied;
- *ownership*: property rights on software/systems to be developed;
- *collusion/conflict of interest*: proper behavior towards others involved including public servants and competitors;
- *amendments*: means for amendment to contract clauses;
- *default and remedies*: the means by which problems with the contract are to be handled, including any penalties to be imposed;
- *termination*: conditions for termination due to convenience or cause (because of inadequate performance);
- *insurance*: cover to be maintained by contractor;
- *indemnification*: of the government agency against liabilities arising from contractor actions; this also covering patent, copyright and trademark infringements;
- *force majeure*: liability exemptions;
- *legal compliance*: the legal jurisdiction covering the contract, plus particular laws that must be complied with, such as equal opportunities.

For relatively minor purchases, some public sector organizations set up period contract arrangements that permit them to keep sourcing from one supplier who, from past experience, has proven reliable and/or good value. This avoids the administrative overheads of tendering or quotation processes.

Public Sector Procurement Issues

IT procurement has been problematic in the public sector, with four issues standing out that require some form of hybrid response.

Centralization/decentralization tensions: These have already been discussed in Chapter 2, which highlighted the problems of centralized procurement (delays, failure to meet needs) and decentralized procurement (high costs, lack of standards and learning). A hybrid approach is probably best. For many governments this has meant, in practice, a reduction in central controls but an increase in review or audit functions.

Length of the procurement process: Public sector procurement has tended to be a lengthy process, mired in both politics and bureaucracy. Procurement cycles of more than a year's duration are not uncommon for major e-government systems (Margetts, 1999; Barrett and Greene, 2001). The predictable result is that technology has moved on in the meantime and so too may the project champions and other staff, bringing in a new agenda.

Public agencies have therefore been concerned to shorten the process. Hybrid-type responses such as central catalogues, framework agreements, government-wide licenses and 'one for all' contracts – mentioned in Chapters 2 and 5 – have been seen as helpful. Other techniques for cutting procurement time include:

- *eProcurement*: Procurement time can be cut by more than half through use of e-procurement (Moon, 2003). Costs are claimed to be cut even more.
- *Request for solution/request for information*: This is essentially the type of request for proposal discussed in the DPWS list above – a half-way house between an expression of interest and the more typical request for proposal used in e-government. User needs, particularly objectives and information needs, are defined internally by the public sector organization, but it is left to suppliers to suggest appropriate solutions, particularly the technology design components. Although necessitating strong communication, this does play to strengths since public agencies tend to be strong on understanding the business, weak on understanding IT, while suppliers are the opposite. Gauteng Province in South Africa made use of this approach and reduced procurement times that had been anything up to two years down to five months (Kahn and Swanborough, 1999). It also produced a better final e-government system.
- *Standardizing documents*: Many public agencies reinvent the wheel when developing request and contract documents. Sharing document templates between public organizations can save both time and money.

- *Pre-qualification*: Cutting down the number of vendors who can submit for an RFP by filtering them through a set of basic pre-qualification criteria similar to those listed in the Appendix below.
- *Shifting to customized*: Shifting from custom-built e-government systems to customized versions of standard packages can save time.
- *Alternative suppliers*: Making use of high street shops, computer supermarkets and direct mail order rather than traditional public sector suppliers.

Cost versus other criteria: Lowest cost does not necessarily mean best. Apparently cheap deals often return to haunt public sector organizations (Finlay, 2004). Price should be traded off against qualitative factors: quality of meeting requirements; quality of product; quality of service. The problem is that price is easy to judge – especially by the non-IT specialists who become involved in public sector IT procurements – while qualitative factors are not.

The UK government made a concerted effort to change mindsets from the concept of 'lowest price' to 'best value', and the Canadian government has tried to push from price-driven to benefits-driven procurement. In both cases, though, there has been a struggle to break the grip of cost- centrality. Even when best value considerations are held in mind, bid differences can mean public managers are trying to compare 'apples and oranges' since suppliers will exhibit strengths in different criteria.

Open source: Concerns about proprietary software have led to a growth of public sector interest in open source software for e-government systems (Cross, 2004). No purchase or license fee is payable for open source software, which is 'free for anyone to use and open for anyone to inspect and alter' (Mathieson, 2004: 4). Of course, initial software costs are only one relatively small part of total e-government system costs, so cost savings should not be exaggerated – someone still has to design, install, operate, maintain and upgrade the software. Nonetheless, there do appear to be cost savings. These may come direct, or they may be obtainable by using talk of open source to leverage discounts from proprietary vendors: Microsoft has been the highest-profile target for such tactics. Open source has also been attractive because it avoids the vendor lock-in associated with proprietary products, offering public agencies greater flexibility.

11.2 FINAL CONSTRUCTION OF THE ᴇGOVERNMENT SYSTEM

The final construction of the system involves the steps below.

1. System Installation

Once the technology has been acquired, it will need to be installed. For larger e-government systems, this will require considerable pre-planning and site preparation. Features such as furnishings, burglar alarms, UPS (uninterruptible power supply), air-conditioning, fire control systems, access control systems, network cabling, and so on will all need to be in place.[1]

2. Detailed System Design

If the software chosen as the basis for the e-government application is an off-the-shelf package, the system development process can proceed fairly directly to implementation (though testing and documentation

will be required to some extent). If not, more detailed design work is required as a precursor to system construction or customization.

It is at this point that specific design decisions can be made relating to issues already discussed in Chapters 4 and 6,[2] including design of:

- data-gathering exercises that will produce the required data for the organization;
- general controls to protect data quality;
- specific application controls, including validation parameters for each data element;
- codes to be used for particular data elements;
- other detailed operational procedures that may be required;
- input forms and screens;
- processing techniques required to produce information from data, with an emphasis on simplicity and flexibility;
- output screens and other output formats;
- other system interfaces, such as query screens; and
- system ergonomics.

Based on all these designs, the information system for e-government can now be constructed.

3. System Testing

Most people would be unwilling to be the first person to fly in a new plane that had never flown before, or to be the first person to try an untested new medicine. Yet some of those same people will try to rush straight into use of an untested e-government system.

If the purpose of system development is to produce a working system, then the system should be tested to see if it works as intended. Most system testing focuses on testing whether the output produced by the system is correct, either in terms of the information it produces or the transactions it supports.

If, say, a new license application system is being tested, a set of known applicant data can be input. The transactional component of the system can be checked by looking at the license details that would be issued. This would check, for example, that the same licenses cannot be issued twice to the same person if they re-enter their data. It would also check that licenses are only issued where all information is correct and validated. The management information component of the system can also be checked through a series of searches and reports, and checked against the data that has been input.

As well as covering the direct information and process components of the e-government system, many other aspects can also be tested, such as:

- whether the system interfaces are acceptable to users;
- whether the documentation (typically online help) matches the system and can be understood by users;
- whether any new work processes associated with the system work correctly; and
- whether the hardware functions properly.

Some systems are tested using special test data, but others can be tested simply by getting users to sit down with real data and with real documentation (in which case, data conversion and documentation will need to be undertaken now). In this way, testing becomes merely one form of prototyping, assessing user reactions to interfaces, documentation, and processes. Modifications can be made if required. This type of user-oriented approach to testing is seen to improve the likely success of

e-government systems, but it will only work well if the internal or external users are properly engaged in planning and evaluating testing, as well as implementing it (Prins and Dahanayake, 2001).

Errors picked up at a late stage in the system lifecycle are generally far more costly to correct than those eliminated earlier on. With this in mind, there has been concern to follow a 'quality approach' to systems development. This is often interpreted as a requirement for highly structured development methodologies and the quantification of anything that moves on the project. Such a hard approach may have something to recommend it as regards system construction. However, for the analysis and design stages, a less rigid and more hybrid approach seems more likely to reduce errors if it ensures that analysis and design are taken seriously and not skimped, takes account of human and organizational factors, and includes techniques to close design–reality gaps, particularly early prototyping. Further discussion about taking a hybrid rather than hard approach to e-government project management can be found in Chapter 5.

4. System Documentation

There are three main types of system documentation on which work can be started right from the early stages of the development lifecycle.

Overall Project Documentation

This is a collection of all the project documents used in developing the new e-government system. It can include things like project proposals, analysis and general design information, details of tendering and outsourcing procedures, and minutes of relevant meetings.

The purpose of this documentation is to act as a corporate memory that can be referred back to. It can be used, for example, to check initially agreed objectives against current performance, or as a good/bad practice guide to help subsequent e-government projects.

System Design Documentation

This records technical information about the design and workings of the new e-government system. It mainly includes quite specific design information, such as the programming languages used to create the system, the structure of any system modules, the design of system interfaces and of data storage, plus a full and annotated list of any programming code used.

It would also be likely to include original DVD/CDs of any programs created, with details of who created them and when. The purpose of this documentation is also to act as a corporate memory. It can be used, for example, if the system needs to be maintained or re-engineered at some later date. This is primarily needed because those who created the system may subsequently leave the organization.

System Operation Documentation

This records details about how to use the e-government system. Apart from acting as a corporate memory, this documentation is also used as the basis for training materials and for manuals and online support that help users answer their own operational queries. Such documentation is often best written by a user rather than a technical member of staff. Best practice guidelines include (Smith and Fletcher, 2001; Kendall and Kendall, 2005):

- customization to audience – for a welfare-claim system, say, guidance for citizen-users would not be the same as the

more detailed operational guidance for staff who maintain the system database;
- a logical structure covering elements such as: the overall purpose of the system; an overview of what the system does, with an online tutorial; clear guidance on the steps in using the system; system errors and problems;
- good accessibility of material via a clearly structured table of contents, a keyword index, and a search facility (ideally with some natural language capability), allowing users to find information quickly;
- a consistent format and style;
- writing in plain language that is clear, simple and brief, and that includes definitions of jargon and concepts (e.g. through hyperlinks);
- plentiful use of diagrams, including pictures of the screens that users encounter;
- creation information on the documentation making it clear who wrote it and when;
- clear details of whom to contact for further help and support.

Such documentation will need to cover the direct usage of the system, but also the type of broader guidelines driven by policies such as those raised in Chapter 6.

11.3 INTRODUCTION OF THE εGOVERNMENT SYSTEM

Operational Training

As indicated in Box 11.3, good training can make all the difference.

Training for e-government can be planned by answering a series of questions, as described below (adapted from Kendall and Kendall, 2005). As with many other stages in systems development, this assumes some degree of organizational rationality that may not be present. For example, internal

---

Box 11.3   Peer Tutoring in the New York State Department of Agriculture and Markets

New York State developed a new system for electronic handling of dog licenses. Training was provided on a voluntary basis by other users. 'Town Clerks who have adopted the automated dog license process volunteer to train their colleagues from other towns in issuing licenses electronically. They are even willing to travel to other municipalities to do on-site one-to-one training' (Dawes et al., 1997: 74). Those involved 'cited this volunteer training program as a real plus that encourages new users to adopt a system that is strictly voluntary. Good training is to the point, meets personal user needs, and comes from credible sources such as experienced users. Excellent training is customized to meet users' immediate and long-term needs. The individualized training given by Town Clerks involved in the Automated Dog Licensing information system meets all of these criteria' (ibid.: 74).

---

staff sent for training might be self-selecting or selected on the basis of 'Buggin's turn' rather than training need.

The questions also tend to leave aside the question of cost and time. Yet these are critical constraints that interfere with good training practice in the public sector. They push organizations towards cheaper and/or quicker rather than better training. They also mean that public managers always find excuses not to send their staff for training (Barrett and Greene, 2001). Building funds for training into e-government implementation budgets is an important part of overcoming these barriers, as is integrating training into staff appraisal and career development planning.

Who is to be Trained?

It is likely that all internal primary system users (those using the system hands-on) will be trained. Internal secondary users (those using only the outputs of the e-government system) normally require training, though they are often ignored. Training may also be needed for staff in more specialized and technical jobs. Examples include data

administration, systems management, systems operation and maintenance. External system users (e.g. citizens, entrepreneurs, users in other agencies) may also need training, though delivery is more challenging than for internal staff.

Why are they being Trained?

Training objectives can focus quite narrowly on just providing the skills necessary to perform the direct operational task within the e-government system. However, other objectives may be equally important:

- giving users the confidence to use the new technology or new information;
- persuading users to use the new system; and/or
- giving users the knowledge and skills to troubleshoot simple problems.

Training will therefore by no means be restricted to IT issues, but will cover information systems and wider management areas, perhaps even stretching to encompass issues of public sector reform (Mundy et al., 2001).

Who will Deliver the Training?

For user training, the main options include:

- *IT suppliers*, who tend to cover technical training;
- *system developers*, who have in-depth knowledge of the e-government system but who may lack training skills or sensitivity to non-technical users;
- *external trainers*, who may lack understanding of public sector realities and who may need to work with internal staff to produce truly customized training;
- *in-house trainers*, who may or may not have good understanding of e-government;
- *other users*, who will have the best understanding of context and of user needs, but who may need support to give them intensive trainer training and system skills training;
- *self-paced training*, which will often be delivered online; development costs can be high, but delivery costs are low, training can be delivered on-demand, and well-designed material customizes the training delivery to individual needs and abilities.

Many successful e-government systems seem to have adopted an approach of employing users as trainers (Lynn, 2000; Holmes, 2001).

When and Where will Training be Delivered?

Training should be timed just at the moment when users are about to use the system, allowing them to move directly from training to use. Any earlier than this and elements of training may be forgotten. Any later than this, and system capacity is wasted through underuse. The further from their PC that users are trained, the more costly it is. On the other hand, there will be fewer distractions, more control over training,

and possibly better access to training resources. Some public agencies adopt a hybrid approach, using PC-based training but running it for groups during specific classroom sessions with an instructor on hand (Hiscock, 1999). This provides the in-built motivation via group and trainer pressure, and the interactivity that PC-based training lacks.

For training of external client users, choice depends on group size/dispersion. For small, discrete groups – say training tax advisers to use a new tax portal – physical training (i.e. a training workshop or seminar) may be feasible. But for most groups – say citizens using a new public health information system – training will have to be virtual and probably multi-channel: a combination of online help, online tutorials, plus leaflets or guidebooks, plus access to phone-based support.

What will be the Specific Content of Training Sessions?

The content of training is normally expected to derive from training objectives combined with an analysis of users' existing capabilities. Where appropriate, a more formal training needs analysis can be undertaken. This will lead to a plan of training activities, each of which has a set of learning objectives.

Time pressures, and the growth of external clients for e-government systems, has led to a great increase in on-demand training of the online help variety. This essentially just tells users which button to press to complete a particular operation. The problem with this approach is that it does not really help users to:

- understand the general purpose and role of the e-government application;
- know what it is possible to do with the application using its various functions;

- be confident to use trial and error methods; and
- know how to use online help and other support systems effectively.

These latter competencies are less easily forgotten and are more future-proofed, giving users a set of 'portable' competencies that they can take forward to other e-government applications (SOCITM and IDEA, 2002). Thus, simultaneous with moves to the 'light bite' approach of very specific, on-demand skill transfer, there are also attempts to encourage 'full meal' training where the emphasis is:

- away from providing new specific e-government skills and towards providing new generic knowledge, attitudes and skills;
- away from 'how do I do it?' and towards 'what can I do and why am I doing it?'; and
- away from 'do what the tutorial system (or teacher) says' and towards 'find out how to do it yourself'.

Where more formalized training of this type is delivered, the content trend has been towards customized courses that match users' particular work process and organizational context. Such training typically includes a continuous mix of teaching new competencies, trainee practice, and review of what has been learned. Practice exercises are seen as especially important. For self-confidence and self-reliance to be built, and so that the trained skills can be repeated in the workplace, training normally includes points where participants work on their own, and undertake trial runs of just-taught skills, or reinforce previously practiced skills in longer, more work-like exercises (Bell and Wood-Harper, 2003). These latter exercises may serve as identifiable achievement milestones that provide trainees with a clear sense of progress and learning.

Where internal staff users are involved, some public agencies assess progress and learning at the end of training, requiring further training for those who do not pass. Other agencies prefer systems of self-assessment. In either case, trainees frequently like to be issued with some kind of certificate of achievement. There has been an enormous growth in such certification from private sector providers (such as Microsoft- and Novell-certified training), colleges (such as the Tek.Xam in the US, a Standard Achievement Test-equivalent for IT), and professional bodies (such as the International Computer Driving License). However, these only cover skills rather than knowledge or attitude change, and they are not specific to particular e-government systems.

The other main problem with training for e-government is that it tends to focus on technical issues and not on deeper, more significant issues of information, information systems and management (Nilsson and Ranerup, 2002). Unless these other areas improve, the gains from simply introducing new technology may be very limited: entrepreneurs might access new health and safety guidelines from an e-government portal, but have no clue how to apply them; forest rangers might access new statistics from a geographic information system, but not know how to interpret those statistics; public managers might be unable to manage the new staff requirements and work processes that a new e-licensing system requires; and so on. eGovernment training therefore has to move well beyond the 'e' if it is to deliver effective new systems for the public sector.

Handover Method

At this point, the new technology, new work processes, new structures and so on are introduced into the public sector organization. In some cases, the new e-government system is just adding an additional channel, in which case it runs alongside existing systems. In other cases, though, a new information system is taking over from an old one. There are five different methods for switching over from old to new. The first four of these help diminish the amount of change the organization has to cope with at any one time.

Parallel Running

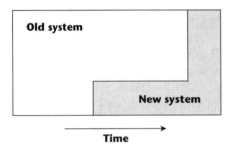

The new system runs alongside the old one for a period of time. During this time, outputs from the old can be compared with the new to ensure it is producing the right results. For example, when introducing an automated crime recording system, a police force might continue to record all crime details on paper at the same time as entering them into the new database. If there are ever problems with the new system, the old one is there as a permanent backup. This is a very safe, secure and relatively low-stress method. However, it can be costly running the two systems together and users who do not like the new system can easily revert to the old one.

Phased Volume Approach

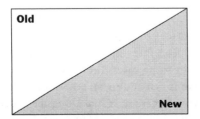

The old system keeps all its existing data, but the new system takes all new transactions. In this way it is phased in, gradually taking over a larger proportion of transactions from the old system. For example, a licensing department might keep records of all existing applications on the current database, but store details of all new applications on the database integrated with their new e-licensing system. The advantage here is that the new system is of only limited importance during any initial teething troubles and that, in case of crisis, the old system can be re-activated for new transactions. The problem is that data is split between two systems for a long time.

Phased Functional Approach

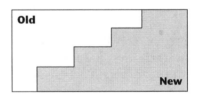

Aspects of the new system are substituted for the old one on a function-by-function basis. For example, a new online customs system could put import licensing first onto the new system followed later by import duty payments, then export licensing, then export payments. Though a bit less so than the previous approach, this still has the advantage of being relatively gradual. It also has the problem that data is split across different functions during the changeover, which may cause problems.

Pilot Approach

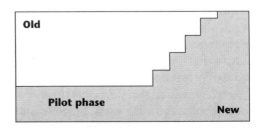

Where the organization is to install a new system at several sites, one is chosen to try out the new system. When and if this pilot is successful, the system is then introduced at the other sites, possibly in a phased manner. For example, a state government introducing a new district-level sports/leisure information portal can pilot it in one district, then spread it to other districts at a rate of two districts per month. The benefit of this approach is that the new system is tried out in a real environment, but one in which problems can be identified and corrected without major risk. On the down side, the method can be slow; there may be problems about selection of the pilot site; and the site may turn out to be unrepresentative of others, and so provide misleading feedback.

'Big Bang'

A complete and immediate switchover from the old to the new system on a given date. For example, the removal of all old call center CRM (customer relationship management) software one evening and its overnight replacement with a new set of packages. The advantage of this approach is that it avoids all the problems of other approaches. However, it can be very risky and very stressful for users. No matter how exhaustive pre-changeover testing has been, there are inevitably going to be unexpected problems that have to be solved 'on the hoof'. Any major problems may lead to complete system collapse without any old system backup. Such problems hit the State of California when – to save money – it

rejected parallel running in favor of big bang when introducing an automated property title search system (Alter, 2002). The new system proved 'buggy' and got rapidly logjammed with thousands of requests, leading to search delays of up to ten weeks. The old system had to be revived in order to save the day.

Data Conversion

This involves converting old system data so that it can be used by the new system. It may be a time-consuming process, such as scanning or typing in manual records. For example, when Vijayawada Municipal Corporation – a city government in South India – wanted to provide basic government services via the web, design and construction of the system front-end took just a few months (Veldanda, 2004). But the overall project timescale was far longer because it took more than three years to digitize the underlying data: more than 1.5 million database records.

Once governments have moved beyond the stage of initial digitization, data conversion should get easier. Increasingly, data files can be automatically converted from an old to a new file format. However, there are still conversion tasks to undertake; not just checking the basic conversion, but also weeding out data inaccuracies, duplications and redundancies.

11.4 POST-IMPLEMENTATION TASKS

Marketing and Support

Many eGovernment initiatives have been based upon a 'build it and they will come' mentality ... Few incentives have been built in to encourage use. Governments have seldom incorporated marketing into their eGovernment activities, nor have they targeted specific segments of their user base to encourage them to take advantage of those services. (Jupp, 2003: 135)

As discussed in Chapter 6, this has been one of e-government's blind spots because 'globally, e-government services provided online have not been embraced with the enthusiasm characteristic of their planners and designers' (UNDESA, 2003a: 64). In Texas, for example, 'only 2 percent of drivers renew their vehicle registrations online' (Eggers, 2004). Worse, one US city government 'invested over $200,000 to put the building permit process online but, after two years, not one person had used the system' (Jorgensen and Cable, 2002: 18). Demand-focused surveys make the problem clear – a current majority of external users (even Internet users) still want to interact with government in traditional ways (Graafland-Essers and Ettedgui, 2003).

There are two often parallel responses to this. The first, and reactive, recognizes this demand and continues to support and develop traditional channels. The second, and more proactive, seeks to modify the nature of demand through active and ongoing marketing campaigns that promote use of e-government systems. Such campaigns are generally related to external users, but they can equally be targeted at internal staff. Marketing of e-government can use much the same guidelines as other forms of marketing:

- Publicizing simple messages for mass awareness raising through all forms of advertising from print to radio/TV to email/web.
- Carrying out targeted marketing through direct mail, direct e-mail or call center marketing to specific client groups.
- Using word-of-mouth by getting staff when dealing with clients or with colleagues, or managers when giving presentations, to keep selling the system.

- Selling benefits not features, for example not 'we've got a portal' but 'now you don't have to queue'.
- Providing incentives. Some examples of these 'carrots for clients' were discussed in Chapter 10. Online tax systems worldwide use a variety of incentives: faster refunds (US), extended tax filing deadlines (Australia) and financial payments (Denmark) (Margetts and Yared, 2003). Incentives may also arise because users find it quicker to use an e-government system. More drastic still is the incentive of compulsion: this tends to be easier with internal systems than those involving external clients, but even here some governments are moving to only accept online transactions (e.g. tax returns from businesses or tax accountants).

In terms of content, marketing must address three key issues that shape e-government usage (adapted from Chaffey, 2002):

- *Cost*: Users must be reassured that the financial and time costs of accessing the e-government system are low.
- *Value*: Users must be shown how use of the system will provide value for them (answering the perennial 'Why should I: what's in it for me?' question).
- *Trust*: Where relevant, users must be reassured that security and privacy issues have been addressed by the system.

Marketing alone, though, is not enough. In addition, there must be continuous provision of user support. This can take the form of a user support/information center.[3] More typically, it is a staffed help desk and help line plus supporting documentation such as short 'crib sheets' plus more detailed manuals. Increasingly, support is going online – documentation can be provided online, supplemented by frequently asked questions and discussion fora. Computer-based training can play a more relevant role here than perhaps in the actual launch of a system, and has been found to reduce the number of user calls to help desks (Willis, 2003b). There may also be an ongoing role for more individualized or small group training or question and answer sessions to maintain the momentum of learning and acceptance of a new system.

Upgrades

One of the problems that public agencies face over time with e-government systems is that many items of IT are subject to rapid technical change, particularly software packages. The producers of such packages feel the need, because of competitive pressures, to bring out continuous upgrades to these packages. Such upgrades may be minor amendments every few months or major new versions every year or so.

Yet they create significant problems for public agencies (Kennedy, 2003). An amended set of skills is required for each upgrade: staff (and external users who cannot be shielded from the upgrade) may feel they are only just getting to grips with one version when an upgrade appears. Given staff time costs, learning may cost more than the technology itself. New bugs or incompatibilities may appear with new versions of software and hardware. In addition, existing data files may need to be converted; even procedures may need to be changed.

Some public sector organizations therefore try to adopt a centralized upgrade policy that chooses to avoid obtaining every upgrade. Instead, it sticks with one version for a number of years. The organization concentrates on deepening staff

skills in that version rather than providing shallow skills in each new upgrade. When the time comes to change, the organization leapfrogs several upgrades that it has missed to purchase a more recent version.

In practice, upgrading decisions may not be made on quite such rational grounds since they are influenced by a number of factors, including:

- *Speed of technical change*: For applications experiencing rapid technical change, upgrades are likely to come sooner.
- *Organizational needs*: If the existing version of an e-government application is not doing an adequate job, or if the latest version could clearly bring new benefits, upgrading is more likely. (One pressure here might be to remain compatible with clients, businesses or other organizations with whom data is exchanged within the application.)
- *Organizational credibility demands*: If the age of application used is a matter of client or public awareness, there are pressures to upgrade.
- *User and IT staff demands*: Regardless of the merits of upgrades, if users or IT staff are demanding them, the organization is more likely to have to acquiesce.
- *Cost and difficulty*: Easier, cheaper upgrades happen faster than costlier, harder ones.
- *Contractual obligations*: Some supplier contracts lock agencies into taking each upgrade, wanted or not.

Public agencies may therefore find themselves pressurized into upgrading both packages and skills according to less than optimum timetables. Concerns about this partly explain the growing interest in open source software, which removes at least some of the pressures noted above (Greig, 2003).

11.5 eGOVERNMENT MONITORING, EVALUATION AND MAINTENANCE

Once a new e-government system has been implemented, an immediate evaluation can be carried out to see (a) whether it is operating, and (b) whether it is operating as intended. This may be regarded as the process of acceptance testing referred to above. It will typically involve discussions with users, user questionnaires and, possibly, observation of system use. These findings can then be compared with the objectives and requirements for the system that were originally set. An example of such an approach is given in Box 11.4. Any gap can lead either to a re-evaluation of system objectives or to alterations to the system.

Such monitoring and evaluation can continue for some months to investigate how the system is used and for what; when and how much it is used; why it is used; what problems there are with it; and what users' opinions are about it. This may lead to an initial evaluation report, covering:

- The extent to which original objectives have been achieved; details of any amendments to objectives; and any unexpected outcomes.
- Future system changes that would be needed to meet existing and emergent objectives.
- Reflections on the process of e-government introduction, suggesting how the process would be done the same or differently next time round.

Box 11.4   Monitoring and Evaluation Criteria for New York State's Immunization Information System (NYSIIS)

The information system set out to assist the immunization of children in New York State (Dawes et al., 1997). During the design process, two sets of objectives were created that were readily made into criteria for formal monitoring and evaluation. The first set addressed the necessary functionality of the system, for example:

- Each child's immunization record must contain a unique identifier that could be reconstructed by the parent from information they have readily to hand.
- The system will capture only necessary data elements and automatically generate reports and reminders based on that data set.

It was relatively easy to evaluate whether or not these objectives had been met. The second set addressed specific system targets, for example:

- By 2000, have a least 400,000 immunization records of children under age 5 captured in the NYSIIS.

Again, this was easy to evaluate. Additional evaluation questions posed by those involved with the system included:

- How many immunizers are electronically exchanging immunization records with a regional IIS server?
- Of the immunization records captured, what percent are accurate and complete?

A true learning approach would ensure not merely that knowledge was captured through evaluation and reporting, but also that it was effectively transferred (through training exercises, 'lessons learned' meetings, online discussion lists, etc.) and also effectively applied (e.g. by building some ring-fenced time into all new e-government projects for learning lessons from past projects).

But evaluation and learning of this type are relatively rare on e-government projects (Barrett and Greene, 2001). This is first because evaluation and learning are costly. They require time and money; often a lot of time and money if they are to be done properly. Public services lack both those resources. eGovernment systems may cost more than most to evaluate because they are so complex, involving so many stakeholders in a situation that is typically politicized.

Perhaps even stronger is the fact that most e-government stakeholders do not want to evaluate and learn after systems have been implemented, for many possible reasons (Heeks, 2003b):

- *Irrelevance of outcomes*: Some stakeholders are only interested in association with the high-profile inception of an e-government project, not with the implementation and outcomes. Others see the project as a means of achieving specific personal goals, not as a means to achieve e-government goals. In these and similar cases, the outcome is of no importance to the stakeholders, so they have no interest in trying to evaluate or learn from the project.
- *Fear of exposure*: Some stakeholders fear that an evaluation process will expose their shortcomings: their ignorance about IT, their self-serving behaviors, and so on.

- *Stakeholder absence*: By the time an e-government project ends, key stakeholders have often moved on to other jobs or projects and have no continuing interest in the original project.
- *External ownership*: Some e-government projects are driven from outside their focal agency – for example, by central government agencies or by external consultants or by IT vendors – and are not owned by local stakeholders, who therefore feel disempowered or disinterested in any evaluation or learning process.
- *Environmental instability/uncertainty*: A characteristic of some public sectors at some times is political (or even socio-economic) instability; for example in the run-up to an election. Such a situation reduces the value of, and incentives for, learning since often the 'goalposts will have moved' from one e-government project to the next.

If the e-government initiative has been some kind of failure, there may be additional problems for evaluation and learning:

- *Skewing of incentives*: In some situations, there may be incentives for ongoing failure. With some e-government applications, 'success' can mean that the public agency is downsized or loses financial resources because of its efficiency gains. By contrast, failure may mean maintenance of resource levels, or even continuing investment in renewed e-government efforts. Likewise, vendors and consultants may see ongoing income from failures in a way they will not if an application succeeds. In these cases, stakeholders do not want to learn how not to fail; they want to continue failing. Alongside this may be a set of disincentives – such as audit, censure, litigation – that discourage evaluation or admission of failure.

- *Cultural inappropriateness*: In some risk-averse public sector cultures, it is not acceptable to admit or learn from failure: failures are to be ignored or denied, not evaluated and discussed for the purposes of learning.

Only in certain situations will e-government evaluation and learning therefore be feasible or valuable. If those situations do arise, then the most obvious way to evaluate an application is against its originally stated objectives as per the example given in Box 11.4. Alternatively, it can be evaluated using more standardized frameworks. Reflecting the ideas on performance discussed in Chapter 6, these frameworks can be input/process focused, such as those looking at design of e-government web sites.[4] More broadly applicable is evaluation that is process/output focused. For example:

- *Information systems evaluation*: Treating the e-government system as an information system and evaluating it according to the CIPSODA checklist presented in Chapter 1; asking questions about each information system task – the capture, input, processing and storage of data – but especially focusing on the output of information and the way that information is used for decisions and actions/transactions. The latter element can reuse the questions identified in Chapter 8: *Who* is getting *what* information? *When* and *where* do they get it? *How* do they use it for decisions and (trans)actions and *why*?

- *Data quality evaluation*: Treating the e-government system as an information system, and evaluating it according to the CARTA checklist presented in Chapter 4; asking questions about the completeness, accuracy, relevance, timeliness, and appropriateness of presentation of the information that it produces.

Alternatively, the frameworks for evaluation could be more outcome-focused. Desirable outcomes are defined differently by different governments but there is a general sense that they should relate to public sector reform goals and to the creation of 'public value' (UNDESA, 2003a). Two examples are presented in Box 11.5.

Box 11.5   Outcome Evaluation Criteria for eGovernment Projects

The US Intergovernmental Advisory Board has identified the following possible outcome-related criteria that can be used for evaluation of e-government projects (IAB, 2003):

- *financial*: reducing costs or increasing revenues;
- *economic*: increasing income of businesses or regions;
- *process*: consolidating and integrating systems to produce greater efficiency and effectiveness;
- *societal*: improving the transparency and accountability of government;
- *service*: providing more efficient or more effective services to citizens.

It should be noted that these criteria overlap; for example, most of the 'process' criteria could be reclassified under 'financial' and 'service'. Only in part have these ideas been incorporated into formal evaluation models, such as the US federal government's Performance Reference Model (OMB, 2005c).

Canada has also adopted an outcome-focused approach, for specific use with online service delivery applications (d'Auray, 2003). This divides 11 evaluation indicators into three main areas:

- *Citizen-/client-centered government*: Convenience; accessibility; credibility.
- *Better, more responsive service*: Critical mass of services; take-up; service transformation; citizen/client satisfaction.
- *Capacity for online delivery*: Security; privacy; efficiency; innovation.

There are two further variants. The first is *multi-stakeholder evaluation* that moves beyond the formally stated objectives for the system to ask representatives of all key stakeholder groups what they wanted to get out of the new e-government system. It then evaluates whether or not those goals have been achieved. Such an approach is critical for a balanced, truthful view on e-government, particularly where there is a genuine interest in system outcomes. It must include – even prioritize – the view of system clients: as the old adage goes: 'If you want to know the quality of dog biscuits, ask the dog'.

The second is an assessment of the implementation process, rather than the actual outcome, with a view to learning more than evaluation. This can be a simple factoral approach, identifying the critical success or failure factors that arose during the assessment, analysis, design, construction and implementation of the e-government application. It could alternatively use the design–reality gap techniques in a post hoc mode. Areas where there are small design–reality gaps tend to be critical success factors. Dimensions where gaps are large tend to be critical failure factors.[5]

One key to successful evaluation of e-government will be its hybridization: combining hard measures, such as finances and IT performance, with soft measures such as user evaluations; and combining different perspectives so that something closer to the 'truth' about the system can be uncovered.

System Maintenance

Perhaps even more important than gathering data about the e-government system through monitoring and evaluation, is ensuring that something is done about the results produced, which may point to desirable system changes. Any fairly minor changes that have to be made to the e-government system after its introduction are regarded as *system maintenance*. They may be:

- *Debugging*: A response to ways in which the system does not perform as originally intended; this typically involves removing programming code errors that have been accidentally included.
- *Tweaking*: Improving system performance to make it operate more efficiently.
- *Updating*: Altering the system because of changes in its original parameters.

Maintenance can also include:

- *Correcting*: Making the system run as it was intended to, but does not, due to poor system development.

Traditional approaches to maintenance would see such work discussed, prioritized and scheduled for some future point. This would be particularly true of more serious maintenance fixes, which may require revisions to work roles and processes, data formats, documentation, and training. They may therefore need to be carefully controlled to prioritize, document and then release changed versions.

Traditional approaches are, however, in tension with the immediacy, visibility and importance of many e-government systems, which require immediate fixing. This can particularly be the case for web-based systems,

where the updating element of system maintenance can be seen as more important than initial development: the most-used sites need to update their content on a daily basis. For some public sector organizations, the result is that maintenance is not only a management challenge, but an activity that begins to absorb more IT staff and budget than new systems development.

Finally, alongside ongoing fixes and improvements, requirements may start to emerge for more fundamental changes. This may signal the need for more comprehensive assessment of emergent problems and for mapping of the e-government system along the lines detailed in Chapters 7 and 8. In other words, the system lifecycle can be started again to see if the current e-government system needs to be substantially revised or even replaced with a new system.

ACTIVITIES

Shorter In-Class Activities[6]

Section 11.1

a. Place the following four e-government system selection criteria in ranked order of importance: speed of response; cost; security features; interface user-friendliness. Be prepared to justify your selection.

b. Consider the weighting criteria provided in Box 11.1. Discuss: (a) whether there are other criteria for e-government systems you feel are more important, that are not used here; (b) whether or not you agree with the weightings used.

c. Discuss which of the elements in Box 11.2 you feel are most important for an e-government contract, and why.

d. You have to decide which of several different e-government packages you wish to purchase. User-friendliness of the interface has emerged as an important selection criterion. How would you assess – even measure – each of the packages against this criterion?

Section 11.2

a. Discuss who is best placed to undertake site preparation and system installation for an e-government application: an in-house team of public servants, or an externally contracted IT firm.

b. 'No-one ever reads e-government systems documentation, so it's not worth bothering with.' Discuss.

Section 11.3

a. Discuss the pros and cons for e-government of the peer tutoring approach described in Box 11.3.

b. Think of the last e-government (or other IT-based) system you used. Did you have training to use this system or not? What conclusions can you draw about training for e-government?

c. 'In a world of online help and e-learning, there is no place left in e-government implementation for classroom-based teaching.' Discuss.

d. You are part of a team planning to introduce the use of wireless PDAs (personal digital assistants) by farm inspectors, to replace their existing use of paper and pen when out in the field. Which one of the five handover methods would you recommend?

Section 11.4

a. 'Citizens should be compelled to use e-government systems in order to drive up usage rates.' Discuss.

b. Discuss whether software package upgrades present more of a problem or more of an opportunity for e-government systems.

Section 11.5

a. Brainstorm a quick list of at least three performance indicators that could be used to measure the public value of e-government systems.

Assignment Questions

Sections 11.1–11.2

a. Use case evidence to develop a set of best practices in e-government procurement, construction and installation.

Sections 11.1–11.4

a. What particular factors make procurement, implementation and operation of an e-government system different from procurement, implementation and operation of an e-business system?

b. Identify at least three case studies of e-government implementation and analyze the extent to which these implementations can or cannot be said to have followed a hybrid approach.

Sections 11.1–11.5

a. Compare and contrast a hybrid approach and a hard approach to e-government system implementation.

Sections 11.3–11.5

a. Use case evidence to develop a set of best practices in e-government handover method, training, marketing, and monitoring and evaluation.

Practitioner Exercises

Sections 11.1–11.5

a. What is the relevance and applicability to your public sector organization of all the system procurement, construction, introduction and post-implementation techniques described in this chapter? Note down any implications of your answer for e-government systems development in the organization.

eGovernment Project Development Exercises

1   If appropriate, determine how requirements checklists will be validated; set software, hardware and supplier requirements checklists (see Appendix below); detail the process

of procurement to be followed; then outline the main installation activities required.

2 Undertake detailed design work on the issues listed in the main text:

- data-gathering exercises that will produce the required data for the organization;
- general controls to protect data quality;
- specific application controls, including validation parameters for each data element;
- codes to be used for particular data elements;
- other detailed operational procedures that may be required;
- input forms and screens;
- processing techniques required to produce information from data;
- output screens and other output formats;

- other system interfaces, such as query screens; and
- system ergonomics.

3 Plan how the new system will be tested to ensure that it is functioning as required.

4 Plan what documentation will be required for the new system.

5 Plan the operational training for the new e-government system.

6 Plan which handover method will be most suitable for the new system.

7 Plan how any data will be converted.

8 Plan how post-implementation system upgrades, marketing and user support will be managed.

9 Plan how the e-government system will be monitored, evaluated and maintained.

NOTES

1. Some of these are discussed in the Online Appendix for Chapter 4.

2. Checklists for more detailed design decisions about networks for e-government are provided in the Online Appendix for Chapter 3. Checklists related to databases, email systems and web sites for e-government can be found in the Online Appendix for this chapter.

3. Further details of information center operations are provided in the Online Appendix for Chapter 5.

4. See this chapter's Online Appendix for further details on e-government web site evaluation.

5. More details of this technique are provided in the Online Appendix to this chapter.

6. Details of longer group activities are provided in the Online Appendix to this chapter.

APPENDIX: REQUIREMENTS CHECKLISTS

The following are a set of checklists that can be used in setting out more detailed

requirements for the procurement of an e-government system.

General Software Requirements

In addition to the system-specific requirements already identified in Chapter 9, general checklist items when purchasing a system based on a software package can include:

- How flexible/upgradable/expandable is this software? How compatible is it with other programs? Both of these questions aim at coping with future changes in requirements that have not been anticipated.
- How user-friendly is the package's interface? (How does it compare, for example, to the input interface guidelines in the Online Appendix for Chapter 4?)
- How clear and instructive is the documentation? This would include the online

help and tutorial facilities provided with the package.

- How new is the software? In general, it may be best to try to avoid software packages that have only just been released. These are sometimes referred to as 'bleeding-edge' technologies since they may contain lots of bugs and their producer may be 'here today and gone tomorrow'. On the other hand, packages produced a number of years ago may not contain some useful features. It may therefore be best to aim for packages that have been released, say, between six months and two years previously. These are likely to be modern but also tried and tested.
- How long has the producer been in business? IT firms do come and go quite rapidly, often with little warning. Nonetheless, a producer who has been in business for five years is probably preferable to one who has only been around for five months.
- How popular is the software? In general, the more popular the package selected, the better. Bugs are more likely to have been ironed out, support and training materials are more widespread and, if needed, outside staff with appropriate skills are easier to find. Popular packages are also likely to be cheaper since they sell in larger volumes. The only downside is that organizational staff trained to use or develop the packages will find it easier to move to other jobs because their skills are in greater demand.
- Is the package available from local suppliers and, if so, what type of support can they provide?
- Does the software run well on existing hardware that the agency has? Is it already in use in other parts of the organization?
- How much does the package cost? Cost is deliberately placed last. Decisions are better made first on technical and qualitative grounds. Where price comes first, the technology chosen may be inadequate or the supplier may claw back costs by providing inadequate support for implementation and maintenance.

General Hardware Requirements

As it did in technology design, hardware comes second to guard against the problem of over-emphasizing hardware in the procurement process. The system-specific requirements already identified from Chapter 9 can be grouped into: capture/input, processing, storage, output and communication technology requirements. In addition, general checklist items when purchasing new hardware can include:

- How flexible/upgradable/expandable is the hardware? For a computer system, part of its flexibility comes from its capacities in three particular areas: the central processing unit (CPU), its memory, and storage capacity. For a network, the flexibility comes mainly from its bandwidth. These will need to be sufficient to run the planned e-government system, but may also be provided with spare capacity to cope with unanticipated future needs.
- How compatible is it with other hardware already used by the organization and/or collaborating institutions and/or clients?
- How clear and instructive is the documentation?
- How new is the hardware? Comments apply as for software.
- How long has the producer been in business? Comments apply as for software.
- How popular is the hardware? Comments apply as for software.

- Is the hardware available from local suppliers and, if so, what type of support can they provide?
- How well can the hardware cope with particular local factors? These could include factors such as heat, cold, humidity, electricity supply problems, if the hardware is to be used in particular climate/infrastructural locations.
- To what extent will spares and maintenance services be conveniently available locally?
- How much does the hardware cost?

General Supplier Requirements

There may be no room for maneuver in choosing a supplier. If there is, though, typical checklist items include:

- How long has the supplier been operating? Note that the supplier and producer of the technology may well be different, with the former being an agent for the latter.
- How easily can they be contacted? A physical office in the next street may be worth much more than promises of fax or telephone contact.
- Who is on their client list? If in doubt and/or for major purchases, it can be important to contact the supplier's clients to see what they think. One key element may be whether or not the supplier has worked with public sector clients in the past. Such clients can provide very useful formal and informal feedback on the supplier.
- What is the content and length of any guarantee and maintenance or post-installation support agreement?
- What support can they offer in terms of: systems development, training, and installation assistance?
- What troubleshooting and repair service do they provide: a telephone hotline, onsite or offsite repairs, local stocks of spares, any guaranteed response time, loan of equipment while original equipment is being repaired? How likely are they to keep their service promises? If in doubt, training in-house staff or using a third-party maintenance service may be a better option.

12

Developing eGovernment Hybrids

Key Points

- The hybrid approach to managing e-government is a successful third way between two less successful extremes, covering six 'POSSET' aspects: philosophy, organizational level, stakeholders, sector, extent of change, and technology.
- A hybrid approach must unite the 'e' and the 'government' of e-government, avoiding failures that arise through divisions between IT staff and mainstream public officials.
- An e-government hybrid is not a single entity; instead hybridization is a way to plan skills and knowledge development for current and future staff based around a 'wheel of competencies' model.
- Hybridization means a greater focus on e-government change agents, who may be created more easily from mainstream staff than from existing IT professionals.
- Both e-government leaders and IT managers are needed, with the former requiring a hybrid skill set that encompasses politics, vision, business issues and change as well as a grasp of technology's capabilities.

Goldilocks walks into the bears' kitchen. She sees a bowl of porridge and takes a taste. 'Yuk' she cries, 'This porridge is far too hot.' Then she spies a second bowl, and eats a spoonful from that. 'Yuk' she cries, 'This porridge is far too cold.' Finally, she sees a third bowl of porridge, and starts to eat from it. This time she says nothing because this time the porridge is *just right*.

So ... Goldilocks was one of the first hybrids, finding a successful 'third way' between two unsuccessful extremes. This has been one of the core concepts of this book – the hybrid approach to management of e-government as a successful third way between two less successful extremes.

As emphasized in Chapter 1, hybrid management is not a guarantee of e-government success. For one thing, the assumptions and requirements within a particular hybrid approach may mismatch the realities of a particular public sector organization. In that case, the hybrid approach may not work – one of the more 'extreme' management approaches may be more appropriate for successful e-government.

Hybrid management also runs the risk of being a grab-bag into which so much is dumped that it starts to lose meaning. We can try to avoid this by categorizing the grab-bag that has emerged within the book with one final acronym: POSSET.[1]

- *Philosophy*: eGovernment hybrids steer a middle way between the 'hard' ideas of objectivity and rationalism, and the 'soft' ideas of subjectivity and personalized politics.
- *Organizational level*: eGovernment hybrids steer a middle way between top-level centralized approaches, and bottom-up decentralized approaches.
- *Stakeholders*: eGovernment hybrids steer a middle way between the interests of external stakeholders (such as clients, taxpayers, voters), and internal stakeholders (such as staff and senior officials).
- *Sector*: eGovernment hybrids steer a middle way between respecting the particular goals and values of the public sector, and accepting that some lessons and ideas can be adapted from the private sector.
- *Extent of change*: eGovernment hybrids steer a middle way between the apathy of sticking with the current status quo/reality, and the risks of failure that can be associated with new system designs.
- *Technology*: eGovernment hybrids steer a middle way between idolizing technology so much that it is the central focus of public sector change, and ignoring the technology so much that it is unable to make a contribution to change.

Despite its shortcomings, the notion of the e-government hybrid is valuable, with the evidence from earlier chapters suggesting that a more hybrid approach to management will reduce the risks of e-government failure. What, then, do public sector organizations need to do?

All of the POSSET dimensions are important, but we will investigate this issue further by focusing on one of the most-commonly discussed challenges that creates problems for e-government. This is the division

between an understanding of technology and an understanding of the workings and purposes of the public sector (Holmes, 2001; Cross, 2002; see also quote below). This is a division reflected particularly in the first and last POSSET dimensions, and a division that can be summarized as being between the 'e' and the 'government' of 'e-government'.

12.1 UNITING THE 'E' AND THE 'GOVERNMENT' OF εGOVERNMENT THROUGH HYBRIDS

In Chapter 2, the 'IT square' was presented (Figure 2.2). Within this square, as just noted, one division is perennially discussed. This is the division between IT staff on the one hand (often the developers of e-government) and public officials, especially senior managers and politicians, on the other (often the users or owners of e-government). This division lies at the heart of many design–reality gaps, and it can thus be seen as an underlying cause for many e-government failures. For example, one Arkansas legislator described the problems of trying to cross the divide in understanding the challenges facing a troubled ERP (enterprise resource planning) application:

> We had meeting after meeting after meeting in my committee; at one end of the table were all the suits from the Department of Finance and Administration, from the Department of Information Systems, the consultants and one bearded guy in blue jeans from SAP [*the IT vendors*] ... Every time someone from the committee asked a question, all the suits would look at each other in puzzlement until, finally, they all looked at the guy with the beard. He would say something that nobody understood, and we'd just say, 'Ok, whatever' and go on. (Peterson, 2003)

One way to address the division is through the creation of hybrid public servants. The

Figure 12.1   The basic competencies of an e-government hybrid

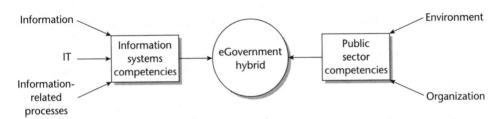

Figure 12.2   The competencies of public hybrids

simplest way to understand these hybrids would be as a combination of expertise in IT ('e') and expertise in the workings of the public sector ('government'), to create the e-government hybrid shown in Figure 12.1. For example, when the US State Department developed an e-government system to support arms control, there was an insistence on using only hybrid managers: any IT manager had also to be an expert in arms control, equally able to work in the policy office as on an IT project (Fulton, 2003). Case studies continuously identify the importance of hybrids in successful e-government projects (Parrado, 2002; Chandrasena, 2003; Foster and Griffin, 2003; Levin and Dingley, 2003).

As a basic working model for understanding e-government hybrids, Figure 12.1 is fine. However, it does have a significant shortcoming. It fails to take in one of the main arguments of this book: that e-government systems are not just IT, but information systems. If we are to properly take on this and other implications of the onion-ring model in Chapter 1, then a more thorough profile

of the kind of hybrid we need would look like that presented in Figure 12.2 (a development of the 'tribrid' concept presented in Figure 10.4). It might even be more appropriate to change the terminology from e-government to 'i-government' hybrid.

This kind of hybrid should not be thought of as a single entity. Rather, the notion of hybridization should be seen as a way to plan skills and knowledge development for current and future staff. For example, IT professionals need to be hybridized into broader change agents who combine IT skills with a better understanding of information systems, and a better understanding of public sector procedures, clients, values, and so on.

Public sector managers need to be hybridized towards a broader skill set that includes an understanding of information systems and IT. This would aim to make them confident about using IT, aware of what the technology can and cannot do, and aware of the role of information and information-related processes in the public sector. This will allow them to take greater control over, or make a more direct contribution to, e-government projects and overall strategies for IT-enabled reform.

Job roles can also be hybridized, not just at the managerial level but for others whose work becomes part information systems-related, part something else, such as:

- trainers who spend part of their time teaching public management skills, part of their time teaching public information systems; or
- a clerk who is also a technical support officer.

All of this clearly has extensive implications for training provision, which itself needs to be hybridized. Yet much of the current training supply for the public sector – both short professional programs, and undergraduate and postgraduate programs – is too narrow in focus. IT is increasingly covered for all groups, but not information systems. The role of information and the broader organizational context and processes that IT is intended to support are rarely included. Thus the majority of training currently available is not enabling staff to engage effectively in the process of information age reform.

We will end by looking at some further implications of the notion of hybrids.

12.2 IMPLICATIONS OF HYBRIDIZATION FOR εGOVERNMENT

New Profiles for IT Professionals in the Public Sector

As noted above, the IT professionals who serve the public sector need to be hybridized into broader change agents. This type of e-government hybrid offers the public sector several advantages (adapted from Earl, 1989). They are better able to:

- recognize the opportunity to introduce new e-government systems;
- make the case for a new e-government system;
- see how it fits into existing organizational operations and systems;
- anticipate the implementation issues associated with the new system.

In order to achieve this, they must develop a set of competencies that include (Mundy et al., 2001):

- *Knowledge*: Up-to-date knowledge of IT and options for systems development; knowledge about the role of information, IT and information systems in the public sector; knowledge about organizational systems, processes and clients; and knowledge about organizational strategies, policies and context.
- *Skills*: eGovernment systems skills relating to 'identification of opportunities for new information systems, analysis of the current use of information, redesign of existing processes, design and construction of software systems, and installation of hardware and software systems' (ibid.: 286). More generic skills relating to 'project and change management, communication and negotiation, problem-solving' are also going to be of value.
- *Attitudes*: Positive attitudes towards involving a broad range of stakeholders in the process of IT-enabled public sector reform.

Where will this type of e-government hybrid come from? Traditionally, it has been assumed that it will come from the

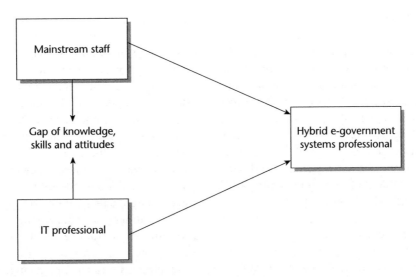

Figure 12.3   Creating hybrid e-government systems professionals for the public sector

hybridization of existing IT staff. However, as illustrated in Figure 12.3 (adapted from Heeks, 2001), there is an alternative route: hybridization of existing mainstream staff (functional managers, operational staff, etc.).

Some public agencies are finding the 'hybridization gap' to be smaller for mainstream staff than it is for some IT professionals. Put simply, it can be easier to teach some mainstream staff the necessary technical skills than it is to teach some IT specialists the necessary management, organizational and interpersonal competencies. Agencies also find that this approach to hybridization addresses some of the recruitment and retention problems identified in Chapter 5.

The Maltese government, for example, has found it much more effective to take public servants from line ministries who are interested in IT and turn them into e-government hybrids rather than trying to develop the required competencies in IT professionals hired externally. Likewise, a critical success factor for the UK Inland

Revenue's pay-as-you-earn computerization was the training of large numbers of office staff to become programmers, building strong links between end users and developers (Margetts, 1999).

It is too early to sound the death knell for IT professionals in the public sector. However, they face many challenges. The higher-level hybrids who provide the glue that holds planning and implementation for e-government in place can be developed from mainstream staff. The spread of user-friendly application-building tools means that simple e-government systems can be created in-house by hybridized end users. More complex systems are increasingly being outsourced, using IT professionals external to the public sector.

None of these trends is without its downsides for the public sector, but IT professionals need to respond: planning how to hybridize their own competency profiles and their own career paths in order to help address the divisions and failures that impede too many e-government projects.

New Competency Profile

A valuable basis for planning staff training, staff development and recruitment in the public sector can be an organizational competency profile: the set of overall competencies (knowledge, skills, attitudes) that are required by the organization. If we now focus on the competency profile needed for e-government, we can see from the discussion above that it must contain a number of the POSSET hybrid elements:

- It must bridge the gap between information systems and government through expertise in IT, in information, and in the workings of the public sector.
- It must bridge the gap between hard and soft through an understanding of data, formal procedures, and technology alongside expertise in the political arts of negotiating and influencing.
- It must bridge the gap between top and bottom by combining high-level vision, with low-level understanding of service tasks and processes.
- It must bridge the gap between inside and outside by understanding both the workings of the public sector, but also the needs, interests and ideas of clients and of the private sector.
- In addition to these structural elements, it must also be able to deal with the kind of e-government processes described in Part 2: change, projects, procurement, and so on.

Putting all these things together, we can create the total 'wheel of competencies' for an information age public sector, as shown in Figure 12.4 (developed from CGNTO, 2001; Haynes, 2002; OGC, 2004).

These are not the competencies that every individual involved with e-government should have: they are too many to be found within a single person. The wheel can help

individuals identify areas of weakness in their own profile that require strengthening. However, its main purpose – as noted – is as a planning tool; as a profile for teams or even whole public sector organizations. When coming up to an e-government project, for instance, one can ask, 'We need all these competencies for the project; where are we going to find them?'

Alternatively, the wheel can be used somewhat longer-term to identify competency areas that need strengthening through training, recruitment or outsourcing. The UK government, for example, identified priority e-government competencies that needed developing as: leadership, change/project management, 'intelligent customer' (i.e. better procurement and contract management), and IT skills (Cabinet Office, 2000). While particular needs will vary from country to country and agency to agency, all four areas do tend to recur – alongside the need for gap-bridging hybrids – in analyses of competency weaknesses related to e-government (Parrado, 2002; Willis, 2003b).

Because of its repeated appearance in e-government analyses, we will end by looking at one of these areas: leadership.

New eGovernment Leadership Requirements

The 'nuts and bolts' of e-government projects require a good project manager. However, perhaps even more critical to the success of such projects is a strong project leader; for leaders and managers are not the same thing:

> The difference between leadership and management was once summed up in the following way by someone looking out of our office window in Covent Garden in central London:
> 'Imagine there's a sudden power failure on the tube [*London underground rail system*]. The system halts and all the lights go out. In the central control room someone

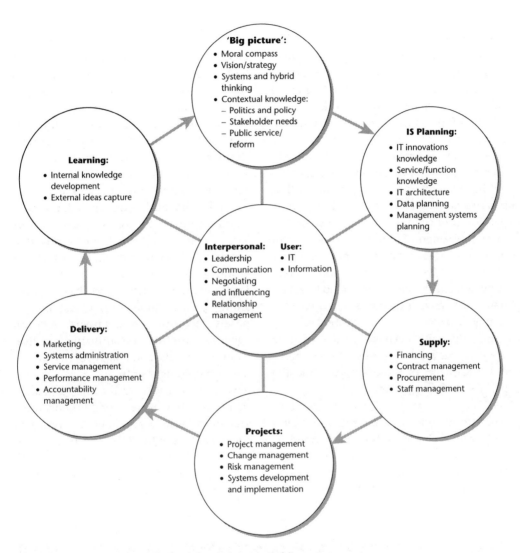

Figure 12.4   Competencies for an information age public sector

is marshalling resources, implementing the standby facilities, rescheduling the trains, calling the emergency services. That's management. Someone else is walking along the darkened platform with a torch bringing a trainload of people to safety. That's leadership. (Yeates and Cadle, 2002: 288)

Perhaps more than any other factor, it is the presence of an e-government leader that will contribute to the success of e-government

projects: this is 'the key role of an IT champion who has the vision and force of personality to inspire, cajole, and lead the transformation of work practices.' (Fulton, 2003: 163). Within this quote is a clue to the need for these leaders to also be hybrids – understanding IT, yet also able to transform work practices.

There is no set identity or locus for these e-government leaders: they may be drawn from the IT or mainstream staffs; they may be senior or middle-ranking. However, as noted above in relation to other types of hybrid, those with an IT background may face greater hurdles. Holmes (2001: 81) puts it bluntly: 'If an IT guy's in charge, it won't work.'

Thus, officials identified as 'e-government champions' are typically drawn from the ranks of non-IT-based senior public officials. They do *not* to come from an IT background, but have long-term work experience within a particular public agency, and have strong political connections that have been critical in gaining support for initiatives and then in insulating those initiatives from interference (Peterson, 1998; Foster and Griffin, 2003). eGovernment champions are found to understand and have experience of IT-enabled change. However, they are hybrids in combining this with deep knowledge of their agencies; the work processes of those agencies; the clients of those agencies; and the politics of those agencies.

It may therefore be that we need to separate out roles of e-government champion from IT leader. While both would be hybridized to some degree, the former would focus on politics, vision, business issues and change; the latter would focus on managing and harnessing the growing IT architecture. Certainly, e-government champions must move well beyond the old 'public sector IT manager' role. In terms of the wheel of competencies, their strengths will be found mainly in the area of big picture, change management, and interpersonal skills. Other aspects, such as information systems, need only be satisficed.

Above all, e-government champions must be political players. In the US, for example, the Bush Administration's lukewarm approach to e-government can be seen rooted in a Republican agenda that sought 'smaller government, not better government.' (Atkinson and Leigh, 2003: 178). Fighting against such views has required strong political nous – repackaging proposals according to dominant political agendas, finding and utilizing political counter-currents, and making opportunistic use of unfolding events.

We end, then, with a repeat of Strassmann's point made in Chapter 5 of this book: those seeking to lead e-government forward in the remainder of the 21st century are better served studying the works of Machiavelli and Sun Tzu than in reading the latest IT magazines and textbooks.

ACTIVITIES

Shorter In-Class Activities[2]

Pre-chapter

a. Before reading any of the chapter, note down as many senses of 'hybrid' in the management of e-government as you can recall. How close did this come to the POSSET checklist?

Introduction

a. Which of the POSSET components of being a hybrid do you think are most important for e-government, and why?

Section 12.1

a. You wish to persuade a committee of senior officials in a public agency that hybrid management is the approach they need to adopt for e-government. Prepare a slide with a maximum of four bullet points that you think will persuade them.

b. 'We should stop talking about e-government, and talk instead about i-government.' Discuss.

Sections 12.1–12.2

a. Reflect on your current study program. Identify two ways in which it could be hybridized.

Section 12.2

a. 'It is not possible to cram all the necessary hybrid competencies into a single person. We need to plan hybrid teams not hybrid individuals.' Discuss.

b. Discuss which components of the wheel of competencies you feel are most important, and why.

c. Identify the qualities of an e-government leader you feel are most important. Discuss how these do/do not relate to those listed in the main text.

Assignment Questions

Introduction, Sections 12.1 and 12.2

a. Explain the concept of a hybrid management approach to e-government. What are the key implications of such an approach?

b. How are the requirements of an e-government hybrid likely to differ from those of an e-business hybrid working in the private sector?

Practitioner Exercises

Section 12.1

a. How many of the staff in your organization could be considered hybrids? Is there a need for more hybrids in your organization? If so, what roles would they fulfill and how could they be created?

Section 12.2

a. Look at your own competency profile. Should it be more hybridized? If so, how could you achieve that?

b. Reflect on the wheel of competencies. What implications does it have for staff training, staff development and recruitment in your organization?

c. If you wished to become an e-government leader in your organization, what competencies would you require and what practices would you need to follow? What are the implications of your answer for your self-development?

NOTES

1. Posset is a hybrid drink that mixes milk and alcohol. Unfortunately, it is also used to describe baby vomit. The reader can decide which meaning is more appropriate here.

2. Details of longer group activities are provided in the Online Appendix to this chapter.

References

Abramson, M.A. and Morin, T.L. (eds) (2003) *E-Government 2003*. Lanham, MD: Rowman & Littlefield.

Accenture (2003) *eGovernment Leadership: Engaging the Customer*. Accenture.

Access Board (2001) *Standards for Electronic and Information Technology*, Washington, DC: Access Board. http://www.access-board.gov/sec508/summary.htm.

Afferson, M., Muhlemann, A., Price, D. and Rushworth, T. (1995) 'Determining management information requirements within a health sector organisation', *Information Infrastructure and Policy*, 4: 67–86.

Alter, S. (2002) *Information Systems*, 4th edition. Upper Saddle River, NJ: Pearson Education.

ANAO (2003) *Outsourcing and Partnerships in the Public Sector*. Canberra: Australian National Audit Office.

Andersen, K.V. (2001) 'Reengineering public sector organisations using information technology', in R.B. Heeks (ed.), *Reinventing Government in the Information Age*. London: Routledge. pp. 312–330.

Anttiroiko, A.-V. (2002) 'Strategic knowledge management in local government', in A. Grönlund (ed.), *Electronic Government*. Hershey, PA: Idea Group Publishing. pp. 268–98.

AOIT (2003) *Best Practices Statement – Project Management*. Little Rock, AR: Arkansas Office of Information Technology.

APM (2005) *Management Overview*. High Wycombe: APM Group. http://www.prince2.org.uk/Web/Site/AboutPRINCE2/Management_Overview3.asp.

Armstrong, M. (2003) *Human Resource Management Practice*, 9th edition. London: Kogan Page.

Arnott, S. (2003) 'UK pays £16bn to outsourcers', *Computing*, 2 October: 1, 5.

Aslund, A. (1995) *How Russia Became a Market Economy*. Washington, DC: Brookings Institute.

Atkinson, R.D. and Leigh, A. (2003) 'Customer-oriented e-government: Can we ever get there?', in G.G. Curtin, M.H. Sommer and V. Vis-Sommer (eds), *The World of E-Government*. New York: Haworth Press. pp. 159–81.

Avison, D. and Fitzgerald, G. (2003) *Information Systems Development*, 3rd edition. Maidenhead, UK: McGraw-Hill.

Baker, R.K. (1998) *Technophobia and Computer-Related Stress*. Tampa, FL: University of Tampa.

Ballantine, J. and Cunningham, N. (2001) 'Strategic information systems planning', in R.B. Heeks (ed.), *Reinventing Government in the Information Age* London: Routledge. pp. 293–311.

Bannister, F. (2003) 'Turf wars: the hidden menace', in F. Bannister and D. Remenyi (eds), *Third European Conference on eGovernment*. Reading: MCIL. pp. 31–42.

Barrett, K. and Greene, R. (2001) *Powering Up*. Washington, DC: CQ Press.

Bell, A. (2000) *Transforming your Workplace*. London: Institute for Personnel and Development.

Bell, S. and Wood-Harper, T. (2003) *How to Set Up Information Systems*. London: Earthscan.

Bellamy, C. and Taylor, J. (1998) *Governing in the Information Age*. Buckingham: Open University Press.

Bentley, C. (2002) *Practical PRINCE2*. London: The Stationery Office.

Berman, E.M., Bowman, J.S., West, J.P. and Van Wart, M. (2001) *Human Resource Management in Public Service*. Thousand Oaks, CA: Sage.

Bhambhani, D. (2002) 'A crisis in slow motion', *Government Computer News*, 3 June. http://www.gcn.com.

Bierstedt, R. (1950) 'An analysis of social power', *American Sociological Review*, 15: 730–8.

Bishop, S. (2001) 'Outsourcing and government information technology strategy', in R.B. Heeks (ed.), *Reinventing Government in the Information Age*. London: Routledge. pp. 253–70.

Blair, G. and Meadows, S. (1996) *Winning at Change*. London: Pitman Publishing.

Bocij, P., Chaffey, D., Greasley, A. and Hickie, S. (2003) *Business Information Systems*, 2nd edition. Harlow: Pearson Education.

Boddy, D., Boonstra, A. and Kennedy, G. (2005) *Managing Information Systems*, 2nd edition. Harlow: Pearson Education.

Bretschneider, S. (1990) 'Management information systems in public and private organizations', *Public Administration Review*, September/October: 536–45.

Broadbent, M. (2002) 'CIO futures', ICA 36th conference, 22–24 October, Singapore. http://ica-it.org/conf36/docs/Broadbented. pdf.

Brown, D.M. (2001) 'Information systems for improved performance management', in R.B. Heeks (ed.), *Reinventing Government in the Information Age*. London: Routledge. pp. 113–34.

Brown, M.M. (2000) 'Mitigating the risk of IT initiatives', in G.D. Garson (ed.), *Handbook of Public Information Systems*. New York: Marcel Dekker. pp. 153–63.

Buchanan, D. and Huczynski, A. (2004) *Organizational Behaviour*, 5th edition. Harlow: Pearson Education.

Burkitt-Gray, A. (1998) 'Lost in cyberspace', *Government Computing*, May: 18–19.

BVPL (2003) *The State of Local Authority Procurement in England Today*. Barnard Castle: Best Value Procurement.

Bygrave, L.A. (2003) *Ensuring Right Information on the Right Person(s)*. University of Oslo: Avdeling for Forvaltningsinformatikk.

Cabinet Office (2000) *e-Government: A Strategic Framework for Public Services in the Information Age*. London: Cabinet Office.

Caffrey, L. (2003) 'Round table discussion: Session 1', ICA 36th conference, 22–24 October, Singapore. http://ica-it.org/conf36/ docs/RT1ed.pdf.

Cain, P. (2001) 'Automating personnel records for improved management of human resources', in R.B. Heeks (ed.), *Reinventing Government in the Information Age*. London: Routledge. pp. 135–55.

Campbell, D. (1999) 'You've got mail (and so have we)', *Guardian (London)*, 18 March, Online supplement: 2–7.

Cats-Baril, W. and Thompson, R. (1995) 'Managing information projects in the public sector', *Public Administration Review*, 55 (6): 559–66.

CBR (2001) 'Weight watchers', *Computer Business Review*, 12 January. http://www. cbronline.com.

CCBC (2003) *Web Content Management System*. Evans, GA: Columbia County Board of Commissioners. http://www.lgov.org/document/ doclist.asp.

CCTA (1997) *PRINCE 2: An Outline*. London: Central Computer and Telecommunications Agency.

CDPUC (2003) *Streetlight Audit of Connecticut Light & Power*. New Britain, CT: Connecticut Department of Public Utility Control.

CEG (2001) *eGovernment: The Next American Revolution*. Washington, DC: Council for Excellence in Government.

CGNTO (2001) *Developing 21st Century Skills*. London: Central Government National Training Organisation.

Chaffey, D. (2002) *E-Business and E-Commerce Management*, Harlow: Pearson Education.

Chambers, R. (1994) 'All power deceives', *IDS Bulletin*, 25 (2): 14–26.

Chambers, R. (1997) *Whose Reality Counts?* London: Intermediate Technology Publications.

Champlain, J.J. (2003) *Auditing Information Systems*. Chichester, UK: John Wiley.

Chandrasena, A.M.S.K. (2003) *Web-Based Access to User-Friendly Government Financial Statements in Sri Lanka*, eTransparency Case Study No.10, eGovernment for Development Information Exchange. http://www.egov4dev. org/lankasad.htm

Checkland, P. and Scholes, J. (1999) *Soft Systems Methodology in Action*. Chichester, UK: Wiley.

Chen, Y.-C. and Perry, J.L. (2003) *IT Outsourcing: A Primer for Public Managers*. Washington, DC: IBM Endowment for the Business of Government.

Chepaitis, E. (2002) 'Soft barriers to ICT application in development: Trust and information quality in Russia', *Journal of International Development*, 14 (1): 51–60.

CITU (2000) *Successful IT: Modernising Government in Action*. London: Central IT Unit, Cabinet Office.

City of Dayton (2001) *Internal and External Electronic Communication Policy*, Dayton, OH: City of Dayton.

City of Richmond (2001) *Electronic Media Systems*, Richmond, VA: City of Richmond.

Cohen, S. and Eimicke, W. (1998) *Tools for Innovators*. San Francisco, CA: Jossey-Bass.

Cohen, S. and Eimicke, W. (2002) *The Effective Public Manager*, 3rd edition. San Francisco, CA: Jossey-Bass.

CoK (2003) *The Direction of Enterprise Information Technology*. Frankfort, KY: Commonwealth of Kentucky.

Computer Weekly (1999) 'Government hit by skills crisis', *Computer Weekly*, 14 January. http://www.computerweekly.com.

Computing (1998) 'The vanishing world of data', *Computing*, 30 April: 48–50.

Computing (2002) 'Public Sector 2002', *Computing*, 23 May: 39–55.

Connell, R. (2001) 'Child Nutrition Management System', *Open Forum*, 15 (3): 1–8.

Cook, M.E., LaVigne, M.F., Pagano, C.M., Dawes, S.S. and Pardo, T.A. (2002) *Making a Case for Local E-Government*. Albany, NY: Center for Technology in Government, University at Albany, SUNY.

Coursey, D. and Killingsworth, J. (2000) 'Managing government Web services in Florida: issues and lessons', in G. David Garson (ed.), *Handbook of Public Information Systems*. New York: Marcel Dekker. pp. 331–43.

Cross, M. (2002) 'Why do government IT projects go wrong?', *Computing*, 12 September: 37–40.

Cross, M. (2004) 'The credible alternative', *Government IT*, March: 8–10.

CSB (2001) *Request for Proposal: Computer Aided Dispatch System*. San Bernadino, CA: County of San Bernardino. http://www.lgov.org/document/doclist.asp.

CSD (1971) *Computers in Government Ten Years Ahead*. London: Civil Service Department, Her Majesty's Stationery Office.

Curthoys, N. and Crabtree, J. (2003) *SmartGov*. London: The Work Foundation.

DAFS (2000) *Ergonomics Policy for Computer Use and other Repetitive Motion Tasks*. Augusta, ME: Dept. of Administrative & Financial Services.

d'Auray, M. (2003) 'The dual challenge of integration and inclusion: Canada's experience with Government Online', in G.G. Curtin, M.H. Sommer and V. Vis-Sommer (eds), *The World of E-Government*. New York: Haworth Press. pp. 31–49.

Davenport, T. (1997) *Information Ecology*. New York: Oxford University Press.

Dawes, S.S., Pardo, T.A., Green, D.E., McInerney, C.R., Connelly, D.R. and

DiCaterino, A. (1997) *Tying a Sensible Knot: A Practical Guide to State-Local Information Systems*. Albany, NY: Center for Technology in Government, University at Albany, SUNY.

Destatis (2002) *E-Strategy, Process Analysis and Design at the Federal Statistical Office*. Bonn: Destatis/Federal Statistical Office.

Detlor, B. and Finn, K. (2002) 'Towards a framework for government portal design', in A. Grönlund (ed.), *Electronic Government*. Hershey, PA: Idea Group Publishing. pp. 99–119.

Devlin, J. (2003) *The IT Career Continuum Progress Report*. Ottawa, ON: IT Champions Committee, Treasury Board of Canada Secretariat.

DFA (2001) *Enhanced 9-1-1 Systems Equipment and Services*. Santa Fe, NM: Department of Finance and Administration, State of New Mexico. http://www.lgov.org/document/doclist.asp.

Dhillon, G. (1998) *The Clinical Information System: A Case of Misleading Design Decisions*. Hershey, PA: Idea Group Publishing.

DHS (2003) *The National Strategy to Secure Cyberspace*. Washington, DC: Department of Homeland Security.

DIS (1995) *Biennial Information Technology Performance Report, 1993–1995*. Seattle, WA: Department of Information Systems.

Doherty, T.L. and Horne, T. (2002) *Managing Public Services*. London: Routledge.

DOI (2002) 'Revision of the FOIA regulations and implementation of the EFOIA amendments of 1996', *Federal Register*, 67 (203): 64527–52.

DOI (2003) *E-Government Strategy FY2004–FY2008*. Washington, DC: Department of the Interior.

DOJ (2000) *IT and People with Disabilities*. Washington, DC: Department of Justice.

DOJ (2001) *Section 508 Self-Evaluation*. Washington, DC: Department of Justice.

DOL (2002) *IT Project Management*. Washington, DC: Department of Labor.

DOL (2003) *E-Government Strategic Plan*. Washington, DC: Department of Labor.

DPWS (1998) *Acquisition of Information Management and Technology*, Sydney: Department of Public Works and Services, New South Wales Government.

Drake, D.B, Koch, M.J. and Steckler, N.A. (2003) 'Scientist, politician, and bureaucrat subcultures as barriers to information-sharing in government agencies', paper presented at *dg.o2003*, 18–21 May, Boston, MA.

Dussault, R. (1999) 'An open and shut case', *Government Technology*, November. http://www.govtech.net/

Earl, M.J. (1989) *Management Strategies for Information Technology*. Hemel Hempstead: Prentice-Hall.

Ebrahim, Z., Irani, Z. and Al-Shawi, S. (2003) 'E-government adoption: Analysis of adoption staged models', in F. Bannister and D. Remenyi (eds), *Third European Conference on eGovernment*. Reading: MCIL. pp. 91–102.

e-Envoy (2001) *International Benchmarking Report*. London: Office of the e-Envoy, Cabinet Office. http://www.cabinetoffice.gov.uk/e-government.

Eggers, W.D. (2003) *Cutting Fat, Adding Muscle*. New York: Deloitte Consulting.

Eggers, W.D. (2004) 'Adoption dilemma', *Public CIO*, February. http://www.public-cio.com.

E-Government Bulletin (2002a) 'Error prone', *E-Government Bulletin*, 1126, 25 November.

E-Government Bulletin (2002b) 'We need architects as well as plumbers', *E-Government Bulletin*, 124, 25 October.

E-Government Bulletin (2004) 'Public sector sites failing on accessibility', *E-Government Bulletin*, 159, 16 April.

Emery, Y. (2004) 'Rewarding civil service performance through team bonuses', *International Review of Administrative Sciences*, 70 (1): 157–68.

Eversheds (2000) *E-Government, Best Value and the Law*. Northampton: Society of Information Technology Management.

FEAPMO (2003) *Federal Enterprise Architecture*. Washington, DC: Federal Enterprise Architecture Program Management Office. http://feapmo.gov/fea.asp.

Finlay, D. (2004) 'Project management', *Government IT*, April: 13–14.

Fisher, C.W. and Kingma, B.R. (2001) 'Criticality of data quality as exemplified in two disasters', *Information & Management*, 39 (2): 109–16.

Fletcher, P.D. (2000) 'Governmental information systems and emerging computer technologies', in G. David Garson (ed.), *Handbook of Public Information Systems*. New York: Marcel Dekker. pp. 577–90.

Flynn, N. (2002) *Public Sector Management*, 4th edition., Harlow: Pearson Education.

Foot, P. (2004) *P.F. Eye*, Special Report for *Private Eye*, 1102, 19 March.

Foster, A. and Griffin, D. (2003) 'The local authority e-champion: The hybrid manager needed to make joined-up government a reality', in F. Bannister and D. Remenyi (eds), *Third European Conference on eGovernment*. Reading: MCIL. pp. 131–42.

Fountain, J.E. (2001) *Building the Virtual State*. Washington, DC: Brookings Institution Press.

Fountain, J.E. (2002) 'Towards a theory of federal bureaucracy for the twenty-first century', in E.C. Kamarck and J.S. Nye (eds), *Governance.com*. Washington, DC: Brookings Institution Press. pp. 117–40.

Fowler, A. (1998) *Negotiating, Persuading and Influencing*. London: Chartered Institute of Personnel and Development.

French, M. (2003a) 'Navy purchase cards hacked', *Federal Computer Week*, 21 August. http://www.fcw.com.

French, M. (2003b) 'GAO sees weak discipline of DOD purchase offenders', *Federal Computer Week*, 3 December. http://www.fcw.com.

Fulton, B. (2003) 'Leveraging technology in the service of diplomacy', in M.A. Abramson and T.L. Morin (eds), *E-Government 2003*. Lanham, MD: Rowman & Littlefield. pp. 127–76.

GAO (2001) *Management Planning Guide for Information Systems Security Auditing*. Washington, DC: General Accounting Office. http://www.gao.gov/special.pubs/mgmtpln.pdf.

Gartner (2002) 'GartnerEXP Says a Majority of E-Government Initiatives Fail or Fall Short of Expectations'. http://symposium.gartner.com/story.php.id.1367.s.5.html.

GHK (2002) *Evaluation of MES*. London: GHK.

Goddard, T.D. and Riback, C. (1998) 'The eight traits of highly successful public officials', *The Hill* 6 May.

GOT (2003) *Annual Report 2002–3*. Frankfort, KY: Governor's Office of Technology.

Government Computing (2002) 'DfES picks at learning failure', *Government Computing*, March: 6.

Government Computing (2003a) 'Managing change', *Government Computing*, March: 31–2.

Government Computing (2003b) 'The Home Office approach', *Government Computing*, April: 30.

Government Computing (2004) 'The 6% dichotomy', Government Computing, February: 34.

Government Technology (1999) 'Feds award first contract for Internet security', 18 September. http://www.govtech.net/.

Graafland-Essers, I. and Ettedgui, E. (2003) Benchmarking e-Government in Europe and the US. Santa Monica, CA: RAND.

Greenwood, M. (1999) 'Using IT to modernise local government', paper presented at SOCITM regional meeting, 10 August, Manchester, UK.

Greig, B. (2003) 'Meeting real needs', CIO, 7 October. http://www.cio.com.au.

Grindley, K. (1991) Managing Information Technology at Board Level. London: Pitman.

Grönlund, A. (2002) 'Electronic government – efficiency, service quality and democracy', in A. Grönlund (ed.), Electronic Government. Hershey, PA: Idea Group Publishing. pp. 23–50.

GSA (1999) 'Limited Personal Use' of Government Office Equipment. Washington, DC: Federal CIO Council, General Services Administration.

GSA (2003) Federal E-Government Initiatives: Are We Headed in the Right Direction? Washington, DC: General Services Administration.

Gubbins, M. (2004) 'Global IT spending by sector', Computing, 8 April: 28.

Gupta, M.P., Kumar, P. and Bhattacharya, J. (2004) Government Online: Opportunities and Challenges. New Delhi: Tata McGraw-Hill.

Hafeez, K. and Savani, H. (2003) 'Innovation, knowledge management and e-government initiatives in the public sector', in F. Bannister and D. Remenyi (eds), Third European Conference on eGovernment. Reading: MCIL. pp. 175–84.

Hammitt, H. (2000) 'The legislative foundation of information access policy', in G. David Garson (ed.), Handbook of Public Information Systems. New York: Marcel Dekker. 27–39.

Handy, C. (1992) Understanding Organizations, 4th edition. Harmondsworth: Penguin.

Hanrahan, M. (2003) 'Working wonders?', Government Computing, May: 39–40.

Harris, B. (2002) 'New tech partnership legislation passes', Government Technology, April. http://www.govtech.net/.

Harris, B. (2003) 'Building the winning team', Government Technology, October. http://www.govtech.net/.

Hauschild, T. (2002) Evaluation Criteria for Potentially Online-Capable Services. Bonn,

Germany: Federal Office for Information Security.

Haynes, C. (2002) 'An ICT skills and resources framework for developing egovernment', paper presented at SOCITM workshop on The Impact of the eGovernment Agenda on HR, 10 January, Lilleshall, UK.

Hayward, D. (1997) 'Battlezone', Computing, 27 March: 36–37.

HCPD (2000) Human Resources Information System RFP Stage 2. Hillsborough County, FL: Hillsborough County Purchasing Department. http://www.lgov.org/document/doclist. asp.

HCTI (2003) 'Modernization of Air Traffic Control Programs to be Focus of Congressional Hearing', press release, House Committee on Transportation and Infrastructure, Washington, DC.

Heeks, R.B. (1997) 'Human resource development for public sector information systems', COMNET-IT conference 'Enhancing Public Service Delivery Through Information Technology', 2–5 December, Sliema, Malta.

Heeks, R.B. (1999a) 'Management information systems in the public sector', in G. David Garson (ed.), Information Technology, and Computer Applications in Public Administration. Hershey, PA: Idea Group Publishing. pp. 157–73.

Heeks, R.B. (1999b) 'La connexion africaine sous-estimée', Liaison Francophone, 25 January. http://www.francophonie.org/liaison.

Heeks, R.B. (1999c) 'The Tyranny of Participation in Information Systems', IDPM Development Informatics Working Paper no. 4, University of Manchester, UK.

Heeks, R.B. (2000a) 'The approach of senior public officials to information technology-related reform', Public Administration and Development, 20: 197–205.

Heeks, R.B. (2000b) 'A core-periphery approach to centralization/decentralization issues in public information systems', in G. David Garson (ed.), Handbook of Public Information Systems. New York: Marcel Dekker. pp. 127–40.

Heeks, R.B. (2000c) 'Information technology and the management of corruption', in T. Wallace (ed.), Development and Management. Oxford: Oxfam Publishing. pp. 252–60.

Heeks, R.B. (2000d) 'Information technology, information systems and public sector accountability', in C. Avgerou and

G. Walsham (eds), *Information Technology in Context*. Aldershot: Ashgate. pp. 201–19.

Heeks, R.B. (2001) 'Explaining success and failure of e-government', in D. Remenyi and F. Bannister (eds), *First European Conference on eGovernment*. Reading: MCIL. pp. 163–74.

Heeks, R.B. (2003a) *Avoiding eGov Failure: Ideas About Politics & Self-Interest*. Manchester: IDPM, University of Manchester. http://www.egov4dev.org/ideapolitics.htm.

Heeks, R.B. (2003b) *The Impact of eGovernment Failure*. Manchester: IDPM, University of Manchester. http://www.egov4dev.org/impactfailure.htm.

Heeks, R.B. (2005) 'eGovernment as a Carrier of Context', *Journal of Public Policy*, 25 (1): 51–74.

Heeks, R.B. and Bhatnagar, S.C. (2001) 'Understanding success and failure in information age reform', in R.B. Heeks (ed.), *Reinventing Government in the Information Age*. London: Routledge. 49–74.

Heeks, R.B. and Wilson, G. (2000) 'Technology, poverty and development', in T. Allen and A. Thomas (eds), *Poverty and Development into the 21st Century*. Oxford: Oxford University Press. pp. 403–24.

Herzberg, F. (1987) 'Workers' needs: the same around the world', *Industry Week*, 234 (6): 29–32.

Hesselmark, O. (2002) *eReadings and eGovernment*. Stockhalm, Sweden.

Hill, S. (2004) 'Socitm consulting update', *Socitm News*, 77: 8.

Hiscock, J. (1999) 'Online crime watch', *IT Training*, 14 July: 20–2.

Hobbs, V.J. and Pigott, D.J. (2001) 'Facilitating end user database development by working with users' natural representations of data', in M. Khosrowpour (ed.), *Managing Information Technology in a Global Environment*. Hershey, PA: Idea Group Publishing. pp. 650–6.

Holden, S.H., Norris, D.F. and Fletcher, P.D. (2003) 'Electronic government at the grass roots', paper presented at the 36th Hawaii International Conference on System Sciences, 6–9 January, Hawaii.

Holmes, D. (2001) *eGov: eBusiness Strategies for Government*. London: Nicholas Brealey.

Horejs, I. (1996) 'IT in rural development planning', in E.M. Roche and M.J. Blaine (eds), *Information Technology, Development and Policy*. Aldershot: Avebury. pp. 209–28.

Horton, K.S. and Dewar, R.G. (2001) 'Evaluating creative practice in information systems strategy formation', paper presented at the 34th Hawaii International Conference on System Sciences, 3–6 January, Hawaii.

Houtari, M.-L. and Wilson, T.D. (2001) 'Determining organizational information needs', *Information Research*, 6 (3). http://informationr.net/ir/6-3/paper108.html.

Howell, J. (2001) 'E-inclusion: designing for diversity', in D. Remenyi and F. Bannister (eds), *First European Conference on eGovernment*. Reading: MCIL. pp. 197–202.

HPG (2001) *Imperative 3: Utilize Best Practices for Implementing IT Initiatives*. Cambridge, MA: Harvard Policy Group on Network-Enabled Services and Government, Kennedy School of Government, Harvard University.

Huang, M. and Smithson, S. (2003) 'Government online in China', in F. Bannister and D. Remenyi (eds), *Third European Conference on eGovernment*. Reading: MCIL. pp. 193–200.

HUD (2001) *Electronic Government Strategic Plan 2001–2005*. Washington, DC: Department of Housing and Urban Development.

IAB (2003) *High Payoff in Electronic Government*. Washington, DC: Intergovernmental Advisory Board.

IDLO (2002) *Legal and Regulatory Aspects of E-Commerce and E-Government*. Rome: International Development Law Organization.

IES (2004) *Information Engineering Overview*. Hillarys, Australia: Information Engineering Services.

Infosys (1994) 'News items', 1 (36): 2.

INK (2005) *AccessKansas*. Topeka, KS: Information Network of Kansas. http://www.accesskansas.org/index.html.

Internetworldstats (2005) *Internet Usage Statistics*, Internet-World-Stats. http://internetworldstats.com/stats.htm.

Isaac-Henry, K. (1997) 'Management of information technology in the public sector', in K. Isaac-Henry, C. Painter and C. Barnes (eds), *Management in the Public Sector*, 2nd edition. London: International Thomson Business Press. pp. 147–59.

ITO (2002) *Illinois Web Accessibility Standards*. Springfield, IL: Illinois Technology Office. http://www100.state.il.us/ito/iwas1_2.cfm.

James, G. (1997) 'IT fiascoes … and how to avoid them', *Datamation*, November. http://

www.datamation.com/PlugIn/issues/1997/
november/11disas.html.

Jessup, L. and Valacich, J. (2006) *Information Systems Today*, 2nd edition. Upper Saddle River, NJ: Pearson Education.

Johnson, N. (2001) 'Recruiting and retaining information systems staff for information age reform', in R.B. Heeks (ed.), *Reinventing Government in the Information Age*. London: Routledge. pp. 350–62.

Jorgensen, D.J. and Cable, S. (2002) 'Facing the challenges of e-government', *SAM Advanced Management Journal*, Summer: 15–30.

Jupp, V. (2003) 'Realizing the vision of e-government', in G.G. Curtin, M.H. Sommer and V. Vis-Sommer (eds), *The World of E-Government*. New York: Haworth Press. pp. 129–45.

Kable (2003) *e-Government Cost Savings Report*. London: Kable.

Kahn, M. and Swanborough, R. (1999) 'Information Management, IT and Government Transformation', iGovernment working paper no. 8, IDPM, University of Manchester, UK.

Keen, K. (2000) *Document Management and Imaging System RFP*. Sedgwick County, KS: Sedgwick County. http://www.lgov.org/document/doclist.asp.

Kendall, K.E. and Kendall, J.E. (2005) *Systems Analysis and Design*, 6th edition. Upper Saddle River, NJ: Prentice Hall.

Kennedy, R. (2003) 'Securing savings on software', *Government IT*, July: 78–9.

Kieley, B., Lane, G., Paquet, G. and Roy, J. (2002) 'e-Government in Canada', in A. Grönlund (ed.), *Electronic Government*. Hershey, PA: Idea Group Publishing. pp. 340–55.

Kipnis, D., Schmidt, S.M., Swaffin-Smith, C. and Wilkinson, I. (1984) 'Patterns of managerial influence: shotgun managers, tacticians and bystanders', *Organizational Dynamics*, Winter: 58–67.

Klein, B.D., Goodhue, D.L. and Davis, G.B. (1997) 'Can humans detect errors in data?', *MIS Quarterly*, 21 (2): 169–94.

Knight, A.V. and Silk, D.J. (1990) *Managing Information*. London: McGraw-Hill.

Knight, S. (2001) 'N.L.P', *Training Journal*, June: 14–17.

Korac-Boisvert, N. and Kouzmin, A. (1995) 'Transcending soft-core IT disasters in public sector organizations', *Information Infrastructure and Policy*, 4: 131–61.

Korac-Kakabadse, A. and Korac-Kakabadse, N. (2001) 'Information technology's impact on the quality of democracy', in R.B. Heeks (ed.), *Reinventing Government in the Information Age*. London: Routledge. pp. 211–28.

Kuk, G. (2003) 'The digital divide and the quality of electronic service delivery in local government in the United Kingdom', *Government Information Quarterly*, 20 (4): 353–63.

Laegreid, P. (2002) 'Transforming top civil servant systems', in T. Christensen and P. Laegreid (eds), *New Public Management*. Aldershot: Ashgate. pp. 147–71.

LaPlante, J.M. (2000) 'Building relevant policy data systems for multiple stakeholders', in G. David Garson (ed.), *Handbook of Public Information Systems*. New York: Marcel Dekker. pp. 315–29.

Latta, B. (2002) 'The quiet revolution', *Summit*, Autumn: 4–6.

Laudon, K.C. and Laudon, J.P. (1995) *Information Systems*, 3rd edition. Fort Worth, TX: Dryden Press.

Laudon, K.C. and Laudon, J.P. (1998) *Management Information Systems*, 5th edition. Upper Saddle River, NJ: Prentice Hall.

Laudon, K.C. and Laudon, J.P. (2004) *Management Information Systems*, 8th edition. Upper Saddle River, NJ: Prentice Hall.

Laudon, K.C. and Laudon, J.P. (2005) *Essentials of Management Information Systems*, 6th edition. Upper Saddle River, NJ: Pearson Education.

Lazer, D. and Binz-Scharf, M.C. (2004) *Information Sharing in E-Government Projects*, Boston, MA: National Center for Digital Government, Harvard University.

Leenes, R.E. (2002) 'The Enschede Virtual Public Counter', in A. Grönlund (ed.), *Electronic Government*. Hershey, PA: Idea Group Publishing. pp. 205–25.

Lenk, K., Traunmüller, R. and Wimmer, M. (2002) 'The significance of law and knowledge for electronic government', in A. Grönlund (ed.), *Electronic Government*. Hershey, PA: Idea Group Publishing. pp. 61–77.

Leslie, S. (1999) 'Modern government should know where it's at', *Government IT*, May: 68–9.

Levin, A. and Dingley, R. (2003) 'Opening Government Information via the Cape Gateway', eTransparency Case Study No. 1, eGovernment for Development Information

Exchange. http://www.egov4dev.org/cape.htm.

Lewis, J.R.T. (2000) 'Electronic access to public records', in G. David Garson (ed.), *Handbook of Public Information Systems*. New York: Marcel Dekker. pp. 197–214.

Longford, G. (2002) 'Rethinking e-government', paper presented at workshop on Public Sector Innovation, 9–10 February, University of Ottawa, Ontario.

Lynn, B. (2000) 'Technology launch in government', in G.D. Garson (ed.), *Handbook of Public Information Systems*. New York: Marcel Dekker. pp. 113–25.

Mahler, J.G. and Regan, P.M. (2003) 'Federal intranet work sites', in M.A. Abramson and T.L. Morin (eds), *E-Government 2003*. Lanham, MD: Rowman & Littlefield. 81–124.

Malstrom, C.W. (1999) *University of Tennessee at Chattanooga IT Report*. Chattanooga, TN: Technology Committee, University of Tennessee at Chattanooga.

Mansell-Lewis, E. (1999) 'Cleaning up?', *Government IT*, May: pp. 60–1.

March, J.G. (1986) 'Theories of choice and making decisions', in R. Wolff (ed.), *Organizing Industrial Development*. Berlin: Walter de Gruyter. pp. 305–25.

Margetts, H. (1999) *Information Technology in Government: Britain and America*, London: Routledge.

Margetts, H. and Yared, H. (2003) *Incentivization of E-government*. London: School of Public Policy, University College.

Martin, L.L. and Singh, K.K. (2004) 'Using government performance management data to identify new business opportunities', *International Review of Administrative Sciences*, 70 (1): 65–76.

Mathieson, S.A. (2002) 'Back from disaster', *Government Computing*, April: 16–17.

Mathieson, S.A. (2004) 'Source of a little irritation', *ePublic*, 28 January: 4–5.

MCC (2003) *Request for Proposals: Web Site Management Software and Services*. Murray, UT: Murray City Corporation. http://www.lgov.org/document/doclist.asp

McCalla, J. (2003) 'Transforming public service in Ontario', in F. Bannister and D. Remenyi (eds), *Third European Conference on eGovernment*. Reading: MCIL. pp. 309–16.

McCue, A. (2002) 'Hackers target vital organisations', *Computing*, 29 March: 8.

McCue, C.P. (2001) 'Organizing the public purchasing function', *Government Finance Review*, February: 1–5.

McGinnis, P. (2003) 'Creating a blueprint for e-government', in G.G. Curtin, M.H. Sommer and V. Vis-Sommer (eds), *The World of E-Government*. New York: Haworth Press. pp. 51–63.

Meijer, A.J. (2003) 'Transparent government', *Information Polity*, 8 (1/2): 67–78.

Milne, A.A. (1926) *Winnie-the-Pooh*. London: Methuen.

Milner, E.M. (2000) *Managing Information and Knowledge in the Public Sector*. London: Routledge.

Moon, M.J. (2003) 'State government e-procurement in the information age', in M.A. Abramson and T.L. Morin (eds), *E-Government 2003*. Lanham, MD: Rowman & Littlefield. pp. 177–235.

Morgan, G. (2004) 'Council tenders £550m contract', *Computing*, 4 March: 13.

Mortleman, J. and Thomas, D. (2004) 'IT staff ditch private work for buoyant public sector', *Computing*, 25 March: 60.

Mosquera, M. (2004) 'FAA slows down display system deployment', *Government Computer News*, 26 April. http://www.gcn.com.

Mullins, L.J. (2002) *Management and Organisational Behaviour*, 6th edition. Harlow: Pearson Education.

Mundy, D., Kanjo, C. and Mtema, P. (2001) 'Meeting training needs for information age reform', in R.B. Heeks (ed.), *Reinventing Government in the Information Age*. London: Routledge. pp. 271–89.

NCC (2001) *Salary and Staff Issues in IT 2001*. Manchester: National Computing Centre.

NECCC (2002) *Creating and Maintaining Proper Systems for Electronic Record Keeping*. Lexington, KY: National Electronic Commerce Co-ordinating Council.

NIC (2002) *e-Government: A Strategic Planning Guide for Local Officials*. Olathe, KS: NIC.

Nicolle, L. (2000) 'How to prevent a staff exodus', *Computer Weekly*, 20 January. http://www.computerweekly.com.

Nilsson, A. and Ranerup, A. (2002) 'Improvisational change management', in A. Grönlund (ed.), *Electronic Government*. Hershey, PA: Idea Group Publishing. pp. 299–319.

Nolan, R.L. (1979) 'Managing the crises in data processing', *Harvard Business Review*, 57 (2): 115–26.

NTIA (1999) *Falling Through the Net: Defining the Digital Divide*. Washington, DC: National Telecommunications and Information Administration, Dept. of Commerce. http://www.ntia.doc.gov/ntiahome/fttn99/contents.html.

OCIPEP (2002) 'Securing Publicly Available Information', Information Note No. IN02-005, Office of Critical Infrastructure Protection and Emergency Preparedness, Ottawa, ON. http://www.ocipep-bpiepc.gc.ca/.

OECD (2001) *Management of Large Public IT Projects*. Paris: OECD.

OECD (2003a) *2nd OECD Symposium on E-Government*. Paris: OECD.

OECD (2003b) *e-Government in Finland*. Paris: OECD.

OGC (2004) *Successful Delivery Toolkit*. London: Office of Government Commerce.

OIG (2002) *Streamlined Processes and Better Automation Can Improve Munitions License Reviews*. Washington, DC: Office of Inspector General. http://oig.state.gov/documents/organization/9575.pdf,

OISC (1998) *Statewide Administrative and Financial Management Control System*. Boise, ID: Office of the Idaho State Controller.

OMB (2002) *eGovernment Strategy: Simplified Delivery of Services to Citizens*. Washington, DC: Office of Management and Budget.

OMB (2003) *E-Government Strategy*. Washington, DC: Office of Management and Budget. http://www.whitehouse.gov/omb/egov/2003egov_strat.pdf.

OMB (2005a) *President's Management Agenda*. Washington, DC: Office of Management and Budget. http://www.whitehouse.gov/omb/egov/g-8-pma.html

OMB (2005b) *Federal Information Security Management Act (FISMA) 2004 Report to Congress*. Washington, DC: Office of Management and Budget.

OMB (2005c) *Performance Reference Model*. Washington, DC: Office of Management and Budget. http://www.whitehouse.gov/omb/egov/a-2-prm.html.

Onley, D.S. (2003) 'DLA system led hackers to credit card records', *Government Computer News*, 1 September. http://www.gcn.com.

Osborne, D. and Plastrik, P. (1997) *Banishing Bureaucracy*. New York: Plume.

OSC (1997) *Information Technology Project Management Resource Book*. Boston, MA: Office of the State Comptroller.

Paquet, G. and Roy, J. (2000) 'Information technology, public policy, and Canadian governance', in G. David Garson (ed.), *Handbook of Public Information Systems*. New York: Marcel Dekker. pp. 53–70.

Parrado, S. (2002) 'ICT-related skills for e-government', paper presented at OECD seminar 'Reform of Public Administration', 23–24 September, Paris.

Pascual, P.J. (2003) *e-Government*. Kuala Lumpur: UNDP-APDIP.

Patching, K. and Chatham, R. (2000) *Corporate Politics for IT Managers*. Oxford: Butterworth-Heinemann.

Pearlson, K.E. (2001) *Managing and Using Information Systems*. New York: Wiley.

Peled, A. (2000a) 'The politics of outsourcing: bureaucrats, vendors, and public information technology projects', *Information Infrastructure and Policy*, 6: 209–25.

Peled, A. (2000b) 'First-class technology – third-rate bureaucracy: the case of Israel', *Information Technology for Development*, 9 (1): 45–58.

Pell, J.D. (1999) *Internet Acceptable Use Policy*. Kern County, CA: Kern County. http://www.lgov.org/document/doclist.asp.

Peterson, S. (2003) 'Lost signals', *Government Technology*, February. http://www.govtech.net/

Peterson, S.B. (1998) 'Saints, demons, wizards and systems', *Public Administration and Development*, 18: 37–60.

Pinder, A. (2004) 'Driving digital take-up', *Government IT*, April: 17.

Pollitt, C. and Harrison, S. (1992) 'Introduction', in C. Pollitt and S. Harrison (eds), *Handbook of Public Services Management*. Oxford: Blackwell. pp. 1–22.

POST (1998) *Electronic Government: Information Technology and the Citizen*. London: Parliamentary Office of Science and Technology. http://www.parliament.uk/post/egov.htm

Prins, L. and Dahanayake, A. (2001) 'Formal testing: a survey at the Dutch Ministry of Social Affairs and Employment', in M. Khosrowpour (ed.), *Managing Information Technology in a Global Environment*. Hershey, PA: Idea Group Publishing. pp. 843–7.

PTI (2004) *Information Technology, Telecommunications and the Web*. Washington, DC: Public Technology Inc. http://pti.nw.dc.us/members/library/titf/titf_docs.html.

PWC (1999) *Government Leadership Survey*. New York, NY: PricewaterhouseCoopers.

Quanjel, M. and Wenzler, I. (1998) 'A participative approach to organizational design: The case of the Royal Netherlands Air Force', paper presented at the Association for Information Systems 1998 Americas conference, 14–16 August, Baltimore, MD.

Rabone, T. (1999) 'Bringing down the total cost of ownership', *IMIS Journal*, 9 (1): 12–14.

Reddick, C. (2005) 'Citizen interaction with e-government', *Government Information Quarterly*, 22 (1): 38–57.

Reeder, F.S. (1998) 'The art of project management', *Government Executive*, April. http://www.govexec.com/tech/articles/0498tech2.htm.

Riley, T. (2002) *E-Government, E-Governance and E-Democracy*. Ottawa, ON: Commonwealth Centre for Electronic Governance.

RIU (2003) *Code of Practice on Consultation – Guidance*. London: Regulatory Impact Unit, Cabinet Office.

Robb, D. (2000) 'Rules of engagement', *Government Technology*, July. http://www.govtech.net/.

Robson, W. (1997) *Strategic Management and Information Systems*, 2nd edition. Harlow: Pearson Education.

Rocheleau, B. (2000) 'Guidelines for public sector acquisition', in G. David Garson (ed.), *Handbook of Public Information Systems*. New York: Marcel Dekker. pp. 377–90.

Salazar, A. (2001) 'Evaluating information systems for decentralisation', in R.B. Heeks (ed.), *Reinventing Government in the Information Age*. London: Routledge. pp. 156–74.

Santos, R. and Heeks, R.B. (2003) *ICTs and Intra-Governmental Structures at Local, Regional and Central Levels: Updating Conventional Ideas*. Manchester: Manchester Centre for eGovernment. http://www.mceg.org.uk

Say, M. (2002a) 'Here come the e-leaders', *Government Computing*, March: 16–17.

Say, M. (2002b) 'Open questions', *Government Computing*, June: 31–2.

Seifert, J.W. and Petersen, R.E. (2002) 'The promise of all things E? Expectations and challenges of emergent electronic government', *Perspectives on Global Development and Technology*, 1 (2): 193–212.

Skaarup, S. (1997) 'Intra- and Internet services for the public', paper presented at the ICA conference 'Integrated Service Delivery: Changing the Role of Government', 26–30 October, Sydney.

SMH (2002) 'E-government week to be held in Canberra', *Sydney Morning Herald*, 6 November. http://www.smh.com.au/.

Smith, D.V.L. and Fletcher, J.H. (2001) *Inside Information*. Chichester: Wiley.

Smith, K. (2004) 'Effective records management', presentation at the seminar 'Freedom of Information Compliance', 25 February, London.

Smith, P. (1999) 'Work and training', *Government Computing*, September: 30–31.

Smith, R.G. (1999) *Defrauding Governments in the Twenty-First Century*. Canberra: Australian Institute of Criminology.

SOCITM (2002) *Key Performance Indicators for ICT*. Northampton: Society of Information Technology Management.

SOCITM and IDEA (2002) *Local e-Government Now*. London: Society of IT Management & Improvement and Development Agency.

State of Hawaii (2001) *Audit of the Department of Human Services' Information System*. Honolulu, HI: The Auditor, State of Hawaii.

Stevens, T. (1999) *Contractual Agreement for Data Communication Lines*. Chesapeake, VA: City of Chesapeake. http://www.lgov.org/document/doclist.asp.

Stewart, T. (2000) 'Ergonomics user interface standards', *Ergonomics*, 43 (7): 1030–44.

Stowers, G.N.L. (2003) 'The state of federal Websites', in M.A. Abramson and T.L. Morin (eds), *E-Government 2003*. Lanham, MD: Rowman & Littlefield. pp. 17–52.

Strassmann, P. (1997) 'Strategic maneuvers', *Business Computer World*, January: 82–83.

Svensson, J.S. (2002) 'The use of legal expert systems in administrative decision making', in A. Grönlund (ed.), *Electronic Government*. Hershey, PA: Idea Group Publishing. pp. 151–69.

Symonds, M. (2000) 'Government and the Internet', survey, *Economist*, 355: 24 June.

Taylor, J.A. and Webster, C.W.R. (1996) 'Universalism: public services and citizenship in the information age', *Information Infrastructure and Policy*, 5: 217–33.

TBCS (2000) *e-Government Capacity Check*. Ottawa, ON: Treasury Board of Canada Secretariat.

TBCS (2002) *Privacy Impact Assessment Guidelines*. Ottawa, ON: Treasury Board of Canada Secretariat. http://www.cio-dpi.gc.ca.

TDWI (2002) *Data Quality and the Bottom Line*. Seattle, WA: The Data Warehousing Institute.

Te'eni, D. (1993) 'Behavioral aspects of data production and their impact on data quality', *Journal of Database Management*, 4 (2): 30–38.

TGIC (2002) *Digital Texas*. Austin, TX: Texas Geographic Information Council.

Turban, E., McLean, E. and Wetherbe, J. (1996) *Information Technology for Management*. New York: Wiley.

Turban, E., McLean, E. and Wetherbe, J. (2001) *Information Technology for Management*, 2nd edition. New York: Wiley.

Turner, T. (2003) 'Reordering priorities for e-government integration across tiers of government', in F. Bannister and D. Remenyi (eds), *Third European Conference on e-Government*. Reading: MCIL. pp. 439–450.

UNDESA (2003a) *eGovernment at the Crossroads*. New York: UN Department for Economic and Social Affairs.

UNDESA (2003b) 'E-government as a "free lunch"?', *Development Administration*, 106: 6–8.

US Congress (2003) 'Federal eGovernment Initiatives: Are We Headed in the Right Direction?', hearing by the House Government Reform Committee Subcommittee on Technology, Information Policy, Intergovernmental Relations and the Census, 13 March, US Congress, Washington, DC. http://estrategy.gov/it_legis.cfm.

US Courts (2001) *Report on Privacy and Public Access to Electronic Case Files*. Washington, DC: US Courts.

Veldanda, S. (2004) 'VOICE: Using Interactive Television to Improve Local Government Services in India', eTransparency Case Study No. 16, eGovernment for Development Information Exchange. http://www.egov4dev.org/voice.htm.

Walker, R.W. (2003) 'The work force transforms', *Government Computer News*, 18 August. http://www.gcn.com.

Walsham, G. (1989) 'The application of information technology in organisations', *Information Technology for Development*, 4 (2): 627–44.

Weaver, P.L., Lambrou, N. and Walkley, M. (1998) *Practical SSADM Version 4+*, 2nd edition. London: Financial Times Pitman Publishing.

Wessmiller, R. (2002) 'Facing the data integrity challenge', *IRMA SG Journal*, 12 (4): 5–6.

Westholm, H. and Aichholzer, G. (2003) 'eAdministration', Strategic Guideline 1, PRISMA. http://www.prisma-eu.net.

WF (2002) *The State of the Office*. London: Work Foundation.

Whalen, J. and Bahree, B. (2000) 'How a Siberian oil field turned into a minefield', *Wall Street Journal*, 9 February: A21.

Willcocks, L. (1994) 'Managing information systems in UK public administration: issues and prospects', *Public Administration*, 72 (Spring): 13–32.

Willis, D. (2003a) 'The green office', *Government Computing*, June: 45–47.

Willis, D. (2003b) 'Filling the skills gap', *Government Computing*, April: 27–28.

Wittkemper, G. and Kleindiek, R. (2003) 'BundOnline 2005', in G.G. Curtin, M.H. Sommer and V. Vis-Sommer (eds), *The World of E-Government*. New York: Haworth Press. pp. 107–126.

Wolfe, L. (2001) 'Transforming accountability for government information technology projects', in R. Heeks (ed.), *Reinventing Government in the Information Age*. London: Routledge. pp. 389–427.

Yeates, D. and Cadle, J. (2002) *Project Management for Information Systems*, 3rd edition. Harlow: Pearson Education.

Yildiz, M. (2003) 'Examining the motivations for e-government from an institutional theory perspective', paper presented at *dg.o2003*, 18–21 May, Boston, MA.

Zammit, J. (2000) *Report on the Online Governance Survey Report*. Blata I-Bajda, Malta: COMNET-IT.

Index